Mediterranean
Diet Cookbook for Beginners

1200+

Easy and Flavorful Recipes,

30-Day Meal Plan to Help You Build Healthy Habits

Maureen Hussey

Contents

Vegetable Mains And Meatless Recipes 33

Beans , Grains, And Pastas Recipes 52

Fish And Seafood Recipes 72

Poultry And Meats Recipes 90

Sides , Salads, And Soups Recipes 108

Fruits, Desserts And Snacks Recipes 125

Introduction

I was born in Patras, Greece, when my family moved there before I was born. Due to the unique Mediterranean climate, which is perfect for growing fruits and vegetables, various fruits and vegetables have also become an important part of the Greek diet, so I grew up cooking and eating Mediterranean food.

The Mediterranean diet isn't just a diet - it's a lifestyle. Originally formulated in the 1960s, it drew on Greek, Italian, French and Spanish cuisines. In the decades since, it has also incorporated other Mediterranean cuisines such as those from the Balkans, the Middle East, North Africa and Portugal. While tasty plant protein, tasty fish, occasional red meat, and plenty of fresh fruits and vegetables are the hallmarks of a diet, you can also enjoy grains, or even a glass of red wine, while getting major health benefits. The Mediterranean diet has been shown to be effective for weight loss, it may even prevent disease and increase your life expectancy.

This cookbook is about the most popular Mediterranean diet recommendations for 2022. See Mediterranean Food Recipes for foods from the surrounding Mediterranean region that maximize your body's sources of vitamins, minerals, and other micronutrients. Overall, food combinations in a healthy lifestyle are associated with improved health.

I look forward to this Mediterranean diet cookbook guiding you to better understand the Mediterranean diet and embarking on this exciting journey with you to achieve a holistic health makeover.

What is the Mediterranean Diet?

The Mediterranean diet or way of eating is a plant-heavy diet that focuses more on vegetables, fruits, whole grains, beans, nuts and legumes, as well as some lean proteins from fish and poultry, and good fats from things like extra virgin olive oil. As you see at the very top of the Mediterranean diet pyramid are red meats and sweets which are enjoyed less frequently.

The Mediterranean diet originates in the food cultures of ancient civilizations which developed around the Mediterranean Basin and is based on the regular consumption of olive oil (as the main source of added fat), plant foods (cereals, fruits, vegetables, legumes, tree nuts, and seeds), the moderate consumption of fish, seafood, and dairy, and low-to-moderate alcohol (mostly red wine) intake, balanced by a comparatively limited use of red meat and other meat products.

Traditional eating habits seen in geographical territories surrounding the Mediterranean Sea, although differentiated by some food choices and cooking practices specific to each country and culture, share a common set of basic features :emphasizes vegetables, fruits, whole grains, beans and legumes; includes low-fat or fat-free dairy products, fish, poultry, non-tropical vegetable oils and nuts; and limits added sugars, sugary drinks, sodium, highly processed foods, refined carbohydrates, saturated fats, and fatty or processed meats.

This diet can play an important role in preventing heart disease and stroke and in reducing risk factors such as obesity, diabetes, high cholesterol and high blood pressure. There is some evidence that a Mediterranean diet rich in virgin olive oil may help your body remove excess cholesterol from your arteries and keep your blood vessels open, helping you achieve the American Heart Association's recommendations for a healthy dietary pattern.

The Mediterranean Diet Pyramid

Scientific research has shown that the benefits brought by Mediterranean-derived dietary interventions not only in the primary and secondary prevention of cardiovascular disease, but also in the therapeutic approach of obesity, type 2 diabetes, metabolic syndrome, cancer or neurodegenerative diseases.

MEDITERRANEAN DIET

8 Easy Ways to Follow the Mediterranean Diet for Better Health

Cook with Olive Oil

If you've been cooking with vegetable oil or coconut oil, make the switch to extra-virgin olive oil. Olive oil is rich in monounsaturated fatty acids, which may improve HDL cholesterol, the "good" type of cholesterol. Use olive oil in homemade salad dressings and vinaigrettes. Drizzle it on finished dishes like fish or chicken to boost flavor. Swap olive oil for butter in mashed potatoes, pasta and more.

Eat More Fish

The go-to protein in the Mediterranean diet is fish. In particular, this diet emphasizes fatty fish like salmon, sardines and mackerel. These fish are rich in heart- and brain-healthy omega-3 fatty acids. Even those fish that are leaner and have less fat (like cod or tilapia) are still worth it, as they provide a good source of protein. Cooking fish in parchment paper or foil packets is one no-fuss, no-mess way to put dinner on the table. Or try incorporating it in some of your favorite foods, like tacos, stir-fries and soups.

Eat Veggies All Day Long

Featured Recipe: Baked Vegetable Soup

If you look at your diet and worry that there's barely a green to be seen, this is the perfect opportunity to fit in more veggies. A good way to do this is to eat one serving at snack time, like crunching on bell pepper strips or throwing a handful of spinach into a smoothie, and one at dinner, like these quick and easy side dishes. Aim for at least two servings per day. More is better. At least three servings can help you bust stress, Australian research notes.

Help Yourself to Whole Grains

Featured Recipe: Italian Tarragon Buckwheat

Experiment with "real" whole grains that are still in their "whole" form and haven't been refined. Quinoa cooks up in just 20 minutes, making it a great side dish for week-night meals. Barley is full of fiber and it's filling: pair it with mushrooms for a steamy, satisfying soup. A hot bowl of oatmeal is perfect for breakfast on a cold winter morning.

Snack on Nuts

Featured Recipe: Garlic-yogurt Dip With Walnuts

Nuts are another Mediterranean diet staple. Grabbing a handful, whether that's almonds, cashews or pistachios, can make for a satisfying, on-the-go snack. One study in Nutrition Journal found that if people replaced their standard snack (cookies, chips, crackers, snack mix, cereal bars) with almonds, their diets would be lower in empty calories, added sugar and sodium. Plus, nuts contain more fiber and minerals, such as potassium, than processed snack foods.

Enjoy Fruit for Dessert

Generally a good source of fiber, vitamin C and antioxidants, fresh fruit is a healthy way to indulge your sweet tooth. If it helps you to eat more, add a little sugar-drizzle slices of pear with honey or sprinkle a little brown sugar on grapefruit. Keep fresh fruit visible at home and keep a piece or two at work so you have a healthful snack when your stomach starts growling.

Sip (a Little) Wine

The people who live along the Mediterranean-the Spanish, Italian, French, Greek and others-are not known to shy away from wine, but that doesn't mean you should pour it at your leisure. Dietitians and experts who developed the Mediterranean diet for the New England Journal of Medicine study advised women to stick to a 3-ounce serving, and men to a 5-ounce serving, per day. When you do sip, try to do so with a meal-even better if that meal is shared with loved ones.

Savor Every Bite

Featured Recipe: Bell Pepper & Chickpea Salad

Eating like a Mediterranean is as much lifestyle as it is diet. Instead of gobbling your meal in front of the TV, slow down and sit down at the table with your family and friends to savor what you're eating. You're more apt to eat just until you're satisfied than until you're busting-at-the-seams full.

Measurement Conversions

BASIC KITCHEN CONVERSIONS & EQUIVALENTS

DRY MEASUREMENTS CONVERSION CHART

3 TEASPOONS = 1 TABLESPOON = 1/16 CUP

6 TEASPOONS = 2 TABLESPOONS = 1/8 CUP

12 TEASPOONS = 4 TABLESPOONS = 1/4 CUP

24 TEASPOONS = 8 TABLESPOONS = 1/2 CUP

36 TEASPOONS = 12 TABLESPOONS = 3/4 CUP

48 TEASPOONS = 16 TABLESPOONS = 1 CUP

METRIC TO US COOKING CONVERSIONS

OVEN TEMPERATURES

120 °C = 250 °F

160 °C = 320 °F

180° C = 350 °F

205 °C = 400 °F

220 °C = 425 °F

LIQUID MEASUREMENTS CONVERSION CHART

8 FLUID OUNCES = 1 CUP = 1/2 PINT = 1/4 QUART

16 FLUID OUNCES = 2 CUPS = 1 PINT = 1/2 QUART

32 FLUID OUNCES = 4 CUPS = 2 PINTS = 1 QUART = 1/4 GALLON

128 FLUID OUNCES = 16 CUPS = 8 PINTS = 4 QUARTS= 1 GALLON

BAKING IN GRAMS

1 CUP FLOUR = 140 GRAMS

1 CUP SUGAR = 150 GRAMS

1 CUP POWDERED SUGAR = 160 GRAMS

1 CUP HEAVY CREAM = 235 GRAMS

VOLUME

1 MILLILITER = 1/5 TEASPOON

5 ML = 1 TEASPOON

15 ML = 1 TABLESPOON

240 ML = 1 CUP OR 8 FLUID OUNCES

1 LITER = 34 FL. OUNCES

WEIGHT

1 GRAM = .035 OUNCES

100 GRAMS = 3.5 OUNCES

500 GRAMS = 1.1 POUNDS

1 KILOGRAM = 35 OUNCES

US TO METRIC COOKING CONVERSIONS

1/5 TSP = 1 ML

1 TSP = 5 ML

1 TBSP = 15 ML

1 FL OUNCE = 30 ML

1 CUP = 237 ML

1 PINT (2 CUPS) = 473 ML

1 QUART (4 CUPS) = .95 LITER

1 GALLON (16 CUPS) = 3.8 LITERS

1 OZ = 28 GRAMS

1 POUND = 454 GRAMS

BUTTER

1 CUP BUTTER = 2 STICKS = 8 OUNCES = 230 GRAMS = 8 TABLESPOONS

WHAT DOES 1 CUP EQUAL

1 CUP = 8 FLUID OUNCES

1 CUP = 16 TABLESPOONS

1 CUP = 48 TEASPOONS

1 CUP = 1/2 PINT

1 CUP = 1/4 QUART

1 CUP = 1/16 GALLON

1 CUP = 240 ML

BAKING PAN CONVERSIONS

1 CUP ALL-PURPOSE FLOUR = 4.5 OZ

1 CUP ROLLED OATS = 3 OZ 1 LARGE EGG = 1.7 OZ

1 CUP BUTTER = 8 OZ 1 CUP MILK = 8 OZ

1 CUP HEAVY CREAM = 8.4 OZ

1 CUP GRANULATED SUGAR = 7.1 OZ

1 CUP PACKED BROWN SUGAR = 7.75 OZ

1 CUP VEGETABLE OIL = 7.7 OZ

1 CUP UNSIFTED POWDERED SUGAR = 4.4 OZ

BAKING PAN CONVERSIONS

9-INCH ROUND CAKE PAN = 12 CUPS

10-INCH TUBE PAN =16 CUPS

11-INCH BUNDT PAN = 12 CUPS

9-INCH SPRINGFORM PAN = 10 CUPS

9 X 5 INCH LOAF PAN = 8 CUPS

9-INCH SQUARE PAN = 8 CUPS

Breakfast Recipes

Breakfast Recipes

Oat & Raspberry Pudding
Servings:2 | Cooking Time:5 Minutes
Ingredients:
- 1 cup almond milk
- ½ cup rolled oats
- 1 tbsp chia seeds
- 2 tsp honey
- 1 cup raspberries, pureed
- 1 tbsp yogurt

Directions:
1. Toss the oats, almond milk, chia seeds, honey, and raspberries in a bowl. Serve in bowls topped with yogurt.

Nutrition:
- Info Per Serving: Calories: 410;Fat: 32g;Protein: 7g;Carbs: 34g.

5-Ingredient Quinoa Breakfast Bowls
Servings:1 | Cooking Time: 17 Minutes
Ingredients:
- ¼ cup quinoa, rinsed
- ¾ cup water, plus additional as needed
- 1 carrot, grated
- ½ small broccoli head, finely chopped
- ¼ teaspoon salt
- 1 tablespoon chopped fresh dill

Directions:
1. Add the quinoa and water to a small pot over high heat and bring to a boil.
2. Once boiling, reduce the heat to low. Cover and cook for 5 minutes, stirring occasionally.
3. Stir in the carrot, broccoli, and salt and continue cooking for 1o to 12 minutes, or until the quinoa is cooked though and the vegetables are fork-tender. If the mixture gets too thick, you can add additional water as needed.
4. Add the dill and serve warm.

Nutrition:
- Info Per Serving: Calories: 219;Fat: 2.9g;Protein: 10.0g;Carbs: 40.8g.

Tomato And Egg Breakfast Pizza
Servings:2 | Cooking Time: 15 Minutes
Ingredients:
- 2 slices of whole-wheat naan bread
- 2 tablespoons prepared pesto
- 1 medium tomato, sliced
- 2 large eggs

Directions:
1. Heat a large nonstick skillet over medium-high heat. Place the naan bread in the skillet and let warm for about 2 minutes on each side, or until softened.
2. Spread 1 tablespoon of the pesto on one side of each slice and top with tomato slices.
3. Remove from the skillet and place each one on its own plate.
4. Crack the eggs into the skillet, keeping them separated, and cook until the whites are no longer translucent and the yolk is cooked to desired doneness.
5. Using a spatula, spoon one egg onto each bread slice. Serve warm.

Nutrition:
- Info Per Serving: Calories: 429;Fat: 16.8g;Protein: 18.1g;Carbs: 12.0g.

Roasted Vegetable Panini
Servings:4 | Cooking Time: 15 Minutes
Ingredients:
- 2 tablespoons extra-virgin olive oil, divided
- 1½ cups diced broccoli
- 1 cup diced zucchini
- ¼ cup diced onion
- ¼ teaspoon dried oregano
- ⅛ teaspoon kosher or sea salt
- ⅛ teaspoon freshly ground black pepper
- 1 jar roasted red peppers, drained and finely chopped
- 2 tablespoons grated Parmesan or Asiago cheese
- 1 cup fresh Mozzarella, sliced
- 1 whole-grain Italian loaf, cut into 4 equal lengths
- Cooking spray

Directions:
1. Place a large, rimmed baking sheet in the oven. Preheat the oven to 450°F with the baking sheet inside.
2. In a large bowl, stir together 1 tablespoon of the oil, broccoli, zucchini, onion, oregano, salt and pepper.
3. Remove the baking sheet from the oven and spritz the baking sheet with cooking spray. Spread the vegetable mixture on the baking sheet and roast for 5 minutes, stirring once halfway through cooking.
4. Remove the baking sheet from the oven. Stir in the red peppers and Parmesan cheese.
5. In a large skillet over medium-high heat, heat the remaining 1 tablespoon of the oil.
6. Cut open each section of bread horizontally, but don't cut all the way through. Fill each with the vegetable mix (about ½ cup), and layer 1 ounce of sliced Mozzarella cheese on top. Close the sandwiches, and place two of them on the skillet. Place a heavy object on top and grill for 2½ minutes. Flip the sandwiches and grill for another 2½ minutes.
7. Repeat the grilling process with the remaining two sandwiches.
8. Serve hot.

Nutrition:
- Info Per Serving: Calories: 116;Fat: 4.0g;Protein: 12.0g;Carbs: 9.0g.

Zucchini & Ricotta Egg Muffins
Servings:4 | Cooking Time:20 Minutes
Ingredients:
- 3 tbsp olive oil
- ½ cup ricotta cheese, crumbled
- 1 lb zucchini, spiralized
- ¼ cup sweet onion, chopped
- 4 large eggs
- ½ tsp hot paprika
- 2 tbsp fresh parsley, chopped
- Salt and black pepper to taste

Directions:
1. Preheat oven to 350°F.Combine the zucchini and sweet onion with olive oil, salt, and black pepper in a bowl. Divide between greased muffin cups. Crack an egg in each one; scatter some salt and hot paprika. Bake for 12 minutes or until set. Serve topped with ricotta cheese and parsley.

Nutrition:
- Info Per Serving: Calories: 226;Fat: 4.6g;Protein: 11g;Carbs: 6.6g.

Banana Corn Fritters

Servings:2 | Cooking Time: 10 Minutes

Ingredients:
- ½ cup yellow cornmeal
- ¼ cup flour
- 2 small ripe bananas, peeled and mashed
- 2 tablespoons unsweetened almond milk
- 1 large egg, beaten
- ½ teaspoon baking powder
- ¼ to ½ teaspoon ground chipotle chili
- ¼ teaspoon ground cinnamon
- ¼ teaspoon sea salt
- 1 tablespoon olive oil

Directions:
1. Stir together all ingredients except for the olive oil in a large bowl until smooth.
2. Heat a nonstick skillet over medium-high heat. Add the olive oil and drop about 2 tablespoons of batter for each fritter. Cook for 2 to 3 minutes until the bottoms are golden brown, then flip. Continue cooking for 1 to 2 minutes more, until cooked through. Repeat with the remaining batter.
3. Serve warm.

Nutrition:
- Info Per Serving: Calories: 396;Fat: 10.6g;Protein: 7.3g;Carbs: 68.0g.

Samosas In Potatoes

Servings:8 | Cooking Time: 30 Minutes

Ingredients:
- 4 small potatoes
- 1 teaspoon coconut oil
- 1 small onion, finely chopped
- 1 small piece ginger, minced
- 2 garlic cloves, minced
- 2 to 3 teaspoons curry powder
- Sea salt and freshly ground black pepper, to taste
- ¼ cup frozen peas, thawed
- 2 carrots, grated
- ¼ cup chopped fresh cilantro

Directions:
1. Preheat the oven to 350°F.
2. Poke small holes into potatoes with a fork, then wrap with aluminum foil.
3. Bake in the preheated oven for 30 minutes until tender.
4. Meanwhile, heat the coconut oil in a nonstick skillet over medium-high heat until melted.
5. Add the onion and sauté for 5 minutes or until translucent.
6. Add the ginger and garlic to the skillet and sauté for 3 minutes or until fragrant.
7. Add the curry power, salt, and ground black pepper, then stir to coat the onion. Remove them from the heat.
8. When the cooking of potatoes is complete, remove the potatoes from the foil and slice in half.
9. Hollow to potato halves with a spoon, then combine the potato fresh with sautéed onion, peas, carrots, and cilantro in a large bowl. Stir to mix well.
10. Spoon the mixture back to the tomato skins and serve immediately.

Nutrition:
- Info Per Serving: Calories: 131;Fat: 13.9g;Protein: 3.2g;Carbs: 8.8g.

Maple Peach Smoothie

Servings:2 | Cooking Time:5 Minutes

Ingredients:
- 2 cups almond milk
- 2 cups peaches, chopped
- 1 cup crushed ice
- ½ tsp ground ginger
- 1 tbsp maple syrup

Directions:
1. In a food processor, mix milk, peaches, ice, maple syrup, and ginger until smooth. Serve.

Nutrition:
- Info Per Serving: Calories: 639;Fat: 58g;Protein: 7g;Carbs: 34.2g.

Almond-Cherry Oatmeal Bowls

Servings:2 | Cooking Time:45 Minutes

Ingredients:
- ½ cup old-fashioned oats
- ¾ cup almond milk
- ½ tsp almond extract
- ½ tsp vanilla
- 1 egg, beaten
- 2 tbsp maple syrup
- ½ cup dried cherries, chopped
- 2 tbsp slivered raw almonds

Directions:
1. In a microwave-safe bowl, combine oats, almond milk, almond extract, vanilla, egg, and maple syrup and mix well.
2. Microwave for 5-6 minutes, stirring every 2 minutes until oats are soft. Spoon the mixture into 2 bowls. Top with cherries and almonds and serve. Enjoy!

Nutrition:
- Info Per Serving: Calories: 287;Fat: 9g;Protein: 11g;Carbs: 43g.

Roasted Tomato Panini

Servings:2 | Cooking Time: 3 Hours 6 Minutes

Ingredients:
- 2 teaspoons olive oil
- 4 Roma tomatoes, halved
- 4 cloves garlic
- 1 tablespoon Italian seasoning
- Sea salt and freshly ground pepper, to taste
- 4 slices whole-grain bread
- 4 basil leaves
- 2 slices fresh Mozzarella cheese

Directions:
1. Preheat the oven to 250°F. Grease a baking pan with olive oil.
2. Place the tomatoes and garlic in the baking pan, then sprinkle with Italian seasoning, salt, and ground pepper. Toss to coat well.
3. Roast in the preheated oven for 3 hours or until the tomatoes are lightly wilted.
4. Preheat the panini press.
5. Make the panini: Place two slices of bread on a clean work surface, then top them with wilted tomatoes. Sprinkle with basil and spread with Mozzarella cheese. Top them with remaining two slices of bread.
6. Cook the panini for 6 minutes or until lightly browned and the cheese melts. Flip the panini halfway through the cooking.
7. Serve immediately.

Nutrition:
- Info Per Serving: Calories: 323;Fat: 12.0g;Protein: 17.4g;Carbs: 37.5g.

Classic Spanish Tortilla With Tuna

Servings:4 | Cooking Time:30 Minutes

Ingredients:
- 7 oz canned tuna packed in water, flaked
- 2 plum tomatoes, seeded and diced
- 2 tbsp olive oil
- 6 large eggs, beaten
- 2 small potatoes, diced
- 2 green onions, chopped
- 1 roasted red bell pepper, sliced
- 1 tsp dried tarragon

Directions:
1. Preheat your broiler to high. Heat the olive oil in a skillet over medium heat. Fry the potatoes for 7 minutes until slightly soft. Add the green onions and cook for 3 minutes. Stir in the tuna, tomatoes, peppers, tarragon, and eggs. Cook for 8-10 minutes until the eggs are bubbling from the bottom and the bottom is slightly brown. Place the skillet under the preheated broiler for 5-6 minutes or until the middle is set and the top is slightly brown. Serve sliced into wedges.

Nutrition:
- Info Per Serving: Calories: 422;Fat: 21g;Protein: 14g;Carbs: 46g.

Feta And Spinach Frittata

Servings:2 | Cooking Time: 15 Minutes

Ingredients:
- 4 large eggs, beaten
- 2 tablespoons fresh chopped herbs, such as rosemary, thyme, oregano, basil or 1 teaspoon dried herbs
- ¼ teaspoon salt
- Freshly ground black pepper, to taste
- 4 tablespoons extra-virgin olive oil, divided
- 1 cup fresh spinach, arugula, kale, or other leafy greens
- 4 ounces quartered artichoke hearts, rinsed, drained, and thoroughly dried
- 8 cherry tomatoes, halved
- ½ cup crumbled soft goat cheese

Directions:
1. Preheat the broiler to Low.
2. In a small bowl, combine the beaten eggs, herbs, salt, and pepper and whisk well with a fork. Set aside.
3. In an ovenproof skillet, heat 2 tablespoons of olive oil over medium heat. Add the spinach, artichoke hearts, and cherry tomatoes and sauté until just wilted, 1 to 2 minutes.
4. Pour in the egg mixture and let it cook undisturbed over medium heat for 3 to 4 minutes, until the eggs begin to set on the bottom.
5. Sprinkle the goat cheese across the top of the egg mixture and transfer the skillet to the oven.
6. Broil for 4 to 5 minutes, or until the frittata is firm in the center and golden brown on top.
7. Remove from the oven and run a rubber spatula around the edge to loosen the sides. Slice the frittata in half and serve drizzled with the remaining 2 tablespoons of olive oil.

Nutrition:
- Info Per Serving: Calories: 529;Fat: 46.5g;Protein: 21.4g;Carbs: 7.1g.

Crustless Tiropita (Greek Cheese Pie)

Servings:6 | Cooking Time: 35 To 40 Minutes

Ingredients:
- 4 tablespoons extra-virgin olive oil, divided
- ½ cup whole-milk ricotta cheese
- 1¼ cups crumbled feta cheese
- 1 tablespoon chopped fresh dill

- 2 tablespoons chopped fresh mint
- ½ teaspoon lemon zest
- ¼ teaspoon freshly ground black pepper
- 2 large eggs
- ½ teaspoon baking powder

Directions:
1. Preheat the oven to 350°F. Coat the bottom and sides of a baking dish with 2 tablespoons of olive oil. Set aside.
2. Mix together the ricotta and feta cheese in a medium bowl and stir with a fork until well combined. Add the dill, mint, lemon zest, and black pepper and mix well.
3. In a separate bowl, whisk together the eggs and baking powder. Pour the whisked eggs into the bowl of cheese mixture. Blend well.
4. Slowly pour the mixture into the coated baking dish and drizzle with the remaining 2 tablespoons of olive oil.
5. Bake in the preheated oven for about 35 to 40 minutes, or until the pie is browned around the edges and cooked through.
6. Cool for 5 minutes before slicing into wedges.

Nutrition:
- Info Per Serving: Calories: 181;Fat: 16.6g;Protein: 7.0g;Carbs: 1.8g.

Goat Cheese & Sweet Potato Tart

Servings:6 | Cooking Time:1 Hour 20 Minutes

Ingredients:
- ¼ cup olive oil
- 2 eggs, whisked
- 2 lb sweet potatoes, cubed
- 7 oz goat cheese, crumbled
- 1 white onion, chopped
- ¼ cup milk
- Salt and black pepper to taste
- 6 phyllo sheets

Directions:
1. Preheat the oven to 380 °F. Line a baking sheet with parchment paper. Place potatoes, half of the olive oil, salt, and pepper in a bowl and toss to combine. Arrange on the sheet and roast for 25 minutes.
2. In the meantime, warm half of the remaining oil in a skillet over medium heat and sauté onion for 3 minutes. Whisk eggs, milk, goat cheese, salt, pepper, onion, sweet potatoes, and remaining oil in a bowl.
3. Place phyllo sheets in a tart dish and rub with oil. Spoon sweet potato mixture, cover with foil and bake for 20 minutes. Remove the foil and bake another 20 minutes. Let cool for a few minutes. Serve sliced.

Nutrition:
- Info Per Serving: Calories: 513;Fat: 23g;Protein: 17g;Carbs: 60g.

Tomato & Prosciutto Sandwiches

Servings:4 | Cooking Time:10 Minutes

Ingredients:
- 1 large, ripe tomato, sliced into 8 rounds
- 8 whole-wheat bread slices
- 1 avocado, halved and pitted
- Salt and black pepper to taste
- 8 romaine lettuce leaves
- 8 thin prosciutto slices
- 1 tbsp cilantro, chopped

Directions:
1. Toast the bread and place on a large platter. Scoop the avocado flesh out of the skin into a small bowl. Season with pepper and salt. With a fork, gently mash the avocado until it resembles a creamy spread. Smear 4 bread slices with the avocado mix. Top with a layer of lettuce leaves, tomato slices, and prosciutto slices.

Repeat the layers one more time, sprinkle with cilantro, then cover with the remaining bread slices. Serve and enjoy!

Nutrition:
• Info Per Serving: Calories: 262;Fat: 12.2g;Protein: 8g;Carbs: 35g.

Grilled Caesar Salad Sandwiches

Servings:2 | Cooking Time: 5 Minutes

Ingredients:
• ¾ cup olive oil, divided
• 2 romaine lettuce hearts, left intact
• 3 to 4 anchovy fillets
• Juice of 1 lemon
• 2 to 3 cloves garlic, peeled
• 1 teaspoon Dijon mustard
• ¼ teaspoon Worcestershire sauce
• Sea salt and freshly ground pepper, to taste
• 2 slices whole-wheat bread, toasted
• Freshly grated Parmesan cheese, for serving

Directions:
1. Preheat the grill to medium-high heat and oil the grates.
2. On a cutting board, drizzle the lettuce with 1 to 2 tablespoons of olive oil and place on the grates.
3. Grill for 5 minutes, turning until lettuce is slightly charred on all sides. Let lettuce cool enough to handle.
4. In a food processor, combine the remaining olive oil with the anchovies, lemon juice, garlic, mustard, and Worcestershire sauce.
5. Pulse the ingredients until you have a smooth emulsion. Season with sea salt and freshly ground pepper to taste. Chop the lettuce in half and place on the bread.
6. Drizzle with the dressing and serve with a sprinkle of Parmesan cheese.

Nutrition:
• Info Per Serving: Calories: 949;Fat: 85.6g;Protein: 12.9g;Carbs: 34.1g.

Quick & Easy Bread In A Mug

Servings:1 | Cooking Time:10 Minutes

Ingredients:
• 1 tbsp olive oil
• 3 tbsp flour
• 1 large egg
• ½ tsp dried thyme
• ¼ tsp baking powder
• ½ tsp salt

Directions:
1. In a heat-resistant ramekin, mix the flour, olive oil, egg, thyme, baking powder, and salt with a fork. Place in the microwave and heat for 80 seconds on high. Run a knife around the edges and flip around to remove the bread. Slice in half to use it to make sandwiches.

Nutrition:
• Info Per Serving: Calories: 232;Fat: 22.2g;Protein: 8g;Carbs: 1.1g.

Creamy Vanilla Oatmeal

Servings:4 | Cooking Time: 40 Minutes

Ingredients:
• 4 cups water
• Pinch sea salt
• 1 cup steel-cut oats
• ¾ cup unsweetened almond milk
• 2 teaspoons pure vanilla extract

Directions:
1. Add the water and salt to a large saucepan over high heat and bring to a boil.

2. Once boiling, reduce the heat to low and add the oats. Mix well and cook for 30 minutes, stirring occasionally.
3. Fold in the almond milk and vanilla and whisk to combine. Continue cooking for about 10 minutes, or until the oats are thick and creamy.
4. Ladle the oatmeal into bowls and serve warm.

Nutrition:
• Info Per Serving: Calories: 117;Fat: 2.2g;Protein: 4.3g;Carbs: 20.0g.

Apple & Pumpkin Muffins

Servings:12 | Cooking Time:30 Minutes

Ingredients:
• ½ cup butter, melted
• 1 ½ cups granulated sugar
• ½ cup sugar
• ¾ cup flour
• 2 tsp pumpkin pie spice
• 1 tsp baking soda
• ¼ tsp salt
• ¼ tsp nutmeg
• 1 apple, grated
• 1 can pumpkin puree
• ½ cup full-fat yogurt
• 2 large egg whites

Directions:
1. Preheat the oven to 350 F. In a bowl, mix sugars, flour, pumpkin pie spice, baking soda, salt, and nutmeg. In a separate bowl, mix apple, pumpkin puree, yogurt, and butter.
2. Slowly mix the wet ingredients into the dry ingredients. Using a mixer on high, whip the egg whites until stiff and fold them into the batter. Pour the batter into a greased muffin tin, filling each cup halfway. Bake for 25 minutes or until a fork inserted in the center comes out clean. Let cool.

Nutrition:
• Info Per Serving: Calories: 259;Fat: 8.2g;Protein: 3g;Carbs: 49.1g.

Herby Artichoke Frittata With Ricotta

Servings:2 | Cooking Time:20 Minutes

Ingredients:
• 4 oz canned artichoke hearts, quartered
• 2 tbsp olive oil
• 4 large eggs
• 1 tsp dried herbs
• Salt and black pepper to taste
• 1 cup kale, chopped
• 8 cherry tomatoes, halved
• ½ cup crumbled ricotta cheese

Directions:
1. Preheat oven to 360 °F. In a bowl, whisk the eggs, herbs, salt, and pepper and whisk well with a fork. Set aside. Warm the olive oil in a skillet over medium heat. Sauté the kale, artichoke, and cherry tomatoes until just wilted, 1-2 minutes.
2. Pour the egg mixture over and let it cook for 3-4 minutes until the eggs begin to set on the bottom. Sprinkle with ricotta cheese on top. Place the skillet under the preheated broiler for 5 minutes until the frittata is firm in the center and golden brown on top. Invert the frittata onto a plate and slice in half. Serve warm.

Nutrition:
• Info Per Serving: Calories: 527;Fat: 47g;Protein: 21g;Carbs: 10g.

Cream Peach Smoothie

Servings:1 | Cooking Time:5 Minutes

Ingredients:
- 1 large peach, sliced
- 6 oz peach Greek yogurt
- 2 tbsp almond milk
- 2 ice cubes

Directions:
1. Blend the peach, yogurt, almond milk, and ice cubes in your food processor until thick and creamy. Serve and enjoy!

Nutrition:
- Info Per Serving: Calories: 228;Fat: 3g;Protein: 11g;Carbs: 41.6g.

Tomato & Avocado Toast

Servings:2 | Cooking Time:15 Minutes

Ingredients:
- 3 tbsp olive oil
- 2 tbsp ground flaxseed
- ½ tsp baking powder
- 2 large eggs
- Salt and black pepper to taste
- ½ tsp garlic powder
- 1 avocado, peeled and sliced
- 5 chopped cherry tomatoes
- 1 tsp cilantro, chopped

Directions:
1. Place the flaxseed and baking powder in a bowl and mix, breaking up any lumps in the baking powder. Add eggs, salt, pepper, and garlic powder. Whisk well. Let sit for 2 minutes.
2. Warm 1 tablespoon of the olive oil in a small skillet over medium heat. Pour in the egg mixture cook for 2-3 minutes until the eggs are set on the bottom. Using a rubber spatula, scrape down the sides to allow the uncooked egg to reach the bottom. Cook for another 2-3 minutes.
3. Flip like a pancake and cook for 1-2 more minutes. Allow to cool slightly. Slice into 2 pieces. Top each toast with avocado slices, cherry tomatoes, and cilantro and drizzle with the remaining olive oil.

Nutrition:
- Info Per Serving: Calories: 287;Fat: 25g;Protein: 9g;Carbs: 10g.

Easy Zucchini & Egg Stuffed Tomatoes

Servings:4 | Cooking Time:40 Minutes

Ingredients:
- 1 tbsp olive oil
- 1 small zucchini, grated
- 8 tomatoes, insides scooped
- 8 eggs
- Salt and black pepper to taste

Directions:
1. Preheat the oven to 360 °F. Place tomatoes on a greased baking dish. Mix the zucchini with olive oil, salt, and pepper. Divide the mixture between the tomatoes and crack an egg on each one. Bake for 20-25 minutes. Serve warm.

Nutrition:
- Info Per Serving: Calories: 280;Fat: 22g;Protein: 14g;Carbs: 12g.

Cinnamon Oatmeal With Dried Cranberries

Servings:2 | Cooking Time: 8 Minutes

Ingredients:
- 1 cup almond milk
- 1 cup water
- Pinch sea salt
- 1 cup old-fashioned oats
- ½ cup dried cranberries
- 1 teaspoon ground cinnamon

Directions:
1. In a medium saucepan over high heat, bring the almond milk, water, and salt to a boil.
2. Stir in the oats, cranberries, and cinnamon. Reduce the heat to medium and cook for 5 minutes, stirring occasionally.
3. Remove the oatmeal from the heat. Cover and let it stand for 3 minutes. Stir before serving.

Nutrition:
- Info Per Serving: Calories: 107;Fat: 2.1g;Protein: 3.2g;Carbs: 18.2g.

Feta And Olive Scrambled Eggs

Servings:2 | Cooking Time: 5 Minutes

Ingredients:
- 4 large eggs
- 1 tablespoon unsweetened almond milk
- Sea salt and freshly ground pepper, to taste
- 1 tablespoon olive oil
- ¼ cup crumbled feta cheese
- 10 Kalamata olives, pitted and sliced
- Small bunch fresh mint, chopped, for garnish

Directions:
1. Beat the eggs in a bowl until just combined. Add the milk and a pinch of sea salt and whisk well.
2. Heat a medium nonstick skillet over medium-high heat and add the olive oil.
3. Pour in the egg mixture and stir constantly, or until they just begin to curd and firm up, about 2 minutes. Add the feta cheese and olive slices, and stir until evenly combined. Season to taste with salt and pepper.
4. Divide the mixture between 2 plates and serve garnished with the fresh chopped mint.

Nutrition:
- Info Per Serving: Calories: 244;Fat: 21.9g;Protein: 8.4g;Carbs: 3.5g.

Cheesy Broccoli And Mushroom Egg Casserole

Servings:4 | Cooking Time: 40 Minutes

Ingredients:
- 2 tablespoons extra-virgin olive oil
- ½ sweet onion, chopped
- 1 teaspoon minced garlic
- 1 cup sliced button mushrooms
- 1 cup chopped broccoli
- 8 large eggs
- ¼ cup unsweetened almond milk
- 1 tablespoon chopped fresh basil
- 1 cup shredded Cheddar cheese
- Sea salt and freshly ground black pepper, to taste

Directions:
1. Preheat the oven to 375°F.
2. Heat the olive oil in a large ovenproof skillet over medium-high heat.
3. Add the onion, garlic, and mushrooms to the skillet and sauté for about 5 minutes, stirring occasionally.
4. Stir in the broccoli and sauté for 5 minutes until the vegetables start to soften.
5. Meanwhile, beat the eggs with the almond milk and basil in a small bowl until well mixed.
6. Remove the skillet from the heat and pour the egg mixture over the top. Scatter the Cheddar cheese all over.
7. Bake uncovered in the preheated oven for about 30 minutes, or

until the top of the casserole is golden brown and a fork inserted in the center comes out clean.
8. Remove from the oven and sprinkle with the sea salt and pepper. Serve hot.
Nutrition:
• Info Per Serving: Calories: 326;Fat: 27.2g;Protein: 14.1g;Carbs: 6.7g.

Spicy Black Bean And Poblano Dippers
Servings:8 | Cooking Time: 21 Minutes
Ingredients:
• 2 tablespoons avocado oil, plus more for brushing the dippers
• 1 can black beans, drained and rinsed
• 1 poblano, deseeded and quartered
• 1 jalapeño, halved and deseeded
• ½ cup fresh cilantro, leaves and tender stems
• 1 yellow onion, quartered
• 2 garlic cloves
• 1 teaspoon chili powder
• 1 teaspoon ground cumin
• 1 teaspoon sea salt
• 24 organic corn tortillas
Directions:
1. Preheat the oven to 400°F. Line a baking sheet with parchment paper and grease with avocado oil.
2. Combine the remaining ingredients, except for the tortillas, in a food processor, then pulse until chopped finely and the mixture holds together. Make sure not to purée the mixture.
3. Warm the tortillas on the baking sheet in the preheated oven for 1 minute or until softened.
4. Add a tablespoon of the mixture in the middle of each tortilla. Fold one side of the tortillas over the mixture and tuck to roll them up tightly to make the dippers.
5. Arrange the dippers on the baking sheet and brush them with avocado oil. Bake in the oven for 20 minutes or until well browned. Flip the dippers halfway through the cooking time.
6. Serve immediately.
Nutrition:
• Info Per Serving: Calories: 388;Fat: 6.5g;Protein: 16.2g;Carbs: 69.6g.

Strawberry Basil Mascarpone Toast
Servings:2 | Cooking Time:15 Minutes
Ingredients:
• 4 fresh basil leaves, sliced into thin shreds
• 4 whole-grain bread slices, toasted
• ½ cup mascarpone cheese
• 1 tbsp honey
• 1 cup strawberries, sliced
Directions:
1. In a small bowl, combine the mascarpone and honey. Spread the mixture evenly over each slice of bread. Top with sliced strawberries and basil.
Nutrition:
• Info Per Serving: Calories: 275;Fat: 8g;Protein: 16g;Carbs: 41g.

Eggs Florentine With Pancetta
Servings:2 | Cooking Time:20 Minutes
Ingredients:
• 1 English muffin, toasted and halved
• ¼ cup chopped pancetta
• 2 tsp hollandaise sauce
• 1 cup spinach
• Salt and black pepper to taste
• 2 large eggs
Directions:

1. Place pancetta in a pan over medium heat and cook for 5 minutes until crispy; reserve. Add the baby spinach and cook for 2-3 minutes in the same pan until the spinach wilts. Fill a pot with 3 inches of water over medium heat and bring to a boil. Add 1 tbsp of vinegar and reduce the heat.
2. Crack the eggs one at a time into a small dish and gently pour into the simmering water. Poach the eggs for 2-3 minutes until the whites are set, but the yolks are still soft; remove with a slotted spoon. Divide the spinach between muffin halves and top with pancetta and poached eggs. Spoon the hollandaise sauce on top and serve.
Nutrition:
• Info Per Serving: Calories: 173;Fat: 7g;Protein: 11g;Carbs: 17g.

Zucchini Hummus Wraps
Servings:2 | Cooking Time: 6 Minutes
Ingredients:
• 1 zucchini, ends removed, thinly sliced lengthwise
• ½ teaspoon dried oregano
• ¼ teaspoon freshly ground black pepper
• ¼ teaspoon garlic powder
• ¼ cup hummus
• 2 whole wheat tortillas
• 2 Roma tomatoes, cut lengthwise into slices
• 1 cup chopped kale
• 2 tablespoons chopped red onion
• ½ teaspoon ground cumin
Directions:
1. In a skillet over medium heat, place the zucchini slices and cook for 3 minutes per side. Sprinkle with the oregano, pepper, and garlic powder and remove from the heat.
2. Spread 2 tablespoons of hummus on each tortilla. Lay half the zucchini in the center of each tortilla. Top with tomato slices, kale, red onion, and ¼ teaspoon of cumin. Wrap tightly and serve.
Nutrition:
• Info Per Serving: Calories: 248;Fat: 8.1g;Protein: 9.1g;Carbs: 37.1g.

Garlic Bell Pepper Omelet
Servings:2 | Cooking Time:10 Minutes
Ingredients:
• 2 tbsp olive oil
• 2 red bell peppers, chopped
• ¼ tsp nutmeg
• 4 eggs, beaten
• 2 garlic cloves, crushed
• 1 tsp Italian seasoning
Directions:
1. Heat the oil in a skillet over medium heat. Stir-fry the peppers for 3 minutes or until lightly charred; reserve. Add the garlic to the skillet and sauté for 1 minute. Pour the eggs over the garlic, sprinkle with Italian seasoning and nutmeg, and cook for 2-3 minutes or until set. Using a spatula, loosen the edges and gently slide onto a plate. Add charred peppers and fold over. Serve hot.
Nutrition:
• Info Per Serving: Calories: 272;Fat: 22g;Protein: 12g;Carbs: 6.4g.

Mozzarella & Olive Cakes
Servings:6 | Cooking Time:25 Minutes
Ingredients:
• 4 tbsp olive oil, softened
• ¼ cup mozzarella, shredded
• ¼ cup black olives, chopped
• ½ cup milk
• 1 egg, beaten

- 1 cup cornflour
- 1 tsp baking powder
- 3 sun-dried tomatoes, chopped
- 2 tbsp fresh cilantro, chopped
- ¼ tsp kosher salt

Directions:

1. Preheat oven to 360 °F. In a bowl, whisk the egg with milk and olive oil. In a separate bowl, mix the salt, cornflour, cilantro, and baking powder. Combine the wet ingredients with the dry mixture. Stir in black olives, tomatoes, and mozzarella cheese. Pour the mixture into greased ramekins and bake for 18-20 minutes or until cooked and golden.

Nutrition:

- Info Per Serving: Calories: 189;Fat: 11.7g;Protein: 4g;Carbs: 19g.

Lime Watermelon Yogurt Smoothie

Servings:6 | Cooking Time:5 Minutes

Ingredients:

- ½ cup almond milk
- 2 cups watermelon, cubed
- ½ cup Greek yogurt
- ½ tsp lime zest

Directions:

1. In a food processor, blend watermelon, almond milk, lime zest, and yogurt until smooth. Serve into glasses.

Nutrition:

- Info Per Serving: Calories: 260;Fat: 10g;Protein: 2g;Carbs: 6g.

Red Pepper Coques With Pine Nuts

Servings:4 | Cooking Time: 45 Minutes

Ingredients:

- Dough:
- 3 cups almond flour
- ½ teaspoon instant or rapid-rise yeast
- 2 teaspoons raw honey
- 1⅓ cups ice water
- 3 tablespoons extra-virgin olive oil
- 1½ teaspoons sea salt
- Red Pepper Topping:
- 4 tablespoons extra-virgin olive oil, divided
- 2 cups jarred roasted red peppers, patted dry and sliced thinly
- 2 large onions, halved and sliced thin
- 3 garlic cloves, minced
- ¼ teaspoon red pepper flakes
- 2 bay leaves
- 3 tablespoons maple syrup
- 1½ teaspoons sea salt
- 3 tablespoons red whine vinegar
- For Garnish:
- ¼ cup pine nuts (optional)
- 1 tablespoon minced fresh parsley

Directions:

1. Make the Dough:
2. Combine the flour, yeast, and honey in a food processor, pulse to combine well. Gently add water while pulsing. Let the dough sit for 10 minutes.
3. Mix the olive oil and salt in the dough and knead the dough until smooth. Wrap in plastic and refrigerate for at least 1 day.
4. Make the Topping:
5. Heat 1 tablespoon of olive oil in a nonstick skillet over medium heat until shimmering.
6. Add the red peppers, onions, garlic, red pepper flakes, bay leaves, maple syrup, and salt. Sauté for 20 minutes or until the onion is caramelized.
7. Turn off the heat and discard the bay leaves. Remove the onion from the skillet and baste with wine vinegar. Let them sit until

ready to use.

8. Make the Coques:
9. Preheat the oven to 500°F. Grease two baking sheets with 1 tablespoon of olive oil.
10. Divide the dough ball into four balls, then press and shape them into equal-sized oval. Arrange the ovals on the baking sheets and pierce each dough about 12 times.
11. Rub the ovals with 2 tablespoons of olive oil and bake for 7 minutes or until puffed. Flip the ovals halfway through the cooking time.
12. Spread the ovals with the topping and pine nuts, then bake for an additional 15 minutes or until well browned.
13. Remove the coques from the oven and spread with parsley. Allow to cool for 10 minutes before serving.

Nutrition:

- Info Per Serving: Calories: 658;Fat: 23.1g;Protein: 3.4g;Carbs: 112.0g.

Chia & Almond Oatmeal

Servings:2 | Cooking Time:10 Min + Chilling Time

Ingredients:

- ¼ tsp almond extract
- ½ cup milk
- ½ cup rolled oats
- 2 tbsp almonds, sliced
- 2 tbsp sugar
- 1 tsp chia seeds
- ¼ tsp ground cardamom
- ¼ tsp ground cinnamon

Directions:

1. Combine the milk, oats, almonds, sugar, chia seeds, cardamom, almond extract, and cinnamon in a mason jar and shake well. Keep in the refrigerator for 4 hours. Serve.

Nutrition:

- Info Per Serving: Calories: 131;Fat: 6.2g;Protein: 4.9g;Carbs: 17g.

Honey & Feta Frozen Yogurt

Servings:4 | Cooking Time:5 Minutes + Freezing Time

Ingredients:

- 1 tbsp honey
- 1 cup Greek yogurt
- ½ cup feta cheese, crumbled
- 2 tbsp mint leaves, chopped

Directions:

1. In a food processor, blend yogurt, honey, and feta cheese until smooth. Transfer to a wide dish, cover with plastic wrap, and put in the freezer for 2 hours or until solid. When frozen, spoon into cups, sprinkle with mint, and serve.

Nutrition:

- Info Per Serving: Calories: 170;Fat: 12g;Protein: 7g;Carbs: 13g.

Banana & Chocolate Porridge

Servings:4 | Cooking Time:20 Minutes

Ingredients:

- 2 bananas
- 4 dried apricots, chopped
- 1 cup barley, soaked
- 2 tbsp flax seeds
- 1 tbsp cocoa powder
- 1 cup coconut milk
- ¼ tsp mint leaves
- 2 oz dark chocolate bars, grated
- 2 tbsp coconut flakes

Directions:

1. Place the barley in a saucepan along with the flaxseeds and

two cups of water. Bring to a boil, then lower the heat and simmer for 12 minutes, stirring often.

2. Meanwhile, in a food processor, blend bananas, cocoa powder, coconut milk, apricots, and mint leaves until smooth. Once the barley is ready, stir in chocolate. Add in banana mixture. Garnish with coconut flakes. Serve.

Nutrition:
• Info Per Serving: Calories: 476;Fat: 22g;Protein: 10g;Carbs: 65g.

Baked Ricotta With Honey Pears

Servings:4 | Cooking Time: 22 To 25 Minutes

Ingredients:
• 1 container whole-milk ricotta cheese
• 2 large eggs
• ¼ cup whole-wheat pastry flour
• 1 tablespoon sugar
• 1 teaspoon vanilla extract
• ¼ teaspoon ground nutmeg
• 1 pear, cored and diced
• 2 tablespoons water
• 1 tablespoon honey
• Nonstick cooking spray

Directions:
1. Preheat the oven to 400°F. Spray four ramekins with nonstick cooking spray.
2. Beat together the ricotta, eggs, flour, sugar, vanilla, and nutmeg in a large bowl until combined. Spoon the mixture into the ramekins.
3. Bake in the preheated oven for 22 to 25 minutes, or until the ricotta is just set.
4. Meanwhile, in a small saucepan over medium heat, simmer the pear in the water for 10 minutes, or until slightly softened. Remove from the heat, and stir in the honey.
5. Remove the ramekins from the oven and cool slightly on a wire rack. Top the ricotta ramekins with the pear and serve.

Nutrition:
• Info Per Serving: Calories: 329;Fat: 19.0g;Protein: 17.0g;Carbs: 23.0g.

Artichoke Omelet With Goat Cheese

Servings:2 | Cooking Time:20 Minutes

Ingredients:
• 1 cup canned artichoke hearts, chopped
• 1 tsp butter
• 4 eggs
• Salt and black pepper to taste
• 2 small tomato, chopped
• 4 oz goat cheese, crumbled

Directions:
1. Whisk the eggs with salt and pepper in a bowl. Melt butter in a skillet over medium heat and pour in the eggs, swirling the skillet until the base is golden, 4 minutes. Add the tomato, artichoke, and goat cheese and fold over the omelet. Serve.

Nutrition:
• Info Per Serving: Calories: 310;Fat: 20g;Protein: 23g;Carbs: 16g.

Maple-Vanilla Yogurt With Walnuts

Servings:4 | Cooking Time:10 Minutes

Ingredients:
• 2 cups Greek yogurt
• ¾ cup maple syrup
• 1 cup walnuts, chopped
• 1 tsp vanilla extract
• 2 tsp cinnamon powder

Directions:
1. Combine yogurt, walnuts, vanilla, maple syrup, and cinnamon powder in a bowl. Let sit in the fridge for 10 minutes.

Nutrition:
• Info Per Serving: Calories: 400;Fat: 25g;Protein: 11g;Carbs: 40g.

Cheese Egg Quiche

Servings:6 | Cooking Time:45 Minutes

Ingredients:
• 1 tbsp melted butter
• 1 ¼ cups crumbled feta
• ½ cup ricotta, crumbled
• 2 tbsp chopped fresh mint
• 1 tbsp chopped fresh dill
• ½ tsp lemon zest
• Black pepper to taste
• 2 large eggs, beaten

Directions:
1. Preheat the oven to 350 F. In a medium bowl, combine the feta and ricotta cheeses and blend them well with a fork. Stir in the mint, dill, lemon zest, and black pepper. Slowly add the eggs to the cheese mixture and blend well. Pour the batter into a greased baking dish and drizzle with melted butter. Bake until lightly browned, 35-40 minutes. Serve.

Nutrition:
• Info Per Serving: Calories: 182;Fat: 17g;Protein: 7g;Carbs: 2g.

Morning Baklava French Toast

Servings:2 | Cooking Time:20 Minutes

Ingredients:
• 2 tbsp orange juice
• 3 fresh eggs, beaten
• 1 tsp lemon zest
• 1⁄8 tsp vanilla extract
• ¼ cup honey
• 2 tbsp whole milk
• ¾ tsp ground cinnamon
• ¼ cup walnuts, crumbled
• ¼ cup pistachios, crumbled
• 1 tbsp sugar
• 2 tbsp white bread crumbs
• 4 slices bread
• 2 tbsp unsalted butter
• 1 tsp confectioners' sugar

Directions:
1. Combine the eggs, orange juice, lemon zest, vanilla, honey, milk, and cinnamon in a bowl; set aside. Pulse walnuts and pistachios in a food processor until they are finely crumbled. In a small bowl, mix the walnuts, pistachios, sugar, and bread crumbs. Spread the nut mixture on 2 bread slices.
2. Cover with the remaining 2 slices. Melt the butter in a skillet over medium heat. Dip the sandwiches into the egg mixture and fry them for 4 minutes on both sides or until golden. Remove to a plate and cut them diagonally. Dust with confectioners' sugar. Serve immediately.

Nutrition:
• Info Per Serving: Calories: 651;Fat: 30g;Protein: 21g;Carbs: 80g.

Energy Nut Smoothie

Servings:1 | Cooking Time:10 Minutes

Ingredients:
- 1 tbsp extra-virgin olive oil
- ½ cup Greek yogurt
- ½ cup almond milk
- ½ orange, zested and juiced
- 1 tbsp pistachios, chopped
- 1 tsp honey
- ½ tsp ground allspice
- ¼ tsp ground cinnamon
- ¼ tsp vanilla extract

Directions:
1. Place the yogurt, almond milk, orange zest and juice, olive oil, pistachios, honey, allspice, cinnamon, and vanilla in a blender and pulse until smooth and creamy. Add a little water to achieve your desired consistency. Serve in a chilled glass.

Nutrition:
- Info Per Serving: Calories: 264;Fat: 22.2g;Protein: 6g;Carbs: 12g.

Vegetable & Egg Sandwiches

Servings:2 | Cooking Time:15 Minutes

Ingredients:
- 1 Iceberg lettuce, separated into leaves
- 1 tbsp olive oil
- 1 tbsp butter
- 2 fontina cheese slices, grated
- 3 eggs
- 4 slices multigrain bread
- 3 radishes, sliced
- ½ cucumber, sliced
- 2 pimiento peppers, chopped
- Salt and red pepper to taste

Directions:
1. Warm the oil in a skillet over medium heat. Crack in the eggs and cook until the whites are set. Season with salt and red pepper; remove to a plate. Brush the bread slices with butter and toast them in the same skillet for 2 minutes per side.
2. Arrange 2 bread slices on a flat surface and put themover the eggs. Add in the remaining ingredients and top with the remaining slices. Serve immediately.

Nutrition:
- Info Per Serving: Calories: 487;Fat: 13g;Protein: 24g;Carbs: 32g.

Cauliflower Breakfast Porridge

Servings:2 | Cooking Time: 5 Minutes

Ingredients:
- 2 cups riced cauliflower
- ¾ cup unsweetened almond milk
- 4 tablespoons extra-virgin olive oil, divided
- 2 teaspoons grated fresh orange peel (from ½ orange)
- ½ teaspoon almond extract or vanilla extract
- ½ teaspoon ground cinnamon
- ⅛ teaspoon salt
- 4 tablespoons chopped walnuts, divided
- 1 to 2 teaspoons maple syrup (optional)

Directions:
1. Place the riced cauliflower, almond milk, 2 tablespoons of olive oil, orange peel, almond extract, cinnamon, and salt in a medium saucepan.
2. Stir to incorporate and bring the mixture to a boil over medium-high heat, stirring often.
3. Remove from the heat and add 2 tablespoons of chopped walnuts and maple syrup (if desired).

4. Stir again and divide the porridge into bowls. To serve, sprinkle each bowl evenly with remaining 2 tablespoons of walnuts and olive oil.

Nutrition:
- Info Per Serving: Calories: 381;Fat: 37.8g;Protein: 5.2g;Carbs: 10.9g.

Carrot & Pecan Cupcakes

Servings:6 | Cooking Time:30 Minutes

Ingredients:
- 2 tbsp olive oil
- 1 ½ cups grated carrots
- ¼ cup pecans, chopped
- 1 cup oat bran
- 1 cup wholewheat flour
- ½ cup all-purpose flour
- ½ cup old-fashioned oats
- 3 tbsp light brown sugar
- 1 tsp vanilla extract
- ½ lemon, zested
- 1 tsp baking powder
- 2 tsp ground cinnamon
- 2 tsp ground ginger
- ½ tsp ground nutmeg
- ¼ tsp salt
- 1¼ cups soy milk
- 2 tbsp honey
- 1 egg

Directions:
1. Preheat oven to 350 °F. Mix whole-wheat flour, all-purpose flour, oat bran, oats, sugar, baking powder, cinnamon, nutmeg, ginger, and salt in a bowl; set aside.
2. Beat egg with soy milk, honey, vanilla, lemon zest, and olive oil in another bowl. Pour this mixture into the flour mixture and combine to blend, leaving some lumps. Stir in carrots and pecans. Spoon batter into greased muffin cups. Bake for about 20 minutes. Prick with a toothpick and if it comes out easily, the cakes are cooked done. Let cool and serve.

Nutrition:
- Info Per Serving: Calories: 346;Fat: 10g;Protein: 13g;Carbs: 59g.

Walnut & Berry Parfait

Servings:1 | Cooking Time:10 Minutes

Ingredients:
- ½ cup Greek yogurt
- 2 tbsp heavy whipping cream
- ¼ cup frozen berries, thawed
- ½ tsp vanilla extract
- 1 tbsp ground flaxseed
- 2 tbsp chopped walnuts
- ¼ mint leaves, chopped

Directions:
1. Mix the yogurt, heavy whipping cream, thawed berries in their juice, vanilla extract, and flaxseed in a small bowl and stir well until smooth. Pour into a glass and top with chopped walnuts and mint. Serve and enjoy!

Nutrition:
- Info Per Serving: Calories: 267;Fat: 19g;Protein: 12g;Carbs: 12g.

Hummus Toast With Pine Nuts & Ricotta

Servings:2 | Cooking Time:5 Minutes

Ingredients:
- 2 whole-wheat bread slices, toasted
- 1 tsp water
- 1 tbsp hummus
- 2 tsp ricotta cheese, crumbled
- ½ lemon, juiced
- 2 tsp pine nuts

Directions:
1. Whisk hummus, water, and lemon juice in a bowl and spread over toasted slices. Sprinkle ricotta cheese and pine nuts.

Nutrition:
- Info Per Serving: Calories: 150;Fat: 8g;Protein: 6g;Carbs: 15g.

One-Pan Tomato-Basil Eggs

Servings:2 | Cooking Time:25 Minutes

Ingredients:
- 2 tsp olive oil
- 2 eggs, whisked
- 2 tomatoes, cubed
- 1 tbsp basil, chopped
- 1 green onion, chopped
- Salt and black pepper to taste

Directions:
1. Warm the oil in a skillet over medium heat and sauté tomatoes, green onion, salt, and pepper for 5 minutes. Stir in eggs and cook for another 10 minutes. Serve topped with basil.

Nutrition:
- Info Per Serving: Calories: 310;Fat: 15g;Protein: 12g;Carbs: 18g.

Parmesan Oatmeal With Greens

Servings:2 | Cooking Time: 18 Minutes

Ingredients:
- 1 tablespoon olive oil
- ¼ cup minced onion
- 2 cups greens (arugula, baby spinach, chopped kale, or Swiss chard)
- ¾ cup gluten-free old-fashioned oats
- 1½ cups water, or low-sodium chicken stock
- 2 tablespoons Parmesan cheese
- Salt, to taste
- Pinch freshly ground black pepper

Directions:
1. Heat the olive oil in a saucepan over medium-high heat. Add the minced onion and sauté for 2 minutes, or until softened.
2. Add the greens and stir until they begin to wilt. Transfer this mixture to a bowl and set aside.
3. Add the oats to the pan and let them toast for about 2 minutes. Add the water and bring the oats to a boil.
4. Reduce the heat to low, cover, and let the oats cook for 10 minutes, or until the liquid is absorbed and the oats are tender.
5. Stir the Parmesan cheese into the oats, and add the onion and greens back to the pan. Add additional water if needed, so the oats are creamy and not dry.
6. Stir well and season with salt and black pepper to taste. Serve warm.

Nutrition:
- Info Per Serving: Calories: 257;Fat: 14.0g;Protein: 12.2g;Carbs: 30.2g.

Chocolate-Strawberry Smoothie

Servings:2 | Cooking Time:5 Minutes

Ingredients:
- 1 cup buttermilk
- 2 cups strawberries, hulled
- 1 cup crushed ice
- 3 tbsp cocoa powder
- 3 tbsp honey
- 2 mint leaves

Directions:
1. In a food processor, pulse buttermilk, strawberries, ice, cocoa powder, mint, and honey until smooth. Serve.

Nutrition:
- Info Per Serving: Calories: 209;Fat: 2.6g;Protein: 7g;Carbs: 47.2g.

Vegetable & Hummus Bowl

Servings:4 | Cooking Time:15 Minutes

Ingredients:
- 2 tbsp butter
- 2 tbsp olive oil
- 3 cups green cabbage, shredded
- 3 cups kale, chopped
- 1 lb asparagus, chopped
- ½ cup hummus
- 1 avocado, sliced
- 4 boiled eggs, sliced
- 1 tbsp balsamic vinegar
- 1 garlic clove, minced
- 2 tsp yellow mustard
- Salt and black pepper to taste

Directions:
1. Melt butter in a skillet over medium heat and sauté asparagus for 5 minutes. Mix the olive oil, balsamic vinegar, garlic, yellow mustard, salt, and pepper in a bowl. Spoon the hummus onto the center of a salad bowl and arrange in the asparagus, kale, cabbage, and avocado. Top with the egg slices. Drizzle with the dressing and serve.

Nutrition:
- Info Per Serving: Calories: 392;Fat: 31g;Protein: 14g;Carbs: 22g.

Detox Juice

Servings:1 | Cooking Time:5 Minutes

Ingredients:
- ½ grapefruit
- ½ lemon
- 3 cups cavolo nero
- 1 cucumber
- ¼ cup fresh parsley leaves
- ¼ pineapple, cut into wedges
- ½ green apple
- 1 tsp grated fresh ginger

Directions:
1. In a mixer, place the cavolo nero, parsley, cucumber, pineapple, grapefruit, apple, lemon, and ginger and pulse until smooth. Serve in a tall glass.

Nutrition:
- Info Per Serving: Calories: 255;Fat: 0.9g;Protein: 9.5g;Carbs: 60g.

Egg Bake

Servings:2 | Cooking Time: 30 Minutes

Ingredients:
- 1 tablespoon olive oil
- 1 slice whole-grain bread
- 4 large eggs
- 3 tablespoons unsweetened almond milk
- ½ teaspoon onion powder
- ¼ teaspoon garlic powder
- ¾ cup chopped cherry tomatoes
- ¼ teaspoon salt
- Pinch freshly ground black pepper

Directions:
1. Preheat the oven to 375ºF.
2. Coat two ramekins with the olive oil and transfer to a baking sheet. Line the bottom of each ramekin with ½ of bread slice.
3. In a medium bowl, whisk together the eggs, almond milk, onion powder, garlic powder, tomatoes, salt, and pepper until well combined.
4. Pour the mixture evenly into two ramekins. Bake in the preheated oven for 30 minutes, or until the eggs are completely set.
5. Cool for 5 minutes before serving.

Nutrition:
- Info Per Serving: Calories: 240;Fat: 17.4g;Protein: 9.0g;Carbs: 12.2g.

Avocado Bruschetta With Tomatoes

Servings:4 | Cooking Time:5 Minutes

Ingredients:
- 1 tbsp olive oil
- 1 baguette, sliced
- 2 sun-dried tomatoes, chopped
- 1 avocado, chopped
- 2 tbsp lemon juice
- 8 cherry tomatoes, chopped
- ¼ cup red onion, chopped
- 1 tsp dried oregano
- 2 tbsp parsley, chopped
- 4 Kalamata olives, chopped
- Salt and black pepper to taste

Directions:
1. Preheat oven to 360 °F. Arrange the bread slices on a greased baking tray and drizzle with olive oil. Bake until golden, about 6-8 minutes. Mash the avocado in a bowl with lemon juice, salt, and pepper. Stir in sun-dried tomatoes, onion, oregano, parsley, and olives. Spread the avocado mixture on toasted bread slices and top with cherry tomatoes to serve.

Nutrition:
- Info Per Serving: Calories: 120;Fat: 11g;Protein: 2g;Carbs: 7g.

Lemon Cardamom Buckwheat Pancakes

Servings:2 | Cooking Time:20 Minutes

Ingredients:
- ½ cup buckwheat flour
- ½ tsp cardamom
- ½ tsp baking powder
- ½ cup milk
- ¼ cup plain Greek yogurt
- 1 egg
- 1 tsp lemon zest
- 1 tbsp honey

Directions:
1. Mix the buckwheat flour, cardamom, and baking powder in a medium bowl. Whisk the milk, yogurt, egg, lemon zest, and honey in another bowl. Add the wet ingredients to the dry ingredients and stir until the batter is smooth.

2. Spray a frying pan with non-stick cooking oil and cook the pancakes over medium heat until the edges begin to brown. Flip and cook on the other side for 3 more minutes. Serve.

Nutrition:
- Info Per Serving: Calories: 196;Fat: 6g;Protein: 10g;Carbs: 27g.

Honey Breakfast Smoothie

Servings:1 | Cooking Time:10 Minutes

Ingredients:
- 1 tbsp olive oil
- 2 tbsp almond butter
- 1 cup almond milk
- ¼ cup blueberries
- 1 tbsp ground flaxseed
- 1 tsp honey
- ½ tsp vanilla extract
- ¼ tsp ground cinnamon

Directions:
1. In a blender, mix the almond milk, blueberries, almond butter, flaxseed, olive oil, stevia vanilla, and cinnamon and pulse until smooth and creamy. Add more milk or water to achieve your desired consistency. Serve at room temperature.

Nutrition:
- Info Per Serving: Calories: 460;Fat: 40.2g;Protein: 9g;Carbs: 20g.

Tomato & Spinach Egg Wraps

Servings:2 | Cooking Time:15 Minutes

Ingredients:
- 1 tbsp parsley, chopped
- 1 tbsp olive oil
- ¼ onion, chopped
- 3 sun-dried tomatoes, chopped
- 3 large eggs, beaten
- 2 cups baby spinach, torn
- 1 oz feta cheese, crumbled
- Salt to taste
- 2 whole-wheat tortillas, warm

Directions:
1. Warm the olive oil in a pan over medium heat. Sauté the onion and tomatoes for about 3 minutes. Add the beaten eggs and stir to scramble them, about 4 minutes. Add the spinach and parsley stir to combine. Sprinkle the feta cheese over the eggs. Season with salt to taste. Divide the mixture between the tortillas. Roll them up and serve.

Nutrition:
- Info Per Serving: Calories: 435;Fat: 28g;Protein: 17g;Carbs: 31g.

Nut & Plum Parfait

Servings:4 | Cooking Time:10 Minutes

Ingredients:
- 1 tbsp honey
- 1 cup plums, chopped
- 2 cups Greek yogurt
- 1 tsp cinnamon powder
- 1 tbsp almonds, chopped
- 1 tbsp walnuts, chopped
- ¼ cup pistachios, chopped

Directions:
1. Place a skillet over medium heat and add in plums, honey, cinnamon powder, almonds, walnuts, pistachios, and ¼ cup water. Cook for 5 minutes. Share Greek yogurt into serving bowls and top with plum mixture and toss before serving.

Nutrition:
- Info Per Serving: Calories: 200;Fat: 5g;Protein: 4g;Carbs: 42g.

Dulse, Avocado, And Tomato Pitas

Servings:4 | Cooking Time: 30 Minutes

Ingredients:
- 2 teaspoons coconut oil
- ½ cup dulse, picked through and separated
- Ground black pepper, to taste
- 2 avocados, sliced
- 2 tablespoons lime juice
- ¼ cup chopped cilantro
- 2 scallions, white and light green parts, sliced
- Sea salt, to taste
- 4 whole wheat pitas, sliced in half
- 4 cups chopped romaine
- 4 plum tomatoes, sliced

Directions:
1. Heat the coconut oil in a nonstick skillet over medium heat until melted.
2. Add the dulse and sauté for 5 minutes or until crispy. Sprinkle with ground black pepper and turn off the heat. Set aside.
3. Put the avocado, lime juice, cilantro, and scallions in a food processor and sprinkle with salt and ground black pepper. Pulse to combine well until smooth.
4. Toast the pitas in a baking pan in the oven for 1 minute until soft.
5. Transfer the pitas to a clean work surface and open. Spread the avocado mixture over the pitas, then top with dulse, romaine, and tomato slices.
6. Serve immediately.

Nutrition:
- Info Per Serving: Calories: 412;Fat: 18.7g;Protein: 9.1g;Carbs: 56.1g.

Apple & Date Smoothie

Servings:1 | Cooking Time:5 Minutes

Ingredients:
- 1 apple, peeled and chopped
- ½ cup milk
- 4 dates
- 1 tsp ground cinnamon

Directions:
1. In a blender, place the milk, ½ cup of water, dates, cinnamon, and apple. Blitz until smooth. Let chill in the fridge for 30 minutes. Serve in a tall glass.

Nutrition:
- Info Per Serving: Calories: 486;Fat: 29g;Protein: 4.2g;Carbs: 63g.

Anchovy & Spinach Sandwiches

Servings:2 | Cooking Time:5 Minutes

Ingredients:
- 1 avocado, mashed
- 4 anchovies, drained
- 4 whole-wheat bread slices
- 1 cup baby spinach
- 1 tomato, sliced

Directions:
1. Spread the slices of bread with avocado mash and arrange the anchovies over. Top with baby spinach and tomato slices.

Nutrition:
- Info Per Serving: Calories: 300;Fat: 12g;Protein: 5g;Carbs: 10g.

Sumptuous Vegetable And Cheese Lavash Pizza

Servings:4 | Cooking Time: 11 Minutes

Ingredients:
- 2 lavash breads
- 2 tablespoons extra-virgin olive oil
- 10 ounces frozen spinach, thawed and squeezed dry
- 1 cup shredded fontina cheese
- 1 tomato, cored and cut into ½-inch pieces
- ½ cup pitted large green olives, chopped
- ¼ teaspoon red pepper flakes
- 3 garlic cloves, minced
- ¼ teaspoon sea salt
- ¼ teaspoon ground black pepper
- ½ cup grated Parmesan cheese

Directions:
1. Preheat oven to 475ºF.
2. Brush the lavash breads with olive oil, then place them on two baking sheet. Heat in the preheated oven for 4 minutes or until lightly browned. Flip the breads halfway through the cooking time.
3. Meanwhile, combine the spinach, fontina cheese, tomato pieces, olives, red pepper flakes, garlic, salt, and black pepper in a large bowl. Stir to mix well.
4. Remove the lavash bread from the oven and sit them on two large plates, spread them with the spinach mixture, then scatter with the Parmesan cheese on top.
5. Bake in the oven for 7 minutes or until the cheese melts and well browned.
6. Slice and serve warm.

Nutrition:
- Info Per Serving: Calories: 431;Fat: 21.5g;Protein: 20.0g;Carbs: 38.4g.

Cherry Tomato & Mushroom Frittata

Servings:4 | Cooking Time:30 Minutes

Ingredients:
- 1 cup Italian brown mushrooms, sliced
- 2 tbsp olive oil
- 2 spring onions, chopped
- 8 cherry tomatoes, halved
- 6 eggs
- ½ cup milk
- Salt and black pepper to taste
- ¼ cup grated Parmesan
- ½ tbsp Italian seasoning mix

Directions:
1. Preheat oven to 370 F. Mix eggs, milk, Italian seasoning, salt, and pepper in a bowl. Warm olive oil in a skillet over medium heat until sizzling. Add in mushrooms, spring onions, and tomatoes and sauté for 5 minutes.
2. Pour in the egg mixture and cook for 5 minutes until the eggs are set. Scatter Parmesan cheese and bake in the oven for 6-7 minutes until the cheese melts. Slice before serving.

Nutrition:
- Info Per Serving: Calories: 227;Fat: 15g;Protein: 13g;Carbs: 13g.

Raspberry-Yogurt Smoothie

Servings:2 | Cooking Time:10 Minutes

Ingredients:
- 2 cups raspberries
- 1 tsp honey
- 1 cup natural yogurt
- ½ cup milk
- 8 ice cubes

Directions:
1. In a food processor, combine yogurt, raspberries, honey, and milk. Blitz until smooth. Add in ice cubes and pulse until uniform. Serve right away.
Nutrition:
• Info Per Serving: Calories: 187;Fat: 7g;Protein: 8g;Carbs: 26g.

Mushroom & Zucchini Egg Muffins

Servings:4 | Cooking Time:20 Minutes
Ingredients:
• 2 tbsp olive oil
• 1 cup Parmesan, grated
• 1 onion, chopped
• 1 cup mushrooms, sliced
• 1 red bell pepper, chopped
• 1 zucchini, chopped
• Salt and black pepper to taste
• 8 eggs, whisked
• 2 tbsp chives, chopped
Directions:
1. Preheat the oven to 360 °F. Warm the olive oil in a skillet over medium heat and sauté onion, bell pepper, zucchini, mushrooms, salt, and pepper for 5 minutes until tender. Mix with eggs and season with salt and pepper. Distribute the mixture across muffin cups and top with the Parmesan cheese. Sprinkle with chives and bake for 10 minutes. Serve.
Nutrition:
• Info Per Serving: Calories: 60;Fat: 4g;Protein: 5g;Carbs: 4g.

Skillet Eggplant & Kale Frittata

Servings:1 | Cooking Time:20 Minutes
Ingredients:
• 1 tbsp olive oil
• 3 large eggs
• 1 tsp milk
• 1 cup curly kale, torn
• ½ eggplant, peeled and diced
• ¼ red bell pepper, chopped
• Salt and black pepper to taste
• 1 oz crumbled Goat cheese
Directions:
1. Preheat your broiler. Whisk the eggs with milk, salt, and pepper until just combined. Heat the olive oil in a small skillet over medium heat. Spread the eggs on the bottom and add the kale on top in an even layer; top with veggies.
2. Season with salt and pepper. Allow the eggs and vegetables to cook 3 to 5 minutes until the bottom half of the eggs are firm and vegetables are tender. Top with the crumbled Goat cheese and place under the broiler for 5 minutes until the eggs are firm in the middle and the cheese has melted. Slice into wedges and serve immediately.
Nutrition:
• Info Per Serving: Calories: 622;Fat: 39g;Protein: 41g;Carbs: 33g.

Baked Parmesan Chicken Wraps

Servings:6 | Cooking Time: 18 Minutes
Ingredients:
• 1 pound boneless, skinless chicken breasts
• 1 large egg
• ¼ cup unsweetened almond milk
• ⅔ cup whole-wheat bread crumbs
• ½ cup grated Parmesan cheese
• ¾ teaspoon garlic powder, divided
• 1 cup canned low-sodium or no-salt-added crushed tomatoes
• 1 teaspoon dried oregano
• 6 whole-wheat tortillas, or whole-grain spinach wraps
• 1 cup fresh Mozzarella cheese, sliced
• 1½ cups loosely packed fresh flat-leaf (Italian) parsley, chopped
• Cooking spray
Directions:
1. Preheat the oven to 425°F. Line a large, rimmed baking sheet with aluminum foil. Place a wire rack on the aluminum foil, and spritz the rack with nonstick cooking spray. Set aside.
2. Place the chicken breasts into a large plastic bag. With a rolling pin, pound the chicken so it is evenly flattened, about ¼ inch thick. Slice the chicken into six portions.
3. In a bowl, whisk together the egg and milk. In another bowl, stir together the bread crumbs, Parmesan cheese and ½ teaspoon of the garlic powder.
4. Dredge each chicken breast portion into the egg mixture, and then into the Parmesan crumb mixture, pressing the crumbs into the chicken so they stick. Arrange the chicken on the prepared wire rack.
5. Bake in the preheated oven for 15 to 18 minutes, or until the internal temperature of the chicken reads 165°F on a meat thermometer and any juices run clear.
6. Transfer the chicken to a cutting board, and cut each portion diagonally into ½-inch pieces.
7. In a small, microwave-safe bowl, stir together the tomatoes, oregano, and the remaining ¼ teaspoon of the garlic powder. Cover the bowl with a paper towel and microwave for about 1 minute on high, until very hot. Set aside.
8. Wrap the tortillas in a damp paper towel and microwave for 30 to 45 seconds on high, or until warmed through.
9. Assemble the wraps: Divide the chicken slices evenly among the six tortillas and top with the sliced Mozzarella cheese. Spread 1 tablespoon of the warm tomato sauce over the cheese on each tortilla, and top each with about ¼ cup of the parsley.
10. Wrap the tortilla: Fold up the bottom of the tortilla, then fold one side over and fold the other side over the top.
11. Serve the wraps warm with the remaining sauce for dipping.
Nutrition:
• Info Per Serving: Calories: 358;Fat: 12.0g;Protein: 21.0g;Carbs: 41.0g.

Cherry Tomato & Zucchini Scrambled Eggs

Servings:4 | Cooking Time:15 Minutes
Ingredients:
• 2 tbsp olive oil
• 6 cherry tomatoes, halved
• ½ cup chopped zucchini
• ½ chopped green bell pepper
• 8 eggs, beaten
• 1 shallot, chopped
• 1 tbsp chopped fresh parsley
• 1 tbsp chopped fresh basil
• Salt and black pepper to taste
Directions:
1. Warm oil in a pan over medium heat. Place in zucchini, green bell peppers, salt, black pepper, and shallot. Cook for 4-5 minutes to sweat the shallot. Stir in tomatoes, parsley, and basil.
2. Cook for a minute and top with the beaten eggs. Lower the heat and cook for 6-7 minutes until the eggs are set but not runny. Remove to a platter to serve.
Nutrition:
• Info Per Serving: Calories: 205;Fat: 15g;Protein: 12g;Carbs: 4g.

Breakfast Pancakes With Berry Sauce

Servings:4 | Cooking Time: 10 Minutes

Ingredients:
- Pancakes:
- 1 cup almond flour
- 1 teaspoon baking powder
- ¼ teaspoon salt
- 6 tablespoon extra-virgin olive oil, divided
- 2 large eggs, beaten
- Zest and juice of 1 lemon
- ½ teaspoon vanilla extract
- Berry Sauce:
- 1 cup frozen mixed berries
- 1 tablespoon water, plus more as needed
- ½ teaspoon vanilla extract

Directions:
1. Make the Pancakes
2. In a large bowl, combine the almond flour, baking powder, and salt and stir to break up any clumps.
3. Add 4 tablespoons olive oil, beaten eggs, lemon zest and juice, and vanilla extract and stir until well mixed.
4. Heat 1 tablespoon of olive oil in a large skillet. Spoon about 2 tablespoons of batter for each pancake. Cook until bubbles begin to form, 4 to 5 minutes. Flip and cook for another 2 to 3 minutes. Repeat with the remaining 1 tablespoon of olive oil and batter.
5. Make the Berry Sauce
6. Combine the frozen berries, water, and vanilla extract in a small saucepan and heat over medium-high heat for 3 to 4 minutes until bubbly, adding more water as needed. Using the back of a spoon or fork, mash the berries and whisk until smooth.
7. Serve the pancakes with the berry sauce.

Nutrition:
- Info Per Serving: Calories: 275;Fat: 26.0g;Protein: 4.0g;Carbs: 8.0g.

Mediterranean Eggs (Shakshuka)

Servings:4 | Cooking Time: 20 Minutes

Ingredients:
- 2 tablespoons extra-virgin olive oil
- 1 cup chopped shallots
- 1 teaspoon garlic powder
- 1 cup finely diced potato
- 1 cup chopped red bell peppers
- 1 can diced tomatoes, drained
- ¼ teaspoon ground cardamom
- ¼ teaspoon paprika
- ¼ teaspoon turmeric
- 4 large eggs
- ¼ cup chopped fresh cilantro

Directions:
1. Preheat the oven to 350ºF.
2. Heat the olive oil in an ovenproof skillet over medium-high heat until it shimmers.
3. Add the shallots and sauté for about 3 minutes, stirring occasionally, until fragrant.
4. Fold in the garlic powder, potato, and bell peppers and stir to combine.
5. Cover and cook for 10 minutes, stirring frequently.
6. Add the tomatoes, cardamon, paprika, and turmeric and mix well.
7. When the mixture begins to bubble, remove from the heat and crack the eggs into the skillet.
8. Transfer the skillet to the preheated oven and bake for 5 to 10 minutes, or until the egg whites are set and the yolks are cooked to your liking.
9. Remove from the oven and garnish with the cilantro before serving.

Nutrition:
- Info Per Serving: Calories: 223;Fat: 11.8g;Protein: 9.1g;Carbs: 19.5g.

Maple Berry & Walnut Oatmeal

Servings:2 | Cooking Time:10 Minutes

Ingredients:
- 1 cup mixed berries
- 1 ½ cups rolled oats
- 2 tbsp walnuts, chopped
- 2 tsp maple syrup

Directions:
1. Cook the oats according to the package instructions and share in 2 bowls. Microwave the maple syrup and berries for 30 seconds; stir well. Pour over each bowl. Top with walnuts.

Nutrition:
- Info Per Serving: Calories: 262;Fat: 10g;Protein: 15g;Carbs: 57g.

Mashed Grape Tomato Pizzas

Servings:6 | Cooking Time: 20 Minutes

Ingredients:
- 3 cups grape tomatoes, halved
- 1 teaspoon chopped fresh thyme leaves
- 2 garlic cloves, minced
- ¼ teaspoon kosher salt
- ¼ teaspoon freshly ground black pepper
- 1 tablespoon extra-virgin olive oil
- ¾ cup shredded Parmesan cheese
- 6 whole-wheat pita breads

Directions:
1. Preheat the oven to 425ºF.
2. Combine the tomatoes, thyme, garlic, salt, ground black pepper, and olive oil in a baking pan.
3. Roast in the preheated oven for 20 minutes. Remove the pan from the oven, mash the tomatoes with a spatula and stir to mix well halfway through the cooking time.
4. Meanwhile, divide and spread the cheese over each pita bread, then place the bread in a separate baking pan and roast in the oven for 5 minutes or until golden brown and the cheese melts.
5. Transfer the pita bread onto a large plate, then top with the roasted mashed tomatoes. Serve immediately.

Nutrition:
- Info Per Serving: Calories: 140;Fat: 5.1g;Protein: 6.2g;Carbs: 16.9g.

Brown Rice Salad With Cheese

Servings:4 | Cooking Time:10 Minutes

Ingredients:
- 2 tbsp olive oil
- ½ cup brown rice
- 1 lb watercress
- 1 Roma tomato, sliced
- 4 oz feta cheese, crumbled
- 2 tbsp fresh basil, chopped
- Salt and black pepper to taste
- 2 tbsp lemon juice
- ¼ tsp lemon zest

Directions:
1. Bring to a boil salted water in a pot over medium heat. Add in the rice and cook for 15-18 minutes. Drain and let cool completely. Whisk the olive oil, lemon zest, lemon juice, salt, and pepper in a salad bowl. Add in the watercress, cooled rice, and basil and toss to coat. Top with feta cheese and tomato. Serve immediately.

Nutrition:
- Info Per Serving: Calories: 480;Fat: 24g;Protein: 14g;Carbs: 55g.

Spinach & Prosciutto Crostini

Servings:1 | Cooking Time:5 Minutes

Ingredients:
- 1 tsp olive oil
- 2 prosciutto slices
- 2 ciabatta slices, toasted
- 1 tbsp Dijon mustard
- Salt and black pepper to taste
- 1 tomato, sliced
- ¼ cup baby spinach

Directions:
1. Smear Dijon mustard on one side of each ciabatta slice and top with prosciutto, tomato, spinach, salt, and pepper on each slice. Drizzle with olive oil and serve.

Nutrition:
- Info Per Serving: Calories: 250;Fat: 12g;Protein: 9g;Carbs: 18g.

Artichoke & Spinach Frittata

Servings:4 | Cooking Time:55 Minutes

Ingredients:
- 4 oz canned artichokes, chopped
- 2 tsp olive oil
- ½ cup whole milk
- 8 eggs
- 1 cup spinach, chopped
- 1 garlic clove, minced
- ½ cup Parmesan, crumbled
- 1 tsp oregano, dried
- 1 Jalapeño pepper, minced
- Salt to taste

Directions:
1. Preheat oven to 360 F. Warm the olive oil in a skillet over medium heat and sauté garlic and spinach for 3 minutes.
2. Beat the eggs in a bowl. Stir in artichokes, milk, Parmesan cheese, oregano, jalapeño pepper, and salt. Add in spinach mixture and toss to combine. Transfer to a greased baking dish and bake for 20 minutes until golden and bubbling. Slice into wedges and serve.

Nutrition:
- Info Per Serving: Calories: 190;Fat: 14g;Protein: 10g;Carbs: 5g.

Creamy Breakfast Bulgur With Berries

Servings:2 | Cooking Time: 10 Minutes

Ingredients:
- ½ cup medium-grain bulgur wheat
- 1 cup water
- Pinch sea salt
- ¼ cup unsweetened almond milk
- 1 teaspoon pure vanilla extract
- ¼ teaspoon ground cinnamon
- 1 cup fresh berries of your choice

Directions:
1. Put the bulgur in a medium saucepan with the water and sea salt, and bring to a boil.
2. Cover, remove from heat, and let stand for 10 minutes until water is absorbed.
3. Stir in the milk, vanilla, and cinnamon until fully incorporated. Divide between 2 bowls and top with the fresh berries to serve.

Nutrition:
- Info Per Serving: Calories: 173;Fat: 1.6g;Protein: 5.7g;Carbs: 34.0g.

Mushroom-Pesto Baked Pizza

Servings:2 | Cooking Time: 15 Minutes

Ingredients:
- 1 teaspoon extra-virgin olive oil
- ½ cup sliced mushrooms
- ½ red onion, sliced
- Salt and freshly ground black pepper
- ¼ cup store-bought pesto sauce
- 2 whole-wheat flatbreads
- ¼ cup shredded Mozzarella cheese

Directions:
1. Preheat the oven to 350ºF.
2. In a small skillet, heat the oil over medium heat. Add the mushrooms and onion, and season with salt and pepper. Sauté for 3 to 5 minutes until the onion and mushrooms begin to soften.
3. Spread 2 tablespoons of pesto on each flatbread.
4. Divide the mushroom-onion mixture between the two flatbreads. Top each with 2 tablespoons of cheese.
5. Place the flatbreads on a baking sheet and bake for 10 to 12 minutes until the cheese is melted and bubbly. Serve warm.

Nutrition:
- Info Per Serving: Calories: 348;Fat: 23.5g;Protein: 14.2g;Carbs: 28.1g.

Banana & Chia Seed Oats With Walnuts

Servings:2 | Cooking Time:15 Minutes

Ingredients:
- ½ cup walnuts, chopped
- 1 banana, peeled and sliced
- 1 cup Greek yogurt
- 2 dates, pitted and chopped
- 1 cup rolled oats
- 2 tbsp chia seeds

Directions:
1. Place banana, yogurt, dates, oats, and chia seeds in a bowl and blend until smooth. Let sit for 1 hour and spoon onto a bowl. Sprinkle with walnuts and serve.

Nutrition:
- Info Per Serving: Calories: 512;Fat: 24g;Protein: 25g;Carbs: 58g.

Spinach Cheese Pie

Servings:8 | Cooking Time: 25 Minutes

Ingredients:
- 2 tablespoons extra-virgin olive oil
- 1 onion, chopped
- 1 pound frozen spinach, thawed
- ¼ teaspoon ground nutmeg
- ¼ teaspoon garlic salt
- ¼ teaspoon freshly ground black pepper
- 4 large eggs, divided
- 1 cup grated Parmesan cheese, divided
- 2 puff pastry doughs, at room temperature
- 4 hard-boiled eggs, halved
- Nonstick cooking spray

Directions:
1. Preheat the oven to 350ºF. Spritz a baking sheet with nonstick cooking spray and set aside.
2. Heat a large skillet over medium-high heat. Add the olive oil and onion and sauté for about 5 minutes, stirring occasionally, or until translucent.
3. Squeeze the excess water from the spinach, then add to the skillet and cook, uncovered, so that any excess water from the spinach can evaporate.
4. Season with the nutmeg, garlic salt, and black pepper. Remove from heat and set aside to cool.

5. Beat 3 eggs in a small bowl. Add the beaten eggs and ½ cup of Parmesan cheese to the spinach mixture, stirring well.
6. Roll out the pastry dough on the prepared baking sheet. Layer the spinach mixture on top of the dough, leaving 2 inches around each edge.
7. Once the spinach is spread onto the pastry dough, evenly place the hard-boiled egg halves throughout the pie, then cover with the second pastry dough. Pinch the edges closed.
8. Beat the remaining 1 egg in the bowl. Brush the egg wash over the pastry dough.
9. Bake in the preheated oven for 15 to 20 minutes until golden brown.
10. Sprinkle with the remaining ½ cup of Parmesan cheese. Cool for 5 minutes before cutting and serving.
Nutrition:
• Info Per Serving: Calories: 417;Fat: 28.0g;Protein: 17.0g;Carbs: 25.0g.

Warm Bulgur Breakfast Bowls With Fruits
Servings:6 | Cooking Time: 15 Minutes
Ingredients:
• 2 cups unsweetened almond milk
• 1½ cups uncooked bulgur
• 1 cup water
• ½ teaspoon ground cinnamon
• 2 cups frozen (or fresh, pitted) dark sweet cherries
• 8 dried (or fresh) figs, chopped
• ½ cup chopped almonds
• ¼ cup loosely packed fresh mint, chopped
Directions:
1. Combine the milk, bulgur, water, and cinnamon in a medium saucepan, stirring, and bring just to a boil.
2. Cover, reduce the heat to medium-low, and allow to simmer for 10 minutes, or until the liquid is absorbed.
3. Turn off the heat, but keep the pan on the stove, and stir in the frozen cherries (no need to thaw), figs, and almonds. Cover and let the hot bulgur thaw the cherries and partially hydrate the figs, about 1 minute.
4. Fold in the mint and stir to combine, then serve.
Nutrition:
• Info Per Serving: Calories: 207;Fat: 6.0g;Protein: 8.0g;Carbs: 32.0g.

Easy Buckwheat Porridge
Servings:4 | Cooking Time: 40 Minutes
Ingredients:
• 3 cups water
• 2 cups raw buckwheat groats
• Pinch sea salt
• 1 cup unsweetened almond milk
Directions:
1. In a medium saucepan, add the water, buckwheat groats, and sea salt and bring to a boil over medium-high heat.
2. Once it starts to boil, reduce the heat to low. Cook for about 20 minutes, stirring occasionally, or until most of the water is absorbed.
3. Fold in the almond milk and whisk well. Continue cooking for about 15 minutes, or until the buckwheat groats are very softened.
4. Ladle the porridge into bowls and serve warm.
Nutrition:
• Info Per Serving: Calories: 121;Fat: 1.0g;Protein: 6.3g;Carbs: 21.5g.

Pumpkin-Yogurt Parfaits
Servings:4 | Cooking Time:5 Min + Chilling Time
Ingredients:
• 1 can pumpkin puree
• 4 tsp honey
• 1 tsp pumpkin pie spice
• ¼ tsp ground cinnamon
• 2 cups Greek yogurt
• 1 cup honey granola
• 2 tbsp pomegranate seeds
Directions:
1. Mix the pumpkin puree, honey, pumpkin pie spice, and cinnamon in a large bowl. Layer the pumpkin mix, yogurt, and granola in small glasses. Repeat the layers. Top with pomegranate seeds. Chill for at least 3 hours before serving.
Nutrition:
• Info Per Serving: Calories: 264;Fat: 9.2g;Protein: 15g;Carbs: 35g.

Mango-Yogurt Smoothie
Servings:2 | Cooking Time:5 Minutes
Ingredients:
• 6 oz Greek yogurt
• 2 mangoes, chopped
• 2 tbsp milk
• 7-8 ice cubes
Directions:
1. In a food processor, place the mango, milk, yogurt, and ice cubes. Pulse until creamy and smooth. Serve right away.
Nutrition:
• Info Per Serving: Calories: 261;Fat: 2g;Protein: 12g;Carbs: 54g.

Granola & Berry Parfait
Servings:2 | Cooking Time:5 Minutes
Ingredients:
• 2 cups berries
• 1 ½ cups Greek yogurt
• 1 tbsp powdered sugar
• ¼ cup granola
Directions:
1. Divide between two bowls a layer of berries, yogurt, and powdered sugar. Scatter with granola and serve.
Nutrition:
• Info Per Serving: Calories: 244;Fat: 11g;Protein: 21g;Carbs: 43g.

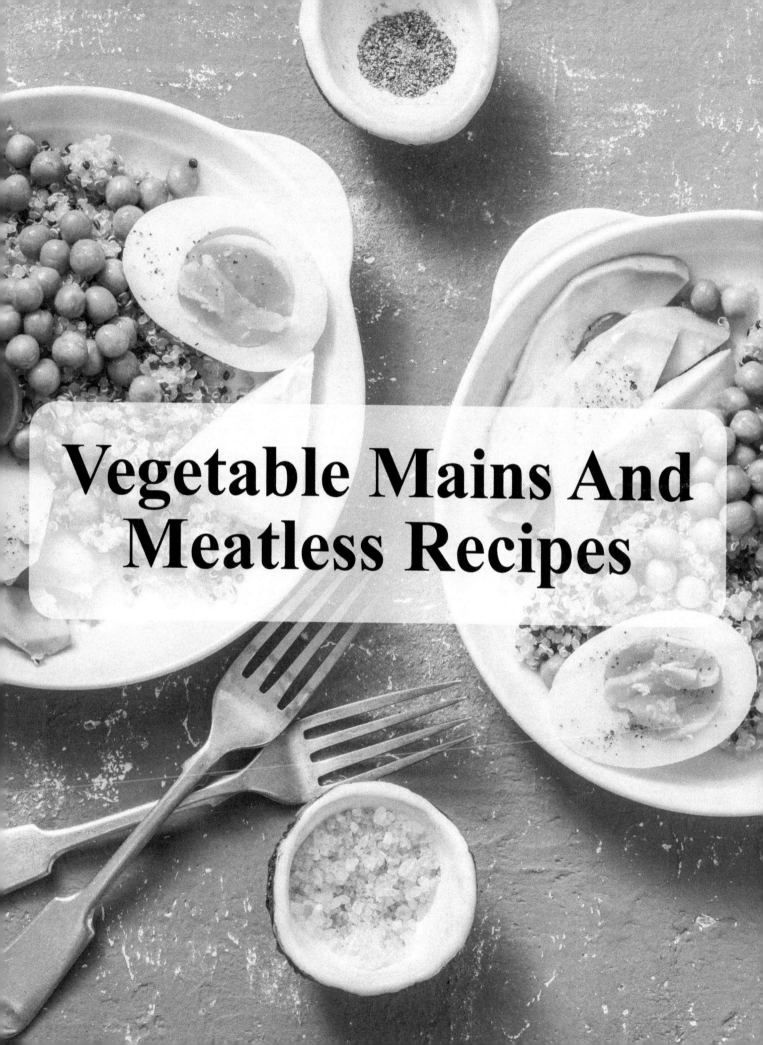

Vegetable Mains And Meatless Recipes

Vegetable Mains And Meatless Recipes

Baked Potato With Veggie Mix

Servings:4 | Cooking Time:45 Minutes

Ingredients:
- 4 tbsp olive oil
- 1 lb potatoes, peeled and diced
- 2 red bell peppers, halved
- 1 lb mushrooms, sliced
- 2 tomatoes, diced
- 8 garlic cloves, peeled
- 1 eggplant, sliced
- 1 yellow onion, quartered
- ½ tsp dried oregano
- ¼ tsp caraway seeds
- Salt to taste

Directions:
1. Preheat the oven to 390°F. In a bowl, combine the bell peppers, mushrooms, tomatoes, eggplant, onion, garlic, salt, olive oil, oregano, and caraway seeds. Set aside. Arrange the potatoes on a baking dish and bake for 15 minutes. Top with the veggies mixture and bake for 15-20 minutes until tender.

Nutrition:
- Info Per Serving: Calories: 302;Fat: 15g;Protein: 8.5g;Carbs: 39g.

Creamy Polenta With Mushrooms

Servings:2 | Cooking Time: 30 Minutes

Ingredients:
- ½ ounce dried porcini mushrooms (optional but recommended)
- 2 tablespoons olive oil
- 1 pound baby bella (cremini) mushrooms, quartered
- 1 large shallot, minced
- 1 garlic clove, minced
- 1 tablespoon flour
- 2 teaspoons tomato paste
- ½ cup red wine
- 1 cup mushroom stock (or reserved liquid from soaking the porcini mushrooms, if using)
- ½ teaspoon dried thyme
- 1 fresh rosemary sprig
- 1½ cups water
- ½ teaspoon salt
- ⅓ cup instant polenta
- 2 tablespoons grated Parmesan cheese

Directions:
1. If using the dried porcini mushrooms, soak them in 1 cup of hot water for about 15 minutes to soften them. When they're softened, scoop them out of the water, reserving the soaking liquid. Mince the porcini mushrooms.
2. Heat the olive oil in a large sauté pan over medium-high heat. Add the mushrooms, shallot, and garlic, and sauté for 10 minutes, or until the vegetables are wilted and starting to caramelize.
3. Add the flour and tomato paste, and cook for another 30 seconds. Add the red wine, mushroom stock or porcini soaking liquid, thyme, and rosemary. Bring the mixture to a boil, stirring constantly until it thickens. Reduce the heat and let it simmer for 10 minutes.
4. Meanwhile, bring the water to a boil in a saucepan and add salt.
5. Add the instant polenta and stir quickly while it thickens. Stir in the Parmesan cheese. Taste and add additional salt, if needed. Serve warm.

Nutrition:
- Info Per Serving: Calories: 450;Fat: 16.0g;Protein: 14.1g;Carbs: 57.8g.

Zoodles With Beet Pesto

Servings:2 | Cooking Time: 50 Minutes

Ingredients:
- 1 medium red beet, peeled, chopped
- ½ cup walnut pieces
- ½ cup crumbled goat cheese
- 3 garlic cloves
- 2 tablespoons freshly squeezed lemon juice
- 2 tablespoons plus 2 teaspoons extra-virgin olive oil, divided
- ¼ teaspoon salt
- 4 small zucchinis, spiralized

Directions:
1. Preheat the oven to 375°F.
2. Wrap the chopped beet in a piece of aluminum foil and seal well.
3. Roast in the preheated oven for 30 to 40 minutes until tender.
4. Meanwhile, heat a skillet over medium-high heat until hot. Add the walnuts and toast for 5 to 7 minutes, or until fragrant and lightly browned.
5. Remove the cooked beets from the oven and place in a food processor. Add the toasted walnuts, goat cheese, garlic, lemon juice, 2 tablespoons of olive oil, and salt. Pulse until smoothly blended. Set aside.
6. Heat the remaining 2 teaspoons of olive oil in a large skillet over medium heat. Add the zucchini and toss to coat in the oil. Cook for 2 to 3 minutes, stirring gently, or until the zucchini is softened.
7. Transfer the zucchini to a serving plate and toss with the beet pesto, then serve.

Nutrition:
- Info Per Serving: Calories: 423;Fat: 38.8g;Protein: 8.0g;Carbs: 17.1g.

Vegetable And Tofu Scramble

Servings:2 | Cooking Time: 10 Minutes

Ingredients:
- 2 tablespoons extra-virgin olive oil
- ½ red onion, finely chopped
- 1 cup chopped kale
- 8 ounces mushrooms, sliced
- 8 ounces tofu, cut into pieces
- 2 garlic cloves, minced
- Pinch red pepper flakes
- ½ teaspoon sea salt
- ⅛ teaspoon freshly ground black pepper

Directions:
1. Heat the olive oil in a medium nonstick skillet over medium-high heat until shimmering.
2. Add the onion, kale, and mushrooms to the skillet and cook for about 5 minutes, stirring occasionally, or until the vegetables start to brown.
3. Add the tofu and stir-fry for 3 to 4 minutes until softened.
4. Stir in the garlic, red pepper flakes, salt, and black pepper and cook for 30 seconds.
5. Let the mixture cool for 5 minutes before serving.

Nutrition:
- Info Per Serving: Calories: 233;Fat: 15.9g;Protein: 13.4g;Carbs: 11.9g.

Balsamic Cherry Tomatoes

Servings:4 | Cooking Time:10 Minutes

Ingredients:
- 2 tbsp olive oil
- 2 lb cherry tomatoes, halved
- 2 tbsp balsamic glaze
- Salt and black pepper to taste
- 1 garlic clove, minced
- 2 tbsp fresh basil, torn

Directions:
1. Warm the olive oil in a skillet over medium heat. Add the cherry tomatoes and cook for 1-2 minutes, stirring occasionally. Stir in garlic, salt, and pepper and cook until fragrant, about 30 seconds. Drizzle with balsamic glaze and decorate with basil. Serve and enjoy!

Nutrition:
- Info Per Serving: Calories: 45;Fat: 2.5g;Protein: 1.1g;Carbs: 5.6g.

Chili Vegetable Skillet

Servings:4 | Cooking Time:30 Minutes

Ingredients:
- 1 cup condensed cream of mushroom soup
- 1 ½ lb eggplants, cut into chunks
- 1 cup cremini mushrooms, sliced
- 4 tbsp olive oil
- 1 carrot, thinly sliced
- 1 can tomatoes
- ½ cup red onion, thinly sliced
- 2 garlic cloves, minced
- 1 tsp fresh rosemary
- 1 tsp chili pepper
- Salt and black pepper to taste
- 2 tbsp parsley, chopped
- ¼ cup Parmesan cheese, grated

Directions:
1. Warm the olive oil in a skillet over medium heat. Add in the eggplant and cook until golden brown on all sides, about 5 minutes; set aside. Add in the carrot, onion, and mushrooms and sauté for 4 more minutes to the same skillet. Add in garlic, rosemary, and chili pepper. Cook for another 30-40 seconds. Add in 1 cup of water, cream of mushroom soup, and tomatoes. Bring to a boil and lower the heat; simmer covered for 5 minutes. Mix in sautéed eggplants and parsley and cook for 10 more minutes. Sprinkle with salt and black pepper. Serve topped with Parmesan cheese.

Nutrition:
- Info Per Serving: Calories: 261;Fat: 18.7g;Protein: 5g;Carbs: 23g.

Baked Tomatoes And Chickpeas

Servings:4 | Cooking Time: 40 To 45 Minutes

Ingredients:
- 1 tablespoon extra-virgin olive oil
- ½ medium onion, chopped
- 3 garlic cloves, chopped
- ¼ teaspoon ground cumin
- 2 teaspoons smoked paprika
- 2 cans chickpeas, drained and rinsed
- 4 cups halved cherry tomatoes
- ½ cup plain Greek yogurt, for serving
- 1 cup crumbled feta cheese, for serving

Directions:
1. Preheat the oven to 425°F.
2. Heat the olive oil in an ovenproof skillet over medium heat.
3. Add the onion and garlic and sauté for about 5 minutes, stirring occasionally, or until tender and fragrant.

4. Add the paprika and cumin and cook for 2 minutes. Stir in the chickpeas and tomatoes and allow to simmer for 5 to 10 minutes.
5. Transfer the skillet to the preheated oven and roast for 25 to 30 minutes, or until the mixture bubbles and thickens.
6. Remove from the oven and serve topped with yogurt and crumbled feta cheese.

Nutrition:
- Info Per Serving: Calories: 411;Fat: 14.9g;Protein: 20.2g;Carbs: 50.7g.

Roasted Veggies And Brown Rice Bowl

Servings:4 | Cooking Time: 20 Minutes

Ingredients:
- 2 cups cauliflower florets
- 2 cups broccoli florets
- 1 can chickpeas, drained and rinsed
- 1 cup carrot slices
- 2 to 3 tablespoons extra-virgin olive oil, divided
- Salt and freshly ground black pepper, to taste
- Nonstick cooking spray
- 2 cups cooked brown rice
- 2 to 3 tablespoons sesame seeds, for garnish
- Dressing:
- 3 to 4 tablespoons tahini
- 2 tablespoons honey
- 1 lemon, juiced
- 1 garlic clove, minced
- Salt and freshly ground black pepper, to taste

Directions:
1. Preheat the oven to 400°F. Spritz two baking sheets with nonstick cooking spray.
2. Spread the cauliflower and broccoli on the first baking sheet and the second with the chickpeas and carrot slices.
3. Drizzle each sheet with half of the olive oil and sprinkle with salt and pepper. Toss to coat well.
4. Roast the chickpeas and carrot slices in the preheated oven for 10 minutes, leaving the carrots tender but crisp, and the cauliflower and broccoli for 20 minutes until fork-tender. Stir them once halfway through the cooking time.
5. Meanwhile, make the dressing: Whisk together the tahini, honey, lemon juice, garlic, salt, and pepper in a small bowl.
6. Divide the cooked brown rice among four bowls. Top each bowl evenly with roasted vegetables and dressing. Sprinkle the sesame seeds on top for garnish before serving.

Nutrition:
- Info Per Serving: Calories: 453;Fat: 17.8g;Protein: 12.1g;Carbs: 61.8g.

Ratatouille

Servings:4 | Cooking Time: 30 Minutes

Ingredients:
- 4 tablespoons extra-virgin olive oil, divided
- 1 cup diced zucchini
- 2 cups diced eggplant
- 1 cup diced onion
- 1 cup chopped green bell pepper
- 1 can no-salt-added diced tomatoes
- ½ teaspoon garlic powder
- 1 teaspoon ground thyme
- Salt and freshly ground black pepper, to taste

Directions:
1. Heat 2 tablespoons of olive oil in a large saucepan over medium heat until it shimmers.
2. Add the zucchini and eggplant and sauté for 10 minutes, stirring occasionally. If necessary, add the remaining olive oil.
3. Stir in the onion and bell pepper and sauté for 5 minutes until softened.

4. Add the diced tomatoes with their juice, garlic powder, and thyme and stir to combine. Continue cooking for 15 minutes until the vegetables are cooked through, stirring occasionally. Sprinkle with salt and black pepper.

5. Remove from the heat and serve on a plate.

Nutrition:
- Info Per Serving: Calories: 189;Fat: 13.7g;Protein: 3.1g;Carbs: 14.8g.

Roasted Celery Root With Yogurt Sauce

Servings:6 | Cooking Time:50 Minutes

Ingredients:
- 3 tbsp olive oil
- 3 celery roots, sliced
- Salt and black pepper to taste
- ¼ cup plain yogurt
- ¼ tsp grated lemon zest
- 1 tsp lemon juice
- 1 tsp sesame seeds, toasted
- 1 tsp coriander seeds, crushed
- ¼ tsp dried thyme
- ¼ tsp chili powder
- ¼ cup fresh cilantro, chopped

Directions:
1. Preheat oven to 425°F. Place the celery slices on a baking sheet. Sprinkle them with olive oil, salt, and pepper. Roast for 25-30 minutes. Flip each piece and continue to roast for 10-15 minutes until celery root is very tender and sides touching sheet are browned. Transfer celery to a serving platter.

2. Whisk yogurt, lemon zest and juice, and salt together in a bowl. In a separate bowl, combine sesame seeds, coriander seeds, thyme, chili powder, and salt. Drizzle celery root with yogurt sauce and sprinkle with seed mixture and cilantro.

Nutrition:
- Info Per Serving: Calories: 75;Fat: 7.5g;Protein: 0.7g;Carbs: 1.8g.

Mini Crustless Spinach Quiches

Servings:6 | Cooking Time: 20 Minutes

Ingredients:
- 2 tablespoons extra-virgin olive oil
- 1 onion, finely chopped
- 2 cups baby spinach
- 2 garlic cloves, minced
- 8 large eggs, beaten
- ¼ cup unsweetened almond milk
- ½ teaspoon sea salt
- ¼ teaspoon freshly ground black pepper
- 1 cup shredded Swiss cheese
- Cooking spray

Directions:
1. Preheat the oven to 375°F. Spritz a 6-cup muffin tin with cooking spray. Set aside.

2. In a large skillet over medium-high heat, heat the olive oil until shimmering. Add the onion and cook for about 4 minutes, or until soft. Add the spinach and cook for about 1 minute, stirring constantly, or until the spinach softens. Add the garlic and sauté for 30 seconds. Remove from the heat and let cool.

3. In a medium bowl, whisk together the eggs, milk, salt and pepper.

4. Stir the cooled vegetables and the cheese into the egg mixture. Spoon the mixture into the prepared muffin tins. Bake for about 15 minutes, or until the eggs are set.

5. Let rest for 5 minutes before serving.

Nutrition:
- Info Per Serving: Calories: 218;Fat: 17.0g;Protein: 14.0g;Carbs: 4.0g.

Sweet Pepper Stew

Servings:2 | Cooking Time: 50 Minutes

Ingredients:
- 2 tablespoons olive oil
- 2 sweet peppers, diced
- ½ large onion, minced
- 1 garlic clove, minced
- 1 tablespoon gluten-free Worcestershire sauce
- 1 teaspoon oregano
- 1 cup low-sodium tomato juice
- 1 cup low-sodium vegetable stock
- ¼ cup brown rice
- ¼ cup brown lentils
- Salt, to taste

Directions:
1. In a Dutch oven, heat the olive oil over medium-high heat.

2. Sauté the sweet peppers and onion for 10 minutes, stirring occasionally, or until the onion begins to turn golden and the peppers are wilted.

3. Stir in the garlic, Worcestershire sauce, and oregano and cook for 30 seconds more. Add the tomato juice, vegetable stock, rice, and lentils to the Dutch oven and stir to mix well.

4. Bring the mixture to a boil and then reduce the heat to medium-low. Let it simmer covered for about 45 minutes, or until the rice is cooked through and the lentils are tender.

5. Sprinkle with salt and serve warm.

Nutrition:
- Info Per Serving: Calories: 378;Fat: 15.6g;Protein: 11.4g;Carbs: 52.8g.

Italian Hot Green Beans

Servings:4 | Cooking Time:25 Minutes

Ingredients:
- 2 tbsp olive oil
- 1 red bell pepper, diced
- 1 ½ lb green beans
- 4 garlic cloves, minced
- ½ tsp mustard seeds
- ½ tsp fennel seeds
- 1 tsp dried dill weed
- 2 tomatoes, chopped
- 1 cup cream of celery soup
- 1 tsp Italian herb mix
- 1 tsp chili powder
- Salt and black pepper to taste

Directions:
1. Warm the olive oil in a saucepan over medium heat. Add and fry the bell pepper and green beans for about 5 minutes, stirring periodically to promote even cooking. Add in the garlic, mustard seeds, fennel seeds, and dill and continue sautéing for an additional 1 minute or until fragrant. Add in the pureed tomatoes, cream of celery soup, Italian herb mix, chili powder, salt, and black pepper. Continue to simmer, covered, for 10-12 minutes until the green beans are tender.

Nutrition:
- Info Per Serving: Calories: 160;Fat: 9g;Protein: 5g;Carbs: 19g.

Vegetable And Red Lentil Stew

Servings:6 | Cooking Time: 35 Minutes

Ingredients:
- 1 tablespoon extra-virgin olive oil
- 2 onions, peeled and finely diced
- 6½ cups water
- 2 zucchinis, finely diced
- 4 celery stalks, finely diced
- 3 cups red lentils
- 1 teaspoon dried oregano
- 1 teaspoon salt, plus more as needed

Directions:
1. Heat the olive oil in a large pot over medium heat.
2. Add the onions and sauté for about 5 minutes, stirring constantly, or until the onions are softened.
3. Stir in the water, zucchini, celery, lentils, oregano, and salt and bring the mixture to a boil.
4. Reduce the heat to low and let simmer covered for 30 minutes, stirring occasionally, or until the lentils are tender.
5. Taste and adjust the seasoning as needed.

Nutrition:
- Info Per Serving: Calories: 387;Fat: 4.4g;Protein: 24.0g;Carbs: 63.7g.

Veggie Rice Bowls With Pesto Sauce

Servings:2 | Cooking Time: 1 Minute

Ingredients:
- 2 cups water
- 1 cup arborio rice, rinsed
- Salt and ground black pepper, to taste
- 2 eggs
- 1 cup broccoli florets
- ½ pound Brussels sprouts
- 1 carrot, peeled and chopped
- 1 small beet, peeled and cubed
- ¼ cup pesto sauce
- Lemon wedges, for serving

Directions:
1. Combine the water, rice, salt, and pepper in the Instant Pot. Insert a trivet over rice and place a steamer basket on top. Add the eggs, broccoli, Brussels sprouts, carrots, beet cubes, salt, and pepper to the steamer basket.
2. Lock the lid. Select the Manual mode and set the cooking time for 1 minute at High Pressure.
3. When the timer beeps, perform a natural pressure release for 10 minutes, then release any remaining pressure. Carefully open the lid.
4. Remove the steamer basket and trivet from the pot and transfer the eggs to a bowl of ice water. Peel and halve the eggs. Use a fork to fluff the rice.
5. Divide the rice, broccoli, Brussels sprouts, carrot, beet cubes, and eggs into two bowls. Top with a dollop of pesto sauce and serve with the lemon wedges.

Nutrition:
- Info Per Serving: Calories: 590;Fat: 34.1g;Protein: 21.9g;Carbs: 50.0g.

Steamed Beetroot With Nutty Yogurt

Servings:4 | Cooking Time:30 Min + Chilling Time

Ingredients:
- ¼ cup extra virgin olive oil
- 1 lb beetroots, cut into wedges
- 1 cup Greek yogurt
- 3 spring onions, sliced
- 5 dill pickles, finely chopped
- 2 garlic cloves, minced
- 2 tbsp fresh parsley, chopped
- 1 oz mixed nuts, crushed
- Salt to taste

Directions:
1. In a pot over medium heat, insert a steamer basket and pour in 1 cup of water. Place in the beetroots and steam for 10-15 minutes until tender. Remove to a plate and let cool. In a bowl, combine the pickles, spring onions, garlic, salt, 3 tbsp of olive oil, Greek yogurt, and nuts and mix well. Spread the yogurt mixture on a serving plate and arrange the beetroot wedges on top. Drizzle with the remaining olive oil and top with parsley. Serve and enjoy!

Nutrition:
- Info Per Serving: Calories: 271;Fat: 18g;Protein: 9.6g;Carbs: 22g.

Cauliflower Steaks With Arugula

Servings:4 | Cooking Time: 20 Minutes

Ingredients:
- Cauliflower:
- 1 head cauliflower
- Cooking spray
- ½ teaspoon garlic powder
- 4 cups arugula
- Dressing:
- 1½ tablespoons extra-virgin olive oil
- 1½ tablespoons honey mustard
- 1 teaspoon freshly squeezed lemon juice

Directions:
1. Preheat the oven to 425ºF.
2. Remove the leaves from the cauliflower head, and cut it in half lengthwise. Cut 1½-inch-thick steaks from each half.
3. Spritz both sides of each steak with cooking spray and season both sides with the garlic powder.
4. Place the cauliflower steaks on a baking sheet, cover with foil, and roast in the oven for 10 minutes.
5. Remove the baking sheet from the oven and gently pull back the foil to avoid the steam. Flip the steaks, then roast uncovered for 10 minutes more.
6. Meanwhile, make the dressing: Whisk together the olive oil, honey mustard and lemon juice in a small bowl.
7. When the cauliflower steaks are done, divide into four equal portions. Top each portion with one-quarter of the arugula and dressing.
8. Serve immediately.

Nutrition:
- Info Per Serving: Calories: 115;Fat: 6.0g;Protein: 5.0g;Carbs: 14.0g.

Beet And Watercress Salad

Servings:4 | Cooking Time: 8 Minutes

Ingredients:
- 2 pounds beets, scrubbed, trimmed and cut into ¾-inch pieces
- ½ cup water
- 1 teaspoon caraway seeds
- ½ teaspoon table salt, plus more for seasoning
- 1 cup plain Greek yogurt
- 1 small garlic clove, minced
- 5 ounces watercress, torn into bite-size pieces
- 1 tablespoon extra-virgin olive oil, divided, plus more for drizzling
- 1 tablespoon white wine vinegar, divided
- Black pepper, to taste
- 1 teaspoon grated orange zest
- 2 tablespoons orange juice
- ¼ cup coarsely chopped fresh dill
- ¼ cup hazelnuts, toasted, skinned and chopped
- Coarse sea salt, to taste

Directions:

1. Combine the beets, water, caraway seeds and table salt in the Instant Pot. Set the lid in place. Select the Manual mode and set the cooking time for 8 minutes on High Pressure. When the timer goes off, do a quick pressure release.
2. Carefully open the lid. Using a slotted spoon, transfer the beets to a plate. Set aside to cool slightly.
3. In a small bowl, combine the yogurt, garlic and 3 tablespoons of the beet cooking liquid. In a large bowl, toss the watercress with 2 teaspoons of the oil and 1 teaspoon of the vinegar. Season with table salt and pepper.
4. Spread the yogurt mixture over a serving dish. Arrange the watercress on top of the yogurt mixture, leaving 1-inch border of the yogurt mixture.
5. Add the beets to now-empty large bowl and toss with the orange zest and juice, the remaining 2 teaspoons of the vinegar and the remaining 1 teaspoon of the oil. Season with table salt and pepper.
6. Arrange the beets on top of the watercress mixture. Drizzle with the olive oil and sprinkle with the dill, hazelnuts and sea salt.
7. Serve immediately.

Nutrition:
• Info Per Serving: Calories: 240;Fat: 15.0g;Protein: 9.0g;Carbs: 19.0g.

Cauliflower Cakes With Goat Cheese

Servings:4 | Cooking Time:50 Minutes

Ingredients:
• ¼ cup olive oil
• 10 oz cauliflower florets
• 1 tsp ground turmeric
• 1 tsp ground coriander
• Salt and black pepper to taste
• ½ tsp ground mustard seeds
• 4 oz Goat cheese, softened
• 2 scallions, sliced thin
• 1 large egg, lightly beaten
• 2 garlic cloves, minced
• 1 tsp grated lemon zest
• 4 lemon wedges
• ¼ cup flour

Directions:

1. Preheat oven to 420°F. In a bowl, whisk 1 tablespoon oil, turmeric, coriander, salt, ground mustard, and pepper. Add in the cauliflower and toss to coat. Transfer to a greased baking sheet and spread it in a single layer. Roast for 20-25 minutes until cauliflower is well browned and tender. Transfer the cauliflower to a large bowl and mash it coarsely with a potato masher. Stir in Goat cheese, scallions, egg, garlic, and lemon zest until well combined. Sprinkle flour over cauliflower mixture and stir to incorporate. Shape the mixture into 10-12 cakes and place them on a sheet pan. Chill to firm, about 30 minutes. Warm the remaining olive oil in a skillet over medium heat. Fry the cakes for 5-6 minutes on each side until deep golden brown and crisp. Serve with lemon wedges.

Nutrition:
• Info Per Serving: Calories: 320;Fat: 25g;Protein: 13g;Carbs: 12g.

Grilled Vegetable Skewers

Servings:4 | Cooking Time: 10 Minutes

Ingredients:
• 4 medium red onions, peeled and sliced into 6 wedges
• 4 medium zucchini, cut into 1-inch-thick slices
• 2 beefsteak tomatoes, cut into quarters
• 4 red bell peppers, cut into 2-inch squares
• 2 orange bell peppers, cut into 2-inch squares
• 2 yellow bell peppers, cut into 2-inch squares
• 2 tablespoons plus 1 teaspoon olive oil, divided
• SPECIAL EQUIPMENT:
• 4 wooden skewers, soaked in water for at least 30 minutes

Directions:

1. Preheat the grill to medium-high heat.
2. Skewer the vegetables by alternating between red onion, zucchini, tomatoes, and the different colored bell peppers. Brush them with 2 tablespoons of olive oil.
3. Oil the grill grates with 1 teaspoon of olive oil and grill the vegetable skewers for 5 minutes. Flip the skewers and grill for 5 minutes more, or until they are cooked to your liking.
4. Let the skewers cool for 5 minutes before serving.

Nutrition:
• Info Per Serving: Calories: 115;Fat: 3.0g;Protein: 3.5g;Carbs: 18.7g.

Zoodles With Walnut Pesto

Servings:4 | Cooking Time: 10 Minutes

Ingredients:
• 4 medium zucchinis, spiralized
• ¼ cup extra-virgin olive oil, divided
• 1 teaspoon minced garlic, divided
• ½ teaspoon crushed red pepper
• ¼ teaspoon freshly ground black pepper, divided
• ¼ teaspoon kosher salt, divided
• 2 tablespoons grated Parmesan cheese, divided
• 1 cup packed fresh basil leaves
• ¾ cup walnut pieces, divided

Directions:

1. In a large bowl, stir together the zoodles, 1 tablespoon of the olive oil, ½ teaspoon of the minced garlic, red pepper, ⅛ teaspoon of the black pepper and ⅛ teaspoon of the salt. Set aside.
2. Heat ½ tablespoon of the oil in a large skillet over medium-high heat. Add half of the zoodles to the skillet and cook for 5 minutes, stirring constantly. Transfer the cooked zoodles into a bowl. Repeat with another ½ tablespoon of the oil and the remaining zoodles. When done, add the cooked zoodles to the bowl.
3. Make the pesto: In a food processor, combine the remaining ½ teaspoon of the minced garlic, ⅛ teaspoon of the black pepper and ⅛ teaspoon of the salt, 1 tablespoon of the Parmesan, basil leaves and ¼ cup of the walnuts. Pulse until smooth and then slowly drizzle the remaining 2 tablespoons of the oil into the pesto. Pulse again until well combined.
4. Add the pesto to the zoodles along with the remaining 1 tablespoon of the Parmesan and the remaining ½ cup of the walnuts. Toss to coat well.
5. Serve immediately.

Nutrition:
• Info Per Serving: Calories: 166;Fat: 16.0g;Protein: 4.0g;Carbs: 3.0g.

5-Ingredient Zucchini Fritters

Servings:14 | Cooking Time: 5 Minutes

Ingredients:
• 4 cups grated zucchini
• Salt, to taste
• 2 large eggs, lightly beaten
• ⅓ cup sliced scallions (green and white parts)
• ⅔ all-purpose flour
• ⅛ teaspoon black pepper
• 2 tablespoons olive oil

Directions:

1. Put the grated zucchini in a colander and lightly season with salt. Set aside to rest for 10 minutes. Squeeze out as much liquid from the grated zucchini as possible.
2. Pour the grated zucchini into a bowl. Fold in the beaten eggs,

scallions, flour, salt, and pepper and stir until everything is well combined.

3. Heat the olive oil in a large skillet over medium heat until hot.
4. Drop 3 tablespoons mounds of the zucchini mixture onto the hot skillet to make each fritter, pressing them lightly into rounds and spacing them about 2 inches apart.
5. Cook for 2 to 3 minutes. Flip the zucchini fritters and cook for 2 minutes more, or until they are golden brown and cooked through.
6. Remove from the heat to a plate lined with paper towels. Repeat with the remaining zucchini mixture.
7. Serve hot.

Nutrition:
• Info Per Serving: Calories: 113;Fat: 6.1g;Protein: 4.0g;Carbs: 12.2g.

Chargrilled Vegetable Kebabs
Servings:4 | Cooking Time:26 Minutes

Ingredients:
• 2 red bell peppers, cut into squares
• 2 zucchinis, sliced into half-moons
• 6 portobello mushroom caps, quartered
• ¼ cup olive oil
• 1 tsp Dijon mustard
• 1 tsp fresh rosemary, chopped
• 1 garlic clove, minced
• Salt and black pepper to taste
• 2 red onions, cut into wedges

Directions:
1. Preheat your grill to High. Mix the olive oil, mustard, rosemary, garlic, salt, and pepper in a bowl. Reserve half of the oil mixture for serving. Thread the vegetables in alternating order onto metal skewers and brush them with the remaining oil mixture. Grill them for about 15 minutes until browned, turning occasionally. Transfer the kebabs to a serving platter and remove the skewers. Drizzle with reserved oil mixture and serve.

Nutrition:
• Info Per Serving: Calories: 96;Fat: 9.2g;Protein: 1.1g;Carbs: 3.6g.

Lentil And Tomato Collard Wraps
Servings:4 | Cooking Time: 0 Minutes

Ingredients:
• 2 cups cooked lentils
• 5 Roma tomatoes, diced
• ½ cup crumbled feta cheese
• 10 large fresh basil leaves, thinly sliced
• ¼ cup extra-virgin olive oil
• 1 tablespoon balsamic vinegar
• 2 garlic cloves, minced
• ½ teaspoon raw honey
• ½ teaspoon salt
• ¼ teaspoon freshly ground black pepper
• 4 large collard leaves, stems removed

Directions:
1. Combine the lentils, tomatoes, cheese, basil leaves, olive oil, vinegar, garlic, honey, salt, and black pepper in a large bowl and stir until well blended.
2. Lay the collard leaves on a flat work surface. Spoon the equal-sized amounts of the lentil mixture onto the edges of the leaves. Roll them up and slice in half to serve.

Nutrition:
• Info Per Serving: Calories: 318;Fat: 17.6g;Protein: 13.2g;Carbs: 27.5g.

Roasted Vegetables And Chickpeas
Servings:2 | Cooking Time: 30 Minutes

Ingredients:
• 4 cups cauliflower florets (about ½ small head)
• 2 medium carrots, peeled, halved, and then sliced into quarters lengthwise
• 2 tablespoons olive oil, divided
• ½ teaspoon garlic powder, divided
• ½ teaspoon salt, divided
• 2 teaspoons za'atar spice mix, divided
• 1 can chickpeas, drained, rinsed, and patted dry
• ¾ cup plain Greek yogurt
• 1 teaspoon harissa spice paste

Directions:
1. Preheat the oven to 400ºF. Line a sheet pan with foil or parchment paper.
2. Place the cauliflower and carrots in a large bowl. Drizzle with 1 tablespoon olive oil and sprinkle with ¼ teaspoon of garlic powder, ¼ teaspoon of salt, and 1 teaspoon of za'atar. Toss well to combine.
3. Spread the vegetables onto one half of the sheet pan in a single layer.
4. Place the chickpeas in the same bowl and season with the remaining 1 tablespoon of oil, ¼ teaspoon of garlic powder, and ¼ teaspoon of salt, and the remaining za'atar. Toss well to combine.
5. Spread the chickpeas onto the other half of the sheet pan.
6. Roast for 30 minutes, or until the vegetables are tender and the chickpeas start to turn golden. Flip the vegetables halfway through the cooking time, and give the chickpeas a stir so they cook evenly.
7. The chickpeas may need an extra few minutes if you like them crispy. If so, remove the vegetables and leave the chickpeas in until they're cooked to desired crispiness.
8. Meanwhile, combine the yogurt and harissa in a small bowl. Taste and add additional harissa as desired, then serve.

Nutrition:
• Info Per Serving: Calories: 468;Fat: 23.0g;Protein: 18.1g;Carbs: 54.1g.

Rainbow Vegetable Kebabs
Servings:4 | Cooking Time:30 Minutes

Ingredients:
• 1 cup mushrooms, cut into quarters
• 6 mixed bell peppers, cut into squares
• 4 red onions, cut into 6 wedges
• 4 zucchini, cut into half-moons
• 2 tomatoes, cut into quarters
• 3 tbsp herbed oil

Directions:
1. Preheat your grill to medium-high. Alternate the vegetables onto bamboo skewers. Grill them for 5 minutes on each side until the vegetables begin to char. Remove them from heat and drizzle with herbed oil.

Nutrition:
• Info Per Serving: Calories: 238;Fat: 12g;Protein: 6g;Carbs: 34.2g.

Stir-Fried Eggplant

Servings:2 | Cooking Time: 15 Minutes

Ingredients:
- 1 cup water, plus more as needed
- ½ cup chopped red onion
- 1 tablespoon finely chopped garlic
- 1 tablespoon dried Italian herb seasoning
- 1 teaspoon ground cumin
- 1 small eggplant, peeled and cut into ½-inch cubes
- 1 medium carrot, sliced
- 2 cups green beans, cut into 1-inch pieces
- 2 ribs celery, sliced
- 1 cup corn kernels
- 2 tablespoons almond butter
- 2 medium tomatoes, chopped

Directions:
1. Heat 1 tablespoon of water in a large soup pot over medium-high heat until it sputters.
2. Cook the onion for 2 minutes, adding a little more water as needed.
3. Add the garlic, Italian seasoning, cumin, and eggplant and stir-fry for 2 to 3 minutes, adding a little more water as needed.
4. Add the carrot, green beans, celery, corn kernels, and ½ cup of water and stir well. Reduce the heat to medium, cover, and cook for 8 to 10 minutes, stirring occasionally, or until the vegetables are tender.
5. Meanwhile, in a bowl, stir together the almond butter and ½ cup of water.
6. Remove the vegetables from the heat and stir in the almond butter mixture and chopped tomatoes. Cool for a few minutes before serving.

Nutrition:
- Info Per Serving: Calories: 176;Fat: 5.5g;Protein: 5.8g;Carbs: 25.4g.

Greek-Style Eggplants

Servings:4 | Cooking Time:25 Minutes

Ingredients:
- 1 ½ lb eggplants, sliced into rounds
- ¼ cup olive oil
- Salt and black pepper to taste
- 4 tsp balsamic vinegar
- 1 tbsp capers, minced
- 1 garlic clove, minced
- ½ tsp lemon zest
- ½ tsp fresh oregano, minced
- 3 tbsp fresh mint, minced

Directions:
1. Preheat oven to 420°F. Arrange the eggplant rounds on a greased baking dish and drizzle with some olive oil. Sprinkle with salt and pepper. Bake for 10-12 per side until mahogany lightly charred. Whisk remaining olive oil, balsamic vinegar, capers, garlic, lemon zest, oregano, salt, and pepper together in a bowl. Drizzle the mixture all over the eggplants and sprinkle with mint. Serve and enjoy!

Nutrition:
- Info Per Serving: Calories: 111;Fat: 9.2g;Protein: 1.2g;Carbs: 7g.

Spicy Roasted Tomatoes

Servings:2 | Cooking Time:50 Minutes

Ingredients:
- ¼ cup olive oil
- 1 lb mixed cherry tomatoes
- 10 garlic cloves, minced
- Salt to taste
- 1 fresh rosemary sprig
- 1 fresh thyme sprig
- 2 crusty bread slices

Directions:
1. Preheat oven to 350°F. Toss the cherry tomatoes, garlic, olive oil, and salt in a baking dish. Top with the herb sprigs. Roast the tomatoes for about 45 minutes until they are soft and begin to caramelize. Discard the herbs and serve with bread.

Nutrition:
- Info Per Serving: Calories: 271;Fat: 26g;Protein: 3g;Carbs: 12g.

Authentic Mushroom Gratin

Servings:4 | Cooking Time:25 Minutes

Ingredients:
- 2 lb Button mushrooms, cleaned
- 2 tbsp olive oil
- 2 tomatoes, sliced
- 2 tomato paste
- ½ cup Parmesan cheese, grated
- ½ cup dry white wine
- ¼ tsp sweet paprika
- ½ tsp dried basil
- ½ tsp dried thyme
- Salt and black pepper to taste

Directions:
1. Preheat oven to 360°F. Combine tomatoes, tomato paste, wine, oil, mushrooms, paprika, black pepper, salt, basil, and thyme in a baking dish. Bake for 15 minutes. Top with Parmesan and continue baking for 5 minutes until the cheese melts.

Nutrition:
- Info Per Serving: Calories: 162;Fat: 8.6g;Protein: 9g;Carbs: 12.3g.

Parmesan Stuffed Zucchini Boats

Servings:4 | Cooking Time: 15 Minutes

Ingredients:
- 1 cup canned low-sodium chickpeas, drained and rinsed
- 1 cup no-sugar-added spaghetti sauce
- 2 zucchinis
- ¼ cup shredded Parmesan cheese

Directions:
1. Preheat the oven to 425°F.
2. In a medium bowl, stir together the chickpeas and spaghetti sauce.
3. Cut the zucchini in half lengthwise and scrape a spoon gently down the length of each half to remove the seeds.
4. Fill each zucchini half with the chickpea sauce and top with one-quarter of the Parmesan cheese.
5. Place the zucchini halves on a baking sheet and roast in the oven for 15 minutes.
6. Transfer to a plate. Let rest for 5 minutes before serving.

Nutrition:
- Info Per Serving: Calories: 139;Fat: 4.0g;Protein: 8.0g;Carbs: 20.0g.

Baked Vegetable Stew

Servings:6 | Cooking Time:70 Minutes

Ingredients:
- 1 can diced tomatoes, drained with juice reserved
- 3 tbsp olive oil
- 1 onion, chopped
- 2 tbsp fresh oregano, minced
- 1 tsp paprika
- 4 garlic cloves, minced
- 1 ½ lb green beans, sliced
- 1 lb Yukon Gold potatoes, peeled and chopped
- 1 tbsp tomato paste
- Salt and black pepper to taste
- 3 tbsp fresh basil, chopped

Directions:
1. Preheat oven to 360°F. Warm the olive oil in a skillet over medium heat. Sauté onion and garlic for 3 minutes until softened. Stir in oregano and paprika for 30 seconds. Transfer to a baking dish and add in green beans, potatoes, tomatoes, tomato paste, salt, pepper, and 1 ½ cups of water; stir well. Bake for 40-50 minutes. Sprinkle with basil. Serve.

Nutrition:
- Info Per Serving: Calories: 121;Fat: 0.8g;Protein: 4.2g;Carbs: 26g.

Braised Cauliflower With White Wine

Servings:4 | Cooking Time: 12 To 16 Minutes

Ingredients:
- 3 tablespoons plus 1 teaspoon extra-virgin olive oil, divided
- 3 garlic cloves, minced
- ⅛ teaspoon red pepper flakes
- 1 head cauliflower, cored and cut into 1½-inch florets
- ¼ teaspoon salt, plus more for seasoning
- Black pepper, to taste
- ⅓ cup vegetable broth
- ⅓ cup dry white wine
- 2 tablespoons minced fresh parsley

Directions:
1. Combine 1 teaspoon of the oil, garlic and pepper flakes in small bowl.
2. Heat the remaining 3 tablespoons of the oil in a skillet over medium-high heat until shimmering. Add the cauliflower and ¼ teaspoon of the salt and cook for 7 to 9 minutes, stirring occasionally, or until florets are golden brown.
3. Push the cauliflower to sides of the skillet. Add the garlic mixture to the center of the skillet. Cook for about 30 seconds, or until fragrant. Stir the garlic mixture into the cauliflower.
4. Pour in the broth and wine and bring to simmer. Reduce the heat to medium-low. Cover and cook for 4 to 6 minutes, or until the cauliflower is crisp-tender. Off heat, stir in the parsley and season with salt and pepper.
5. Serve immediately.

Nutrition:
- Info Per Serving: Calories: 143;Fat: 11.7g;Protein: 3.1g;Carbs: 8.7g.

Easy Zucchini Patties

Servings:2 | Cooking Time: 5 Minutes

Ingredients:
- 2 medium zucchinis, shredded
- 1 teaspoon salt, divided
- 2 eggs
- 2 tablespoons chickpea flour
- 1 tablespoon chopped fresh mint
- 1 scallion, chopped
- 2 tablespoons extra-virgin olive oil

Directions:
1. Put the shredded zucchini in a fine-mesh strainer and season with ½ teaspoon of salt. Set aside.
2. Beat together the eggs, chickpea flour, mint, scallion, and remaining ½ teaspoon of salt in a medium bowl.
3. Squeeze the zucchini to drain as much liquid as possible. Add the zucchini to the egg mixture and stir until well incorporated.
4. Heat the olive oil in a large skillet over medium-high heat.
5. Drop the zucchini mixture by spoonful into the skillet. Gently flatten the zucchini with the back of a spatula.
6. Cook for 2 to 3 minutes or until golden brown. Flip and cook for an additional 2 minutes.
7. Remove from the heat and serve on a plate.

Nutrition:
- Info Per Serving: Calories: 264;Fat: 20.0g;Protein: 9.8g;Carbs: 16.1g.

Tradicional Matchuba Green Beans

Servings:4 | Cooking Time:15 Minutes

Ingredients:
- 1 ¼ lb narrow green beans, trimmed
- 3 tbsp butter, melted
- 1 cup Moroccan matbucha
- 2 green onions, chopped
- Salt and black pepper to taste

Directions:
1. Steam the green beans in a pot for 5-6 minutes until tender. Remove to a bowl, reserving the cooking liquid. In a skillet over medium heat, melt the butter. Add in green onions, salt, and black pepper and cook until fragrant. Lower the heat and put in the green beans along with some of the reserved water. Simmer for 3-4 minutes. Serve the green beans with the Sabra Moroccan matbucha as a dip.

Nutrition:
- Info Per Serving: Calories: 125;Fat: 8.6g;Protein: 2.2g;Carbs: 9g.

Grilled Eggplant "Steaks" With Sauce

Servings:6 | Cooking Time:20 Minutes

Ingredients:
- 2 lb eggplants, sliced lengthways
- 6 tbsp olive oil
- 5 garlic cloves, minced
- 1 tsp dried oregano
- ½ tsp red pepper flakes
- ½ cup Greek yogurt
- 3 tbsp chopped fresh parsley
- 1 tsp grated lemon zest
- 2 tsp lemon juice
- 1 tsp ground cumin
- Salt and black pepper to taste

Directions:
1. In a bowl, whisk half of the olive oil, yogurt, parsley, lemon zest and juice, cumin, and salt; set aside until ready to serve. Preheat your grill to High. Rub the eggplant steaks with the remaining olive oil, oregano, salt, and pepper. Grill them for 4-6 minutes per side until browned and tender; transfer to a serving platter. Drizzle yogurt sauce over eggplant.

Nutrition:
- Info Per Serving: Calories: 112;Fat: 7g;Protein: 2.6g;Carbs: 11.3g.

Sautéed Green Beans With Tomatoes

Servings:4 | Cooking Time: 20 Minutes

Ingredients:
- ¼ cup extra-virgin olive oil
- 1 large onion, chopped
- 4 cloves garlic, finely chopped
- 1 pound green beans, fresh or frozen, cut into 2-inch pieces
- 1½ teaspoons salt, divided
- 1 can diced tomatoes
- ½ teaspoon freshly ground black pepper

Directions:
1. Heat the olive oil in a large skillet over medium heat.
2. Add the onion and garlic and sauté for 1 minute until fragrant.
3. Stir in the green beans and sauté for 3 minutes. Sprinkle with ½ teaspoon of salt.
4. Add the tomatoes, remaining salt, and pepper and stir to mix well. Cook for an additional 12 minutes, stirring occasionally, or until the green beans are crisp and tender.
5. Remove from the heat and serve warm.

Nutrition:
- Info Per Serving: Calories: 219;Fat: 13.9g;Protein: 4.0g;Carbs: 17.7g.

Balsamic Grilled Vegetables

Servings:4 | Cooking Time:20 Minutes

Ingredients:
- ¼ cup olive oil
- 4 carrots, cut in half
- 2 onions, quartered
- 1 zucchini, cut into rounds
- 1 eggplant, cut into rounds
- 1 red bell pepper, chopped
- Salt and black pepper to taste
- Balsamic vinegar to taste

Directions:
1. Heat your grill to medium-high. Brush the vegetables lightly with olive oil, and season with salt and pepper. Grill the vegetables for 3–4 minutes per side. Transfer to a serving dish and drizzle with balsamic vinegar. Serve and enjoy!

Nutrition:
- Info Per Serving: Calories: 184;Fat: 14g;Protein: 2.1g;Carbs: 14g.

Parmesan Asparagus With Tomatoes

Servings:6 | Cooking Time:30 Minutes

Ingredients:
- 3 tbsp olive oil
- 2 garlic cloves, minced
- 12 oz cherry tomatoes, halved
- 1 tsp dried oregano
- 10 Kalamata olives, chopped
- 2 lb asparagus, trimmed
- 2 tbsp fresh basil, chopped
- ¼ cup Parmesan cheese, grated
- Salt and black pepper to taste

Directions:
1. Warm 2 tbsp of olive oil in a skillet over medium heat sauté the garlic for 1-2 minutes, stirring often, until golden. Add tomatoes, olives, and oregano and cook until tomatoes begin to break down, about 3 minutes; transfer to a bowl.
2. Coat the asparagus with the remaining olive oil and cook in a grill pan over medium heat for about 5 minutes, turning once until crisp-tender. Sprinkle with salt and pepper. Transfer asparagus to a serving platter, top with tomato mixture, and sprinkle with basil and Parmesan cheese. Serve and enjoy!

Nutrition:

- Info Per Serving: Calories: 157;Fat: 7g;Protein: 7.3g;Carbs: 19g.

Garlicky Zucchini Cubes With Mint

Servings:4 | Cooking Time: 10 Minutes

Ingredients:
- 3 large green zucchinis, cut into ½-inch cubes
- 3 tablespoons extra-virgin olive oil
- 1 large onion, chopped
- 3 cloves garlic, minced
- 1 teaspoon salt
- 1 teaspoon dried mint

Directions:
1. Heat the olive oil in a large skillet over medium heat.
2. Add the onion and garlic and sauté for 3 minutes, stirring constantly, or until softened.
3. Stir in the zucchini cubes and salt and cook for 5 minutes, or until the zucchini is browned and tender.
4. Add the mint to the skillet and toss to combine, then continue cooking for 2 minutes.
5. Serve warm.

Nutrition:
- Info Per Serving: Calories: 146;Fat: 10.6g;Protein: 4.2g;Carbs: 11.8g.

Baby Kale And Cabbage Salad

Servings:6 | Cooking Time: 0 Minutes

Ingredients:
- 2 bunches baby kale, thinly sliced
- ½ head green savoy cabbage, cored and thinly sliced
- 1 medium red bell pepper, thinly sliced
- 1 garlic clove, thinly sliced
- 1 cup toasted peanuts
- Dressing:
- Juice of 1 lemon
- ¼ cup apple cider vinegar
- 1 teaspoon ground cumin
- ¼ teaspoon smoked paprika

Directions:
1. In a large mixing bowl, toss together the kale and cabbage.
2. Make the dressing: Whisk together the lemon juice, vinegar, cumin and paprika in a small bowl.
3. Pour the dressing over the greens and gently massage with your hands.
4. Add the pepper, garlic and peanuts to the mixing bowl. Toss to combine.
5. Serve immediately.

Nutrition:
- Info Per Serving: Calories: 199;Fat: 12.0g;Protein: 10.0g;Carbs: 17.0g.

Quick Steamed Broccoli

Servings:2 | Cooking Time: 0 Minutes

Ingredients:
- ¼ cup water
- 3 cups broccoli florets
- Salt and ground black pepper, to taste

Directions:
1. Pour the water into the Instant Pot and insert a steamer basket. Place the broccoli florets in the basket.
2. Secure the lid. Select the Manual mode and set the cooking time for 0 minutes at High Pressure.
3. Once cooking is complete, do a quick pressure release. Carefully open the lid.
4. Transfer the broccoli florets to a bowl with cold water to keep bright green color.

5. Season the broccoli with salt and pepper to taste, then serve.
Nutrition:
• Info Per Serving: Calories: 16;Fat: 0.2g;Protein: 1.9g;Carbs: 1.7g.

Spicy Kale With Almonds
Servings:4 | Cooking Time:25 Minutes
Ingredients:
• 2 tbsp olive oil
• ¼ cup slivered almonds
• 1 lb chopped kale
• ¼ cup vegetable broth
• 1 lemon, juiced and zested
• 1 garlic clove, minced
• 1 tbsp red pepper flakes
• Salt and black pepper to taste
Directions:
1. Warm olive oil in a pan over medium heat and sauté garlic, kale, salt, and pepper for 8-9 minutes until soft. Add in lemon juice, lemon zest, red pepper flakes, and vegetable broth and continue cooking until the liquid evaporates, about 3-5 minutes. Garnish with almonds and serve.
Nutrition:
• Info Per Serving: Calories: 123;Fat: 8.1g;Protein: 4g;Carbs: 10.8g.

Eggplant Rolls In Tomato Sauce
Servings:4 | Cooking Time:60 Minutes
Ingredients:
• 2 tbsp olive oil
• 1 ½ cups ricotta cheese
• 2 cans diced tomatoes
• 1 shallot, finely chopped
• 2 garlic cloves, minced
• 1 tbsp Italian seasoning
• 1 tsp dried oregano
• 2 eggplants
• ½ cup grated mozzarella
• Salt to taste
• ¼ tsp red pepper flakes
Directions:
1. Preheat oven to 350ºF. Warm olive oil in a pot over medium heat and sauté shallot and garlic for 3 minutes until tender and fragrant. Mix in tomatoes, oregano, Italian seasoning, salt, and red flakes and simmer for 6 minutes.
2. Cut the eggplants lengthwise into 1,5-inch slices and season with salt. Grill them for 2-3 minutes per side until softened. Place them on a plate and spoon 2 tbsp of ricotta cheese. Wrap them and arrange on a greased baking dish. Pour over the sauce and scatter with the mozzarella cheese. Bake for 15-20 minutes until golden-brown and bubbling.
Nutrition:
• Info Per Serving: Calories: 362;Fat: 17g;Protein: 19g;Carbs: 38g.

Grilled Za´Atar Zucchini Rounds
Servings:4 | Cooking Time:20 Minutes
Ingredients:
• 2 tbsp olive oil
• 4 zucchinis, sliced
• 1 tbsp za'atar seasoning
• Salt to taste
• 2 tbsp parsley, chopped
Directions:
1. Preheat the grill on high. Cut the zucchini lengthways into ½-inch thin pieces. Brush the zucchini 'steaks' with olive oil and season with salt and za'atar seasoning. Grill for 6 minutes on both sides. Sprinkle with parsley and serve.
Nutrition:
• Info Per Serving: Calories: 91;Fat: 7.4g;Protein: 2.4g;Carbs: 6.6g.

Cheesy Sweet Potato Burgers
Servings:4 | Cooking Time: 19 To 20 Minutes
Ingredients:
• 1 large sweet potato
• 2 tablespoons extra-virgin olive oil, divided
• 1 cup chopped onion
• 1 large egg
• 1 garlic clove
• 1 cup old-fashioned rolled oats
• 1 tablespoon dried oregano
• 1 tablespoon balsamic vinegar
• ¼ teaspoon kosher salt
• ½ cup crumbled Gorgonzola cheese
Directions:
1. Using a fork, pierce the sweet potato all over and microwave on high for 4 to 5 minutes, until softened in the center. Cool slightly before slicing in half.
2. Meanwhile, in a large skillet over medium-high heat, heat 1 tablespoon of the olive oil. Add the onion and sauté for 5 minutes.
3. Spoon the sweet potato flesh out of the skin and put the flesh in a food processor. Add the cooked onion, egg, garlic, oats, oregano, vinegar and salt. Pulse until smooth. Add the cheese and pulse four times to barely combine.
4. Form the mixture into four burgers. Place the burgers on a plate, and press to flatten each to about ¾-inch thick.
5. Wipe out the skillet with a paper towel. Heat the remaining 1 tablespoon of the oil over medium-high heat for about 2 minutes. Add the burgers to the hot oil, then reduce the heat to medium. Cook the burgers for 5 minutes per side.
6. Transfer the burgers to a plate and serve.
Nutrition:
• Info Per Serving: Calories: 290;Fat: 12.0g;Protein: 12.0g;Carbs: 43.0g.

Grilled Romaine Lettuce
Servings:4 | Cooking Time: 3 To 5 Minutes
Ingredients:
• Romaine:
• 2 heads romaine lettuce, halved lengthwise
• 2 tablespoons extra-virgin olive oil
• Dressing:
• ½ cup unsweetened almond milk
• 1 tablespoon extra-virgin olive oil
• ¼ bunch fresh chives, thinly chopped
• 1 garlic clove, pressed
• 1 pinch red pepper flakes
Directions:
1. Heat a grill pan over medium heat.
2. Brush each lettuce half with the olive oil. Place the lettuce halves, flat-side down, on the grill. Grill for 3 to 5 minutes, or until the lettuce slightly wilts and develops light grill marks.
3. Meanwhile, whisk together all the ingredients for the dressing in a small bowl.
4. Drizzle 2 tablespoons of the dressing over each romaine half and serve.
Nutrition:
• Info Per Serving: Calories: 126;Fat: 11.0g;Protein: 2.0g;Carbs: 7.0g.

Tomatoes Filled With Tabbouleh

Servings:4 | Cooking Time:25 Minutes

Ingredients:
- 3 tbsp olive oil, divided
- 8 medium tomatoes
- ½ cup water
- ½ cup bulgur wheat
- 1 ½ cups minced parsley
- ⅓ cup minced fresh mint
- 2 scallions, chopped
- 1 tsp sumac
- Salt and black pepper to taste
- 1 lemon, zested

Directions:
1. Place the bulgur wheat and 2 cups of salted water in a pot and bring to a boil. Lower the heat and simmer for 10 minutes or until tender. Remove the pot from the heat and cover with a lid. Let it sit for 15 minutes.
2. Preheat the oven to 400°F. Slice off the top of each tomato and scoop out the pulp and seeds using a spoon into a sieve set over a bowl. Drain and discard any excess liquid; chop the remaining pulp and place it in a large mixing bowl. Add in parsley, mint, scallions, sumac, lemon zest, lemon juice, bulgur, pepper, and salt, and mix well.
3. Spoon the filling into the tomatoes and place the lids on top. Drizzle with olive oil and bake for 15-20 minutes until the tomatoes are tender. Serve and enjoy!

Nutrition:
- Info Per Serving: Calories: 160;Fat: 7g;Protein: 5g;Carbs: 22g.

Roasted Artichokes

Servings:4 | Cooking Time:50 Minutes

Ingredients:
- 4 artichokes, stalk trimmed and large leaves removed
- 2 lemons, freshly squeezed
- 4 tbsp extra-virgin olive oil
- 4 cloves garlic, chopped
- 1 tsp fresh rosemary
- 1 tsp fresh basil
- 1 tsp fresh parsley
- 1 tsp fresh oregano
- Salt and black pepper to taste
- 1 tsp red pepper flakes
- 1 tsp paprika

Directions:
1. Preheat oven to 395°F. In a small bowl, thoroughly combine the garlic with herbs and spices; set aside. Cut the artichokes in half vertically and scoop out the fibrous choke to expose the heart with a teaspoon.
2. Rub the lemon juice all over the entire surface of the artichoke halves. Arrange them on a parchment-lined baking dish, cut side up, and brush them evenly with olive oil. Stuff the cavities with the garlic/herb mixture. Cover them with aluminum foil and bake for 30 minutes. Discard the foil and bake for another 10 minutes until lightly charred. Serve.

Nutrition:
- Info Per Serving: Calories: 220;Fat: 14g;Protein: 6g;Carbs: 21g.

Vegan Lentil Bolognese

Servings:2 | Cooking Time: 50 Minutes

Ingredients:
- 1 medium celery stalk
- 1 large carrot
- ½ large onion
- 1 garlic clove
- 2 tablespoons olive oil
- 1 can crushed tomatoes
- 1 cup red wine
- ½ teaspoon salt, plus more as needed
- ½ teaspoon pure maple syrup
- 1 cup cooked lentils (prepared from ½ cup dry)

Directions:
1. Add the celery, carrot, onion, and garlic to a food processor and process until everything is finely chopped.
2. In a Dutch oven, heat the olive oil over medium-high heat. Add the chopped mixture and sauté for about 10 minutes, stirring occasionally, or until the vegetables are lightly browned.
3. Stir in the tomatoes, wine, salt, and maple syrup and bring to a boil.
4. Once the sauce starts to boil, cover, and reduce the heat to medium-low. Simmer for 30 minutes, stirring occasionally, or until the vegetables are softened.
5. Stir in the cooked lentils and cook for an additional 5 minutes until warmed through.
6. Taste and add additional salt, if needed. Serve warm.

Nutrition:
- Info Per Serving: Calories: 367;Fat: 15.0g;Protein: 13.7g;Carbs: 44.5g.

Sweet Potato Chickpea Buddha Bowl

Servings:2 | Cooking Time: 10 To 15 Minutes

Ingredients:
- Sauce:
- 1 tablespoon tahini
- 2 tablespoons plain Greek yogurt
- 2 tablespoons hemp seeds
- 1 garlic clove, minced
- Pinch salt
- Freshly ground black pepper, to taste
- Bowl:
- 1 small sweet potato, peeled and finely diced
- 1 teaspoon extra-virgin olive oil
- 1 cup from 1 can low-sodium chickpeas, drained and rinsed
- 2 cups baby kale

Directions:
1. Make the Sauce
2. Whisk together the tahini and yogurt in a small bowl.
3. Stir in the hemp seeds and minced garlic. Season with salt pepper. Add 2 to 3 tablespoons water to create a creamy yet pourable consistency and set aside.
4. Make the Bowl
5. Preheat the oven to 425°F. Line a baking sheet with parchment paper.
6. Place the sweet potato on the prepared baking sheet and drizzle with the olive oil. Toss well
7. Roast in the preheated oven for 10 to 15 minutes, stirring once during cooking, or until fork-tender and browned.
8. In each of 2 bowls, place ½ cup of chickpeas, 1 cup of baby kale, and half of the cooked sweet potato. Serve drizzled with half of the prepared sauce.

Nutrition:
- Info Per Serving: Calories: 323;Fat: 14.1g;Protein: 17.0g;Carbs: 36.0g.

Tasty Lentil Burgers

Servings:4 | Cooking Time:25 Minutes

Ingredients:
- 1 cup cremini mushrooms, finely chopped
- 1 cup cooked green lentils
- ½ cup Greek yogurt
- ½ lemon, zested and juiced
- ½ tsp garlic powder
- ½ tsp dried oregano
- 1 tbsp fresh cilantro, chopped
- Salt to taste
- 3 tbsp extra-virgin olive oil
- ¼ tsp tbsp white miso
- ¼ tsp smoked paprika
- ¼ cup flour

Directions:
1. Pour ½ cup of lentils in your blender and puree partially until somewhat smooth, but with many whole lentils still remaining. In a small bowl, mix the yogurt, lemon zest and juice, garlic powder, oregano, cilantro, and salt. Season and set aside. In a medium bowl, mix the mushrooms, 2 tablespoons of olive oil, miso, and paprika. Stir in all the lentils. Add in flour and stir until the mixture everything is well incorporated. Shape the mixture into patties about ¾-inch thick. Warm the remaining olive oil in a skillet over medium heat. Fry the patties until browned and crisp, about 3 minutes. Turn and fry on the second side. Serve with the reserved yogurt mixture.

Nutrition:
- Info Per Serving: Calories: 215;Fat: 13g;Protein: 10g;Carbs: 19g.

Roasted Caramelized Root Vegetables

Servings:6 | Cooking Time:40 Minutes

Ingredients:
- 1 sweet potato, peeled and cut into chunks
- 3 tbsp olive oil
- 2 carrots, peeled
- 2 beets, peeled
- 1 turnip, peeled
- 1 tsp cumin
- 1 tsp sweet paprika
- Salt and black pepper to taste
- 1 lemon, juiced
- 2 tbsp parsley, chopped

Directions:
1. Preheat oven to 400°F. Cut the vegetables into chunks and toss them with olive oil and seasonings in a sheet pan. Drizzle with lemon juice and roast them for 35-40 minutes until vegetables are tender and golden. Serve topped with parsley.

Nutrition:
- Info Per Serving: Calories: 80;Fat: 4.8g;Protein: 1.5g;Carbs: 8.9g.

Zucchini Crisp

Servings:2 | Cooking Time: 20 Minutes

Ingredients:
- 4 zucchinis, sliced into ½-inch rounds
- ½ cup unsweetened almond milk
- 1 teaspoon fresh lemon juice
- 1 teaspoon arrowroot powder
- ½ teaspoon salt, divided
- ½ cup whole wheat bread crumbs
- ¼ cup nutritional yeast
- ¼ cup hemp seeds
- ½ teaspoon garlic powder
- ¼ teaspoon crushed red pepper

- ¼ teaspoon black pepper

Directions:
1. Preheat the oven to 375°F. Line two baking sheets with parchment paper and set aside.
2. Put the zucchini in a medium bowl with the almond milk, lemon juice, arrowroot powder, and ¼ teaspoon of salt. Stir to mix well.
3. In a large bowl with a lid, thoroughly combine the bread crumbs, nutritional yeast, hemp seeds, garlic powder, crushed red pepper and black pepper. Add the zucchini in batches and shake until the slices are evenly coated.
4. Arrange the zucchini on the prepared baking sheets in a single layer.
5. Bake in the preheated oven for about 20 minutes, or until the zucchini slices are golden brown.
6. Season with the remaining ¼ teaspoon of salt before serving.

Nutrition:
- Info Per Serving: Calories: 255;Fat: 11.3g;Protein: 8.6g;Carbs: 31.9g.

Stuffed Portobello Mushrooms With Spinach

Servings:4 | Cooking Time: 20 Minutes

Ingredients:
- 8 large portobello mushrooms, stems removed
- 3 teaspoons extra-virgin olive oil, divided
- 1 medium red bell pepper, diced
- 4 cups fresh spinach
- ¼ cup crumbled feta cheese

Directions:
1. Preheat the oven to 450°F.
2. Using a spoon to scoop out the gills of the mushrooms and discard them. Brush the mushrooms with 2 teaspoons of olive oil.
3. Arrange the mushrooms (cap-side down) on a baking sheet. Roast in the preheated oven for 20 minutes.
4. Meantime, in a medium skillet, heat the remaining olive oil over medium heat until it shimmers.
5. Add the bell pepper and spinach and sauté for 8 to 10 minutes, stirring occasionally, or until the spinach is wilted.
6. Remove the mushrooms from the oven to a paper towel-lined plate. Using a spoon to stuff each mushroom with the bell pepper and spinach mixture. Scatter the feta cheese all over.
7. Serve immediately.

Nutrition:
- Info Per Serving: Calories: 115;Fat: 5.9g;Protein: 7.2g;Carbs: 11.5g.

Minty Broccoli & Walnuts

Servings:2 | Cooking Time:10 Minutes

Ingredients:
- 1 garlic clove, minced
- ½ cups walnuts, chopped
- 3 cups broccoli florets, steamed
- 1 tbsp mint, chopped
- ½ lemon, juiced
- Salt and black pepper to taste

Directions:
1. Mix walnuts, broccoli, garlic, mint, lemon juice, salt, and pepper in a bowl. Serve chilled.

Nutrition:
- Info Per Serving: Calories: 210;Fat: 7g;Protein: 4g;Carbs: 9g.

Sautéed Spinach And Leeks

Servings:2 | Cooking Time: 8 Minutes

Ingredients:
- 3 tablespoons olive oil
- 2 garlic cloves, crushed
- 2 leeks, chopped
- 2 red onions, chopped
- 9 ounces fresh spinach
- 1 teaspoon kosher salt
- ½ cup crumbled goat cheese

Directions:
1. Coat the bottom of the Instant Pot with the olive oil.
2. Add the garlic, leek, and onions and stir-fry for about 5 minutes, on Sauté mode.
3. Stir in the spinach. Sprinkle with the salt and sauté for an additional 3 minutes, stirring constantly.
4. Transfer to a plate and scatter with the goat cheese before serving.

Nutrition:
- Info Per Serving: Calories: 447;Fat: 31.2g;Protein: 14.6g;Carbs: 28.7g.

Spicy Potato Wedges

Servings:4 | Cooking Time:30 Minutes

Ingredients:
- 1 ½ lb potatoes, peeled and cut into wedges
- 3 tbsp olive oil
- 1 tbsp minced fresh rosemary
- 2 tsp chili powder
- 3 garlic cloves, minced
- Salt and black pepper to taste

Directions:
1. Preheat the oven to 370ºF. Toss the wedges with olive oil, garlic, salt, and pepper. Spread out in a roasting sheet. Roast for 15-20 minutes until browned and crisp at the edges. Remove and sprinkle with chili powder and rosemary.

Nutrition:
- Info Per Serving: Calories: 152;Fat: 7g;Protein: 2.5g;Carbs: 21g.

Simple Zoodles

Servings:2 | Cooking Time: 5 Minutes

Ingredients:
- 2 tablespoons avocado oil
- 2 medium zucchinis, spiralized
- ¼ teaspoon salt
- Freshly ground black pepper, to taste

Directions:
1. Heat the avocado oil in a large skillet over medium heat until it shimmers.
2. Add the zucchini noodles, salt, and black pepper to the skillet and toss to coat. Cook for 1 to 2 minutes, stirring constantly, until tender.
3. Serve warm.

Nutrition:
- Info Per Serving: Calories: 128;Fat: 14.0g;Protein: 0.3g;Carbs: 0.3g.

Tahini & Feta Butternut Squash

Servings:6 | Cooking Time:50 Minutes

Ingredients:
- 3 lb butternut squash, peeled, halved lengthwise, and seeded
- 3 tbsp olive oil
- Salt and black pepper to taste
- 2 tbsp fresh thyme, chopped
- 1 tbsp tahini
- 1 ½ tsp lemon juice
- 1 tsp honey
- 1 oz feta cheese, crumbled
- ¼ cup pistachios, chopped

Directions:
1. Preheat oven to 425ºF. Slice the squash halves crosswise into ½-inch-thick pieces. Toss them with 2 tablespoons of olive oil, salt, and pepper and arrange them on a greased baking sheet in an even layer. Roast for 45-50 minutes or until golden and tender. Transfer squash to a serving platter. Whisk tahini, lemon juice, honey, remaining oil, and salt together in a bowl. Drizzle squash with tahini dressing and sprinkle with feta, pistachios, and thyme. Serve and enjoy!

Nutrition:
- Info Per Serving: Calories: 212;Fat: 12g;Protein: 4.1g;Carbs: 27g.

Sautéed Mushrooms With Garlic & Parsley

Servings:6 | Cooking Time:15 Minutes

Ingredients:
- 3 tbsp butter
- 2 lb cremini mushrooms, sliced
- 2 tbsp garlic, minced
- Salt and black pepper to taste
- 1 tbsp fresh parsley, chopped

Directions:
1. Melt the butter in a skillet over medium heat. Cook the garlic for 1-2 minutes until soft. Stir in the mushrooms and season with salt. Sauté for 7-8 minutes, stirring often. Remove to a serving dish. Top with pepper and parsley to serve.

Nutrition:
- Info Per Serving: Calories: 183;Fat: 9g;Protein: 8.9g;Carbs: 10.1g.

Fried Eggplant Rolls

Servings:4 | Cooking Time: 10 Minutes

Ingredients:
- 2 large eggplants, trimmed and cut lengthwise into ¼-inch-thick slices
- 1 teaspoon salt
- 1 cup shredded ricotta cheese
- 4 ounces goat cheese, shredded
- ¼ cup finely chopped fresh basil
- ½ teaspoon freshly ground black pepper
- Olive oil spray

Directions:
1. Add the eggplant slices to a colander and season with salt. Set aside for 15 to 20 minutes.
2. Mix together the ricotta and goat cheese, basil, and black pepper in a large bowl and stir to combine. Set aside.
3. Dry the eggplant slices with paper towels and lightly mist them with olive oil spray.
4. Heat a large skillet over medium heat and lightly spray it with olive oil spray.
5. Arrange the eggplant slices in the skillet and fry each side for 3 minutes until golden brown.
6. Remove from the heat to a paper towel-lined plate and rest for 5 minutes.
7. Make the eggplant rolls: Lay the eggplant slices on a flat work surface and top each slice with a tablespoon of the prepared cheese mixture. Roll them up and serve immediately.

Nutrition:
- Info Per Serving: Calories: 254;Fat: 14.9g;Protein: 15.3g;Carbs: 18.6g.

Baked Honey Acorn Squash

Servings:4 | Cooking Time:35 Minutes

Ingredients:
- 1 acorn squash, cut into wedges
- 2 tbsp olive oil
- 2 tbsp honey
- 2 tbsp rosemary, chopped
- 2 tbsp walnuts, chopped

Directions:
1. Preheat oven to 400°F. In a bowl, mix honey, rosemary, and olive oil. Lay the squash wedges on a baking sheet and drizzle with the honey mixture. Bake for 30 minutes until squash is tender and slightly caramelized, turning each slice over halfway through. Serve cooled sprinkled with walnuts.

Nutrition:
- Info Per Serving: Calories: 136;Fat: 6g;Protein: 0.9g;Carbs: 20g.

Celery And Mustard Greens

Servings:4 | Cooking Time: 15 Minutes

Ingredients:
- ½ cup low-sodium vegetable broth
- 1 celery stalk, roughly chopped
- ½ sweet onion, chopped
- ½ large red bell pepper, thinly sliced
- 2 garlic cloves, minced
- 1 bunch mustard greens, roughly chopped

Directions:
1. Pour the vegetable broth into a large cast iron pan and bring it to a simmer over medium heat.
2. Stir in the celery, onion, bell pepper, and garlic. Cook uncovered for about 3 to 5 minutes, or until the onion is softened.
3. Add the mustard greens to the pan and stir well. Cover, reduce the heat to low, and cook for an additional 10 minutes, or until the liquid is evaporated and the greens are wilted.
4. Remove from the heat and serve warm.

Nutrition:
- Info Per Serving: Calories: 39;Fat: 0g;Protein: 3.1g;Carbs: 6.8g.

Parsley & Olive Zucchini Bake

Servings:6 | Cooking Time:1 Hour 40 Minutes

Ingredients:
- 3 tbsp olive oil
- 1 can tomatoes, diced
- 2 lb zucchinis, sliced
- 1 onion, chopped
- Salt and black pepper to taste
- 3 garlic cloves, minced
- ¼ tsp dried oregano
- ¼ tsp red pepper flakes
- 10 Kalamata olives, chopped
- 2 tbsp fresh parsley, chopped

Directions:
1. Preheat oven to 325°F. Warm the olive oil in a saucepan over medium heat. Sauté zucchini for about 3 minutes per side; transfer to a bowl. Stir-fry the onion and salt in the same saucepan for 3-5 minutes, stirring occasionally until onion soft and lightly golden. Stir in garlic, oregano, and pepper flakes and cook until fragrant, about 30 seconds.
2. Add in olives, tomatoes, salt, and pepper, bring to a simmer, and cook for about 10 minutes, stirring occasionally. Return the zucchini, cover, and transfer the pot to the oven. Bake for 10-15 minutes. Sprinkle with parsley and serve.

Nutrition:
- Info Per Serving: Calories: 164;Fat: 6g;Protein: 1.5g;Carbs: 7.7g.

Roasted Vegetables

Servings:2 | Cooking Time: 35 Minutes

Ingredients:
- 6 teaspoons extra-virgin olive oil, divided
- 12 to 15 Brussels sprouts, halved
- 1 medium sweet potato, peeled and cut into 2-inch cubes
- 2 cups fresh cauliflower florets
- 1 medium zucchini, cut into 1-inch rounds
- 1 red bell pepper, cut into 1-inch slices
- Salt, to taste

Directions:
1. Preheat the oven to 425°F.
2. Add 2 teaspoons of olive oil, Brussels sprouts, sweet potato, and salt to a large bowl and toss until they are completely coated.
3. Transfer them to a large roasting pan and roast for 10 minutes, or until the Brussels sprouts are lightly browned.
4. Meantime, combine the cauliflower florets with 2 teaspoons of olive oil and salt in a separate bowl.
5. Remove from the oven. Add the cauliflower florets to the roasting pan and roast for 10 minutes more.
6. Meanwhile, toss the zucchini and bell pepper with the remaining olive oil in a medium bowl until well coated. Season with salt.
7. Remove the roasting pan from the oven and stir in the zucchini and bell pepper. Continue roasting for 15 minutes, or until the vegetables are fork-tender.
8. Divide the roasted vegetables between two plates and serve warm.

Nutrition:
- Info Per Serving: Calories: 333;Fat: 16.8g;Protein: 12.2g;Carbs: 37.6g.

Buttery Garlic Green Beans

Servings:6 | Cooking Time:25 Minutes

Ingredients:
- 2 tbsp butter
- 1 lb green beans, trimmed
- 4 cups water
- 6 garlic cloves, minced
- 1 shallot, chopped
- Celery salt to taste
- ½ tsp red pepper flakes

Directions:
1. Pour 4 cups of water in a pot over high heat and bring to a boil. Cut the green beans in half crosswise. Reduce the heat and add in the green beans. Simmer for 6-8 minutes until crisp-tender but still vibrant green. Drain beans and set aside.
2. Melt the butter in a pan over medium heat and sauté garlic and shallot for 3 minutes until the garlic is slightly browned and fragrant. Stir in the beans and season with celery salt. Cook for 2–3 minutes. Serve topped with red pepper flakes.

Nutrition:
- Info Per Serving: Calories: 65;Fat: 4g;Protein: 2g;Carbs: 7g.

Veggie-Stuffed Portabello Mushrooms

Servings:6 | Cooking Time: 24 To 25 Minutes

Ingredients:
- 3 tablespoons extra-virgin olive oil, divided
- 1 cup diced onion
- 2 garlic cloves, minced
- 1 large zucchini, diced
- 3 cups chopped mushrooms
- 1 cup chopped tomato
- 1 teaspoon dried oregano
- ¼ teaspoon kosher salt
- ¼ teaspoon crushed red pepper
- 6 large portabello mushrooms, stems and gills removed
- Cooking spray

- 4 ounces fresh Mozzarella cheese, shredded

Directions:
1. In a large skillet over medium heat, heat 2 tablespoons of the oil. Add the onion and sauté for 4 minutes. Stir in the garlic and sauté for 1 minute.
2. Stir in the zucchini, mushrooms, tomato, oregano, salt and red pepper. Cook for 10 minutes, stirring constantly. Remove from the heat.
3. Meanwhile, heat a grill pan over medium-high heat.
4. Brush the remaining 1 tablespoon of the oil over the portabello mushroom caps. Place the mushrooms, bottom-side down, on the grill pan. Cover with a sheet of aluminum foil sprayed with non-stick cooking spray. Cook for 5 minutes.
5. Flip the mushroom caps over, and spoon about ½ cup of the cooked vegetable mixture into each cap. Top each with about 2½ tablespoons of the Mozzarella.
6. Cover and grill for 4 to 5 minutes, or until the cheese is melted.
7. Using a spatula, transfer the portabello mushrooms to a plate. Let cool for about 5 minutes before serving.

Nutrition:
- Info Per Serving: Calories: 111;Fat: 4.0g;Protein: 11.0g;Carbs: 11.0g.

Hot Turnip Chickpeas

Servings:4 | Cooking Time:50 Minutes

Ingredients:
- 2 tbsp olive oil
- 2 onions, chopped
- 2 red bell peppers, chopped
- Salt and black pepper to taste
- ¼ cup tomato paste
- 1 jalapeño pepper, minced
- 5 garlic cloves, minced
- ¾ tsp ground cumin
- ¼ tsp cayenne pepper
- 2 cans chickpeas
- 12 oz potatoes, chopped
- ¼ cup chopped fresh parsley
- 1 lemon, juiced

Directions:
1. Warm the olive oil in a saucepan oven over medium heat. Sauté the onions, bell peppers, salt, and pepper for 6 minutes until softened and lightly browned. Stir in tomato paste, jalapeño pepper, garlic, cumin, and cayenne pepper and cook for about 30 seconds until fragrant. Stir in chickpeas and their liquid, potatoes, and 1 cup of water. Bring to simmer and cook for 25-35 minutes until potatoes are tender and the sauce has thickened. Stir in parsley and lemon juice.

Nutrition:
- Info Per Serving: Calories: 124;Fat: 5.3g;Protein: 3.7g;Carbs: 17g.

Garlicky Broccoli Rabe

Servings:4 | Cooking Time: 5 To 6 Minutes

Ingredients:
- 14 ounces broccoli rabe, trimmed and cut into 1-inch pieces
- 2 teaspoons salt, plus more for seasoning
- Black pepper, to taste
- 2 tablespoons extra-virgin olive oil
- 3 garlic cloves, minced
- ¼ teaspoon red pepper flakes

Directions:
1. Bring 3 quarts water to a boil in a large saucepan. Add the broccoli rabe and 2 teaspoons of the salt to the boiling water and cook for 2 to 3 minutes, or until wilted and tender.
2. Drain the broccoli rabe. Transfer to ice water and let sit until

chilled. Drain again and pat dry.
3. In a skillet over medium heat, heat the oil and add the garlic and red pepper flakes. Sauté for about 2 minutes, or until the garlic begins to sizzle.
4. Increase the heat to medium-high. Stir in the broccoli rabe and cook for about 1 minute, or until heated through, stirring constantly. Season with salt and pepper.
5. Serve immediately.

Nutrition:
- Info Per Serving: Calories: 87;Fat: 7.3g;Protein: 3.4g;Carbs: 4.0g.

Sweet Mustard Cabbage Hash

Servings:4 | Cooking Time:30 Minutes

Ingredients:
- 1 head Savoy cabbage, shredded
- 3 tbsp olive oil
- 1 onion, finely chopped
- 2 garlic cloves, minced
- ½ tsp fennel seeds
- ¼ cup red wine vinegar
- 1 tbsp mustard powder
- 1 tbsp honey
- Salt and black pepper to taste

Directions:
1. Warm olive oil in a pan over medium heat and sauté onion, fennel seeds, cabbage, salt, and pepper for 8-9 minutes.
2. In a bowl, mix vinegar, mustard, and honey; set aside. Sauté garlic in the pan for 30 seconds. Pour in vinegar mixture and cook for 10-15 minutes until the liquid reduces by half.

Nutrition:
- Info Per Serving: Calories: 181;Fat: 12g;Protein: 3.4g;Carbs: 19g.

Baked Veggie Medley

Servings:4 | Cooking Time:70 Minutes

Ingredients:
- 2 tbsp olive oil
- ½ lb green beans, trimmed
- 1 tomato, chopped
- 1 potato, sliced
- ½ tbsp tomato paste
- 2 tbsp chopped fresh parsley
- 1 tsp sweet paprika
- 1 onion, sliced
- 1 cup mushrooms, sliced
- 1 celery stalk, chopped
- 1 red bell pepper, sliced
- 1 eggplant, sliced
- ½ cup vegetable broth
- Salt and black pepper to taste

Directions:
1. Preheat oven to 375°F. Warm oil in a skillet over medium heat and sauté onion, bell pepper, celery, and mushrooms for 5 minutes until tender. Stir in paprika and tomato paste for 1 minute. Pour in the vegetable broth and stir. Combine the remaining ingredients in a baking pan and mix in the sautéed vegetable. Bake covered with foil for 40-50 minutes.

Nutrition:
- Info Per Serving: Calories: 175;Fat: 8g;Protein: 5.2g;Carbs: 25.2g.

Pea & Carrot Noodles

Servings:4 | Cooking Time:25 Minutes

Ingredients:
- 2 tbsp olive oil
- 4 carrots, spiralized
- 1 sweet onion, chopped
- 2 cups peas
- 2 garlic cloves, minced
- ¼ cup chopped fresh parsley
- Salt and black pepper to taste

Directions:
1. Warm 2 tbsp of olive oil in a pot over medium heat and sauté the onion and garlic for 3 minutes until just tender and fragrant. Add in spiralized carrots and cook for 4 minutes. Mix in peas, salt, and pepper and cook for 4 minutes. Drizzle with the remaining olive oil and sprinkle with parsley.

Nutrition:
- Info Per Serving: Calories: 157;Fat: 7g;Protein: 4.8g;Carbs: 19.6g.

Asparagus & Mushroom Farro

Servings:2 | Cooking Time:40 Minutes

Ingredients:
- ½ oz dried porcini mushrooms, soaked
- 2 tbsp olive oil
- 1 cup hot water
- 3 cups vegetable stock
- ½ large onion, minced
- 1 garlic clove
- 1 cup fresh mushrooms, sliced
- ½ cup farro
- ½ cup dry white wine
- ½ tsp dried thyme
- ½ tsp dried marjoram
- 4 oz asparagus, chopped
- 2 tbsp grated Parmesan cheese

Directions:
1. Drain the soaked mushrooms, reserving the liquid, and cut them into slices. Warm the olive oil in a saucepan oven over medium heat. Sauté the onion, garlic, and soaked and fresh mushrooms for 8 minutes. Stir in the farro for 1-2 minutes. Add the wine, thyme, marjoram, reserved mushroom liquid, and a ladleful of stock. Bring it to a boil.
2. Lower the heat and cook for about 20 minutes, stirring occasionally and adding another ladleful of stock, until the farro is cooked through but not overcooked. Stir in the asparagus and the remaining stock. Cook for 3-5 more minutes or until the asparagus is softened. Sprinkle with Parmesan cheese and serve warm.

Nutrition:
- Info Per Serving: Calories: 341;Fat: 16g;Protein: 13g;Carbs: 26g.

Spinach & Lentil Stew

Servings:4 | Cooking Time:40 Minutes

Ingredients:
- 2 tbsp olive oil
- 1 cup dry red lentils, rinsed
- 1 carrot, chopped
- 1 celery stalk, chopped
- 1 red onion, chopped
- 4 garlic cloves, minced
- 3 tomatoes, puréed
- 3 cups vegetable broth
- 1 tsp cayenne pepper
- ½ tsp ground cumin
- ½ tsp thyme
- 1 tsp turmeric
- 1 tbsp sweet paprika
- 1 cup spinach, chopped
- 1 cup fresh cilantro, chopped
- Salt and black pepper to taste

Directions:
1. Heat the olive oil in a pot over medium heat and sauté the garlic, carrot, celery, and onion until tender, about 4-5 minutes. Stir in cayenne pepper, cumin, thyme, paprika, and turmeric for 1 minute and add tomatoes; cook for 3 more minutes. Pour in vegetable broth and lentils and bring to a boil. Reduce the heat and simmer covered for 15 minutes. Stir in spinach and cook for 5 minutes until wilted. Adjust the seasoning and divide between bowls. Top with cilantro.

Nutrition:
- Info Per Serving: Calories: 310;Fat: 9g;Protein: 18.3g;Carbs: 41g.

Chickpea Lettuce Wraps With Celery

Servings:4 | Cooking Time: 0 Minutes

Ingredients:
- 1 can low-sodium chickpeas, drained and rinsed
- 1 celery stalk, thinly sliced
- 2 tablespoons finely chopped red onion
- 2 tablespoons unsalted tahini
- 3 tablespoons honey mustard
- 1 tablespoon capers, undrained
- 12 butter lettuce leaves

Directions:
1. In a bowl, mash the chickpeas with a potato masher or the back of a fork until mostly smooth.
2. Add the celery, red onion, tahini, honey mustard, and capers to the bowl and stir until well incorporated.
3. For each serving, place three overlapping lettuce leaves on a plate and top with ¼ of the mashed chickpea filling, then roll up. Repeat with the remaining lettuce leaves and chickpea mixture.

Nutrition:
- Info Per Serving: Calories: 182;Fat: 7.1g;Protein: 10.3g;Carbs: 19.6g.

Garlic-Butter Asparagus With Parmesan

Servings:2 | Cooking Time: 8 Minutes

Ingredients:
- 1 cup water
- 1 pound asparagus, trimmed
- 2 cloves garlic, chopped
- 3 tablespoons almond butter
- Salt and ground black pepper, to taste
- 3 tablespoons grated Parmesan cheese

Directions:
1. Pour the water into the Instant Pot and insert a trivet.
2. Put the asparagus on a tin foil add the butter and garlic. Season to taste with salt and pepper.
3. Fold over the foil and seal the asparagus inside so the foil doesn't come open. Arrange the asparagus on the trivet.
4. Secure the lid. Select the Manual mode and set the cooking time for 8 minutes at High Pressure.
5. Once cooking is complete, do a quick pressure release. Carefully open the lid.
6. Unwrap the foil packet and serve sprinkled with the Parmesan cheese.

Nutrition:
- Info Per Serving: Calories: 243;Fat: 15.7g;Protein: 12.3g;Carbs: 15.3g.

Roasted Vegetable Medley

Servings:2 | Cooking Time:65 Minutes

Ingredients:
- 1 head garlic, cloves split apart, unpeeled
- 3 tbsp olive oil
- 2 carrots, cut into strips
- ¼ lb asparagus, chopped
- ½ lb Brussels sprouts, halved
- 2 cups broccoli florets
- 1 cup cherry tomatoes
- ½ fresh lemon, sliced
- Salt and black pepper to taste

Directions:
1. Preheat oven to 375°F. Drizzle the garlic cloves with some olive oil and lightly wrap them in a small piece of foil. Place the packet in the oven and roast for 30 minutes. Place all the vegetables and the lemon slices into a large mixing bowl. Drizzle with the remaining olive oil and season with salt and pepper. Increase the oven to 400 F. Pour the vegetables on a sheet pan in a single layer, leaving the packet of garlic cloves on the pan. Roast for 20 minutes, shaking occasionally until tender. Remove the pan from the oven. Let the garlic cloves sit until cool enough to handle, then remove the skins. Top the vegetables with roasted garlic and serve.

Nutrition:
- Info Per Serving: Calories: 256;Fat: 15g;Protein: 7g;Carbs: 31g.

Mushroom & Cauliflower Roast

Servings:4 | Cooking Time:35 Minutes

Ingredients:
- 2 tbsp olive oil
- 4 cups cauliflower florets
- 1 celery stalk, chopped
- 1 cup mushrooms, sliced
- 10 cherry tomatoes, halved
- 1 yellow onion, chopped
- 2 garlic cloves, minced
- 2 tbsp dill, chopped
- Salt and black pepper to taste

Directions:
1. Preheat the oven to 340°F. Line a baking sheet with parchment paper. Place in cauliflower florets, olive oil, mushrooms, celery, tomatoes, onion, garlic, salt, and pepper and mix to combine. Bake for 25 minutes. Serve topped with dill.

Nutrition:
- Info Per Serving: Calories: 380;Fat: 15g;Protein: 12g;Carbs: 17g.

Simple Honey-Glazed Baby Carrots

Servings:2 | Cooking Time: 6 Minutes

Ingredients:
- ⅔ cup water
- 1½ pounds baby carrots
- 4 tablespoons almond butter
- ½ cup honey
- 1 teaspoon dried thyme
- 1½ teaspoons dried dill
- Salt, to taste

Directions:
1. Pour the water into the Instant Pot and add a steamer basket. Place the baby carrots in the basket.
2. Secure the lid. Select the Manual mode and set the cooking time for 4 minutes at High Pressure.
3. Once cooking is complete, do a quick pressure release. Carefully open the lid.
4. Transfer the carrots to a plate and set aside.
5. Pour the water out of the Instant Pot and dry it.
6. Press the Sauté button on the Instant Pot and heat the almond butter.
7. Stir in the honey, thyme, and dill.
8. Return the carrots to the Instant Pot and stir until well coated. Sauté for another 1 minute.
9. Taste and season with salt as needed. Serve warm.

Nutrition:
- Info Per Serving: Calories: 575;Fat: 23.5g;Protein: 2.8g;Carbs: 90.6g.

Baked Beet & Leek With Dilly Yogurt

Servings:4 | Cooking Time:40 Minutes

Ingredients:
- 5 tbsp olive oil
- ½ lb leeks, thickly sliced
- 1 lb red beets, sliced
- 1 cup yogurt
- 2 garlic cloves, finely minced
- ¼ tsp cumin, ground
- ¼ tsp dried parsley
- ¼ cup parsley, chopped
- 1 tsp dill
- Salt and black pepper to taste

Directions:
1. Preheat the oven to 390°F. Arrange the beets and leeks on a greased roasting dish. Sprinkle with some olive oil, cumin, dried parsley, black pepper, and salt. Bake in the oven for 25-30 minutes. Transfer to a serving platter. In a bowl, stir in yogurt, dill, garlic, and the remaining olive oil. Whisk to combine. Drizzle the veggies with the yogurt sauce and top with fresh parsley to serve.

Nutrition:
- Info Per Serving: Calories: 281;Fat: 18.7g;Protein: 6g;Carbs: 24g.

Zucchini Ribbons With Ricotta

Servings:4 | Cooking Time:10 Minutes

Ingredients:
- 3 tbsp olive oil
- 1 garlic clove, minced
- 1 tsp lemon zest
- 1 tbsp lemon juice
- 4 zucchinis, cut into ribbons
- Salt and black pepper to taste
- 2 tbsp chopped fresh parsley
- ½ ricotta cheese, crumbled

Directions:
1. Whisk 2 tablespoons oil, garlic, salt, pepper, and lemon zest, and lemon juice in a bowl. Warm the remaining olive oil in a skillet over medium heat. Season the zucchini ribbons with salt and pepper and add them to the skillet; cook for 3-4 minutes per side. Transfer to a serving bowl and drizzle with the dressing, sprinkle with parsley and cheese and serve.

Nutrition:
- Info Per Serving: Calories: 134;Fat: 2g;Protein: 2g;Carbs: 4g.

Simple Broccoli With Yogurt Sauce

Servings:4 | Cooking Time:25 Minutes

Ingredients:
- 2 tbsp olive oil
- 1 head broccoli, cut into florets
- 2 garlic cloves, minced
- ½ cup Greek yogurt
- Salt and black pepper to taste
- 2 tsp fresh dill, chopped

Directions:
1. Warm olive oil in a pan over medium heat and sauté broccoli, salt, and pepper for 12 minutes. Mix Greek yogurt, dill, and garlic in a small bowl. Drizzle the broccoli with the sauce.

Nutrition:
- Info Per Serving: Calories: 104;Fat: 7.7g;Protein: 4.5g;Carbs: 6g.

Sautéed Cabbage With Parsley

Servings:4 | Cooking Time: 12 To 14 Minutes

Ingredients:
- 1 small head green cabbage, cored and sliced thin
- 2 tablespoons extra-virgin olive oil, divided
- 1 onion, halved and sliced thin
- ¾ teaspoon salt, divided
- ¼ teaspoon black pepper
- ¼ cup chopped fresh parsley
- 1½ teaspoons lemon juice

Directions:
1. Place the cabbage in a large bowl with cold water. Let sit for 3 minutes. Drain well.
2. Heat 1 tablespoon of the oil in a skillet over medium-high heat until shimmering. Add the onion and ¼ teaspoon of the salt and cook for 5 to 7 minutes, or until softened and lightly browned. Transfer to a bowl.
3. Heat the remaining 1 tablespoon of the oil in now-empty skillet over medium-high heat until shimmering. Add the cabbage and sprinkle with the remaining ½ teaspoon of the salt and black pepper. Cover and cook for about 3 minutes, without stirring, or until cabbage is wilted and lightly browned on bottom.
4. Stir and continue to cook for about 4 minutes, uncovered, or until the cabbage is crisp-tender and lightly browned in places, stirring once halfway through cooking. Off heat, stir in the cooked onion, parsley and lemon juice.
5. Transfer to a plate and serve.

Nutrition:
- Info Per Serving: Calories: 117;Fat: 7.0g;Protein: 2.7g;Carbs: 13.4g.

Feta & Zucchini Rosti Cakes

Servings:4 | Cooking Time:25 Minutes

Ingredients:
- 5 tbsp olive oil
- 1 lb zucchini, shredded
- 4 spring onions, chopped
- Salt and black pepper to taste
- 4 oz feta cheese, crumbled
- 1 egg, lightly beaten
- 2 tbsp minced fresh dill
- 1 garlic clove, minced
- ¼ cup flour
- Lemon wedges for serving

Directions:
1. Preheat oven to 380ºF. In a large bowl, mix the zucchini, spring onions, feta cheese, egg, dill, garlic, salt, and pepper. Sprinkle flour over the mixture and stir to incorporate.
2. Warm the oil in a skillet over medium heat. Cook the rosti mixture in small flat fritters for about 4 minutes per side until crisp and golden on both sides, pressing with a fish slice as they cook. Serve with lemon wedges.

Nutrition:
- Info Per Serving: Calories: 239;Fat: 19.8g;Protein: 7.8g;Carbs: 9g.

Beans , Grains, And Pastas Recipes

Beans , Grains, And Pastas Recipes

Swiss Chard Couscous With Feta Cheese

Servings:4 | Cooking Time:20 Minutes

Ingredients:
- 2 tbsp olive oil
- 10 oz couscous
- 2 garlic cloves, minced
- 1 cup raisins
- ½ cup feta cheese, crumbled
- 1 bunch of Swiss chard, torn

Directions:
1. In a bowl, place couscous and cover with hot water. Let sit covered for 10 minutes. Using a fork, fluff it. Warm the olive oil in a skillet over medium heat and sauté garlic for a minute. Stir in couscous, raisins, and chard. Top with feta.

Nutrition:
- Info Per Serving: Calories: 310;Fat: 8g;Protein: 7g;Carbs: 18g.

Mustard Vegetable Millet

Servings:6 | Cooking Time:35 Minutes

Ingredients:
- 6 oz okra, cut into 1-inch lengths
- 3 tbsp olive oil
- 6 oz asparagus, chopped
- Salt and black pepper to taste
- 1 ½ cups whole millet
- 2 tbsp lemon juice
- 2 tbsp minced shallot
- 1 tsp Dijon mustard
- 6 oz cherry tomatoes, halved
- 3 tbsp chopped fresh dill
- 2 oz goat cheese, crumbled

Directions:
1. In a large pot, bring 4 quarts of water to a boil. Add asparagus, snap peas, and salt and cook until crisp-tender, about 3 minutes. Using a slotted spoon, transfer vegetables to a large plate and let cool completely, about 15 minutes. Add millet to water, return to a boil, and cook until grains are tender, 15-20 minutes.
2. Drain millet, spread in rimmed baking sheet, and let cool completely, 15 minutes. Whisk oil, lemon juice, shallot, mustard, salt, and pepper in a large bowl. Add vegetables, millet, tomatoes, dill, and half of the goat cheese and toss gently to combine. Season with salt and pepper. Sprinkle with remaining goat cheese to serve.

Nutrition:
- Info Per Serving: Calories: 315;Fat: 19g;Protein: 13g;Carbs: 35g.

Chicken Linguine A La Toscana

Servings:4 | Cooking Time:35 Minutes

Ingredients:
- 1 cup sundried tomatoes in oil, chopped
- ¾ cup grated Pecorino Romano cheese
- 2 tbsp olive oil
- 16 oz linguine
- 4 chicken breasts
- 1 white onion, chopped
- 1 red bell pepper, chopped
- 5 garlic cloves, minced
- ¾ cup chicken broth
- 1 ½ cups heavy cream
- 1 cup baby kale, chopped
- Salt and black pepper to taste

Directions:
1. In a pot of boiling water, cook the linguine pasta for 8-10 minutes until al dente. Drain and set aside.
2. Heat the olive oil in a large skillet, season the chicken with salt, black pepper, and cook in the oil until golden brown on the outside and cooked within, 7 to 8 minutes. Transfer the chicken to a plate and cut into 4 slices each. Set aside.
3. Add the onion, sundried tomatoes, bell pepper to the skillet and sauté until softened, 5 minutes. Mix in the garlic and cook until fragrant, 1 minute. Deglaze the skillet with the chicken broth and mix in the heavy cream. Simmer for 2 minutes and stir in the Pecorino Romano cheese until melted, 2 minutes. Once the cheese melts, stir in the kale to wilt and adjust the taste with salt and black pepper. Mix in the linguine and chicken until well coated in the sauce. Dish the food and serve warm.

Nutrition:
- Info Per Serving: Calories: 941;Fat: 61g;Protein: 79g;Carbs: 11g.

Eggplant & Chickpea Casserole

Servings:6 | Cooking Time:75 Minutes

Ingredients:
- ¼ cup olive oil
- 2 onions, chopped
- 1 green bell pepper, chopped
- Salt and black pepper to taste
- 3 garlic cloves, minced
- 1 tsp dried oregano
- ½ tsp ground cumin
- 1 lb eggplants, cubed
- 1 can tomatoes, diced
- 2 cans chickpeas

Directions:
1. Preheat oven to 400° F. Warm the olive oil in a skillet over medium heat. Add the onions, bell pepper, salt, and pepper.
2. Cook for about 5 minutes until softened. Stir in garlic, oregano, and cumin for about 30 seconds until fragrant. Transfer to a baking dish and add the eggplants, tomatoes, and chickpeas and stir. Place in the oven and bake for 45-60 minutes, shaking the dish twice during cooking. Serve.

Nutrition:
- Info Per Serving: Calories: 260;Fat: 12g;Protein: 8g;Carbs: 33.4g.

Harissa Vegetable Couscous

Servings:4 | Cooking Time:60 Minutes

Ingredients:
- Salt and black pepper to taste 1 large sweet potato
- 2 red bell peppers, sliced
- 2 zucchini, chopped
- 1 garlic clove, minced
- 3 tbsp olive oil
- 1 tsp harissa paste
- 1 cup couscous
- 8 oz spinach leaves, torn
- ½ lemon, juiced

Directions:
1. Preheat oven to 350 F. Whisk the garlic, harissa paste, salt, pepper, and olive oil in a large bowl. Add all the vegetables, except for the spinach, and toss to coat. Transfer to a baking dish. Roast for 35-40 minutes until the vegetables are tender.
2. Cover the couscous in a bowl with 1 ½ cups of boiling water and plut a lid. Let stand for 5 minutes to absorb the water.Fluff the

couscous with a fork, then stir through the spinach and the lemon zest and juice. Stir through the roasted vegetables. Serve immediately.

Nutrition:
• Info Per Serving: Calories: 301;Fat: 11g;Protein: 9g;Carbs: 43g.

Classic Garidomakaronada (Shrimp & Pasta)

Servings:4 | Cooking Time:45 Minutes

Ingredients:
• 2 tbsp olive oil
• 16 medium shrimp, shelled and deveined
• Salt and black pepper to taste
• 1 onion, finely chopped
• 3 garlic cloves, minced
• 4 tomatoes, puréed
• ½ tsp sugar
• 1 tbsp tomato paste
• 1 tbsp ouzo
• 1 lb whole-wheat spaghetti
• ½ tsp crushed red pepper
• ¼ tsp dried Greek oregano
• 2 tbsp chopped fresh parsley

Directions:
1. Bring a large pot of salted water to a boil, add the spaghetti, and cook for 7-9 minutes until al dente. Drain the pasta and set aside. Warm the olive oil in a large skillet over medium heat. Sauté the shrimp for 2 minutes, flipping once or until pink; set aside. Add the onion and garlic to the skillet and cook for 3-5 minutes or until tender.
2. Add tomatoes, sugar, oregano, and tomato paste. Bring the sauce to a boil. Reduce the heat and simmer for 15–20 minutes or until thickened. Stir in ouzo and season with salt and black pepper. Add the pasta along with crushed red pepper and cooked shrimp. Remove from heat and toss to coat the pasta. Sprinkle with parsley and serve immediately.

Nutrition:
• Info Per Serving: Calories: 319;Fat: 9g;Protein: 10g;Carbs: 51g.

Tortellini & Cannellini With Meatballs

Servings:4 | Cooking Time:30 Minutes

Ingredients:
• 2 tbsp parsley, chopped
• 12 oz fresh tortellini
• 3 tbsp olive oil
• 5 cloves garlic, minced
• ½ lb meatballs
• 1 can cannellini beans
• 1 can roasted tomatoes
• Salt and black pepper to taste

Directions:
1. Bring to a boil salted water in a pot over high heat. Add the tortellini and cook according to package directions. Drain and set aside. Warm the olive oil in a large skillet over medium heat and sauté the garlic for 1 minute. Stir in meatballs and brown for 4–5 minutes on all sides. Add the tomatoes and cannellini and continue to cook for 5 minutes or until heated through. Adjust the seasoning with salt and pepper. Stir in tortellini. Sprinkle with parsley and serve.

Nutrition:
• Info Per Serving: Calories: 578;Fat: 30g;Protein: 25g;Carbs: 58g.

Power Green Barley Pilaf

Servings:6 | Cooking Time:25 Minutes

Ingredients:
• 3 tbsp olive oil
• 1 small onion, chopped fine
• Salt and black pepper to taste
• 1 ½ cups pearl barley, rinsed
• 2 garlic cloves, minced
• ½ tsp dried thyme
• 2 ½ cups water
• ¼ cup parsley, minced
• 2 tbsp cilantro, chopped
• 1 ½ tsp lemon juice

Directions:
1. Warm the olive oil in a saucepan over medium heat. Stir-fry onion for 5 minutes until soft. Stir in barley, garlic, and thyme and cook, stirring frequently, until barley is lightly toasted and fragrant, 3-4 minutes. Stir in water and bring to a simmer. Reduce heat to low, cover, and simmer until barley is tender and water is absorbed, 25-35 minutes. Lay clean dish towel underneath the lid and let pilaf sit for 10 minutes. Add parsley, cilantro, and lemon juice and fluff gently with a fork to mix. Season with salt and pepper and serve warm.

Nutrition:
• Info Per Serving: Calories: 275;Fat: 21g;Protein: 12g;Carbs: 32g.

Papaya, Jicama, And Peas Rice Bowl

Servings:4 | Cooking Time: 45 Minutes

Ingredients:
• Sauce:
• Juice of ¼ lemon
• 2 teaspoons chopped fresh basil
• 1 tablespoon raw honey
• 1 tablespoon extra-virgin olive oil
• Sea salt, to taste
• Rice:
• 1½ cups wild rice
• 2 papayas, peeled, seeded, and diced
• 1 jicama, peeled and shredded
• 1 cup snow peas, julienned
• 2 cups shredded cabbage
• 1 scallion, white and green parts, chopped

Directions:
1. Combine the ingredients for the sauce in a bowl. Stir to mix well. Set aside until ready to use.
2. Pour the wild rice in a saucepan, then pour in enough water to cover. Bring to a boil.
3. Reduce the heat to low, then simmer for 45 minutes or until the wild rice is soft and plump. Drain and transfer to a large serving bowl.
4. Top the rice with papayas, jicama, peas, cabbage, and scallion. Pour the sauce over and stir to mix well before serving.

Nutrition:
• Info Per Serving: Calories: 446;Fat: 7.9g;Protein: 13.1g;Carbs: 85.8g.

Lemony Farro And Avocado Bowl

Servings:4 | Cooking Time: 25 Minutes

Ingredients:
• 1 tablespoon plus 2 teaspoons extra-virgin olive oil, divided
• ½ medium onion, chopped
• 1 carrot, shredded
• 2 garlic cloves, minced
• 1 cup pearled farro
• 2 cups low-sodium vegetable soup

- 2 avocados, peeled, pitted, and sliced
- Zest and juice of 1 small lemon
- ¼ teaspoon sea salt

Directions:
1. Heat 1 tablespoon of olive oil in a saucepan over medium-high heat until shimmering.
2. Add the onion and sauté for 5 minutes or until translucent.
3. Add the carrot and garlic and sauté for 1 minute or until fragrant.
4. Add the farro and pour in the vegetable soup. Bring to a boil over high heat. Reduce the heat to low. Put the lid on and simmer for 20 minutes or until the farro is al dente.
5. Transfer the farro in a large serving bowl, then fold in the avocado slices. Sprinkle with lemon zest and salt, then drizzle with lemon juice and 2 teaspoons of olive oil.
6. Stir to mix well and serve immediately.

Nutrition:
- Info Per Serving: Calories: 210;Fat: 11.1g;Protein: 4.2g;Carbs: 27.9g.

Oregano Chicken Risotto

Servings:4 | Cooking Time:45 Minutes

Ingredients:
- 4 chicken thighs, bone-in and skin-on
- 2 tbsp olive oil
- 1 cup arborio rice
- 2 lemons, juiced
- 1 tsp oregano, dried
- 1 red onion, chopped
- Salt and black pepper to taste
- 2 garlic cloves, minced
- 2 ½ cups chicken stock
- 1 cup green olives, sliced
- 2 tbsp parsley, chopped
- ½ cup Parmesan, grated

Directions:
1. Warm the olive oil in a skillet over medium heat and brown chicken thighs skin-side down for 3-4 minutes, turn, and cook for 3 minutes. Remove to a plate. Place garlic and onion in the same skillet and sauté for 3 minutes. Stir in rice, salt, pepper, oregano, and lemon juice. Add 1 cup of chicken stock, reduce the heat and simmer the rice while stirring until it is absorbed. Add another cup of chicken broth and continue simmering until the stock is absorbed. Pour in the remaining chicken stock and return the chicken; cook until the rice is tender. Turn the heat off. Stir in Parmesan cheese and top with olives and parsley. Serve into plates. Enjoy!

Nutrition:
- Info Per Serving: Calories: 450;Fat: 19g;Protein: 26g;Carbs: 28g.

Macaroni & Cauliflower Gratin

Servings:4 | Cooking Time:45 Minutes

Ingredients:
- 16 oz elbow pasta
- 20 oz cauliflower florets
- 1 cup heavy cream
- 1 cup grated mozzarella
- 1 tsp dried thyme
- 1 tsp smoked paprika
- Salt to taste
- ½ tsp red chili flakes

Directions:
1. In a pot of boiling water, cook the macaroni for 8-10 minutes until al dente. Drain and set aside.
2. Preheat the oven to 350° F. Grease a baking dish with cooking spray. Set aside. Bring 4 cups of water to a boil in a large pot and blanch the cauliflower for 4 minutes. Drain through a colander. In a large bowl, mix the cauliflower, macaroni, heavy cream, half of the mozzarella cheese, thyme, paprika, salt, and red chili flakes until well-combined. Transfer the mixture to the baking dish and top with the remaining cheese. Bake for 30 minutes. Allow cooling for 2 minutes and serve afterwards.

Nutrition:
- Info Per Serving: Calories: 301;Fat: 21g;Protein: 11g;Carbs: 13g.

Swoodles With Almond Butter Sauce

Servings:4 | Cooking Time: 20 Minutes

Ingredients:
- Sauce:
- 1 garlic clove
- 1-inch piece fresh ginger, peeled and sliced
- ¼ cup chopped yellow onion
- ¾ cup almond butter
- 1 tablespoon tamari
- 1 tablespoon raw honey
- 1 teaspoon paprika
- 1 tablespoon fresh lemon juice
- ⅛ teaspoon ground red pepper
- Sea salt and ground black pepper, to taste
- ¼ cup water
- Swoodles:
- 2 large sweet potatoes, spiralized
- 2 tablespoons coconut oil, melted
- Sea salt and ground black pepper, to taste
- For Serving:
- ½ cup fresh parsley, chopped
- ½ cup thinly sliced scallions

Directions:
1. Make the Sauce
2. Put the garlic, ginger, and onion in a food processor, then pulse to combine well.
3. Add the almond butter, tamari, honey, paprika, lemon juice, ground red pepper, salt, and black pepper to the food processor. Pulse to combine well. Pour in the water during the pulsing until the mixture is thick and smooth.
4. Make the Swoodles:
5. Preheat the oven to 425°F. Line a baking sheet with parchment paper.
6. Put the spiralized sweet potato in a bowl, then drizzle with olive oil. Toss to coat well. Transfer them on the baking sheet. Sprinkle with salt and pepper.
7. Bake in the preheated oven for 20 minutes or until lightly browned and al dente. Check the doneness during the baking and remove any well-cooked swoodles.
8. Transfer the swoodles on a large plate and spread with sauce, parsley, and scallions. Toss to serve.

Nutrition:
- Info Per Serving: Calories: 441;Fat: 33.6g;Protein: 12.0g;Carbs: 29.6g.

Veggie & Egg Quinoa With Pancetta

Servings:4 | Cooking Time:35 Minutes

Ingredients:
- 4 pancetta slices, cooked and crumbled
- 2 tbsp olive oil
- 1 small red onion, chopped
- 1 red bell pepper, chopped
- 1 sweet potato, grated
- 1 green bell pepper, chopped
- 2 garlic cloves, minced
- 1 cup mushrooms, sliced
- ½ cup quinoa

- 1 cup chicken stock
- 4 eggs, fried
- ¼ tsp red pepper flakes
- Salt and black pepper to taste

Directions:
1. Warm the olive oil in a skillet over medium heat and cook onion, garlic, bell peppers, sweet potato, and mushrooms for 5 minutes, stirring often. Stir in quinoa for another minute. Mix in stock, salt, and pepper for 15 minutes. Share into plates and serve topped with fried eggs, salt, pepper, red pepper flakes, and crumbled pancetta.

Nutrition:
- Info Per Serving: Calories: 310;Fat: 15g;Protein: 16g;Carbs: 26g.

Tomato Sauce And Basil Pesto Fettuccine

Servings:4 | Cooking Time: 15 Minutes

Ingredients:
- 4 Roma tomatoes, diced
- 2 teaspoons no-salt-added tomato paste
- 1 tablespoon chopped fresh oregano
- 2 garlic cloves, minced
- 1 cup low-sodium vegetable soup
- ½ teaspoon sea salt
- 1 packed cup fresh basil leaves
- ¼ cup pine nuts
- ¼ cup grated Parmesan cheese
- 2 tablespoons extra-virgin olive oil
- 1 pound cooked whole-grain fettuccine

Directions:
1. Put the tomatoes, tomato paste, oregano, garlic, vegetable soup, and salt in a skillet. Stir to mix well.
2. Cook over medium heat for 10 minutes or until lightly thickened.
3. Put the remaining ingredients, except for the fettuccine, in a food processor and pulse to combine until smooth.
4. Pour the puréed basil mixture into the tomato mixture, then add the fettuccine. Cook for a few minutes or until heated through and the fettuccine is well coated.
5. Serve immediately.

Nutrition:
- Info Per Serving: Calories: 389;Fat: 22.7g;Protein: 9.7g;Carbs: 40.2g.

Bulgur Pilaf With Garbanzo

Servings:4 | Cooking Time: 20 Minutes

Ingredients:
- 3 tablespoons extra-virgin olive oil
- 1 large onion, chopped
- 1 can garbanzo beans, rinsed and drained
- 2 cups bulgur wheat, rinsed and drained
- 1½ teaspoons salt
- ½ teaspoon cinnamon
- 4 cups water

Directions:
1. In a large pot over medium heat, heat the olive oil. Add the onion and cook for 5 minutes.
2. Add the garbanzo beans and cook for an additional 5 minutes.
3. Stir in the remaining ingredients.
4. Reduce the heat to low. Cover and cook for 10 minutes.
5. When done, fluff the pilaf with a fork. Cover and let sit for another 5 minutes before serving.

Nutrition:
- Info Per Serving: Calories: 462;Fat: 13.0g;Protein: 15.0g;Carbs: 76.0g.

Tasty Beanballs In Marinara Sauce

Servings:4 | Cooking Time:45 Minutes

Ingredients:
- Beanballs
- 2 tbsp olive oil
- ½ yellow onion, minced
- 1 tsp coriander seeds
- ½ tsp dried oregano
- ½ tsp dried thyme
- ½ tsp red pepper flakes
- 1 tsp garlic powder
- 1 can white beans
- ½ cup bread crumbs
- Salt and black pepper to taste
- Marinara
- 1 can diced tomatoes with juice
- 1 tbsp olive oil
- 3 garlic cloves, minced
- 2 tbsp basil leaves
- Salt to taste

Directions:
1. Preheat the oven to 350° F. Warm 2 tbsp of olive oil in a skillet over medium heat. Sauté the onion for 3 minutes. Sprinkle with coriander seeds, oregano, thyme, pepper flakes, and garlic powder, then cook for 1 minute or until aromatic.
2. Pour the sautéed mixture into a food processor and add the beans and bread crumbs. Sprinkle with salt and black pepper and pulse to combine well, and the mixture holds together. Shape the mixture into balls. Arrange them on a greased baking sheet. Bake for 30 minutes or until lightly browned. Flip the balls halfway through the cooking time.
3. Meanwhile, heat 1 tbsp of olive oil in a saucepan over medium heat. Add the garlic and basil and sauté for 2 minutes or until fragrant. Fold in the tomatoes and juice. Bring to a boil. Reduce the heat to low. Put the lid on and simmer for 15 minutes. Sprinkle with salt. Transfer the beanballs to a large plate and drizzle with marinara sauce. Serve.

Nutrition:
- Info Per Serving: Calories: 351;Fat: 16g;Protein: 12g;Carbs: 43g.

Lemony Tuna Barley With Capers

Servings:4 | Cooking Time:50 Minutes

Ingredients:
- 2 tbsp olive oil
- 3 cups chicken stock
- 10 oz canned tuna, flaked
- 1 cup barley
- Salt and black pepper to taste
- 12 cherry tomatoes, halved
- ½ cup pepperoncini, sliced
- ¼ cup capers, drained
- ½ lemon, juiced

Directions:
1. Boil chicken stock in a saucepan over medium heat and add in barley. Cook covered for 40 minutes. Fluff the barley and remove to a bowl. Stir in tuna, salt, pepper, tomatoes, pepperoncini, olive oil, capers, and lemon juice. Serve.

Nutrition:
- Info Per Serving: Calories: 260;Fat: 12g;Protein: 24g;Carbs: 17g.

Creamy Asparagus & Parmesan Linguine

Servings:2 | Cooking Time:30 Minutes

Ingredients:
- 2 tsp olive oil
- 1 bunch of asparagus spears
- 1 yellow onion, thinly sliced
- ¼ cup white wine
- ¼ cup vegetable stock
- 2 cups heavy cream
- ¼ tsp garlic powder
- 8 oz linguine
- ¼ cup Parmesan cheese
- 1 lemon, juiced
- Salt and black pepper to taste
- 2 tbsp chives, chopped

Directions:
1. Bring to a boil salted water in a pot over high heat. Add the linguine and cook according to package directions. Drain and transfer to a bowl. Slice the asparagus into bite-sized pieces. Warm the olive oil in a skillet over medium heat. Add onion and cook 3 minutes until softened. Add asparagus and wine and cook until wine is mostly evaporated, then add the stock. Stir in cream and garlic powder and bring to a boil and simmer until the sauce is slightly thick, 2-3 minutes. Add the linguine and stir until everything is heated through. Remove from the heat and season with lemon juice, salt, and pepper. Top with parmesan cheese and chives and serve.

Nutrition:
- Info Per Serving: Calories: 503;Fat: 55g;Protein: 24g;Carbs: 41g.

Cumin Quinoa Pilaf

Servings:2 | Cooking Time: 5 Minutes

Ingredients:
- 2 tablespoons extra virgin olive oil
- 2 cloves garlic, minced
- 3 cups water
- 2 cups quinoa, rinsed
- 2 teaspoons ground cumin
- 2 teaspoons turmeric
- Salt, to taste
- 1 handful parsley, chopped

Directions:
1. Press the Sauté button to heat your Instant Pot.
2. Once hot, add the oil and garlic to the pot, stir and cook for 1 minute.
3. Add water, quinoa, cumin, turmeric, and salt, stirring well.
4. Lock the lid. Select the Manual mode and set the cooking time for 1 minute at High Pressure.
5. When the timer beeps, perform a natural pressure release for 10 minutes, then release any remaining pressure. Carefully remove the lid.
6. Fluff the quinoa with a fork. Season with more salt, if needed.
7. Sprinkle parsley on top and serve.

Nutrition:
- Info Per Serving: Calories: 384;Fat: 12.3g;Protein: 12.8g;Carbs: 57.4g.

Lemon Couscous With Broccoli

Servings:4 | Cooking Time:20 Minutes

Ingredients:
- 2 tsp olive oil
- Salt and black pepper to taste
- 1 small red onion, sliced
- 1 lemon, zested
- 1 head broccoli, cut into florets
- 1 cup couscous

Directions:
1. Heat a pot filled with salted water over medium heat; bring to a boil. Add in the broccoli and cook for 4-6 minutes until tender. Remove to a boil with a slotted spoon. In another bowl, place the couscous and cover with boiling broccoli water. Cover and let sit for 3-4 minutes until the water is absorbrd. Fluff the couscous with a fork and season with lemon zest, salt. and pepper. Stir in broccoli and top with red onion to serve.

Nutrition:
- Info Per Serving: Calories: 620;Fat: 45g;Protein: 11g;Carbs: 51g.

Lebanese Flavor Broken Thin Noodles

Servings:6 | Cooking Time: 25 Minutes

Ingredients:
- 1 tablespoon extra-virgin olive oil
- 1 cup vermicelli, broken into 1- to 1½-inch pieces
- 3 cups shredded cabbage
- 1 cup brown rice
- 3 cups low-sodium vegetable soup
- ½ cup water
- 2 garlic cloves, mashed
- ¼ teaspoon sea salt
- ⅛ teaspoon crushed red pepper flakes
- ½ cup coarsely chopped cilantro
- Fresh lemon slices, for serving

Directions:
1. Heat the olive oil in a saucepan over medium-high heat until shimmering.
2. Add the vermicelli and sauté for 3 minutes or until toasted.
3. Add the cabbage and sauté for 4 minutes or until tender.
4. Pour in the brown rice, vegetable soup, and water. Add the garlic and sprinkle with salt and red pepper flakes.
5. Bring to a boil over high heat. Reduce the heat to medium low. Put the lid on and simmer for another 10 minutes.
6. Turn off the heat, then let sit for 5 minutes without opening the lid.
7. Pour them on a large serving platter and spread with cilantro. Squeeze the lemon slices over and serve warm.

Nutrition:
- Info Per Serving: Calories: 127;Fat: 3.1g;Protein: 4.2g;Carbs: 22.9g.

Herby Fusilli In Chickpea Sauce

Servings:4 | Cooking Time:35 Minutes

Ingredients:
- 1 can chickpeas, drained, liquid reserved
- ¼ cup olive oil
- ½ large shallot, chopped
- 5 garlic cloves, thinly sliced
- 1 cup whole-grain fusilli
- Salt and black pepper to taste
- ¼ cup Parmesan, shaved
- 2 tsp dried parsley
- 1 tsp dried oregano
- A pinch of red pepper flakes

Directions:

1. Heat the oil in a skillet over medium heat and sauté the shallot and garlic for 3-5 minutes until the garlic is golden. Add ¾ of the chickpeas and 2 tbsp of the water from the can; bring to a simmer. Remove from the heat, transfer to a blender, and pulse until smooth. Add the remaining chickpeas and some more of the reserved liquid if it's too thick.
2. Bring a large pot of salted water to a boil and cook pasta until al dente, 7-8 minutes. Reserve ½ cup of the pasta liquid, drain the pasta and return it to the pot. Add the chickpea sauce to the hot pasta and keep adding ¼ cup of the pasta liquid until your desired consistency is reached. Place the pasta pot over medium heat and mix occasionally until the sauce thickens. Season with salt and pepper. Sprinkle with freshly grated Parmesan cheese, parsley, oregano, and red pepper flakes. Serve and enjoy!
Nutrition:
• Info Per Serving: Calories: 322;Fat: 18g;Protein: 12g;Carbs: 36g.

Cherry Tomato Cannellini Beans
Servings:4 | Cooking Time:10 Minutes
Ingredients:
• 2 tbsp olive oil
• 15 oz canned cannellini beans
• 10 cherry tomatoes, halved
• 2 spring onions, chopped
• 1 tsp paprika
• Salt and black pepper to taste
• ½ tsp ground cumin
• 1 tbsp lime juice
Directions:
1. Place beans, cherry tomatoes, spring onions, olive oil, paprika, salt, pepper, cumin, and lime juice in a bowl and toss to combine. Transfer to the fridge for 10 minutes. Serve.
Nutrition:
• Info Per Serving: Calories: 300;Fat: 8g;Protein: 13g;Carbs: 26g.

Parmesan Beef Rotini With Asparagus
Servings:4 | Cooking Time:40 Minutes
Ingredients:
• 1 lb asparagus, cut into 1-inch pieces
• 3 tbsp olive oil
• 16 oz rotini pasta
• 1 lb ground beef
• 2 large shallots, chopped
• 3 garlic cloves, minced
• Salt and black pepper to taste
• 1 cup grated Parmesan cheese
Directions:
1. In a pot of boiling water, cook the rotini pasta for 8-10 minutes until al dente. Drain and set aside.
2. Heat a large non-stick skillet over medium heat and add the beef. Cook while breaking the lumps that form until brown, 10 minutes. Use a slotted spoon to transfer the beef to a plate and discard the drippings. Heat olive oil in a skillet and sauté asparagus until tender, 7 minutes. Stir in shallots and garlic and cook for 2 minutes. Season with salt and pepper. Stir in the beef and rotini pasta and toss until well combined. Adjust the taste with salt and black pepper as desired. Dish the food between serving plates and garnish with Parmesan.
Nutrition:
• Info Per Serving: Calories: 513;Fat: 25g;Protein: 44g;Carbs: 21g.

Spanish-Style Linguine With Tapenade
Servings:4 | Cooking Time:20 Minutes
Ingredients:
• 1 cup black olives, pitted
• 2 tbsp capers
• 2 tbsp rosemary, chopped
• 1 garlic clove, smashed
• 2 anchovy fillets, chopped
• ½ tsp sugar
• ⅔ cup + 2 tbsp olive oil
• 1 lb linguine
• ½ cup grated Manchego cheese
• 1 tbsp chopped fresh chives
Directions:
1. Process the olives, capers, rosemary, garlic, anchovies, sugar, and ⅔ cup olive oil in your food processor until well incorporated but not smooth; set aside. Bring a large pot of salted water to a boil, add the linguine, and cook for 7-9 minutes until al dente. Drain the pasta in a bowl and add the remaining 2 tablespoons olive oil and Manchego cheese; toss to coat. Arrange pasta on a serving platter and top it with tapenade and chives. Serve and enjoy!
Nutrition:
• Info Per Serving: Calories: 375;Fat: 39g;Protein: 5g;Carbs: 23g.

Minestrone Chickpeas And Macaroni Casserole
Servings:5 | Cooking Time: 7 Hours 20 Minutes
Ingredients:
• 1 can chickpeas, drained and rinsed
• 1 can diced tomatoes, with the juice
• 1 can no-salt-added tomato paste
• 3 medium carrots, sliced
• 3 cloves garlic, minced
• 1 medium yellow onion, chopped
• 1 cup low-sodium vegetable soup
• ½ teaspoon dried rosemary
• 1 teaspoon dried oregano
• 2 teaspoons maple syrup
• ½ teaspoon sea salt
• ¼ teaspoon ground black pepper
• ½ pound fresh green beans, trimmed and cut into bite-size pieces
• 1 cup macaroni pasta
• 2 ounces Parmesan cheese, grated
Directions:
1. Except for the green beans, pasta, and Parmesan cheese, combine all the ingredients in the slow cooker and stir to mix well.
2. Put the slow cooker lid on and cook on low for 7 hours.
3. Fold in the pasta and green beans. Put the lid on and cook on high for 20 minutes or until the vegetable are soft and the pasta is al dente.
4. Pour them in a large serving bowl and spread with Parmesan cheese before serving.
Nutrition:
• Info Per Serving: Calories: 349;Fat: 6.7g;Protein: 16.5g;Carbs: 59.9g.

Spicy Bean Rolls
Servings:4 | Cooking Time:25 Minutes
Ingredients:
• 1 tbsp olive oil
• 1 red onion, chopped
• 2 garlic cloves, minced
• 1 green bell pepper, sliced
• 2 cups canned cannellini beans
• 1 red chili pepper, chopped
• 1 tbsp cilantro, chopped
• 1 tsp cumin, ground

- Salt and black pepper to taste
- 4 whole-wheat tortillas
- 1 cup mozzarella, shredded

Directions:
1. Warm the olive oil in a skillet over medium heat and sauté onion for 3 minutes. Stir in garlic, bell pepper, cannellini beans, red chili pepper, cilantro, cumin, salt, and pepper and cook for 15 minutes. Spoon bean mixture on each tortilla and top with cheese. Roll up and serve right away.

Nutrition:
- Info Per Serving: Calories: 680;Fat: 15g;Protein: 38g;Carbs: 75g.

Roasted Ratatouille Pasta

Servings:2 | Cooking Time: 30 Minutes

Ingredients:
- 1 small eggplant
- 1 small zucchini
- 1 portobello mushroom
- 1 Roma tomato, halved
- ½ medium sweet red pepper, seeded
- ½ teaspoon salt, plus additional for the pasta water
- 1 teaspoon Italian herb seasoning
- 1 tablespoon olive oil
- 2 cups farfalle pasta
- 2 tablespoons minced sun-dried tomatoes in olive oil with herbs
- 2 tablespoons prepared pesto

Directions:
1. Slice the ends off the eggplant and zucchini. Cut them lengthwise into ½-inch slices.
2. Place the eggplant, zucchini, mushroom, tomato, and red pepper in a large bowl and sprinkle with ½ teaspoon of salt. Using your hands, toss the vegetables well so that they're covered evenly with the salt. Let them rest for about 10 minutes.
3. While the vegetables are resting, preheat the oven to 400°F. Line a baking sheet with parchment paper.
4. When the oven is hot, drain off any liquid from the vegetables and pat them dry with a paper towel. Add the Italian herb seasoning and olive oil to the vegetables and toss well to coat both sides.
5. Lay the vegetables out in a single layer on the baking sheet. Roast them for 15 to 20 minutes, flipping them over after about 10 minutes or once they start to brown on the underside. When the vegetables are charred in spots, remove them from the oven.
6. While the vegetables are roasting, fill a large saucepan with water. Add salt and cook the pasta until al dente, about 8 to 10 minutes. Drain the pasta, reserving ½ cup of the pasta water.
7. When cool enough to handle, cut the vegetables into large chunks and add them to the hot pasta.
8. Stir in the sun-dried tomatoes and pesto and toss everything well. Serve immediately.

Nutrition:
- Info Per Serving: Calories: 613;Fat: 16.0g;Protein: 23.1g;Carbs: 108.5g.

Creamy Garlic Parmesan Chicken Pasta

Servings:4 | Cooking Time: 15 Minutes

Ingredients:
- 3 tablespoons extra-virgin olive oil
- 2 boneless, skinless chicken breasts, cut into thin strips
- 1 large onion, thinly sliced
- 3 tablespoons garlic, minced
- 1½ teaspoons salt
- 1 pound fettuccine pasta
- 1 cup heavy whipping cream
- ¾ cup freshly grated Parmesan cheese, divided
- ½ teaspoon freshly ground black pepper

Directions:

1. In a large skillet over medium heat, heat the olive oil. Add the chicken and cook for 3 minutes.
2. Add the onion, garlic and salt to the skillet. Cook for 7 minutes, stirring occasionally.
3. Meanwhile, bring a large pot of salted water to a boil and add the pasta, then cook for 7 minutes.
4. While the pasta is cooking, add the heavy cream, ½ cup of the Parmesan cheese and black pepper to the chicken. Simmer for 3 minutes.
5. Reserve ½ cup of the pasta water. Drain the pasta and add it to the chicken cream sauce.
6. Add the reserved pasta water to the pasta and toss together. Simmer for 2 minutes. Top with the remaining ¼ cup of the Parmesan cheese and serve warm.

Nutrition:
- Info Per Serving: Calories: 879;Fat: 42.0g;Protein: 35.0g;Carbs: 90.0g.

Pesto Fusilli With Broccoli

Servings:4 | Cooking Time:25 Minutes

Ingredients:
- ¼ cup olive oil
- 4 Roma tomatoes, diced
- 1 cup broccoli florets
- 1 lb fusilli
- 2 tsp tomato paste
- 2 garlic cloves, minced
- 1 tbsp chopped fresh oregano
- ½ tsp salt
- 1 cup vegetable broth
- 6 fresh basil leaves
- ¼ cup grated Parmesan cheese
- ¼ cup pine nuts

Directions:
1. Place the pasta in a pot with salted boiling water and cook for 8-10 minutes until al dente. Drain and set aside. In a pan over medium heat, sauté tomato paste, tomatoes, broth, oregano, garlic, and salt for 10 minutes.
2. In a food processor, place basil, broccoli, Parmesan, olive oil, and pine nuts; pulse until smooth. Pour into the tomato mixture. Stir in pasta, cook until heated through and the pasta is well coated. Serve.

Nutrition:
- Info Per Serving: Calories: 385;Fat: 22g;Protein: 12g;Carbs: 38g.

Lush Moroccan Chickpea, Vegetable, And Fruit Stew

Servings:6 | Cooking Time: 6 Hours 4 Minutes

Ingredients:
- 1 large bell pepper, any color, chopped
- 6 ounces green beans, trimmed and cut into bite-size pieces
- 3 cups canned chickpeas, rinsed and drained
- 1 can diced tomatoes, with the juice
- 1 large carrot, cut into ¼-inch rounds
- 2 large potatoes, peeled and cubed
- 1 large yellow onion, chopped
- 1 teaspoon grated fresh ginger
- 2 garlic cloves, minced
- 1¾ cups low-sodium vegetable soup
- 1 teaspoon ground cumin
- 1 tablespoon ground coriander
- ¼ teaspoon ground red pepper flakes
- Sea salt and ground black pepper, to taste
- 8 ounces fresh baby spinach
- ¼ cup diced dried figs

- ¼ cup diced dried apricots
- 1 cup plain Greek yogurt

Directions:
1. Place the bell peppers, green beans, chicken peas, tomatoes and juice, carrot, potatoes, onion, ginger, and garlic in the slow cooker.
2. Pour in the vegetable soup and sprinkle with cumin, coriander, red pepper flakes, salt, and ground black pepper. Stir to mix well.
3. Put the slow cooker lid on and cook on high for 6 hours or until the vegetables are soft. Stir periodically.
4. Open the lid and fold in the spinach, figs, apricots, and yogurt. Stir to mix well.
5. Cook for 4 minutes or until the spinach is wilted. Pour them in a large serving bowl. Allow to cool for at least 20 minutes, then serve warm.

Nutrition:
- Info Per Serving: Calories: 611;Fat: 9.0g;Protein: 30.7g;Carbs: 107.4g.

Quinoa & Watercress Salad With Nuts

Servings:4 | Cooking Time:5 Minutes

Ingredients:
- 2 boiled eggs, cut into wedges
- 2 cups watercress
- 2 cups cherry tomatoes, halved
- 1 cucumber, sliced
- 1 cup quinoa, cooked
- 1 cup almonds, chopped
- 2 tbsp olive oil
- 1 avocado, peeled and sliced
- 2 tbsp fresh cilantro, chopped
- Salt to taste
- 1 lemon, juiced

Directions:
1. Place watercress, cherry tomatoes, cucumber, quinoa, almonds, olive oil, cilantro, salt, and lemon juice in a bowl and toss to combine. Top with egg wedges and avocado slices and serve immediately.

Nutrition:
- Info Per Serving: Calories: 530;Fat: 35g;Protein: 20g;Carbs: 45g.

Mediterranean Brown Rice

Servings:4 | Cooking Time:20 Minutes

Ingredients:
- 1 lb asparagus, steamed and chopped
- 2 tbsp olive oil
- 3 tbsp balsamic vinegar
- 1 cup brown rice
- 2 tsp mustard
- Salt and black pepper to taste
- 5 oz baby spinach
- ½ cup parsley, chopped
- 1 tbsp tarragon, chopped

Directions:
1. Bring to a boil a pot of salted water over medium heat. Add in brown rice and cook for 7-9 minutes until al dente. Drain and place in a bowl. Add the asparagus to the same pot and blanch them for 4-5 minutes. Remove them to the rice bowl. Mix in spinach, olive oil, balsamic vinegar, mustard, salt, pepper, parsley, and tarragon. Serve.

Nutrition:
- Info Per Serving: Calories: 330;Fat: 12g;Protein: 11g;Carbs: 17g.

Hot Chickpea & Faro Stew

Servings:4 | Cooking Time:35 Minutes

Ingredients:
- 3 tbsp olive oil
- 1 cup faro
- Salt and black pepper to taste
- 1 eggplant, cubed
- 1 yellow onion, chopped
- 14 oz canned tomatoes, diced
- 14 oz canned chickpeas
- 3 garlic cloves, minced
- 2 tbsp harissa paste
- 2 tbsp cilantro, chopped

Directions:
1. Warm the olive oil in a skillet over medium heat and sauté eggplant, salt, and pepper for 10 minutes; reserve. In the same skillet, add and sauté onion for 3-4 minutes. Stir in garlic, salt, pepper, harissa paste, chickpeas, tomatoes, and faro, and 2 cups of water. Cook for 20 minutes. Stir in eggplant for 5 minutes. Garnish with cilantro and serve.

Nutrition:
- Info Per Serving: Calories: 680;Fat: 16g;Protein: 28g;Carbs: 88g.

Lentil And Vegetable Curry Stew

Servings:8 | Cooking Time: 4 Hours 7 Minutes

Ingredients:
- 1 tablespoon coconut oil
- 1 yellow onion, diced
- ¼ cup yellow Thai curry paste
- 2 cups unsweetened coconut milk
- 2 cups dry red lentils, rinsed well and drained
- 3 cups bite-sized cauliflower florets
- 2 golden potatoes, cut into chunks
- 2 carrots, peeled and diced
- 8 cups low-sodium vegetable soup, divided
- 1 bunch kale, stems removed and roughly chopped
- Sea salt, to taste
- ½ cup fresh cilantro, chopped
- Pinch crushed red pepper flakes

Directions:
1. Heat the coconut oil in a nonstick skillet over medium-high heat until melted.
2. Add the onion and sauté for 5 minutes or until translucent.
3. Pour in the curry paste and sauté for another 2 minutes, then fold in the coconut milk and stir to combine well. Bring to a simmer and turn off the heat.
4. Put the lentils, cauliflower, potatoes, and carrot in the slow cooker. Pour in 6 cups of vegetable soup and the curry mixture. Stir to combine well.
5. Cover and cook on high for 4 hours or until the lentils and vegetables are soft. Stir periodically.
6. During the last 30 minutes, fold the kale in the slow cooker and pour in the remaining vegetable soup. Sprinkle with salt.
7. Pour the stew in a large serving bowl and spread the cilantro and red pepper flakes on top before serving hot.

Nutrition:
- Info Per Serving: Calories: 530;Fat: 19.2g;Protein: 20.3g;Carbs: 75.2g.

Greek-Style Shrimp & Feta Macaroni

Servings:6 | Cooking Time:50 Minutes

Ingredients:
- 10 Kalamata olives
- 1 ½ lb elbow macaroni
- 2 red chili peppers, minced
- 1 garlic clove, minced
- 2 whole garlic cloves
- 2 tbsp fresh parsley, chopped
- 1 ¼ cups fresh basil, sliced
- ½ cup extra-virgin olive oil
- ½ tsp honey
- ½ lemon, juiced and zested
- ¼ cup butter
- 1 small red onion, chopped
- 1 lb button mushrooms, sliced
- 1 tsp sweet paprika
- 6 ripe plum tomatoes, puréed
- ¼ cup dry white wine
- 1 oz ouzo
- 1 cup heavy cream
- 1 cup feta cheese, crumbled
- 24 shrimp, peeled and deveined
- 1 cup feta cheese, cubed
- 1 tsp dried Greek oregano
- Salt and black pepper to taste

Directions:
1. Bring to a boil salted water in a pot over high heat. Add the macaroni and cook for 6-8 minutes until al dente. Drain. Set aside. Preheat your broiler. Place the chilies, whole garlic, parsley, ¼ cup of basil, ¼ cup of oil, honey, lemon juice, lemon zest, and salt in a food processor and blend until all the ingredients are well incorporated. Set aside.
2. Warm the remaining olive oil and butter in a large skillet over medium heat. Sauté the onion, minced garlic, mushrooms, and paprika for 5 minutes until tender. Pour in the tomatoes, wine, and ouzo and season with salt and pepper. Simmer for 6–7 minutes until most of the liquid evaporates, 5 minutes.
3. Stir in the heavy cream and crumbled feta cheese for 3 minutes until the sauce is thickened. Add in remaining basil and pasta and stir to combine. Pour the mixture into a baking dish and top with shrimp and cubed feta cheese. Broil 5 minutes or until the shrimp turn pink and cheese melts. Drizzle with reserved parsley-basil sauce and sprinkle with oregano. Let cool for 5 minutes. Serve topped with olives.

Nutrition:
- Info Per Serving: Calories: 1004;Fat: 47g;Protein: 47g;Carbs: 97g.

One-Bowl Microwave Lasagna

Servings:2 | Cooking Time:30 Minutes

Ingredients:
- ½ tbsp chopped basil
- ½ lb ground beef, crumbled
- 1 cup tomatoes, diced
- 1 ½ cups marinara sauce
- 1 ½ cups mozzarella, grated
- 1 ½ cups ricotta cheese
- 12 oven-ready lasagna noodles

Directions:
1. Microwave the crumbled beef in a microwave-safe bowl for 5 minutes. Stir and microwave for 4 more minutes until the beef is cooked through. Remove and mix the ground beef with tomatoes and marinara sauce. Stir in cheeses.
2. Place 4 lasagna noodles in a large bowl. Spread 1/3 of the meat mixture over the noodle layer. Repeat until you run out of ingredients. Cover the bowl with parchment paper. Microwave for about

8 minutes until cheeses are cooked. Let lasagna stand for 10 minutes. Top with basil. Serve.

Nutrition:
- Info Per Serving: Calories: 917;Fat: 34g;Protein: 85g;Carbs: 73g.

Paprika Spinach & Chickpea Bowl

Servings:4 | Cooking Time:20 Minutes

Ingredients:
- 2 tbsp olive oil
- 1 lb canned chickpeas
- 10 oz spinach
- 1 tsp coriander seeds
- 1 red onion, finely chopped
- 2 tomatoes, pureed
- 1 garlic clove, minced
- ½ tbsp rosemary
- ½ tsp smoked paprika
- Salt and white pepper to taste

Directions:
1. Heat the olive oil in a pot over medium heat. Add in the onion, garlic, coriander seeds, salt, and pepper and cook for 3 minutes until translucent. Stir in tomatoes, rosemary, paprika, salt, and white pepper. Bring to a boil, then lower the heat, and simmer for 10 minutes. Add in chickpeas and spinach and cook covered until the spinach wilts. Serve.

Nutrition:
- Info Per Serving: Calories: 512;Fat: 1.8g;Protein: 25g;Carbs: 76g.

Jalapeño Veggie Rice Stew

Servings:4 | Cooking Time:45 Minutes

Ingredients:
- 2 tbsp olive oil
- 1 cup rice
- 1 lb green beans, chopped
- 2 zucchinis, sliced
- 1 bell pepper, sliced
- 1 jalapeño pepper, chopped
- 1 carrot, chopped
- 2 spring onions, chopped
- 2 cloves garlic, minced
- 2 tomatoes, pureed
- 1 cup vegetable broth
- ½ tsp dried sage
- 1 tsp paprika
- Salt and black pepper to taste

Directions:
1. Cook the rice in a pot with 2 cups of water for about 20 minutes. Using a fork, fluff the rice and set aside. Heat the olive oil in a pot over medium heat. Add in the zucchinis, green beans, bell pepper, jalapeño pepper, carrot, spring onions, tomatoes, and garlic and stir-fry for 10 minutes or until the veggies are softened. Pour in vegetable broth, sage, paprika, salt, and black pepper. Cook covered for 7 minutes. Distribute the rice across bowls and top with the veggie mixture. Serve hot.

Nutrition:
- Info Per Serving: Calories: 153;Fat: 7.9g;Protein: 5.7g;Carbs: 19g.

Portuguese Thyme & Mushroom Millet

Servings:6 | Cooking Time:35 Minutes

Ingredients:
- 10 oz cremini mushrooms, chopped
- 3 tbsp olive oil
- 1 ½ cups millet
- Salt and black pepper to taste
- 1 shallot, minced
- ½ tsp dried thyme
- 3 tbsp dry sherry
- 3 tbsp parsley, minced
- 1 ½ tsp Port wine

Directions:
1. In a large pot, bring 4 quarts of water to a boil. Add millet and a pinch of salt, return to a boil and cook until tender, 15-20 minutes. Drain millet and cover to keep warm.
2. Warm 2 tablespoons of oil in a large skillet over medium heat. Add mushrooms, shallot, thyme, and salt and stir occasionally, until moisture has evaporated and vegetables start to brown, 10 minutes. Stir in wine, scraping off any browned bits from the bottom until the skillet is almost dry. Add the remaining oil and farro and keep stirring for 2 minutes. Stir in parsley and wine. Season with salt and pepper and serve.

Nutrition:
- Info Per Serving: Calories: 323;Fat: 18g;Protein: 10g;Carbs: 27g.

Easy Bulgur Tabbouleh

Servings:4 | Cooking Time:30 Minutes

Ingredients:
- 1 cucumber, peeled and chopped
- ¼ cup extra-virgin olive oil
- 8 cherry tomatoes, quartered
- 1 cup bulgur, rinsed
- 4 scallions, chopped
- ½ cup fresh parsley, chopped
- 1 lemon, juiced
- Salt and black pepper to taste

Directions:
1. Place the bulgur in a large pot with plenty of salted water, cover, and boil for 13-15 minutes. Drain and let it cool completely. Add scallions, tomatoes, cucumber, and parsley to the cooled bulgur and mix to combine. In another bowl, whisk the lemon juice, olive oil, salt, and pepper. Pour the dressing over the bulgur mixture and toss to combine. Serve.

Nutrition:
- Info Per Serving: Calories: 291;Fat: 13.7g;Protein: 7g;Carbs: 40g.

Slow Cooked Turkey And Brown Rice

Servings:6 | Cooking Time: 3 Hours 10 Minutes

Ingredients:
- 1 tablespoon extra-virgin olive oil
- 1½ pounds ground turkey
- 2 tablespoons chopped fresh sage, divided
- 2 tablespoons chopped fresh thyme, divided
- 1 teaspoon sea salt
- ½ teaspoon ground black pepper
- 2 cups brown rice
- 1 can stewed tomatoes, with the juice
- ¼ cup pitted and sliced Kalamata olives
- 3 medium zucchini, sliced thinly
- ¼ cup chopped fresh flat-leaf parsley
- 1 medium yellow onion, chopped
- 1 tablespoon plus 1 teaspoon balsamic vinegar
- 2 cups low-sodium chicken stock

- 2 garlic cloves, minced
- ½ cup grated Parmesan cheese, for serving

Directions:
1. Heat the olive oil in a nonstick skillet over medium-high heat until shimmering.
2. Add the ground turkey and sprinkle with 1 tablespoon of sage, 1 tablespoon of thyme, salt and ground black pepper.
3. Sauté for 10 minutes or until the ground turkey is lightly browned.
4. Pour them in the slow cooker, then pour in the remaining ingredients, except for the Parmesan. Stir to mix well.
5. Put the lid on and cook on high for 3 hours or until the rice and vegetables are tender.
6. Pour them in a large serving bowl, then spread with Parmesan cheese before serving.

Nutrition:
- Info Per Serving: Calories: 499;Fat: 16.4g;Protein: 32.4g;Carbs: 56.5g.

Rich Cauliflower Alfredo

Servings:4 | Cooking Time: 30 Minutes

Ingredients:
- Cauliflower Alfredo Sauce:
- 1 tablespoon avocado oil
- ½ yellow onion, diced
- 2 cups cauliflower florets
- 2 garlic cloves, minced
- 1½ teaspoons miso
- 1 teaspoon Dijon mustard
- Pinch of ground nutmeg
- ½ cup unsweetened almond milk
- 1½ tablespoons fresh lemon juice
- 2 tablespoons nutritional yeast
- Sea salt and ground black pepper, to taste
- Fettuccine:
- 1 tablespoon avocado oil
- ½ yellow onion, diced
- 1 cup broccoli florets
- 1 zucchini, halved lengthwise and cut into ¼-inch-thick half-moons
- Sea salt and ground black pepper, to taste
- ½ cup sun-dried tomatoes, drained if packed in oil
- 8 ounces cooked whole-wheat fettuccine
- ½ cup fresh basil, cut into ribbons

Directions:
1. Make the Sauce:
2. Heat the avocado oil in a nonstick skillet over medium-high heat until shimmering.
3. Add half of the onion to the skillet and sauté for 5 minutes or until translucent.
4. Add the cauliflower and garlic to the skillet. Reduce the heat to low and cook for 8 minutes or until the cauliflower is tender.
5. Pour them in a food processor, add the remaining ingredients for the sauce and pulse to combine well. Set aside.
6. Make the Fettuccine:
7. Heat the avocado oil in a nonstick skillet over medium-high heat.
8. Add the remaining half of onion and sauté for 5 minutes or until translucent.
9. Add the broccoli and zucchini. Sprinkle with salt and ground black pepper, then sauté for 5 minutes or until tender.
10. Add the sun-dried tomatoes, reserved sauce, and fettuccine. Sauté for 3 minutes or until well-coated and heated through.
11. Serve the fettuccine on a large plate and spread with basil before serving.

Nutrition:
- Info Per Serving: Calories: 288;Fat: 15.9g;Protein: 10.1g;Carbs: 32.5g.

Wild Rice With Cheese & Mushrooms

Servings:4 | Cooking Time:30 Minutes

Ingredients:
- 2 cups chicken stock
- 1 cup wild rice
- 1 onion, chopped
- ½ lb wild mushrooms, sliced
- 2 garlic cloves, minced
- 1 lemon, juiced and zested
- 1 tbsp chives, chopped
- ½ cup mozzarella, grated
- Salt and black pepper to taste

Directions:
1. Warm chicken stock in a pot over medium heat and add in wild rice, onion, mushrooms, garlic, lemon juice, lemon zest, salt, and pepper. Bring to a simmer and cook for 20 minutes. Transfer to a baking tray and top with mozzarella cheese. Place the tray under the broiler for 4 minutes until the cheese is melted. Sprinkle with chives and serve.

Nutrition:
- Info Per Serving: Calories: 230;Fat: 6g;Protein: 6g;Carbs: 13g.

Greek Chicken & Fusilli Bake

Servings:4 | Cooking Time:55 Minutes

Ingredients:
- 2 tbsp olive oil
- 1 cup Provolone cheese, grated
- 16 oz fusilli pasta
- 1 lb ground chicken
- 1 shallot, thinly sliced
- 2 bell peppers, chopped
- 2 tomatoes, pureed
- 1 bay leaf
- 1 tbsp tomato paste
- ½ cup Greek yogurt
- 1 tsp dried oregano, divided
- ½ tsp salt

Directions:
1. To a pot with salted boiling water, add the fusilli pasta and cook until al dente, 8-10 minutes. Reserve ½ cup of the cooking water and drain the pasta. Transfer to a bowl.
2. Preheat oven to 380° F. Warm the olive oil in a skillet over medium heat. Add in the chicken and brown for 3-4 minutes, stirring periodically. Add in shallot, bell peppers, oregano, and bay leaf and cook for 3-4 minutes. Remove the mixture to the pasta bowl and mix in the tomato puree and tomato paste. Sprinkle with the reserved cooking liquid and toss to coat. Transfer the pasta mixture to a baking dish. Spread the yogurt on top and sprinkle with the cheese. Cover with aluminum foil and bake for 20 minutes. Discard the foil and cook for another 5 minutes until the cheese is golden brown.

Nutrition:
- Info Per Serving: Calories: 772;Fat: 28g;Protein: 58g;Carbs: 71g.

Quick Pesto Pasta

Servings:4 | Cooking Time:20 Minutes

Ingredients:
- 1 lb linguine
- 2 tomatoes, chopped
- 10 oz basil pesto
- ½ cup pine nuts, toasted
- ½ cup Parmesan cheese, grated
- 1 lemon, zested

Directions:
1. Bring to a boil salted water in a pot over high heat. Add the linguine and cook according to package directions, 9-11 minutes. Drain and transfer to a serving bowl. Add the tomatoes, pesto, and lemon zest toss gently to coat the pasta. Sprinkle with Parmesan cheese and pine nuts and serve.

Nutrition:
- Info Per Serving: Calories: 617;Fat: 17g;Protein: 23g;Carbs: 94g.

Basic Brown Rice Pilaf With Capers

Servings:4 | Cooking Time:30 Minutes

Ingredients:
- 2 tbsp olive oil
- 1 cup brown rice
- 1 onion, chopped
- 1 celery stalk, chopped
- 2 garlic cloves, minced
- ½ cup capers, rinsed
- Salt and black pepper to taste
- 2 tbsp parsley, chopped

Directions:
1. Warm the olive oil in a skillet over medium heat. Sauté celery, garlic, and onion for 10 minutes. Stir in rice, capers, 2 cups of water, salt, and pepper and cook for 25 minutes. Serve topped with parsley.

Nutrition:
- Info Per Serving: Calories: 230;Fat: 8.9g;Protein: 7g;Carbs: 16g.

Carrot & Caper Chickpeas

Servings:4 | Cooking Time:35 Minutes

Ingredients:
- 3 tbsp olive oil
- 3 tbsp capers, drained
- 1 lemon, juiced and zested
- 1 red onion, chopped
- 14 oz canned chickpeas
- 4 carrots, peeled and cubed
- 1 tbsp parsley, chopped
- Salt and black pepper to taste

Directions:
1. Warm the olive oil in a skillet over medium heat and cook onion, lemon zest, lemon juice, and capers for 5 minutes. Stir in chickpeas, carrots, parsley, salt, and pepper and cook for another 20 minutes. Serve and enjoy!

Nutrition:
- Info Per Serving: Calories: 210;Fat: 5g;Protein: 4g;Carbs: 7g.

Leftover Pasta & Mushroom Frittata

Servings:4 | Cooking Time:25 Minutes

Ingredients:
- 2 tbsp olive oil
- 4 oz leftover spaghetti, cooked
- 8 large eggs, beaten
- ¼ cup heavy cream
- ½ tsp Italian seasoning
- ½ tsp garlic salt
- 1/8 tsp garlic pepper
- 1 cup chopped mushrooms
- 1 cup Pecorino cheese, grated

Directions:
1. Preheat your broiler. Warm the olive oil in a large skillet over medium heat. Add mushrooms and cook for 3–4 minutes, until almost tender. In a large bowl, beat the eggs with cream, Italian seasoning, garlic salt, and garlic pepper. Stir in the leftover spaghetti. Pour the egg mixture over the mushrooms and level with a spatula. Cook for 5–7 minutes until the eggs are almost set. Sprin-

kle with cheese and place under broiler for 3–5 minutes, until the cheese melts. Serve.

Nutrition:
• Info Per Serving: Calories: 400;Fat: 30g;Protein: 23g;Carbs: 11g.

Thyme Spinach & Cannellini Bean Stew

Servings:4 | Cooking Time:40 Minutes

Ingredients:
• 2 tbsp olive oil
• 1 onion, chopped
• 1 can diced tomatoes
• 2 cans cannellini beans
• 1 cup carrots, chopped
• 1 celery stalk, chopped
• 4 cups vegetable broth
• ½ tsp dried thyme
• 1 lb baby spinach
• Salt and black pepper to taste

Directions:
1. Warm the olive oil in a saucepan over medium heat. Sauté the onion, celery, and carrots for 5 minutes until tender. Add the tomatoes, beans, carrots, broth, thyme, pepper, and salt. Stir and cook for 20 minutes. Add the spinach and cook for 5 minutes until the spinach wilts. Serve warm.

Nutrition:
• Info Per Serving: Calories: 256;Fat: 12g;Protein: 15g;Carbs: 47g.

Triple-Green Pasta With Cheese

Servings:4 | Cooking Time: 14 To 16 Minutes

Ingredients:
• 8 ounces uncooked penne
• 1 tablespoon extra-virgin olive oil
• 2 garlic cloves, minced
• ¼ teaspoon crushed red pepper
• 2 cups chopped fresh flat-leaf parsley, including stems
• 5 cups loosely packed baby spinach
• ¼ teaspoon ground nutmeg
• ¼ teaspoon kosher salt
• ¼ teaspoon freshly ground black pepper
• ⅓ cup Castelvetrano olives, pitted and sliced
• ⅓ cup grated Parmesan cheese

Directions:
1. In a large stockpot of salted water, cook the pasta for about 8 to 10 minutes. Drain the pasta and reserve ¼ cup of the cooking liquid.
2. Meanwhile, heat the olive oil in a large skillet over medium heat. Add the garlic and red pepper and cook for 30 seconds, stirring constantly.
3. Add the parsley and cook for 1 minute, stirring constantly. Add the spinach, nutmeg, salt, and pepper, and cook for 3 minutes, stirring occasionally, or until the spinach is wilted.
4. Add the cooked pasta and the reserved ¼ cup cooking liquid to the skillet. Stir in the olives and cook for about 2 minutes, or until most of the pasta water has been absorbed.
5. Remove from the heat and stir in the cheese before serving.

Nutrition:
• Info Per Serving: Calories: 262;Fat: 4.0g;Protein: 15.0g;Carbs: 51.0g.

Simple Lentil Risotto

Servings:2 | Cooking Time: 20 Minutes

Ingredients:
• ½ tablespoon olive oil
• ½ medium onion, chopped
• ½ cup dry lentils, soaked overnight
• ½ celery stalk, chopped
• 1 sprig parsley, chopped
• ½ cup Arborio (short-grain Italian) rice
• 1 garlic clove, lightly mashed
• 2 cups vegetable stock

Directions:
1. Press the Sauté button to heat your Instant Pot.
2. Add the oil and onion to the Instant Pot and sauté for 5 minutes.
3. Add all the remaining ingredients to the Instant Pot.
4. Secure the lid. Select the Manual mode and set the cooking time for 15 minutes at High Pressure.
5. Once cooking is complete, do a natural pressure release for 20 minutes, then release any remaining pressure. Carefully open the lid.
6. Stir and serve hot.

Nutrition:
• Info Per Serving: Calories: 261;Fat: 3.6g;Protein: 10.6g;Carbs: 47.1g.

Sardine & Caper Tagliatelle

Servings:4 | Cooking Time:20 Minutes

Ingredients:
• 1 tbsp olive oil
• 8 oz tagliatelle
• ¼ cup chopped onion
• 2 garlic cloves, minced
• 1 tsp tomato paste
• 16 canned sardines in olive oil
• 1 tbsp capers
• ½ cup grated Parmesan cheese
• Salt and black pepper to taste
• 1 tbsp chopped parsley
• 1 tsp chopped oregano

Directions:
1. Boil water in a pot over medium heat and place in the pasta. Cook for 8-10 minutes for al dente. Drain and set aside; reserve ½ cup of the cooking liquid. Warm the olive oil in a pan over medium heat. Place in onion, garlic, and oregano and cook for 5 minutes until soft. Stir in salt, tomato paste, pepper, and ½ cup of reserved liquid for 1 minute. Mix in cooked pasta, capers, and sardines and toss to coat. Serve topped with Parmesan cheese and parsley.

Nutrition:
• Info Per Serving: Calories: 412;Fat: 13g;Protein: 23g;Carbs: 47g.

Pasta In Dilly Walnut Sauce

Servings:4 | Cooking Time:10 Minutes

Ingredients:
- 3 tbsp extra-virgin olive oil
- 8 oz whole-wheat pasta
- ¼ cup walnuts, chopped
- 3 garlic cloves, finely minced
- ½ cup fresh dill, chopped
- ¼ cup grated Parmesan cheese

Directions:
1. Cook the whole-wheat pasta according to pack instructions, drain and let it cool. Place the olive oil, dill, garlic, Parmesan cheese, and walnuts in a food processor and blend for 15 seconds or until paste forms. Pour over the cooled pasta and toss to combine. Serve immediately.

Nutrition:
- Info Per Serving: Calories: 559;Fat: 17g;Protein: 21g;Carbs: 91g.

Spicy Chicken Lentils

Servings:4 | Cooking Time:1 Hour 20 Minutes

Ingredients:
- 2 tbsp olive oil
- 1 lb chicken thighs, skinless, boneless, and cubed
- 1 tbsp coriander seeds
- 1 bay leaf
- 1 tbsp tomato paste
- 2 carrots, chopped
- 1 onion, chopped
- 2 garlic cloves, chopped
- ½ tsp red chili flakes
- ½ tsp paprika
- 4 cups chicken stock
- 1 cup brown lentils
- Salt and black pepper to taste

Directions:
1. Warm the olive oil in a pot over medium heat and cook chicken, onion, and garlic for 6-8 minutes. Stir in carrots, tomato paste, coriander seeds, bay leaf, red chili pepper, and paprika for 3 minutes. Pour in the chicken stock and bring to a boil. Simmer for 25 minutes. Add in lentils, season with salt and pepper and cook for another 15 minutes. Discard bay leaf and serve right away.

Nutrition:
- Info Per Serving: Calories: 320;Fat: 14g;Protein: 14g;Carbs: 18g.

Hot Collard Green Oats With Parmesan

Servings:4 | Cooking Time:15 Minutes

Ingredients:
- 2 tbsp olive oil
- 2 cups collard greens, torn
- ½ cup black olives, sliced
- 1 cup rolled oats
- 2 tomatoes, diced
- 2 spring onions, chopped
- 1 tsp garlic powder
- ½ tsp hot paprika
- A pinch of salt
- 2 tbsp fresh parsley, chopped
- 1 tbsp lemon juice
- ½ cup Parmesan cheese, grated

Directions:
1. Put 2 cups of water in a pot over medium heat. Bring to a boil, then lower the heat, and add the rolled oats. Cook for 4-5 minutes. Mix in tomatoes, spring onions, hot paprika, garlic powder, salt, collard greens, black olives, parsley, lemon juice, and olive oil.

Cook for another 5 minutes. Ladle into bowls and top with Parmesan cheese. Serve warm.

Nutrition:
- Info Per Serving: Calories: 192;Fat: 11g;Protein: 5g;Carbs: 19.8g.

Ricotta & Olive Rigatoni

Servings:4 | Cooking Time:25 Minutes

Ingredients:
- 2 tbsp extra-virgin olive oil
- 1 lb rigatoni
- ½ lb Ricotta cheese, crumbled
- 3/4 cup black olives, chopped
- 10 sun-dried tomatoes, sliced
- 1 tbsp dried oregano
- Black pepper to taste

Directions:
1. Bring to a boil salted water in a pot over high heat. Add the rigatoni and cook according to package directions; drain. Heat the olive oil in a large saucepan over medium heat. Add the rigatoni, ricotta, olives, and sun-dried tomatoes. Toss mixture to combine and cook 2–3 minutes or until cheese just starts to melt. Season with oregano and pepper.

Nutrition:
- Info Per Serving: Calories: 383;Fat: 28g;Protein: 15g;Carbs: 21g.

Carrot & Barley Risotto

Servings:6 | Cooking Time:1 Hour 20 Minutes

Ingredients:
- 2 tbsp olive oil
- 4 cups vegetable broth
- 4 cups water
- 1 onion, chopped fine
- 1 carrot, chopped
- 1 ½ cups pearl barley
- 1 cup dry white wine
- ¼ tsp dried oregano
- 2 oz Parmesan cheese, grated
- Salt and black pepper to taste

Directions:
1. Bring broth and water to a simmer in a saucepan. Reduce heat to low and cover to keep warm.
2. Heat 1 tbsp of oil in a pot over medium heat until sizzling. Stir-fry onion and carrot until softened, 6-7 minutes. Add barley and cook, stirring often, until lightly toasted and aromatic, 4 minutes. Add wine and cook, stirring frequently for 2 minutes. Stir in 3 cups of water and oregano, bring to a simmer, and cook, stirring occasionally until liquid is absorbed, 25 minutes. Stir in 2 cups of broth, bring to a simmer, and cook until the liquid is absorbed, 15 minutes.
3. Continue cooking, stirring often and adding warm broth as needed to prevent the pot bottom from becoming dry until barley is cooked through but still somewhat firm in the center, 15-20 minutes. Off heat, adjust consistency with the remaining warm broth as needed. Stir in Parmesan and the remaining oil and season with salt and pepper to taste. Serve.

Nutrition:
- Info Per Serving: Calories: 355;Fat: 21g;Protein: 16g;Carbs: 35g.

Green Bean & Pork Fettuccine

Servings:4 | Cooking Time:40 Minutes

Ingredients:
- 1 tbsp olive oil
- 16 oz fettuccine
- 4 pork loin, cut into strips
- Salt and black pepper to taste
- ½ cup green beans, chopped
- 1 lemon, zested and juiced
- ¼ cup chicken broth
- 1 cup crème fraiche
- 6 basil leaves, chopped
- 1 cup shaved Parmesan cheese

Directions:
1. In a pot of boiling water, cook the fettuccine pasta for 8-10 minutes until al dente. Drain and set aside.
2. Heat olive oil in a skillet, season the pork with salt, pepper, and cook for 10 minutes. Mix in green beans and cook for 5 minutes. Stir in lemon zest, lemon juice, and chicken broth. Cook for 5 more minutes or until the liquid reduces by a quarter. Add crème fraiche and mix well. Pour in pasta and basil and cook for 1 minute. Top with Parmesan cheese.

Nutrition:
- Info Per Serving: Calories: 586;Fat: 32g;Protein: 59g;Carbs: 9g.

Brown Rice Pilaf With Pistachios And Raisins

Servings:6 | Cooking Time: 15 Minutes

Ingredients:
- 1 tablespoon extra-virgin olive oil
- 1 cup chopped onion
- ½ cup shredded carrot
- ½ teaspoon ground cinnamon
- 1 teaspoon ground cumin
- 2 cups brown rice
- 1¾ cups pure orange juice
- ¼ cup water
- ½ cup shelled pistachios
- 1 cup golden raisins
- ½ cup chopped fresh chives

Directions:
1. Heat the olive oil in a saucepan over medium-high heat until shimmering.
2. Add the onion and sauté for 5 minutes or until translucent.
3. Add the carrots, cinnamon, and cumin, then sauté for 1 minutes or until aromatic.
4. Pour int the brown rice, orange juice, and water. Bring to a boil. Reduce the heat to medium-low and simmer for 7 minutes or until the liquid is almost absorbed.
5. Transfer the rice mixture in a large serving bowl, then spread with pistachios, raisins, and chives. Serve immediately.

Nutrition:
- Info Per Serving: Calories: 264;Fat: 7.1g;Protein: 5.2g;Carbs: 48.9g.

Bean And Veggie Pasta

Servings:2 | Cooking Time: 15 Minutes

Ingredients:
- 16 ounces small whole wheat pasta, such as penne, farfalle, or macaroni
- 5 cups water
- 1 can cannellini beans, drained and rinsed
- 1 can diced (with juice) or crushed tomatoes
- 1 yellow onion, chopped
- 1 red or yellow bell pepper, chopped
- 2 tablespoons tomato paste

- 1 tablespoon olive oil
- 3 garlic cloves, minced
- ¼ teaspoon crushed red pepper (optional)
- 1 bunch kale, stemmed and chopped
- 1 cup sliced basil
- ½ cup pitted Kalamata olives, chopped

Directions:
1. Add the pasta, water, beans, tomatoes (with juice if using diced), onion, bell pepper, tomato paste, oil, garlic, and crushed red pepper (if desired), to a large stockpot or deep skillet with a lid. Bring to a boil over high heat, stirring often.
2. Reduce the heat to medium-high, add the kale, and cook, continuing to stir often, until the pasta is al dente, about 10 minutes.
3. Remove from the heat and let sit for 5 minutes. Garnish with the basil and olives and serve.

Nutrition:
- Info Per Serving: Calories: 565;Fat: 17.7g;Protein: 18.0g;Carbs: 85.5g.

Florentine Bean & Vegetable Gratin

Servings:4 | Cooking Time:50 Minutes

Ingredients:
- ½ cup Parmigiano Reggiano cheese, grated
- 4 pancetta slices
- 2 tbsp olive oil
- 4 garlic cloves, minced
- 1 onion, chopped
- ½ fennel bulb, chopped
- 1 tbsp brown rice flour
- 2 cans white beans
- 1 can tomatoes, diced
- 1 medium zucchini, chopped
- 1 tsp porcini powder
- 1 tbsp fresh basil, chopped
- ½ tsp dried oregano
- 1 tsp red pepper flakes
- Salt to taste
- 2 tbsp butter, cubed

Directions:
1. Heat the olive in a skillet over medium heat. Fry the pancetta for 5 minutes until crispy. Drain on paper towels, chop, and reserve. Add garlic, onion, and fennel to the skillet and sauté for 5 minutes until softened. Stir in rice flour for 3 minutes.
2. Preheat oven to 350° F. Add the beans, tomatoes, and zucchini to a casserole dish and pour in the sautéed vegetable and chopped pancetta; mix well. Sprinkle with porcini powder, oregano, red pepper flakes, and salt. Top with Parmigiano Reggiano cheese and butter and bake for 25 minutes or until the cheese is lightly browned. Garnish with basil and serve.

Nutrition:
- Info Per Serving: Calories: 483;Fat: 28g;Protein: 19g;Carbs: 42g.

Minty Lamb Risotto

Servings:4 | Cooking Time:90 Minutes

Ingredients:
- 2 tbsp olive oil
- 2 garlic cloves, minced
- 1 onion, chopped
- 1 lb lamb, cubed
- Salt and black pepper to taste
- 2 cups vegetable stock
- 1 cup arborio rice
- 2 tbsp mint, chopped
- 1 cup Parmesan, grated

Directions:
1. Warm the olive oil in a skillet over medium heat and cook the

onion for 5 minutes. Put in lamb and cook for another 5 minutes. Stir in garlic, salt, pepper, and stock and bring to a simmer; cook for 1 hour. Stir in rice and cook for 18-20 minutes. Top with Parmesan cheese and mint and serve.

Nutrition:
- Info Per Serving: Calories: 310;Fat: 14g;Protein: 15g;Carbs: 17g.

Bulgur Pilaf With Kale And Tomatoes

Servings:2 | Cooking Time: 10 Minutes

Ingredients:
- 2 tablespoons olive oil
- 2 cloves garlic, minced
- 1 bunch kale, trimmed and cut into bite-sized pieces
- Juice of 1 lemon
- 2 cups cooked bulgur wheat
- 1 pint cherry tomatoes, halved
- Sea salt and freshly ground pepper, to taste

Directions:
1. Heat the olive oil in a large skillet over medium heat. Add the garlic and sauté for 1 minute.
2. Add the kale leaves and stir to coat. Cook for 5 minutes until leaves are cooked through and thoroughly wilted.
3. Add the lemon juice, bulgur and tomatoes. Season with sea salt and freshly ground pepper to taste, then serve.

Nutrition:
- Info Per Serving: Calories: 300;Fat: 14.0g;Protein: 6.2g;Carbs: 37.8g.

Creamy Shrimp With Tie Pasta

Servings:4 | Cooking Time:25 Minutes

Ingredients:
- 1 lb shrimp, peeled and deveined
- 1 tbsp olive oil
- 2 tbsp unsalted butter
- Salt and black pepper to taste
- 6 garlic cloves, minced
- ½ cup dry white wine
- 1 ½ cups heavy cream
- ½ cup grated Asiago cheese
- 2 tbsp chopped fresh parsley
- 16 oz bow tie pasta
- Salt to taste

Directions:
1. In a pot of boiling salted water, cook the tie pasta for 8-10 minutes until al dente. Drain and set aside.
2. Heat the olive oil in a large skillet, season the shrimp with salt and black pepper, and cook in the oil on both sides until pink and opaque, 2 minutes. Set aside. Melt the butter in the skillet and sauté the garlic until fragrant. Stir in the white wine and cook until reduced by half, scraping the bottom of the pan to deglaze. Reduce the heat to low and stir in the heavy cream. Allow simmering for 1 minute and stir in the Asiago cheese to melt. Return the shrimp to the sauce and sprinkle the parsley on top. Adjust the taste with salt and black pepper, if needed. Top the pasta with sauce and serve.

Nutrition:
- Info Per Serving: Calories: 493;Fat: 32g;Protein: 34g;Carbs: 16g.

Raspberry & Nut Quinoa

Servings:4 | Cooking Time:5 Minutes

Ingredients:
- 1 tbsp honey
- 2 cups almond milk
- 2 cups quinoa, cooked
- ½ tsp cinnamon powder
- 1 cup raspberries
- ¼ cup walnuts, chopped

Directions:
1. Combine quinoa, milk, cinnamon powder, honey, raspberries, and walnuts in a bowl. Serve in individual bowls.

Nutrition:
- Info Per Serving: Calories: 300;Fat: 15g;Protein: 5g;Carbs: 15g.

Spanakopita Macaroni With Cheese

Servings:3 | Cooking Time:15 Minutes

Ingredients:
- ½ lb leftover macaroni, cooked
- 4 tbsp butter
- 1 garlic clove, minced
- 1 lb spinach, torn
- 1 cup whole milk
- 1/3 cup feta cheese, crumbled
- ¼ tsp ground nutmeg
- 1 tsp dried Greek oregano
- 1 tsp lemon juice

Directions:
1. Melt the butter in a saucepan over medium heat. Stir in garlic and nutmeg for 1 minute. Slowly add the milk and spinach and cook for 3 minutes. Add the feta and oregano. Continue stirring with a whisk until the mixture thickens. Add the pasta and lemon juice and stir until everything is heated through. Serve immediately.

Nutrition:
- Info Per Serving: Calories: 499;Fat: 30g;Protein: 19g;Carbs: 42g.

Mediterranean-Style Beans And Greens

Servings:2 | Cooking Time: 15 Minutes

Ingredients:
- 1 can diced tomatoes with juice
- 1 can cannellini beans, drained and rinsed
- 2 tablespoons chopped green olives, plus 1 or 2 sliced for garnish
- ¼ cup vegetable broth, plus more as needed
- 1 teaspoon extra-virgin olive oil
- 2 cloves garlic, minced
- 4 cups arugula
- ¼ cup freshly squeezed lemon juice

Directions:
1. In a medium saucepan, bring the tomatoes, beans and chopped olives to a low boil, adding just enough broth to make the ingredients saucy (you may need more than ¼ cup if your canned tomatoes don't have a lot of juice). Reduce heat to low and simmer for about 5 minutes.
2. Meanwhile, in a large skillet, heat the olive oil over medium-high heat. When the oil is hot and starts to shimmer, add garlic and sauté just until it starts to turn slightly tan, about 30 seconds. Add the arugula and lemon juice, stirring to coat leaves with the olive oil and juice. Cover and reduce heat to low. Simmer for 3 to 5 minutes.
3. Serve beans over the greens and garnish with olive slices.

Nutrition:
- Info Per Serving: Calories: 262;Fat: 5.9g;Protein: 13.2g;Carbs: 40.4g.

Israeli Style Eggplant And Chickpea Salad

Servings:6 | Cooking Time: 20 Minutes

Ingredients:
- 2 tablespoons balsamic vinegar
- 2 tablespoons freshly squeezed lemon juice
- 1 teaspoon ground cumin
- ¼ teaspoon sea salt
- 2 tablespoons olive oil, divided
- 1 medium globe eggplant, stem removed, cut into flat cubes (about ½ inch thick)
- 1 can chickpeas, drained and rinsed
- ¼ cup chopped mint leaves
- 1 cup sliced sweet onion
- 1 garlic clove, finely minced
- 1 tablespoon sesame seeds, toasted

Directions:
1. Preheat the oven to 550ºF or the highest level of your oven or broiler. Grease a baking sheet with 1 tablespoon of olive oil.
2. Combine the balsamic vinegar, lemon juice, cumin, salt, and 1 tablespoon of olive oil in a small bowl. Stir to mix well.
3. Arrange the eggplant cubes on the baking sheet, then brush with 2 tablespoons of the balsamic vinegar mixture on both sides.
4. Broil in the preheated oven for 8 minutes or until lightly browned. Flip the cubes halfway through the cooking time.
5. Meanwhile, combine the chickpeas, mint, onion, garlic, and sesame seeds in a large serving bowl. Drizzle with remaining balsamic vinegar mixture. Stir to mix well.
6. Remove the eggplant from the oven. Allow to cool for 5 minutes, then slice them into ½-inch strips on a clean work surface.
7. Add the eggplant strips in the serving bowl, then toss to combine well before serving.

Nutrition:
- Info Per Serving: Calories: 125;Fat: 2.9g;Protein: 5.2g;Carbs: 20.9g.

Lentil And Mushroom Pasta

Servings:2 | Cooking Time: 50 Minutes

Ingredients:
- 2 tablespoons olive oil
- 1 large yellow onion, finely diced
- 2 portobello mushrooms, trimmed and chopped finely
- 2 tablespoons tomato paste
- 3 garlic cloves, chopped
- 1 teaspoon oregano
- 2½ cups water
- 1 cup brown lentils
- 1 can diced tomatoes with basil (with juice if diced)
- 1 tablespoon balsamic vinegar
- 8 ounces pasta of choice, cooked
- Salt and black pepper, to taste
- Chopped basil, for garnish

Directions:
1. Place a large stockpot over medium heat. Add the oil. Once the oil is hot, add the onion and mushrooms. Cover and cook until both are soft, about 5 minutes. Add the tomato paste, garlic, and oregano and cook 2 minutes, stirring constantly.
2. Stir in the water and lentils. Bring to a boil, then reduce the heat to medium-low and cook for 5 minutes, covered.
3. Add the tomatoes (and juice if using diced) and vinegar. Replace the lid, reduce the heat to low and cook until the lentils are tender, about 30 minutes.
4. Remove the sauce from the heat and season with salt and pepper to taste. Garnish with the basil and serve over the cooked pasta.

Nutrition:
- Info Per Serving: Calories: 463;Fat: 15.9g;Protein: 12.5g;Carbs: 70.8g.

Hot Zucchini Millet

Servings:4 | Cooking Time:30 Minutes

Ingredients:
- 3 tbsp olive oil
- 2 tomatoes, chopped
- 2 zucchinis, chopped
- 1 cup millet
- 2 spring onions, chopped
- ½ cup cilantro, chopped
- 1 tsp chili paste
- ½ cup lemon juice
- Salt and black pepper to taste

Directions:
1. Warm the olive oil in a skillet over medium heat and sauté millet for 1-2 minutes. Pour in 2 cups of water, salt, and pepper and bring to a simmer. Cook for 15 minutes. Mix in spring onions, tomatoes, zucchini, chili paste, and lemon juice. Serve topped with cilantro.

Nutrition:
- Info Per Serving: Calories: 230;Fat: 11g;Protein: 3g;Carbs: 15g.

Fava And Garbanzo Bean Ful

Servings:6 | Cooking Time: 10 Minutes

Ingredients:
- 1 can fava beans, rinsed and drained
- 1 can garbanzo beans, rinsed and drained
- 3 cups water
- ½ cup lemon juice
- 3 cloves garlic, peeled and minced
- 1 teaspoon salt
- 3 tablespoons extra-virgin olive oil

Directions:
1. In a pot over medium heat, cook the beans and water for 10 minutes.
2. Drain the beans and transfer to a bowl. Reserve 1 cup of the liquid from the cooked beans.
3. Add the reserved liquid, lemon juice, minced garlic and salt to the bowl with the beans. Mix to combine well. Using a potato masher, mash up about half the beans in the bowl.
4. Give the mixture one more stir to make sure the beans are evenly mixed.
5. Drizzle with the olive oil and serve.

Nutrition:
- Info Per Serving: Calories: 199;Fat: 9.0g;Protein: 10.0g;Carbs: 25.0g.

Kale & Feta Couscous

Servings:4 | Cooking Time:20 Minutes

Ingredients:
- 2 tbsp olive oil
- 1 cup couscous
- 1 cup kale, chopped
- 1 tbsp parsley, chopped
- 3 spring onions, chopped
- 1 cucumber, chopped
- 1 tsp allspice
- ½ lemon, juiced and zested
- 4 oz feta cheese, crumbled

Directions:
1. In a bowl, place couscous and cover with hot water. Let sit for 10 minutes and fluff. Warm the olive oil in a skillet over medium heat and sauté onions and allspice for 3 minutes. Stir in the remaining ingredients and cook for 5-6 minutes.

Nutrition:
- Info Per Serving: Calories: 210;Fat: 7g;Protein: 5g;Carbs: 16g.

Roasted Butternut Squash And Zucchini With Penne

Servings:6 | Cooking Time: 30 Minutes

Ingredients:
- 1 large zucchini, diced
- 1 large butternut squash, peeled and diced
- 1 large yellow onion, chopped
- 2 tablespoons extra-virgin olive oil
- 1 teaspoon paprika
- ½ teaspoon garlic powder
- ½ teaspoon sea salt
- ½ teaspoon freshly ground black pepper
- 1 pound whole-grain penne
- ½ cup dry white wine
- 2 tablespoons grated Parmesan cheese

Directions:
1. Preheat the oven to 400°F. Line a baking sheet with aluminum foil.
2. Combine the zucchini, butternut squash, and onion in a large bowl. Drizzle with olive oil and sprinkle with paprika, garlic powder, salt, and ground black pepper. Toss to coat well.
3. Spread the vegetables in the single layer on the baking sheet, then roast in the preheated oven for 25 minutes or until the vegetables are tender.
4. Meanwhile, bring a pot of water to a boil, then add the penne and cook for 14 minutes or until al dente. Drain the penne through a colander.
5. Transfer ½ cup of roasted vegetables in a food processor, then pour in the dry white wine. Pulse until smooth.
6. Pour the puréed vegetables in a nonstick skillet and cook with penne over medium-high heat for a few minutes to heat through.
7. Transfer the penne with the purée on a large serving plate, then spread the remaining roasted vegetables and Parmesan on top before serving.

Nutrition:
- Info Per Serving: Calories: 340;Fat: 6.2g;Protein: 8.0g;Carbs: 66.8g.

Vegetable Quinoa & Garbanzo Skillet

Servings:4 | Cooking Time:30 Minutes

Ingredients:
- 2 tbsp olive oil
- 1 shallot, chopped
- 2 garlic cloves, minced
- 1 tomato, chopped
- 1 cup quinoa
- 1 eggplant, cubed
- ¼ cup green olives, chopped
- ½ cup feta cheese, crumbled
- 1 cup canned garbanzo beans
- Salt and black pepper to taste

Directions:
1. Warm the olive oil in a skillet over medium heat and sauté garlic, shallot, tomato, and eggplant for 4-5 minutes until tender. Pour in quinoa and 2 cups of water. Season with salt and pepper and bring to a boil. Reduce the heat to low and cook for 15 minutes. Stir in olives, feta, and garbanzo beans.

Nutrition:
- Info Per Serving: Calories: 320;Fat: 12g;Protein: 12g;Carbs: 45g.

Spicy Farfalle With Zucchini & Tomatoes

Servings:6 | Cooking Time:30 Minutes

Ingredients:
- 2 lb zucchini, halved lengthwise cut into ½ inch
- 2 tbsp Pecorino-Romano cheese, grated
- 5 tbsp extra-virgin olive oil
- Salt and black pepper to taste
- 3 garlic cloves, minced
- ½ tsp red pepper flakes
- 1 lb farfalle
- 12 oz grape tomatoes, halved
- ½ cup fresh basil, chopped
- ¼ cup pine nuts, toasted
- 2 tbsp balsamic vinegar

Directions:
1. Sprinkle zucchini with 1 tablespoon salt and let drain in a colander for 30 minutes; pat dry. Heat 1 tbsp of oil in a large skillet. Add half of the zucchini and cook until golden brown and slightly charred, 5-7 minutes, reducing the heat if the skillet begins to scorch; transfer to plate. Repeat with 1 tbsp of oil and remaining zucchini; set aside. Heat 1 tbsp of oil in the same skillet and stir-fry garlic and pepper flakes for 30 seconds. Add in squash and stir-fry for 40 seconds.
2. Meanwhile, bring a large pot filled with water to a boil. Add pasta, a pinch of salt and cook until al dente. Reserve ½ cup of cooking liquid, drain pasta and return it to pot. Add the zucchini mixture, tomatoes, basil, pine nuts, vinegar, and remaining oil and toss to combine. Season to taste and adjust consistency with the reserved cooking liquid as needed. Serve with freshly grated Pecorino-Romano cheese.

Nutrition:
- Info Per Serving: Calories: 422;Fat: 13g;Protein: 14g;Carbs: 41g.

Mediterranean Lentils

Servings:2 | Cooking Time: 24 Minutes

Ingredients:
- 1 tablespoon olive oil
- 1 small sweet or yellow onion, diced
- 1 garlic clove, diced
- 1 teaspoon dried oregano
- ½ teaspoon ground cumin
- ½ teaspoon dried parsley
- ½ teaspoon salt, plus more as needed
- ¼ teaspoon freshly ground black pepper, plus more as needed
- 1 tomato, diced
- 1 cup brown or green lentils
- 2½ cups vegetable stock
- 1 bay leaf

Directions:
1. Set your Instant Pot to Sauté and heat the olive oil until it shimmers.
2. Add the onion and cook for 3 to 4 minutes until soft. Turn off the Instant Pot and add the garlic, oregano, cumin, parsley, salt, and pepper. Cook until fragrant, about 1 minute.
3. Stir in the tomato, lentils, stock, and bay leaf.
4. Lock the lid. Select the Manual mode and set the cooking time for 18 minutes at High Pressure.
5. When the timer beeps, perform a natural pressure release for 10 minutes, then release any remaining pressure. Carefully open the lid.
6. Remove and discard the bay leaf. Taste and season with more salt and pepper, as needed. If there's too much liquid remaining, select Sauté and cook until it evaporates.
7. Serve warm.

Nutrition:
- Info Per Serving: Calories: 426;Fat: 8.1g;Protein: 26.2g;Carbs: 63.8g.

Couscous With Carrots & Peas

Servings:6 | Cooking Time:33 Minutes

Ingredients:
- ¼ cup olive oil
- 1 ½ cups couscous
- 2 carrots, chopped
- 1 onion, finely chopped
- Salt and black pepper to taste
- 3 garlic cloves, minced
- 1 tsp ground coriander
- ¼ tsp ground anise seed
- 1 can chickpeas
- 1 ½ cups frozen peas
- ½ cup chopped fresh cilantro
- 1 lemon, cut into wedges

Directions:
1. Warm 2 tablespoons of oil in a skillet. Stir in couscous until the grains are just starting to brown, 3-5 minutes. Transfer to bowl and wipe the skillet clean. Heat the remaining oil in the skillet and stir-fry carrots, onion, and salt until softened, 5 minutes. Stir in garlic, coriander, and anise and cook until fragrant, 30 seconds. Stir in 2 cups of water and chickpeas and bring to a simmer. Stir in peas and couscous.
2. Cover, remove the skillet from the heat, and let sit until couscous is tender, 7 minutes. Add the cilantro and fluff gently with a fork to mix well. Season to taste and drizzle with extra olive oil. Serve with lemon wedges.

Nutrition:
- Info Per Serving: Calories: 402;Fat: 11g;Protein: 9g;Carbs: 42g.

Stewed Borlotti Beans

Servings:6 | Cooking Time:25 Minutes

Ingredients:
- 3 tbsp olive oil
- 1 onion, chopped
- 1 can tomato paste
- ¼ cup red wine vinegar
- 8 fresh sage leaves, chopped
- 2 garlic cloves, minced
- ½ cup water
- 2 cans borlotti beans

Directions:
1. Warm the olive oil in a saucepan over medium heat. Sauté the onion and garlic for 5 minutes, stirring frequently. Add the tomato paste, vinegar, and 1 cup of water, and mix well. Turn the heat to low. Drain and rinse one can of the beans in a colander and add to the saucepan. Pour the entire second can of beans (including the liquid) into the saucepan. Simmer for 10 minutes, stirring occasionally. Serve warm sprinkled with sage.

Nutrition:
- Info Per Serving: Calories: 434;Fat: 2g;Protein: 26g;Carbs: 80g.

Home-Style Beef Ragu Rigatoni

Servings:6 | Cooking Time:2 Hours

Ingredients:
- 1 tbsp olive oil
- 1 ½ lb bone-in short ribs
- Salt and black pepper to taste
- 1 onion, finely chopped
- 3 garlic cloves, minced
- 1 tsp fresh thyme, minced
- ½ tsp ground cinnamon
- A pinch of ground cloves
- ½ cup dry red wine
- 1 can tomatoes, diced
- 1 lb rigatoni

- 2 tbsp fresh parsley, minced
- 2 tbsp Pecorino cheese, grated

Directions:
1. Season the ribs with salt and pepper. Heat oil in a large skillet and brown the ribs on all sides, 7-10 minutes; transfer to a plate. Remove all but 1 tsp fat from skillet, add onion, and stir-fry over medium heat for 5 minutes. Stir in garlic, thyme, cinnamon, and cloves and cook until fragrant, 40 seconds. Pour in the wine, scraping off any browned bits, and simmer until almost evaporated, 2 minutes. Stir in tomatoes and their juice.
2. Nestle ribs into the sauce along with any accumulated juices and bring to a simmer. Lower the heat, cover and let simmer, turning the ribs from time to time until the meat is very tender and falling off bones, 2 hours. Transfer the ribs to cutting board, let cool slightly, then shred it using 2 forks; discard excess fat and bones.
3. Skim excess fat from the surface of the sauce with a spoon. Stir shredded meat and any accumulated juices into the sauce and bring to a simmer over medium heat. Season to taste. Meanwhile, bring a large pot filled with salted water to a boil and cook pasta until al dente. Reserve ½ cup of the cooking water, drain pasta and return it to pot. Add sauce and parsley and toss to combine. Season to taste and adjust consistency with reserved cooking water as needed. Serve with freshly grated Pecorino cheese.

Nutrition:
- Info Per Serving: Calories: 415;Fat: 11g;Protein: 12g;Carbs: 42g.

Asparagus & Goat Cheese Rice Salad

Servings:4 | Cooking Time:35 Minutes

Ingredients:
- 3 tbsp olive oil
- ½ cups brown rice
- Salt and black pepper to taste
- ½ lemon, zested and juiced
- 1 lb asparagus, chopped
- 1 shallot, minced
- 2 oz goat cheese, crumbled
- ¼ cup hazelnuts, toasted
- ¼ cup parsley, minced

Directions:
1. In a pot, bring 2 cups of water to a boil. Add rice, a pinch of salt, and cook until tender, 15-18 minutes, stirring occasionally. Drain the rice, spread onto a rimmed baking sheet, and drizzle with 1 tbsp of lemon juice. Let cool completely, 15 minutes.
2. Heat 1 tbsp of olive oil in a skillet over high heat. Add asparagus, salt, and pepper to taste and cook until asparagus is browned and crisp-tender, 4-5 minutes. Transfer to plate and let cool slightly. Whisk the remaining oil, lemon zest and juice, shallot in large a bowl. Add rice, asparagus, half of the goat cheese, half of the hazelnuts, and half of the parsley. Toss to combine and let sit for 10 minutes. Season with salt and pepper to taste. Sprinkle with the remaining goat cheese, hazelnuts, and parsley.

Nutrition:
- Info Per Serving: Calories: 185;Fat: 16g;Protein: 8g;Carbs: 24g.

Parmesan Zucchini Farfalle

Servings:4 | Cooking Time:42 Minutes

Ingredients:
- 3 tbsp olive oil
- 2 garlic cloves, minced
- 4 medium zucchini, diced
- Salt and black pepper to taste
- ½ cup milk
- ¼ tsp ground nutmeg
- 8 oz bow ties
- ½ cup Romano cheese, grated
- 1 tbsp lemon juice

Directions:
1. Heat the oil in a large skillet over medium heat. Stir-fry garlic for 1 minute. Add zucchini, pepper, and salt, stir and cook for 15 minutes, stirring once or twice. In a microwave-safe bowl, warm the milk in the microwave on high for 30 seconds. Stir the milk and nutmeg into the skillet and cook for another 5 minutes, stirring occasionally.
2. Meanwhile, in a large pot, cook the pasta according to the package directions. Drain the pasta in a colander, saving ¼ cup of the pasta liquid. Add the pasta and liquid to the skillet. Mix everything together and remove from the heat. Stir in the grated cheese and lemon juice and serve immediately.

Nutrition:
- Info Per Serving: Calories: 277;Fat: 8g;Protein: 8g;Carbs: 32g.

Curry Apple Couscous With Leeks And Pecans

Servings:4 | Cooking Time: 8 Minutes

Ingredients:
- 2 teaspoons extra-virgin olive oil
- 2 leeks, white parts only, sliced
- 1 apple, diced
- 2 cups cooked couscous
- 2 tablespoons curry powder
- ½ cup chopped pecans

Directions:
1. Heat the olive oil in a skillet over medium heat until shimmering.
2. Add the leeks and sauté for 5 minutes or until soft.
3. Add the diced apple and cook for 3 more minutes until tender.
4. Add the couscous and curry powder. Stir to combine.
5. Transfer them in a large serving bowl, then mix in the pecans and serve.

Nutrition:
- Info Per Serving: Calories: 254;Fat: 11.9g;Protein: 5.4g;Carbs: 34.3g.

Wild Rice, Celery, And Cauliflower Pilaf

Servings:4 | Cooking Time: 45 Minutes

Ingredients:
- 1 tablespoon olive oil, plus more for greasing the baking dish
- 1 cup wild rice
- 2 cups low-sodium chicken broth
- 1 sweet onion, chopped
- 2 stalks celery, chopped
- 1 teaspoon minced garlic
- 2 carrots, peeled, halved lengthwise, and sliced
- ½ cauliflower head, cut into small florets
- 1 teaspoon chopped fresh thyme
- Sea salt, to taste

Directions:
1. Preheat the oven to 350°F. Line a baking sheet with parchment paper and grease with olive oil.
2. Put the wild rice in a saucepan, then pour in the chicken broth. Bring to a boil. Reduce the heat to low and simmer for 30 minutes or until the rice is plump.
3. Meanwhile, heat the remaining olive oil in an oven-proof skillet over medium-high heat until shimmering.
4. Add the onion, celery, and garlic to the skillet and sauté for 3 minutes or until the onion is translucent.
5. Add the carrots and cauliflower to the skillet and sauté for 5 minutes. Turn off the heat and set aside.
6. Pour the cooked rice in the skillet with the vegetables. Sprinkle with thyme and salt.
7. Set the skillet in the preheated oven and bake for 15 minutes or until the vegetables are soft.
8. Serve immediately.

Nutrition:
- Info Per Serving: Calories: 214;Fat: 3.9g;Protein: 7.2g;Carbs: 37.9g.

Fish And Seafood Recipes

Fish And Seafood Recipes

Traditional Tuscan Scallops

Servings:4 | Cooking Time:25 Minutes

Ingredients:
- 2 tbsp olive oil
- 1 lb sea scallops, rinsed
- 4 cups Tuscan kale
- 1 orange, juiced
- Salt and black pepper to taste
- ¼ tsp red pepper flakes

Directions:
1. Sprinkle scallops with salt and pepper.
2. Warm olive oil in a skillet over medium heat and brown scallops for 6-8 minutes on all sides. Remove to a plate and keep warm, covering with foil. In the same skillet, add the kale, red pepper flakes, orange juice, salt, and pepper and cook until the kale wilts, about 4-5 minutes. Share the kale mixture into 4 plates and top with the scallops. Serve warm.

Nutrition:
- Info Per Serving: Calories: 214;Fat: 8g;Protein: 21g;Carbs: 15.2g.

Grilled Sardines With Herby Sauce

Servings:4 | Cooking Time:15 Min + Marinating Time

Ingredients:
- 12 sardines, gutted and cleaned
- 1 lemon, cut into wedges
- 2 garlic cloves, minced
- 2 tbsp capers, finely chopped
- 1 tbsp whole capers
- 1 shallot, diced
- 1 tsp anchovy paste
- 1 lemon, zested and juiced
- 2 tbsp olive oil
- 1 tbsp parsley, finely chopped
- 1 tbsp basil, finely chopped

Directions:
1. In a bowl, blend garlic, chopped capers, shallot, anchovy paste, lemon zest, and olive oil. Add the sardines and toss to coat; let them sit to marinate for about 30 minutes.
2. Preheat your grill to high. Place the sardines on the grill. Cook for 3-4 minutes per side until the skin is browned and beginning to blister. Pour the marinade in a saucepan over medium heat and add the whole capers, parsley, basil, and lemon juice. Cook for 2-3 minutes until thickens. Pour the sauce over grilled sardines. Serve with lemon wedges.

Nutrition:
- Info Per Serving: Calories: 395;Fat: 21g;Protein: 46g;Carbs: 2.1g.

Shrimp & Salmon In Tomato Sauce

Servings:4 | Cooking Time:30 Minutes

Ingredients:
- 1 lb shrimp, peeled and deveined
- 2 tbsp olive oil
- 1 lb salmon fillets
- Salt and black pepper to taste
- 1 cups tomatoes, chopped
- 1 onion, chopped
- 2 garlic cloves, minced
- ¼ tsp red pepper flakes
- 1 cup fish stock
- 1 tbsp cilantro, chopped

Directions:
1. Preheat the oven to 360°F. Line a baking sheet with parchment paper. Season the salmon with salt and pepper, drizzle with some olive oil, and arrange them on the sheet. Bake for 15 minutes. Remove to a serving plate.
2. Warm the remaining olive oil in a skillet over medium heat and sauté onion and garlic for 3 minutes until tender. Pour in tomatoes, fish stock, salt, pepper, and red pepper flakes and bring to a boil. Simmer for 10 minutes. Stir in shrimp and cook for another 8 minutes. Pour the sauce over the salmon and serve sprinkled with cilantro.

Nutrition:
- Info Per Serving: Calories: 240;Fat: 16g;Protein: 18g;Carbs: 22g.

Baked Fish With Pistachio Crust

Servings:4 | Cooking Time: 15 To 20 Minutes

Ingredients:
- ½ cup extra-virgin olive oil, divided
- 1 pound flaky white fish (such as cod, haddock, or halibut), skin removed
- ½ cup shelled finely chopped pistachios
- ½ cup ground flaxseed
- Zest and juice of 1 lemon, divided
- 1 teaspoon ground cumin
- 1 teaspoon ground allspice
- ½ teaspoon salt
- ¼ teaspoon freshly ground black pepper

Directions:
1. Preheat the oven to 400°F.
2. Line a baking sheet with parchment paper or aluminum foil and drizzle 2 tablespoons of olive oil over the sheet, spreading to evenly coat the bottom.
3. Cut the fish into 4 equal pieces and place on the prepared baking sheet.
4. In a small bowl, combine the pistachios, flaxseed, lemon zest, cumin, allspice, salt, and pepper. Drizzle in ¼ cup of olive oil and stir well.
5. Divide the nut mixture evenly on top of the fish pieces. Drizzle the lemon juice and remaining 2 tablespoons of olive oil over the fish and bake until cooked through, 15 to 20 minutes, depending on the thickness of the fish.
6. Cool for 5 minutes before serving.

Nutrition:
- Info Per Serving: Calories: 509;Fat: 41.0g;Protein: 26.0g;Carbs: 9.0g.

Baked Cod With Vegetables

Servings:2 | Cooking Time: 25 Minutes

Ingredients:
- 1 pound thick cod fillet, cut into 4 even portions
- ¼ teaspoon onion powder (optional)
- ¼ teaspoon paprika
- 3 tablespoons extra-virgin olive oil
- 4 medium scallions
- ½ cup fresh chopped basil, divided
- 3 tablespoons minced garlic (optional)
- 2 teaspoons salt
- 2 teaspoons freshly ground black pepper
- ¼ teaspoon dry marjoram (optional)
- 6 sun-dried tomato slices
- ½ cup dry white wine
- ½ cup crumbled feta cheese

- 1 can oil-packed artichoke hearts, drained
- 1 lemon, sliced
- 1 cup pitted kalamata olives
- 1 teaspoon capers (optional)
- 4 small red potatoes, quartered

Directions:
1. Preheat the oven to 375°F.
2. Season the fish with paprika and onion powder (if desired).
3. Heat an ovenproof skillet over medium heat and sear the top side of the cod for about 1 minute until golden. Set aside.
4. Heat the olive oil in the same skillet over medium heat. Add the scallions, ¼ cup of basil, garlic (if desired), salt, pepper, marjoram (if desired), tomato slices, and white wine and stir to combine. Bring to a boil and remove from heat.
5. Evenly spread the sauce on the bottom of skillet. Place the cod on top of the tomato basil sauce and scatter with feta cheese. Place the artichokes in the skillet and top with the lemon slices.
6. Scatter with the olives, capers (if desired), and the remaining ¼ cup of basil. Remove from the heat and transfer to the preheated oven. Bake for 15 to 20 minutes, or until it flakes easily with a fork.
7. Meanwhile, place the quartered potatoes on a baking sheet or wrapped in aluminum foil. Bake in the oven for 15 minutes until fork-tender.
8. Cool for 5 minutes before serving.

Nutrition:
- Info Per Serving: Calories: 1168;Fat: 60.0g;Protein: 63.8g;Carbs: 94.0g.

Lemon Trout With Roasted Beets

Servings:4 | Cooking Time:45 Minutes

Ingredients:
- 1 lb medium beets, peeled and sliced
- 3 tbsp olive oil
- 4 trout fillets, boneless
- Salt and black pepper to taste
- 1 tbsp rosemary, chopped
- 2 spring onions, chopped
- 2 tbsp lemon juice
- ½ cup vegetable stock

Directions:
1. Preheat oven to 390°F. Line a baking sheet with parchment paper. Arrange the beets on the sheet, season with salt and pepper, and drizzle with some olive oil. Roast for 20 minutes.
2. Warm the remaining oil in a skillet over medium heat. Cook trout fillets for 8 minutes on all sides; reserve. Add spring onions to the skillet and sauté for 2 minutes. Stir in lemon juice and stock and cook for 5-6 minutes until the sauce thickens. Remove the beets to a plate and top with trout fillets. Pour the sauce all over and sprinkle with rosemary.

Nutrition:
- Info Per Serving: Calories: 240;Fat: 6g;Protein: 18g;Carbs: 22g.

Avocado & Onion Tilapia

Servings:4 | Cooking Time:10 Minutes

Ingredients:
- 1 tbsp olive oil
- 1 tbsp orange juice
- ¼ tsp kosher salt
- ½ tsp ground coriander seeds
- 4 tilapia fillets, skin-on
- ¼ cup chopped red onions
- 1 avocado, skinned and sliced

Directions:
1. In a bowl, mix together the olive oil, orange juice, ground coriander seeds, and salt. Add the fish and turn to coat on all sides. Arrange the fillets on a greased microwave-safe dish. Top with

onion and cover the dish with plastic wrap, leaving a small part open at the edge to vent the steam. Microwave on high for about 3 minutes. The fish is done when it just begins to separate into chunks when pressed gently with a fork. Top the fillets with the avocado and serve.

Nutrition:
- Info Per Serving: Calories: 210;Fat: 11g;Protein: 25g;Carbs: 5g.

Marinara Mussels

Servings:4 | Cooking Time:25 Minutes

Ingredients:
- 2 lb mussels, cleaned and de-bearded
- 2 tbsp olive oil
- 2 leeks, chopped
- 1 red onion, chopped
- Salt and black pepper to taste
- 1 tbsp parsley, chopped
- 1 tbsp chives, chopped
- ½ cup tomato sauce

Directions:
1. Warm the olive oil in a skillet over medium heat and cook leeks and onion for 5 minutes. Stir in mussels, salt, pepper, parsley, chives, and tomato sauce and cook for 10 minutes. Discard any unopened mussels. Serve right away.

Nutrition:
- Info Per Serving: Calories: 250;Fat: 10g;Protein: 9g;Carbs: 16g.

Wine-Steamed Clams

Servings:4 | Cooking Time:30 Minutes

Ingredients:
- 4 lb clams, scrubbed and debearded
- 3 tbsp butter
- 3 garlic cloves, minced
- ¼ tsp red pepper flakes
- 1 cup dry white wine
- 3 sprigs fresh thyme
- 2 tbsp fresh dill, minced

Directions:
1. Melt the butter in a large saucepan over medium heat and cook garlic and pepper flakes, stirring constantly, until fragrant, about 30 seconds. Stir in wine and thyme sprigs, bring to a boil and cook until wine is slightly reduced, about 1 minute. Stir in clams. Cover the saucepan and simmer for 15-18 minutes. Remove, discard thyme sprigs and any clams that refuse to open. Sprinkle with dill and serve.

Nutrition:
- Info Per Serving: Calories: 326;Fat: 14g;Protein: 36g;Carbs: 12g.

Braised Branzino With Wine Sauce

Servings:2 | Cooking Time: 15 Minutes

Ingredients:
- Sauce:
- ¾ cup dry white wine
- 2 tablespoons white wine vinegar
- 2 tablespoons cornstarch
- 1 tablespoon honey
- Fish:
- 1 large branzino, butterflied and patted dry
- 2 tablespoons onion powder
- 2 tablespoons paprika
- ½ tablespoon salt
- 6 tablespoons extra-virgin olive oil, divided
- 4 garlic cloves, thinly sliced
- 4 scallions, both green and white parts, thinly sliced
- 1 large tomato, cut into ¼-inch cubes

- 4 kalamata olives, pitted and chopped

Directions:

1. Make the sauce: Mix together the white wine, vinegar, cornstarch, and honey in a bowl and keep stirring until the honey has dissolved. Set aside.
2. Make the fish: Place the fish on a clean work surface, skin-side down. Sprinkle the onion powder, paprika, and salt to season. Drizzle 2 tablespoons of olive oil all over the fish.
3. Heat 2 tablespoons of olive oil in a large skillet over high heat until it shimmers.
4. Add the fish, skin-side up, to the skillet and brown for about 2 minutes. Carefully flip the fish and cook for another 3 minutes. Remove from the heat to a plate and set aside.
5. Add the remaining 2 tablespoons olive oil to the skillet and swirl to coat. Stir in the garlic cloves, scallions, tomato, and kalamata olives and sauté for 5 minutes. Pour in the prepared sauce and stir to combine.
6. Return the fish (skin-side down) to the skillet, flipping to coat in the sauce. Reduce the heat to medium-low, and cook for an additional 5 minutes until cooked through.
7. Using a slotted spoon, transfer the fish to a plate and serve warm.

Nutrition:
- Info Per Serving: Calories: 1059;Fat: 71.9g;Protein: 46.2g;-Carbs: 55.8g.

Parsley Salmon Bake

Servings:4 | Cooking Time:20 Minutes

Ingredients:
- 2 tbsp olive oil
- 1 lb salmon fillets
- ¼ fresh parsley, chopped
- 1 garlic clove, minced
- ¼ tsp dried dill
- ¼ tsp chili powder
- ¼ tsp garlic powder
- 1 lemon, grated
- Salt and black pepper to taste

Directions:
1. Preheat oven to 350 °F. Sprinkle the salmon with dill, chili powder, garlic powder, salt, and pepper.
2. Warm olive oil in a pan over medium heat and sear salmon skin-side down for 5 minutes. Transfer to the oven and bake for another 4-5 minutes. Combine parsley, lemon zest, garlic, and salt in a bowl. Serve salmon topped with the mixture.

Nutrition:
- Info Per Serving: Calories: 212;Fat: 14g;Protein: 22g;Carbs: 0.5g.

Peppercorn-Seared Tuna Steaks

Servings:2 | Cooking Time: 10 Minutes

Ingredients:
- 2 ahi tuna steaks
- 1 teaspoon kosher salt
- ¼ teaspoon cayenne pepper
- 2 tablespoons olive oil
- 1 teaspoon whole peppercorns

Directions:
1. On a plate, Season the tuna steaks on both sides with salt and cayenne pepper.
2. In a skillet, heat the olive oil over medium-high heat until it shimmers.
3. Add the peppercorns and cook for about 5 minutes, or until they soften and pop.
4. Carefully put the tuna steaks in the skillet and sear for 1 to 2 minutes per side, depending on the thickness of the tuna steaks, or until the fish is cooked to the desired level of doneness.

5. Cool for 5 minutes before serving.

Nutrition:
- Info Per Serving: Calories: 260;Fat: 14.3g;Protein: 33.4g;Carbs: 0.2g.

Salmon In Thyme Tomato Sauce

Servings:4 | Cooking Time:25 Minutes

Ingredients:
- 2 tbsp olive oil
- 4 salmon fillets, boneless
- 1 tsp thyme, chopped
- Salt and black pepper to taste
- 1 lb cherry tomatoes, halved

Directions:
1. Warm the olive oil in a skillet over medium heat and sear salmon for 6 minutes, turning once; set aside. In the same skillet, stir in cherry tomatoes for 3-4 minutes and sprinkle with thyme, salt, and pepper. Pour the sauce over the salmon.

Nutrition:
- Info Per Serving: Calories: 300;Fat: 18g;Protein: 26g;Carbs: 27g.

Mackerel And Green Bean Salad

Servings:2 | Cooking Time: 10 Minutes

Ingredients:
- 2 cups green beans
- 1 tablespoon avocado oil
- 2 mackerel fillets
- 4 cups mixed salad greens
- 2 hard-boiled eggs, sliced
- 1 avocado, sliced
- 2 tablespoons lemon juice
- 2 tablespoons olive oil
- 1 teaspoon Dijon mustard
- Salt and black pepper, to taste

Directions:
1. Cook the green beans in a medium saucepan of boiling water for about 3 minutes until crisp-tender. Drain and set aside.
2. Melt the avocado oil in a pan over medium heat. Add the mackerel fillets and cook each side for 4 minutes.
3. Divide the greens between two salad bowls. Top with the mackerel, sliced egg, and avocado slices.
4. In another bowl, whisk together the lemon juice, olive oil, mustard, salt, and pepper, and drizzle over the salad. Add the cooked green beans and toss to combine, then serve.

Nutrition:
- Info Per Serving: Calories: 737;Fat: 57.3g;Protein: 34.2g;Carbs: 22.1g.

Tomato Seafood Soup

Servings:4 | Cooking Time:30 Minutes

Ingredients:
- ½ lb cod, skinless and cubed
- 2 tbsp olive oil
- ½ lb shrimp, deveined
- 1 yellow onion, chopped
- 1 carrot, finely chopped
- 1 celery stalk, finely chopped
- 1 small pepper, chopped
- 1 garlic clove, minced
- ½ cup tomatoes, crushed
- 4 cups fish stock
- ¼ tsp rosemary, dried
- Salt and black pepper to taste

Directions:
1. Warm the olive oil in a pot over medium heat. Cook onion,

garlic, carrot, celery, and pepper for 5 minutes until soft, stirring occasionally. Stir in the tomatoes, stock, cod, shrimp, rosemary, salt, and pepper and simmer for 15 minutes.

Nutrition:
- Info Per Serving: Calories: 200;Fat: 9g;Protein: 27g;Carbs: 5g.

Crispy Herb Crusted Halibut

Servings:4 | Cooking Time: 20 Minutes

Ingredients:
- 4 halibut fillets, patted dry
- Extra-virgin olive oil, for brushing
- ½ cup coarsely ground unsalted pistachios
- 1 tablespoon chopped fresh parsley
- 1 teaspoon chopped fresh basil
- 1 teaspoon chopped fresh thyme
- Pinch sea salt
- Pinch freshly ground black pepper

Directions:
1. Preheat the oven to 350°F. Line a baking sheet with parchment paper.
2. Place the fillets on the baking sheet and brush them generously with olive oil.
3. In a small bowl, stir together the pistachios, parsley, basil, thyme, salt, and pepper.
4. Spoon the nut mixture evenly on the fish, spreading it out so the tops of the fillets are covered.
5. Bake in the preheated oven until it flakes when pressed with a fork, about 20 minutes.
6. Serve immediately.

Nutrition:
- Info Per Serving: Calories: 262;Fat: 11.0g;Protein: 32.0g;Carbs: 4.0g.

Vegetable & Shrimp Roast

Servings:4 | Cooking Time:30 Minutes

Ingredients:
- 2 lb shrimp, peeled and deveined
- 4 tbsp olive oil
- 2 bell peppers, cut into chunks
- 2 fennel bulbs, cut into wedges
- 2 red onions, cut into wedges
- 4 garlic cloves, unpeeled
- 8 Kalamata olives, halved
- 1 tsp lemon zest, grated
- 2 tsp oregano, dried
- 2 tbsp parsley, chopped
- Salt and black pepper to taste

Directions:
1. Preheat the oven to 390 °F. Place bell peppers, garlic, fennel, red onions, and olives in a roasting tray. Add in the lemon zest, oregano, half of the olive oil, salt, and pepper and toss to coat; roast for 15 minutes. Coat the shrimp with the remaining olive oil and pour over the veggies; roast for another 7 minutes. Serve topped with parsley.

Nutrition:
- Info Per Serving: Calories: 350;Fat: 20g;Protein: 11g;Carbs: 35g.

Herby Cod Skewers

Servings:4 | Cooking Time:30 Minutes

Ingredients:
- 1 lb cod fillets, cut into chunks
- 2 sweet peppers, cut into chunks
- 2 tbsp olive oil
- 2 oranges, juiced
- 1 tbsp Dijon mustard
- 1 tsp dried dill
- 1 tsp dried parsley
- Salt and black pepper to taste

Directions:
1. Mix olive oil, orange juice, dill, parsley, mustard, salt, and pepper in a bowl. Stir in cod to coat. Allow sitting for 10 minutes. Heat the grill over medium heat. Thread the cod and peppers onto skewers. Grill for 7-8 minutes, turning regularly until the fish is cooked through.

Nutrition:
- Info Per Serving: Calories: 244;Fat: 8g;Protein: 27g;Carbs: 15.5g.

Bell Pepper & Scallop Skillet

Servings:4 | Cooking Time:25 Minutes

Ingredients:
- 3 tbsp olive oil
- 2 celery stalks, sliced
- 2 lb sea scallops, halved
- 3 garlic cloves, minced
- Juice of 1 lime
- 1 red bell pepper, chopped
- 1 tbsp capers, chopped
- 1 tbsp mayonnaise
- 1 tbsp rosemary, chopped
- 1 cup chicken stock

Directions:
1. Warm olive oil in a skillet over medium heat and cook celery and garlic for 2 minutes. Stir in bell pepper, lime juice, capers, rosemary, and stock and bring to a boil. Simmer for 8 minutes. Mix in scallops and mayonnaise and cook for 5 minutes.

Nutrition:
- Info Per Serving: Calories: 310;Fat: 16g;Protein: 9g;Carbs: 33g.

Simple Fried Cod Fillets

Servings:4 | Cooking Time: 10 Minutes

Ingredients:
- ½ cup all-purpose flour
- 1 teaspoon garlic powder
- 1 teaspoon salt
- 4 cod fillets
- 1 tablespoon extra-virgin olive oil

Directions:
1. Mix together the flour, garlic powder, and salt in a shallow dish.
2. Dredge each piece of fish in the seasoned flour until they are evenly coated.
3. Heat the olive oil in a medium skillet over medium-high heat.
4. Once hot, add the cod fillets and fry for 6 to 8 minutes, flipping the fish halfway through, or until the fish is opaque and flakes easily.
5. Remove from the heat and serve on plates.

Nutrition:
- Info Per Serving: Calories: 333;Fat: 18.8g;Protein: 21.2g;Carbs: 20.0g.

Pesto Shrimp Over Zoodles

Servings:4 | Cooking Time: 10 Minutes

Ingredients:
- 1 pound fresh shrimp, peeled and deveined
- Salt and freshly ground black pepper, to taste
- 2 tablespoons extra-virgin olive oil
- ½ small onion, slivered
- 8 ounces store-bought jarred pesto
- ¾ cup crumbled goat or feta cheese, plus additional for serving
- 2 large zucchini, spiralized, for serving

- ¼ cup chopped flat-leaf Italian parsley, for garnish

Directions:
1. In a bowl, season the shrimp with salt and pepper. Set aside.
2. In a large skillet, heat the olive oil over medium-high heat. Sauté the onion until just golden, 5 to 6 minutes.
3. Reduce the heat to low and add the pesto and cheese, whisking to combine and melt the cheese. Bring to a low simmer and add the shrimp. Reduce the heat back to low and cover. Cook until the shrimp is cooked through and pink, about 3 to 4 minutes.
4. Serve the shrimp warm over zoodles, garnishing with chopped parsley and additional crumbled cheese.

Nutrition:
- Info Per Serving: Calories: 491;Fat: 35.0g;Protein: 29.0g;Carbs: 15.0g.

Hazelnut Crusted Sea Bass

Servings:2 | Cooking Time: 15 Minutes

Ingredients:
- 2 tablespoons almond butter
- 2 sea bass fillets
- ⅓ cup roasted hazelnuts
- A pinch of cayenne pepper

Directions:
1. Preheat the oven to 425°F. Line a baking dish with waxed paper.
2. Brush the almond butter over the fillets.
3. Pulse the hazelnuts and cayenne in a food processor. Coat the sea bass with the hazelnut mixture, then transfer to the baking dish.
4. Bake in the preheated oven for about 15 minutes. Cool for 5 minutes before serving.

Nutrition:
- Info Per Serving: Calories: 468;Fat: 30.8g;Protein: 40.0g;Carbs: 8.8g.

Mom's Cod With Mozzarella & Tomatoes

Servings:4 | Cooking Time:35 Minutes

Ingredients:
- 2 tbsp olive oil
- 4 cod fillets, boneless
- Salt and black pepper to taste
- 12 cherry tomatoes, halved
- 1 red chili pepper, chopped
- 1 tbsp cilantro, chopped
- 2 tbsp balsamic vinegar
- 1 oz fresh mozzarella, torn

Directions:
1. Preheat the oven to 380 °F. Drizzle the cod fillets with some olive oil and season with salt and pepper. Place them on a roasting tray, top with mozzarella cheese, and bake for 15 minutes until golden and crispy. Warm the remaining oil in a skillet over medium heat and cook the cherry tomatoes for 5 minutes. Stir in red chili pepper, cilantro, and balsamic vinegar for 1-2 minutes. Serve the fish with sautéed veggies.

Nutrition:
- Info Per Serving: Calories: 270;Fat: 11g;Protein: 21g;Carbs: 25g.

Tarragon Haddock With Capers

Servings:4 | Cooking Time:25 Minutes

Ingredients:
- 2 tbsp olive oil
- 4 haddock fillets, boneless
- ¼ cup capers, drained
- 1 tbsp tarragon, chopped
- Salt and black pepper to taste
- 2 tbsp parsley, chopped
- 1 tbsp lemon juice

Directions:
1. Warm the olive oil in a skillet over medium heat and sear haddock for 6 minutes on both sides. Stir in capers, tarragon, salt, pepper, parsley, and lemon juice and cook for another 6-8 minutes. Serve right away.

Nutrition:
- Info Per Serving: Calories: 170;Fat: 10g;Protein: 18g;Carbs: 13g.

Lime-Orange Squid Meal

Servings:4 | Cooking Time:30 Minutes

Ingredients:
- 1 lb baby squid, cleaned, body and tentacles chopped
- 3 tbsp olive oil
- ½ cup green olives, chopped
- ½ tsp lime zest, grated
- 1 tbsp lime juice
- ½ tsp orange zest, grated
- 1 tsp red pepper flakes
- 1 tbsp parsley, chopped
- 4 garlic cloves, minced
- 1 shallot, chopped
- 1 cup vegetable stock
- 2 tbsp red wine vinegar
- Salt and black pepper to taste

Directions:
1. Warm the olive oil in a skillet over medium heat and stir in lime zest, lime juice, orange zest, red pepper flakes, garlic, shallot, olives, stock, vinegar, salt, and pepper. Bring to a boil and simmer for 10 minutes. Mix in squid and parsley and cook for another 10 minutes. Serve hot.

Nutrition:
- Info Per Serving: Calories: 310;Fat: 10g;Protein: 12g;Carbs: 23g.

Tuna And Zucchini Patties

Servings:4 | Cooking Time: 12 Minutes

Ingredients:
- 3 slices whole-wheat sandwich bread, toasted
- 2 cans tuna in olive oil, drained
- 1 cup shredded zucchini
- 1 large egg, lightly beaten
- ¼ cup diced red bell pepper
- 1 tablespoon dried oregano
- 1 teaspoon lemon zest
- ¼ teaspoon freshly ground black pepper
- ¼ teaspoon kosher or sea salt
- 1 tablespoon extra-virgin olive oil
- Salad greens or 4 whole-wheat rolls, for serving (optional)

Directions:
1. Crumble the toast into bread crumbs with your fingers (or use a knife to cut into ¼-inch cubes) until you have 1 cup of loosely packed crumbs. Pour the crumbs into a large bowl. Add the tuna, zucchini, beaten egg, bell pepper, oregano, lemon zest, black pepper, and salt. Mix well with a fork. With your hands, form the mixture into four (½-cup-size) patties. Place them on a plate, and

press each patty flat to about ¾-inch thick.
2. In a large skillet over medium-high heat, heat the oil until it's very hot, about 2 minutes.
3. Add the patties to the hot oil, then reduce the heat down to medium. Cook the patties for 5 minutes, flip with a spatula, and cook for an additional 5 minutes. Serve the patties on salad greens or whole-wheat rolls, if desired.
Nutrition:
• Info Per Serving: Calories: 757;Fat: 72.0g;Protein: 5.0g;Carbs: 26.0g.

Lemon-Parsley Swordfish
Servings:4 | Cooking Time: 17 To 20 Minutes
Ingredients:
• 1 cup fresh Italian parsley
• ¼ cup lemon juice
• ¼ cup extra-virgin olive oil
• ¼ cup fresh thyme
• 2 cloves garlic
• ½ teaspoon salt
• 4 swordfish steaks
• Olive oil spray
Directions:
1. Preheat the oven to 450°F. Grease a large baking dish generously with olive oil spray.
2. Place the parsley, lemon juice, olive oil, thyme, garlic, and salt in a food processor and pulse until smoothly blended.
3. Arrange the swordfish steaks in the greased baking dish and spoon the parsley mixture over the top.
4. Bake in the preheated oven for 17 to 20 minutes until flaky.
5. Divide the fish among four plates and serve hot.
Nutrition:
• Info Per Serving: Calories: 396;Fat: 21.7g;Protein: 44.2g;Carbs: 2.9g.

Saucy Cod With Calamari Rings
Servings:4 | Cooking Time:20 Minutes
Ingredients:
• 1 lb cod, skinless and cubed
• 2 tbsp olive oil
• 1 mango, peeled and cubed
• ½ lb calamari rings
• 1 tbsp garlic chili sauce
• ¼ cup lime juice
• ½ tsp smoked paprika
• ½ tsp cumin, ground
• 2 garlic cloves, minced
• Salt and black pepper to taste
Directions:
1. Warm the olive oil in a skillet over medium heat and cook chili sauce, lime juice, paprika, cumin, garlic, salt, pepper, and mango for 3 minutes. Stir in cod and calamari and cook for another 7 minutes. Serve warm.
Nutrition:
• Info Per Serving: Calories: 290;Fat: 13g;Protein: 16g;Carbs: 12g.

Oven-Baked Spanish Salmon
Servings:4 | Cooking Time:30 Minutes
Ingredients:
• 15 green pimiento-stuffed olives
• 2 small red onions, sliced
• 1 cup fennel bulbs shaved
• 1 cup cherry tomatoes
• Salt and black pepper to taste
• 1 tsp cumin seeds

• ½ tsp smoked paprika
• 4 salmon fillets
• ½ cup chicken broth
• 3 tbsp olive oil
• 2 cups cooked farro
Directions:
1. Preheat oven to 375 °F. In a bowl, combine the onions, fennel, tomatoes, and olives. Season with salt, pepper, cumin, and paprika and mix well. Spread out on a greased baking dish. Arrange the fish fillets over the vegetables, season with salt, and gently pour the broth over. Drizzle with olive oil and bake for 20 minutes. Serve over farro.
Nutrition:
• Info Per Serving: Calories: 475;Fat: 18g;Protein: 50g;Carbs: 26g.

Anchovy Spread With Avocado
Servings:2 | Cooking Time:5 Minutes
Ingredients:
• 1 avocado, peeled and pitted
• 1 tsp lemon juice
• ¼ celery stalk, chopped
• ¼ cup chopped shallots
• 2 anchovy fillets in olive oil
• Salt and black pepper to taste
Directions:
1. Combine lemon juice, avocado, celery, shallots, and anchovy fillets (with their olive oil) in a food processor. Blitz until smooth. Season with salt and black pepper. Serve.
Nutrition:
• Info Per Serving: Calories: 271;Fat: 20g;Protein: 15g;Carbs: 12g.

Mediterranean Braised Cod With Vegetables
Servings:2 | Cooking Time: 18 Minutes
Ingredients:
• 1 tablespoon olive oil
• ½ medium onion, minced
• 2 garlic cloves, minced
• 1 teaspoon oregano
• 1 can artichoke hearts in water, drained and halved
• 1 can diced tomatoes with basil
• ¼ cup pitted Greek olives, drained
• 10 ounces wild cod
• Salt and freshly ground black pepper, to taste
Directions:
1. In a skillet, heat the olive oil over medium-high heat.
2. Sauté the onion for about 5 minutes, stirring occasionally, or until tender.
3. Stir in the garlic and oregano and cook for 30 seconds more until fragrant.
4. Add the artichoke hearts, tomatoes, and olives and stir to combine. Top with the cod.
5. Cover and cook for 10 minutes, or until the fish flakes easily with a fork and juices run clean.
6. Sprinkle with the salt and pepper. Serve warm.
Nutrition:
• Info Per Serving: Calories: 332;Fat: 10.5g;Protein: 29.2g;Carbs: 30.7g.

Spiced Citrus Sole

Servings:4 | Cooking Time: 10 Minutes

Ingredients:
- 1 teaspoon garlic powder
- 1 teaspoon chili powder
- ½ teaspoon lemon zest
- ½ teaspoon lime zest
- ¼ teaspoon smoked paprika
- ¼ teaspoon freshly ground black pepper
- Pinch sea salt
- 4 sole fillets, patted dry
- 1 tablespoon extra-virgin olive oil
- 2 teaspoons freshly squeezed lime juice

Directions:
1. Preheat the oven to 450°F. Line a baking sheet with aluminum foil and set aside.
2. Mix together the garlic powder, chili powder, lemon zest, lime zest, paprika, pepper, and salt in a small bowl until well combined.
3. Arrange the sole fillets on the prepared baking sheet and rub the spice mixture all over the fillets until well coated. Drizzle the olive oil and lime juice over the fillets.
4. Bake in the preheated oven for about 8 minutes until flaky.
5. Remove from the heat to a plate and serve.

Nutrition:
- Info Per Serving: Calories: 183;Fat: 5.0g;Protein: 32.1g;Carbs: 0g.

Tuna Burgers

Servings:4 | Cooking Time:20 Minutes

Ingredients:
- 2 tbsp olive oil
- 2 cans tuna, flaked
- 4 hamburger buns
- 3 green onions, chopped
- ¼ cup breadcrumbs
- 1 egg, beaten
- 2 tbsp chopped fresh parsley
- 1 tbsp Italian seasoning
- 1 lemon, zested
- ½ cup mayonnaise
- 1 tbsp chopped fresh dill
- 1 tbsp green olives, chopped
- Sea salt to taste

Directions:
1. Combine tuna, breadcrumbs, green onions, eggs, Italian seasoning, parsley, and lemon zest in a bowl. Shape the mixture into 6 patties. Warm olive oil in a skillet over medium heat and brown patties for 8 minutes on both sides. Mix mayonnaise, green olives, dill, and salt in a bowl. Spoon the mixture on the buns and top with the patties.

Nutrition:
- Info Per Serving: Calories: 423;Fat: 24g;Protein: 16g;Carbs: 35g.

Hot Jumbo Shrimp

Servings:4 | Cooking Time:20 Minutes

Ingredients:
- 2 lb shell-on jumbo shrimp, deveined
- ¼ cup olive oil
- Salt and black pepper to taste
- 6 garlic cloves, minced
- 1 tsp anise seeds
- ½ tsp red pepper flakes
- 2 tbsp minced fresh cilantro
- 1 lemon, cut into wedges

Directions:
1. Combine the olive oil, garlic, anise seeds, pepper flakes, and black pepper in a large bowl. Add the shrimp and cilantro and toss well, making sure the oil mixture gets into the interior of the shrimp. Arrange shrimp in a single layer on a baking tray. Set under the preheated broiler for approximately 4 minutes. Flip shrimp and continue to broil until it is opaque and shells are beginning to brown, about 2 minutes, rotating sheet halfway through broiling. Serve with lemon wedges.

Nutrition:
- Info Per Serving: Calories: 218;Fat: 9g;Protein: 30.8g;Carbs: 2.3g.

Juicy Basil-Tomato Scallops

Servings:4 | Cooking Time:20 Minutes

Ingredients:
- 2 tbsp olive oil
- 1 tbsp basil, chopped
- 1 lb scallops, scrubbed
- 1 tbsp garlic, minced
- 1 onion, chopped
- 6 tomatoes, cubed
- 1 cup heavy cream
- 1 tbsp parsley, chopped

Directions:
1. Warm the olive oil in a skillet over medium heat and cook garlic and onion for 2 minutes. Stir in scallops, basil, tomatoes, heavy cream, and parsley and cook for an additional 7 minutes. Serve immediately.

Nutrition:
- Info Per Serving: Calories: 270;Fat: 12g;Protein: 11g;Carbs: 17g.

Prawns With Mushrooms

Servings:4 | Cooking Time:25 Minutes

Ingredients:
- 1 lb tiger prawns, peeled and deveined
- 3 tbsp olive oil
- 2 green onions, sliced
- ½ lb white mushrooms, sliced
- 2 tbsp balsamic vinegar
- 2 tsp garlic, minced

Directions:
1. Warm the olive oil in a skillet over medium heat and cook green onions and garlic for 2 minutes. Stir in mushrooms and balsamic vinegar and cook for an additional 6 minutes. Put in prawns and cook for 4 minutes. Serve right away.

Nutrition:
- Info Per Serving: Calories: 260;Fat: 9g;Protein: 19g;Carbs: 13g.

Baked Salmon With Tarragon Mustard Sauce

Servings:4 | Cooking Time: 12 Minutes

Ingredients:
- 1¼ pounds salmon fillet (skin on or removed), cut into 4 equal pieces
- ¼ cup Dijon mustard
- ¼ cup avocado oil mayonnaise
- Zest and juice of ½ lemon
- 2 tablespoons chopped fresh tarragon
- ½ teaspoon salt
- ¼ teaspoon freshly ground black pepper
- 4 tablespoons extra-virgin olive oil, for serving

Directions:
1. Preheat the oven to 425°F. Line a baking sheet with parchment

paper.

2. Arrange the salmon pieces on the prepared baking sheet, skin-side down.

3. Stir together the mustard, avocado oil mayonnaise, lemon zest and juice, tarragon, salt, and pepper in a small bowl. Spoon the mustard mixture over the salmon.

4. Bake for 10 to 12 minutes, or until the top is golden and salmon is opaque in the center.

5. Divide the salmon among four plates and drizzle each top with 1 tablespoon of olive oil before serving.

Nutrition:
• Info Per Serving: Calories: 386;Fat: 27.7g;Protein: 29.3g;Carbs: 3.8g.

Halibut Confit With Sautéed Leeks

Servings:4 | Cooking Time:45 Minutes

Ingredients:
• 1 tsp fresh lemon zest
• ¼ cup olive oil
• 4 skinless halibut fillets
• Salt and black pepper to taste
• 1 lb leeks, sliced
• 1 tsp Dijon mustard
• ¾ cup dry white wine
• 1 tbsp fresh cilantro, chopped
• 4 lemon wedges

Directions:
1. Warm the olive oil in a skillet over medium heat. Season the halibut with salt and pepper. Sear in the skillet for 6-7 minutes until cooked all the way through. Carefully transfer the halibut to a large plate. Add leeks, mustard, salt, and pepper to the skillet and sauté for 10-12 minutes, stirring frequently, until softened. Pour in the wine and lemon zest and bring to a simmer. Top with halibut. Reduce the heat to low, cover, and simmer for 6-10 minutes. Carefully transfer halibut to a serving platter, tent loosely with aluminum foil, and let rest while finishing leeks. Increase the heat and cook the leeks for 2-4 minutes until the sauce is slightly thickened. Adjust the seasoning with salt and pepper. Pour the leek mixture around the halibut, sprinkle with cilantro, and serve with lemon wedges.

Nutrition:
• Info Per Serving: Calories: 566;Fat: 19g;Protein: 78g;Carbs: 17g.

Dill Chutney Salmon

Servings:2 | Cooking Time: 3 Minutes

Ingredients:
• Chutney:
• ¼ cup fresh dill
• ¼ cup extra virgin olive oil
• Juice from ½ lemon
• Sea salt, to taste
• Fish:
• 2 cups water
• 2 salmon fillets
• Juice from ½ lemon
• ¼ teaspoon paprika
• Salt and freshly ground pepper to taste

Directions:
1. Pulse all the chutney ingredients in a food processor until creamy. Set aside.
2. Add the water and steamer basket to the Instant Pot. Place salmon fillets, skin-side down, on the steamer basket. Drizzle the lemon juice over salmon and sprinkle with the paprika.
3. Secure the lid. Select the Manual mode and set the cooking time for 3 minutes at High Pressure.
4. Once cooking is complete, do a quick pressure release. Care-

fully open the lid.

5. Season the fillets with pepper and salt to taste. Serve topped with the dill chutney.

Nutrition:
• Info Per Serving: Calories: 636;Fat: 41.1g;Protein: 65.3g;Carbs: 1.9g.

Baked Haddock With Rosemary Gremolata

Servings:6 | Cooking Time:35 Min + Marinating Time

Ingredients:
• 1 cup milk
• Salt and black pepper to taste
• 2 tbsp rosemary, chopped
• 1 garlic clove, minced
• 1 lemon, zested
• 1 ½ lb haddock fillets

Directions:
1. In a large bowl, coat the fish with milk, salt, pepper, and 1 tablespoon of rosemary. Refrigerate for 2 hours.
2. Preheat oven to 380ºF. Carefully remove the haddock from the marinade, drain thoroughly, and place in a greased baking dish. Cover and bake 15–20 minutes until the fish is flaky. Remove fish from the oven and let it rest 5 minutes. To make the gremolata, mix the remaining rosemary, lemon zest, and garlic. Sprinkle the fish with gremolata and serve.

Nutrition:
• Info Per Serving: Calories: 112;Fat: 2g;Protein: 20g;Carbs: 3g.

Dill Smoked Salmon & Eggplant Rolls

Servings:4 | Cooking Time:20 Minutes

Ingredients:
• 2 eggplants, lengthwise cut into thin slices
• 2 tbsp olive oil
• 1 cup ricotta cheese, soft
• 4 oz smoked salmon, chopped
• 2 tsp lemon zest, grated
• 1 small red onion, sliced
• Salt and pepper to the taste

Directions:
1. Mix salmon, cheese, lemon zest, onion, salt, and pepper in a bowl. Grease the eggplant with olive oil and grill them on a preheated grill pan for 3-4 minutes per side. Set aside to cool. Spread the cooled eggplant slices with the salmon mixture. Roll out and secure with toothpicks and serve.

Nutrition:
• Info Per Serving: Calories: 310;Fat: 25g;Protein: 12g;Carbs: 16g.

Garlic-Butter Parmesan Salmon And Asparagus

Servings:2 | Cooking Time: 15 Minutes

Ingredients:
• 2 salmon fillets, skin on and patted dry
• Pink Himalayan salt
• Freshly ground black pepper, to taste
• 1 pound fresh asparagus, ends snapped off
• 3 tablespoons almond butter
• 2 garlic cloves, minced
• ¼ cup grated Parmesan cheese

Directions:
1. Preheat the oven to 400ºF. Line a baking sheet with aluminum foil.
2. Season both sides of the salmon fillets with salt and pepper.
3. Put the salmon in the middle of the baking sheet and arrange the asparagus around the salmon.

4. Heat the almond butter in a small saucepan over medium heat.
5. Add the minced garlic and cook for about 3 minutes, or until the garlic just begins to brown.
6. Drizzle the garlic-butter sauce over the salmon and asparagus and scatter the Parmesan cheese on top.
7. Bake in the preheated oven for about 12 minutes, or until the salmon is cooked through and the asparagus is crisp-tender. You can switch the oven to broil at the end of cooking time for about 3 minutes to get a nice char on the asparagus.
8. Let cool for 5 minutes before serving.

Nutrition:
• Info Per Serving: Calories: 435;Fat: 26.1g;Protein: 42.3g;Carbs: 10.0g.

Leek & Olive Cod Casserole

Servings:4 | Cooking Time:30 Minutes

Ingredients:
• ½ cup olive oil
• 1 lb fresh cod fillets
• 1 cup black olives, chopped
• 4 leeks, trimmed and sliced
• 1 cup breadcrumbs
• ¾ cup chicken stock
• Salt and black pepper to taste

Directions:
1. Preheat oven to 350°F. Brush the cod with some olive oil, season with salt and pepper, and bake for 5-7 minutes. Let it cool, then cut it into 1-inch pieces.
2. Warm the remaining olive oil in a skillet over medium heat. Stir-fry the olives and leeks for 4 minutes until the leeks are tender. Add the breadcrumbs and chicken stock, stirring to mix. Fold in the pieces of cod. Pour the mixture into a greased baking dish and bake for 15 minutes or until cooked through.

Nutrition:
• Info Per Serving: Calories: 534;Fat: 33g;Protein: 24g;Carbs: 36g.

Crispy Fish Sticks

Servings:4 | Cooking Time:15 Minutes

Ingredients:
• 2 eggs, lightly beaten
• 1 tbsp milk
• 1 lb skinned tilapia fillet strips
• ½ cup yellow cornmeal
• ½ cup panko bread crumbs
• ¼ tsp smoked paprika
• 1 Spanish Padrón pepper, sliced
• Salt and black pepper to taste

Directions:
1. Put a large, rimmed baking sheet in your oven. Preheat the oven to 400 °F with the pan inside. In a large bowl, mix the eggs and milk. Add the fish strips to the egg mixture and stir gently to coat. Put the cornmeal, bread crumbs, smoked paprika, salt, and black pepper in a zip-top plastic bag. Transfer the fish to the bag, letting the excess egg wash drip off into the bowl before transferring. Seal the bag and shake gently to completely coat each fish stick.
2. Carefully remove the hot baking sheet with oven mitts from the oven and spray it with nonstick cooking spray. Remove the fish sticks from the bag and arrange them on the hot baking sheet. Top with Padrón pepper and bake for 6-8 minutes until gentle pressure with a fork causes the fish to flake.

Nutrition:
• Info Per Serving: Calories: 238;Fat: 3g;Protein: 22g;Carbs: 28g.

Lemon Cioppino

Servings:6 | Cooking Time:6 Minutes

Ingredients:
• 1 lb mussels, scrubbed, debearded
• 1 lb large shrimp, peeled and deveined
• 1 ½ lb haddock fillets, cut into chunks
• 3 tbsp olive oil
• 1 fennel bulb, thinly sliced
• 1 onion, chopped
• 3 large shallots, chopped
• Salt to taste
• 4 garlic cloves, minced
• ¼ tsp red pepper flakes
• ¼ cup tomato paste
• 1 can diced tomatoes
• 1 ½ cups dry white wine
• 5 cups vegetable stock
• 1 bay leaf
• 1 lb clams, scrubbed
• 2 tbsp basil, chopped

Directions:
1. Warm the olive oil in a large pot over medium heat. Sauté the fennel, onion, garlic, and shallots for 8-10 minutes until tender. Add the red pepper flakes and sauté for 2 minutes. Stir in the tomato paste, tomatoes with their juices, wine, stock, salt, and bay leaf. Cover and bring to a simmer. Lower the heat to low and simmer for 30 minutes until the flavors blend.
2. Pour in the clams and mussels and cook for about 5 minutes. Add the shrimp and fish. Simmer gently until the fish and shrimp are just cooked through, 5 minutes. Discard any clams and mussels that refuse to open and bay leaf. Top with basil.

Nutrition:
• Info Per Serving: Calories: 163;Fat: 4.1g;Protein: 22g;Carbs: 8.3g.

Better-For-You Cod & Potatoes

Servings:4 | Cooking Time:35 Minutes

Ingredients:
• 1 tbsp olive oil
• 2 cod fillets
• 1 tbsp basil, chopped
• Salt and black pepper to taste
• 2 potatoes, peeled and sliced
• 2 tsp turmeric powder
• 1 garlic clove, minced

Directions:
1. Preheat the oven to 360°F. Spread the potatoes on a greased baking dish and season with salt and pepper. Bake for 10 minutes. Arrange the cod fillets on top of the potatoes, sprinkle with salt and pepper, and drizzle with some olive oil. Bake for 10-12 more minutes until the fish flakes easily.
2. Warm the remaining olive oil in a skillet over medium heat and sauté garlic for 1 minute. Stir in basil, salt, pepper, turmeric powder, and 3-4 tbsp of water; cook for another 2-3 minutes. Pour the sauce over the cod fillets and serve warm.

Nutrition:
• Info Per Serving: Calories: 300;Fat: 15g;Protein: 33g;Carbs: 28g.

Easy Tomato Tuna Melts

Servings:2 | Cooking Time: 3 To 4 Minutes

Ingredients:
- 1 can chunk light tuna packed in water, drained
- 2 tablespoons plain Greek yogurt
- 2 tablespoons finely chopped celery
- 1 tablespoon finely chopped red onion
- 2 teaspoons freshly squeezed lemon juice
- Pinch cayenne pepper
- 1 large tomato, cut into ¾-inch-thick rounds
- ½ cup shredded Cheddar cheese

Directions:
1. Preheat the broiler to High.
2. Stir together the tuna, yogurt, celery, red onion, lemon juice, and cayenne pepper in a medium bowl.
3. Place the tomato rounds on a baking sheet. Top each with some tuna salad and Cheddar cheese.
4. Broil for 3 to 4 minutes until the cheese is melted and bubbly. Cool for 5 minutes before serving.

Nutrition:
- Info Per Serving: Calories: 244;Fat: 10.0g;Protein: 30.1g;Carbs: 6.9g.

Haddock With Cucumber Sauce

Servings:4 | Cooking Time: 10 Minutes

Ingredients:
- ¼ cup plain Greek yogurt
- ½ scallion, white and green parts, finely chopped
- ½ English cucumber, grated, liquid squeezed out
- 2 teaspoons chopped fresh mint
- 1 teaspoon honey
- Sea salt and freshly ground black pepper, to taste
- 4 haddock fillets, patted dry
- Nonstick cooking spray

Directions:
1. In a small bowl, stir together the yogurt, cucumber, scallion, mint, honey, and a pinch of salt. Set aside.
2. Season the fillets lightly with salt and pepper.
3. Place a large skillet over medium-high heat and spray lightly with cooking spray.
4. Cook the haddock, turning once, until it is just cooked through, about 5 minutes per side.
5. Remove the fish from the heat and transfer to plates.
6. Serve topped with the cucumber sauce.

Nutrition:
- Info Per Serving: Calories: 164;Fat: 2.0g;Protein: 27.0g;Carbs: 4.0g.

Slow Cooker Salmon In Foil

Servings:2 | Cooking Time: 2 Hours

Ingredients:
- 2 salmon fillets
- 1 tablespoon olive oil
- 2 cloves garlic, minced
- ½ tablespoon lime juice
- 1 teaspoon finely chopped fresh parsley
- ¼ teaspoon black pepper

Directions:
1. Spread a length of foil onto a work surface and place the salmon fillets in the middle.
2. Mix together the olive oil, garlic, lime juice, parsley, and black pepper in a small bowl. Brush the mixture over the fillets. Fold the foil over and crimp the sides to make a packet.
3. Place the packet into the slow cooker, cover, and cook on High for 2 hours, or until the fish flakes easily with a fork.
4. Serve hot.

Nutrition:
- Info Per Serving: Calories: 446;Fat: 20.7g;Protein: 65.4g;Carbs: 1.5g.

Shrimp & Gnocchi With Feta Cheese

Servings:4 | Cooking Time:30 Minutes

Ingredients:
- 1 lb shrimp, shells and tails removed
- 1 jar roasted red peppers, chopped
- 2 tbsp olive oil
- 1 cup chopped fresh tomato
- 2 garlic cloves, minced
- ½ tsp dried oregano
- Black pepper to taste
- ¼ tsp crushed red peppers
- 1 lb potato gnocchi
- ½ cup cubed feta cheese
- ⅓ cup fresh basil leaves, torn

Directions:
1. Preheat oven to 425 °F. In a baking dish, mix the tomatoes, olive oil, garlic, oregano, black pepper, and crushed red peppers. Roast in the oven for 10 minutes. Stir in the roasted peppers and shrimp. Roast for 10 minutes until the shrimp turn pink. Bring a saucepan of salted water to the boil and cook the gnocchi for 1-2 mins, until floating. Drain. Remove the dish from the oven. Mix in the cooked gnocchi, sprinkle with feta and basil and serve.

Nutrition:
- Info Per Serving: Calories: 146;Fat: 5g;Protein: 23g;Carbs: 1g.

Scallion Clams With Snow Peas

Servings:4 | Cooking Time:30 Minutes

Ingredients:
- 2 tbsp olive oil
- 1 tbsp basil, chopped
- 2 lb clams
- 1 onion, chopped
- 4 garlic cloves, minced
- Salt and black pepper to taste
- ½ cup vegetable stock
- 1 cup snow peas, sliced
- ½ tbsp balsamic vinegar
- 1 cup scallions, sliced

Directions:
1. Warm olive oil in a skillet over medium heat. Sauté onion and garlic for 2 to 3 minutes until tender and fragrant, stirring often. Add in the clams, salt, pepper, vegetable stock, snow peas, balsamic vinegar, and basil and bring to a boil. Lower the heat and simmer for 10 minutes. Remove from the heat. Discard any unopened clams. Scatter with scallions.

Nutrition:
- Info Per Serving: Calories: 310;Fat: 13g;Protein: 22g;Carbs: 27g.

Cioppino (Seafood Tomato Stew)

Servings:2 | Cooking Time: 20 Minutes

Ingredients:
- 2 tablespoons olive oil
- ½ small onion, diced
- ½ green pepper, diced
- 2 teaspoons dried basil
- 2 teaspoons dried oregano
- ½ cup dry white wine
- 1 can diced tomatoes with basil
- 1 can no-salt-added tomato sauce
- 1 can minced clams with their juice
- 8 ounces peeled, deveined raw shrimp

- 4 ounces any white fish (a thick piece works best)
- 3 tablespoons fresh parsley
- Salt and freshly ground black pepper, to taste

Directions:
1. In a Dutch oven, heat the olive oil over medium heat.
2. Sauté the onion and green pepper for 5 minutes, or until tender.
3. Stir in the basil, oregano, wine, diced tomatoes, and tomato sauce and bring to a boil.
4. Once boiling, reduce the heat to low and bring to a simmer for 5 minutes.
5. Add the clams, shrimp, and fish and cook for about 10 minutes, or until the shrimp are pink and cooked through.
6. Scatter with the parsley and add the salt and black pepper to taste.
7. Remove from the heat and serve warm.

Nutrition:
- Info Per Serving: Calories: 221;Fat: 7.7g;Protein: 23.1g;Carbs: 10.9g.

Mushroom & Shrimp Rice

Servings:4 | Cooking Time:40 Minutes

Ingredients:
- 2 tbsp olive oil
- 1 lb shrimp, peeled, deveined
- 1 cup white rice
- 4 garlic cloves, sliced
- ¼ tsp hot paprika
- 1 cup mushrooms, sliced
- ¼ cup green peas
- Juice of 1 lime
- Sea salt to taste
- ¼ cup chopped fresh chives

Directions:
1. Bring a pot of salted water to a boil. Cook the rice for 15-18 minutes, stirring occasionally. Drain and place in a bowl. Add in the green peas and mix to combine well. Taste and adjust the seasoning. Remove to a serving plate.
2. Heat the olive oil in a saucepan over medium heat and sauté garlic and hot paprika for 30-40 seconds until garlic is light golden brown. Remove the garlic with a slotted spoon. Add the mushrooms to the saucepan and sauté them for 5 minutes until tender. Put in the shrimp, lime juice, and salt and stir for 4 minutes. Turn the heat off. Add the chives and reserved garlic to the shrimp and pour over the rice. Serve and enjoy!

Nutrition:
- Info Per Serving: Calories: 342;Fat: 12g;Protein: 24g;Carbs: 33g.

One-Pot Shrimp With White Beans

Servings:4 | Cooking Time:23 Minutes

Ingredients:
- 1 lb large shrimp, peeled and deveined
- 3 tbsp olive oil
- Salt and black pepper to taste
- 1 red bell pepper, chopped
- 1 small red onion, chopped
- 2 garlic cloves, minced
- ¼ tsp red pepper flakes
- 2 cans cannellini beans
- 2 tbsp lemon zest

Directions:
1. Warm the olive oil in a skillet over medium heat. Add the shrimp and cook, without stirring, until spotty brown and edges turn pink, about 2 minutes. Remove the skillet from the heat, turn over the shrimp, and let sit until opaque throughout, about 30 seconds. Transfer shrimp to a bowl and cover with foil to keep warm.

2. Return the skillet to heat and reheat the olive oil. Sauté the bell pepper, garlic, and onion until softened, about 5 minutes. Stir in pepper flakes and salt for about 30 seconds. Pour in the beans and cook until heated through, 5 minutes. Add the shrimp with any accumulated juices back to the skillet cook for about 1 minute. Stir in lemon zest and serve.

Nutrition:
- Info Per Serving: Calories: 300;Fat: 18g;Protein: 25g;Carbs: 11g.

Shrimp And Pea Paella

Servings:2 | Cooking Time: 60 Minutes

Ingredients:
- 2 tablespoons olive oil
- 1 garlic clove, minced
- ½ large onion, minced
- 1 cup diced tomato
- ½ cup short-grain rice
- ½ teaspoon sweet paprika
- ½ cup dry white wine
- 1¼ cups low-sodium chicken stock
- 8 ounces large raw shrimp
- 1 cup frozen peas
- ¼ cup jarred roasted red peppers, cut into strips
- Salt, to taste

Directions:
1. Heat the olive oil in a large skillet over medium-high heat.
2. Add the garlic and onion and sauté for 3 minutes, or until the onion is softened.
3. Add the tomato, rice, and paprika and stir for 3 minutes to toast the rice.
4. Add the wine and chicken stock and stir to combine. Bring the mixture to a boil.
5. Cover and reduce the heat to medium-low, and simmer for 45 minutes, or until the rice is just about tender and most of the liquid has been absorbed.
6. Add the shrimp, peas, and roasted red peppers. Cover and cook for an additional 5 minutes. Season with salt to taste and serve.

Nutrition:
- Info Per Serving: Calories: 646;Fat: 27.1g;Protein: 42.0g;Carbs: 59.7g.

Roman-Style Cod

Servings:2 | Cooking Time:40 Minutes

Ingredients:
- 2 cod fillets, cut in 4 portions
- ¼ tsp paprika
- ¼ tsp onion powder
- 3 tbsp olive oil
- 4 medium scallions
- 2 tbsp fresh chopped basil
- 3 tbsp minced garlic
- Salt and black pepper to taste
- ¼ tsp dry marjoram
- 6 sun-dried tomato slices
- ½ cup dry white wine
- ½ cup ricotta cheese, crumbled
- 1 can artichoke hearts
- 1 lemon, sliced
- 1 cup pitted black olives
- 1 tsp capers

Directions:
1. Preheat oven to 375 °F. Warm the olive oil in a skillet over medium heat. Sprinkle the cod with paprika and onion powder. Sear it for about 1 minute per side or until golden; reserve. Add the scallions, basil, garlic, salt, pepper, marjoram, tomatoes, and wine to the same skillet. Bring to a boil. Remove the skillet from the

heat. Arrange the fish on top of the sauce and sprinkle with ricotta cheese.

2. Place the artichokes in the pan and top with lemon slices. Sprinkle with black olives and capers. Place the skillet in the oven. Bake for 15-20 minutes until it flakes easily with a fork.

Nutrition:
- Info Per Serving: Calories: 1172;Fat: 59g;Protein: 64g;Carbs: 94g.

Veggie & Clam Stew With Chickpeas

Servings:4 | Cooking Time:40 Minutes

Ingredients:
- 2 tbsp olive oil
- 1 yellow onion, chopped
- 1 fennel bulb, chopped
- 1 carrot, chopped
- 1 red bell pepper, chopped
- 2 garlic cloves, minced
- 3 tbsp tomato paste
- 16 oz canned chickpeas, drained
- 1 tsp dried thyme
- ¼ tsp smoked paprika
- Salt and black pepper to taste
- 1 lb clams, scrubbed

Directions:
1. Warm olive oil in a pot over medium heat and sauté fennel, onion, bell pepper, and carrot for 5 minutes until they're tender. Stir in garlic and tomato paste and cook for another minute. Mix in the chickpeas, thyme, paprika, salt, pepper, and 2 cups of water and bring to a boil; cook for 20 minutes.
2. Rinse the clams under cold, running water. Discard any clams that remain open when tapped with your fingers. Put the unopened clams into the pot and cook everything for 4-5 minutes until the shells have opened. When finished, discard any clams that haven't opened fully during the cooking process. Adjust the seasoning with salt and pepper. Serve.

Nutrition:
- Info Per Serving: Calories: 460;Fat: 13g;Protein: 35g;Carbs: 48g.

Creamy Halibut & Potato Soup

Servings:4 | Cooking Time:25 Minutes

Ingredients:
- 3 gold potatoes, peeled and cubed
- 4 oz halibut fillets, boneless and cubed
- 2 tbsp olive oil
- 2 carrots, chopped
- 1 red onion, chopped
- Salt and white pepper to taste
- 4 cups fish stock
- ½ cup heavy cream
- 1 tbsp dill, chopped

Directions:
1. Warm the olive oil in a skillet over medium heat and cook the onion for 3 minutes. Put in potatoes, salt, pepper, carrots, and stock and bring to a boil. Cook for an additional 5-6 minutes. Stir in halibut, cream, and dill and simmer for another 5 minutes. Serve right away.

Nutrition:
- Info Per Serving: Calories: 215;Fat: 17g;Protein: 12g;Carbs: 7g.

Chili Flounder Parcels

Servings:4 | Cooking Time:20 Minutes

Ingredients:
- 2 tbsp olive oil
- 4 flounder fillets
- ¼ tsp red pepper flakes
- 4 fresh rosemary sprigs
- 2 garlic cloves, thinly sliced
- 1 cup cherry tomatoes, halved
- ½ chopped onion
- 2 tbsp capers
- 8 black olives, sliced
- 2 tbsp dry white wine
- Salt and black pepper to taste

Directions:
1. Preheat oven to 420°F. Drizzle the flounder with olive oil and season with salt, pepper, and red pepper flakes. Divide fillets between 4 pieces of aluminium foil. Top each one with garlic, cherry tomatoes, capers, onion, and olives. Fold the edges to form packets with opened tops. Add in a rosemary sprig in each one and drizzle with the white wine. Seal the packets and arrange them on a baking sheet. Bake for 10 minutes or until the fish is cooked. Serve warm.

Nutrition:
- Info Per Serving: Calories: 242;Fat: 10g;Protein: 31.5g;Carbs: 4g.

Parsley Littleneck Clams In Sherry Sauce

Servings:4 | Cooking Time:20 Minutes

Ingredients:
- 2 tbsp olive oil
- 1 cup dry sherry
- 3 shallots, minced
- 4 garlic cloves, minced
- 4 lb littleneck clams, scrubbed
- 2 tbsp minced fresh parsley
- ½ tsp cayenne pepper
- 1 Lemon, cut into wedges

Directions:
1. Bring the sherry wine, shallots, and garlic to a simmer in a large saucepan and cook for 3 minutes. Add clams, cover, and cook, stirring twice, until clams open, about 7 minutes. With a slotted spoon, transfer clams to a serving bowl, discarding any that refuse to open. Stir in olive oil, parsley, and cayenne pepper. Pour sauce over clams and serve with lemon wedges.

Nutrition:
- Info Per Serving: Calories: 333;Fat: 9g;Protein: 44.9g;Carbs: 14g.

Roasted Cod With Cabbage

Servings:4 | Cooking Time:30 Minutes

Ingredients:
- 2 tbsp olive oil
- 1 head white cabbage, shredded
- 1 tsp garlic powder
- 1 tsp smoked paprika
- 4 cod fillets, boneless
- ½ cup tomato sauce
- 1 tsp Italian seasoning
- 1 tbsp chives, chopped

Directions:
1. Preheat the oven to 390°F. Mix cabbage, garlic powder, paprika, olive oil, tomato sauce, Italian seasoning, and chives in a roasting pan. Top with cod fillets and bake covered with foil for 20 minutes. Serve immediately.

Nutrition:
- Info Per Serving: Calories: 200;Fat: 14g;Protein: 18g;Carbs: 24g.

Lemon Grilled Shrimp

Servings:4 | Cooking Time: 4 To 6 Minutes

Ingredients:
- 2 tablespoons garlic, minced
- 3 tablespoons fresh Italian parsley, finely chopped
- ¼ cup extra-virgin olive oil
- ½ cup lemon juice
- 1 teaspoon salt
- 2 pounds jumbo shrimp, peeled and deveined
- Special Equipment:
- 4 skewers, soaked in water for at least 30 minutes

Directions:
1. Whisk together the garlic, parsley, olive oil, lemon juice, and salt in a large bowl.
2. Add the shrimp to the bowl and toss well, making sure the shrimp are coated in the marinade. Set aside to sit for 15 minutes.
3. When ready, skewer the shrimps by piercing through the center. You can place about 5 to 6 shrimps on each skewer.
4. Preheat the grill to high heat.
5. Grill the shrimp for 4 to 6 minutes, flipping the shrimp halfway through, or until the shrimp are pink on the outside and opaque in the center.
6. Serve hot.

Nutrition:
- Info Per Serving: Calories: 401;Fat: 17.8g;Protein: 56.9g;Carbs: 3.9g.

Parchment Orange & Dill Salmon

Servings:4 | Cooking Time:25 Minutes

Ingredients:
- 2 tbsp butter, melted
- 4 salmon fillets
- Salt and black pepper to taste
- 1 orange, juiced and zested
- 4 tbsp fresh dill, chopped

Directions:
1. Preheat oven to 375 °F. Coat the salmon fillets on both sides with butter. Season with salt and pepper and divide them between 4 pieces of parchment paper. Drizzle the orange juice over each piece of fish and top with orange zest and dill. Wrap the paper around the fish to make packets. Place on a baking sheet and bake for 15-20 minutes until the cod is cooked through. Serve and enjoy!

Nutrition:
- Info Per Serving: Calories: 481;Fat: 21g;Protein: 65g;Carbs: 4.2g.

Spiced Flounder With Pasta Salad

Servings:4 | Cooking Time:25 Minutes

Ingredients:
- 2 tbsp olive oil
- 4 flounder fillets, boneless
- 1 tsp rosemary, dried
- 2 tsp cumin, ground
- 1 tbsp coriander, ground
- 2 tsp cinnamon powder
- 2 tsp oregano, dried
- Salt and black pepper to taste
- 2 cups macaroni, cooked
- 1 cup cherry tomatoes, halved
- 1 avocado, peeled and sliced
- 1 cucumber, cubed
- ½ cup black olives, sliced
- 1 lemon, juiced

Directions:
1. Preheat the oven to 390 °F. Combine rosemary, cumin, cori-
ander, cinnamon, oregano, salt, and pepper in a bowl. Add in the flounder and toss to coat.
2. Warm olive oil in a skillet over medium heat. Brown the fish fillets for 4 minutes on both sides. Transfer to a baking tray and bake in the oven for 7-10 minutes. Combine macaroni, tomatoes, avocado, cucumber, olives, and lemon juice in a bowl; toss to coat. Serve the fish with pasta salad on the side.

Nutrition:
- Info Per Serving: Calories: 370;Fat: 16g;Protein: 26g;Carbs: 57g.

Mediterranean Grilled Sea Bass

Servings:6 | Cooking Time: 20 Minutes

Ingredients:
- ¼ teaspoon onion powder
- ¼ teaspoon garlic powder
- ¼ teaspoon paprika
- Lemon pepper and sea salt to taste
- 2 pounds sea bass
- 3 tablespoons extra-virgin olive oil, divided
- 2 large cloves garlic, chopped
- 1 tablespoon chopped Italian flat leaf parsley

Directions:
1. Preheat the grill to high heat.
2. Place the onion powder, garlic powder, paprika, lemon pepper, and sea salt in a large bowl and stir to combine.
3. Dredge the fish in the spice mixture, turning until well coated.
4. Heat 2 tablespoon of olive oil in a small skillet. Add the garlic and parsley and cook for 1 to 2 minutes, stirring occasionally. Remove the skillet from the heat and set aside.
5. Brush the grill grates lightly with remaining 1 tablespoon olive oil.
6. Grill the fish for about 7 minutes. Flip the fish and drizzle with the garlic mixture and cook for an additional 7 minutes, or until the fish flakes when pressed lightly with a fork.
7. Serve hot.

Nutrition:
- Info Per Serving: Calories: 200;Fat: 10.3g;Protein: 26.9g;Carbs: 0.6g.

Crispy Salmon Patties With Grecian Sauce

Servings:2 | Cooking Time:30 Minutes

Ingredients:
- 1 cup tzatziki sauce
- 2 tsp olive oil
- Salmon cakes
- 6 oz cooked salmon, flaked
- ¼ cup celery, minced
- ¼ cup onion, minced
- ¼ tsp chili powder
- ½ tsp dried dill
- 1 tbsp fresh minced parsley
- Salt and black pepper to taste
- 1 egg, beaten
- ½ cup breadcrumbs

Directions:
1. In a large bowl, mix well all the salmon cake ingredients. Shape the mixture into balls, then press them to form patties.
2. Warm the olive oil in a skillet over medium heat. Cook the patties for 3 minutes per side or until they're golden brown. Serve the salmon cakes topped with the tzatziki sauce.

Nutrition:
- Info Per Serving: Calories: 555;Fat: 41g;Protein: 31g;Carbs: 18g.

Salmon Baked In Foil

Servings:4 | Cooking Time: 25 Minutes

Ingredients:
- 2 cups cherry tomatoes
- 3 tablespoons extra-virgin olive oil
- 3 tablespoons lemon juice
- 3 tablespoons almond butter
- 1 teaspoon oregano
- ½ teaspoon salt
- 4 salmon fillets

Directions:
1. Preheat the oven to 400ºF.
2. Cut the tomatoes in half and put them in a bowl.
3. Add the olive oil, lemon juice, butter, oregano, and salt to the tomatoes and gently toss to combine.
4. Cut 4 pieces of foil, about 12-by-12 inches each.
5. Place the salmon fillets in the middle of each piece of foil.
6. Divide the tomato mixture evenly over the 4 pieces of salmon. Bring the ends of the foil together and seal to form a closed pocket.
7. Place the 4 pockets on a baking sheet. Bake in the preheated oven for 25 minutes.
8. Remove from the oven and serve on a plate.

Nutrition:
- Info Per Serving: Calories: 410;Fat: 32.0g;Protein: 30.0g;Carbs: 4.0g.

Instant Pot Poached Salmon

Servings:4 | Cooking Time: 3 Minutes

Ingredients:
- 1 lemon, sliced ¼ inch thick
- 4 skinless salmon fillets, 1½ inches thick
- ½ teaspoon salt
- ¼ teaspoon pepper
- ½ cup water

Directions:
1. Layer the lemon slices in the bottom of the Instant Pot.
2. Season the salmon with salt and pepper, then arrange the salmon (skin- side down) on top of the lemon slices. Pour in the water.
3. Secure the lid. Select the Manual mode and set the cooking time for 3 minutes at High Pressure.
4. Once cooking is complete, do a quick pressure release. Carefully open the lid.
5. Serve warm.

Nutrition:
- Info Per Serving: Calories: 350;Fat: 23.0g;Protein: 35.0g;Carbs: 0g.

Garlic Shrimp With Mushrooms

Servings:4 | Cooking Time: 15 Minutes

Ingredients:
- 1 pound fresh shrimp, peeled, deveined, and patted dry
- 1 teaspoon salt
- 1 cup extra-virgin olive oil
- 8 large garlic cloves, thinly sliced
- 4 ounces sliced mushrooms (shiitake, baby bella, or button)
- ½ teaspoon red pepper flakes
- ¼ cup chopped fresh flat-leaf Italian parsley

Directions:
1. In a bowl, season the shrimp with salt. Set aside.
2. Heat the olive oil in a large skillet over medium-low heat.
3. Add the garlic and cook for 3 to 4 minutes until fragrant, stirring occasionally.
4. Sauté the mushrooms for 5 minutes, or until they start to exude their juices.
5. Stir in the shrimp and sprinkle with red pepper flakes and sauté

for 3 to 4 minutes more, or until the shrimp start to turn pink.
6. Remove the skillet from the heat and add the parsley. Stir to combine and serve warm.

Nutrition:
- Info Per Serving: Calories: 619;Fat: 55.5g;Protein: 24.1g;Carbs: 3.7g.

Parsley Halibut With Roasted Peppers

Servings:4 | Cooking Time:45 Minutes

Ingredients:
- 3 tbsp olive oil
- 1 tsp butter
- 2 red peppers, cut into wedges
- 4 halibut fillets
- 2 shallots, cut into rings
- 2 garlic cloves, minced
- ¾ cup breadcrumbs
- 2 tbsp chopped fresh parsley
- Salt and black pepper to taste

Directions:
1. Preheat oven to 450 °F. Combine red peppers, garlic, shallots, 1 tbsp of olive oil, salt, and pepper in a bowl. Spread on a baking sheet and bake for 40 minutes. Warm the remaining olive oil in a pan over medium heat and brown the breadcrumbs for 4-5 minutes, stirring constantly. Set aside.
2. Clean the pan and add in the butter to melt. Sprinkle the fish with salt and pepper. Add to the butter and cook for 8-10 minutes on both sides. Divide the pepper mixture between 4 plates and top with halibut fillets. Spread the crunchy breadcrumbs all over and top with parsley. Serve and enjoy!

Nutrition:
- Info Per Serving: Calories: 511;Fat: 19.4g;Protein: 64g;Carbs: 18g.

Mediterranean Cod Stew

Servings:6 | Cooking Time: 20 Minutes

Ingredients:
- 2 tablespoons extra-virgin olive oil
- 2 cups chopped onion
- 2 garlic cloves, minced
- ¾ teaspoon smoked paprika
- 1 can diced tomatoes, undrained
- 1 jar roasted red peppers, drained and chopped
- 1 cup sliced olives, green or black
- ⅓ cup dry red wine
- ¼ teaspoon kosher or sea salt
- ¼ teaspoon freshly ground black pepper
- 1½ pounds cod fillets, cut into 1-inch pieces
- 3 cups sliced mushrooms

Directions:
1. In a large stockpot over medium heat, heat the oil. Add the onion and cook for 4 minutes, stirring occasionally. Add the garlic and smoked paprika and cook for 1 minute, stirring often.
2. Mix in the tomatoes with their juices, roasted peppers, olives, wine, pepper, and salt, and turn the heat to medium-high. Bring the mixture to a boil. Add the cod fillets and mushrooms, and reduce the heat to medium.
3. Cover and cook for about 10 minutes, stirring a few times, until the cod is cooked through and flakes easily, and serve.

Nutrition:
- Info Per Serving: Calories: 167;Fat: 5.0g;Protein: 19.0g;Carbs: 11.0g.

Walnut-Crusted Salmon

Servings:4 | Cooking Time:25 Minutes

Ingredients:
- 2 tbsp olive oil
- 4 salmon fillets, boneless
- 2 tbsp mustard
- 5 tsp honey
- 1 cup walnuts, chopped
- 1 tbsp lemon juice
- 2 tsp parsley, chopped
- Salt and pepper to the taste

Directions:
1. Preheat the oven to 380°F. Line a baking tray with parchment paper. In a bowl, whisk the olive oil, mustard, and honey. In a separate bowl, combine walnuts and parsley. Sprinkle salmon with salt and pepper and place them on the tray. Rub each fillet with mustard mixture and scatter with walnut mixture; bake for 15 minutes. Drizzle with lemon juice.

Nutrition:
- Info Per Serving: Calories: 300;Fat: 16g;Protein: 17g;Carbs: 22g.

Fennel Poached Cod With Tomatoes

Servings:4 | Cooking Time: 20 Minutes

Ingredients:
- 1 tablespoon olive oil
- 1 cup thinly sliced fennel
- ½ cup thinly sliced onion
- 1 tablespoon minced garlic
- 1 can diced tomatoes
- 2 cups chicken broth
- ½ cup white wine
- Juice and zest of 1 orange
- 1 pinch red pepper flakes
- 1 bay leaf
- 1 pound cod

Directions:
1. Heat the olive oil in a large skillet. Add the onion and fennel and cook for 6 minutes, stirring occasionally, or until translucent. Add the garlic and cook for 1 minute more.
2. Add the tomatoes, chicken broth, wine, orange juice and zest, red pepper flakes, and bay leaf, and simmer for 5 minutes to meld the flavors.
3. Carefully add the cod in a single layer, cover, and simmer for 6 to 7 minutes.
4. Transfer fish to a serving dish, ladle the remaining sauce over the fish, and serve.

Nutrition:
- Info Per Serving: Calories: 336;Fat: 12.5g;Protein: 45.1g;Carbs: 11.0g.

Seared Halibut With Moroccan Chermoula

Servings:4 | Cooking Time:30 Min + Marinating Time

Ingredients:
- 2 tbsp olive oil
- 1 tsp dry thyme
- 1 tsp dry rosemary
- 4 halibut steaks
- Salt and black pepper to taste
- Chermoula
- 2 tbsp olive oil
- ¾ cup fresh cilantro
- 2 tbsp lemon juice
- 4 garlic cloves, minced
- ½ tsp ground cumin
- ½ tsp paprika
- ¼ tsp salt
- ½ tsp cayenne pepper

Directions:
1. In a large bowl, coat the fish with 2 tbsp olive oil, rosemary, thyme, salt, and pepper. Let it marinate for 15 minutes. Process cilantro, lemon juice, olive oil, garlic, cumin, paprika, salt, and cayenne pepper in your food processor until smooth, about 1 minute, scraping down sides of the bowl as needed. Set aside the chermoula until ready to serve.
2. Preheat oven to 325 °F. Place the halibut in a baking tray. Bake for 10-12 minutes until halibut flakes apart when gently prodded with a paring knife. Serve with chermoula.

Nutrition:
- Info Per Serving: Calories: 187;Fat: 11g;Protein: 19g;Carbs: 1.1g.

Italian Canned Tuna & Bean Bowl

Servings:6 | Cooking Time:30 Minutes

Ingredients:
- 3 tbsp olive oil
- 1 lb kale, chopped
- 1 onion, chopped
- 3 garlic cloves, minced
- 1 can sliced olives
- ¼ cup capers
- ¼ tsp red pepper flakes
- 2 cans tuna in olive oil
- 1 can cannellini beans
- ½ cup chicken broth
- Salt and black pepper to taste

Directions:
1. Steam the kale for approximately 4 minutes or until crisp-tender and set aside. Warm the olive oil in a saucepan over medium heat. Sauté the onion and garlic for 4 minutes, stirring often. Add the chicken broth, olives, capers, and crushed red pepper flakes and cook for 4-5 minutes, stirring often. Add the kale and stir. Remove to a bowl and mix in the tuna, beans, pepper, and salt. Serve and enjoy!

Nutrition:
- Info Per Serving: Calories: 636;Fat: 60g;Protein: 8g;Carbs: 22g.

Baked Cod With Lemony Rice

Servings:4 | Cooking Time:45 Minutes

Ingredients:
- 2 tbsp olive oil
- 1 cup rice
- 1 garlic clove, minced
- 1 tsp red pepper, crushed
- 2 shallots, chopped
- 1 tsp anchovy paste
- 1 tbsp oregano, chopped
- 6 black olives, chopped
- 2 tbsp capers, drained
- 1 tsp paprika
- 15 oz canned tomatoes, diced
- Salt and black pepper to taste
- 4 cod fillets, boneless
- 1 oz feta cheese, crumbled
- 1 tbsp parsley, chopped
- 2 cups chicken stock
- 1 lemon, zested

Directions:
1. Preheat the oven to 360°F. Warm the olive oil in a skillet over medium heat. Sauté the garlic, red pepper, and shallot for 5 minutes. Stir in anchovy paste, paprika, oregano, olives, capers, tomatoes, salt, and pepper and cook for another 5 minutes. Put in cod fillets and top with the feta cheese and parsley. Bake for 15

minutes.

2. In the meantime, boil chicken stock in a pot over medium heat. Add in rice and lemon zest, bring to a simmer, and cook for 15-18 minutes. When ready, fluff with a fork. Share the rice into plates and top with cod mixture. Serve warm.

Nutrition:
• Info Per Serving: Calories: 410;Fat: 22g;Protein: 32g;Carbs: 22g.

Fried Scallops With Bean Mash

Servings:2 | Cooking Time:20 Minutes

Ingredients:
• 4 tbsp olive oil
• 2 garlic cloves
• 2 tsp fresh thyme, minced
• 1 can cannellini beans
• ½ cup chicken stock
• Salt and black pepper to taste
• 10 oz sea scallops

Directions:
1. Warm 2 tablespoons of olive oil in a saucepan over medium heat. Sauté the garlic for 30 seconds or just until it's fragrant. Stir in the beans and stock and bring to a boil. Simmer for 5 minutes. Remove the beans to a bowl and mash them with a potato mash. Season with thyme, salt, and pepper.

2. Warm the remaining oil in a large sauté pan. Add the scallops, flat-side down, and cook for 2 minutes or until they're golden on the bottom. Flip over and cook for another 1-2 minutes or until opaque and slightly firm. Divide the bean mash between plates and top with scallops.

Nutrition:
• Info Per Serving: Calories: 465;Fat: 29g;Protein: 30g;Carbs: 21g.

Tuna Gyros With Tzatziki

Servings:4 | Cooking Time:15 Minutes

Ingredients:
• 4 oz tzatziki
• ½ lb canned tuna, drained
• ½ cup tahini
• 4 sundried tomatoes, diced
• 2 tbsp warm water
• 2 garlic cloves, minced
• 1 tbsp lemon juice
• 4 pita wraps
• 5 black olives, chopped
• Salt and black pepper to taste

Directions:
1. In a bowl, combine the tahini, water, garlic, lemon juice, salt, and black pepper. Warm the pita wraps in a grilled pan for a few minutes, turning once. Spread the tahini and tzatziki sauces over the warmed pitas and top with tuna, sundried tomatoes, and olives. Fold in half and serve immediately.

Nutrition:
• Info Per Serving: Calories: 334;Fat: 24g;Protein: 21.3g;Carbs: 9g.

Crispy Tilapia With Mango Salsa

Servings:2 | Cooking Time: 10 Minutes

Ingredients:
• Salsa:
• 1 cup chopped mango
• 2 tablespoons chopped fresh cilantro
• 2 tablespoons chopped red onion
• 2 tablespoons freshly squeezed lime juice
• ½ jalapeño pepper, seeded and minced

• Pinch salt
• Tilapia:
• 1 tablespoon paprika
• 1 teaspoon onion powder
• ½ teaspoon dried thyme
• ½ teaspoon freshly ground black pepper
• ¼ teaspoon cayenne pepper
• ½ teaspoon garlic powder
• ¼ teaspoon salt
• ½ pound boneless tilapia fillets
• 2 teaspoons extra-virgin olive oil
• 1 lime, cut into wedges, for serving

Directions:
1. Make the salsa: Place the mango, cilantro, onion, lime juice, jalapeño, and salt in a medium bowl and toss to combine. Set aside.
2. Make the tilapia: Stir together the paprika, onion powder, thyme, black pepper, cayenne pepper, garlic powder, and salt in a small bowl until well mixed. Rub both sides of fillets generously with the mixture.
3. Heat the olive oil in a large skillet over medium heat.
4. Add the fish fillets and cook each side for 3 to 5 minutes until golden brown and cooked through.
5. Divide the fillets among two plates and spoon half of the prepared salsa onto each fillet. Serve the fish alongside the lime wedges.

Nutrition:
• Info Per Serving: Calories: 239;Fat: 7.8g;Protein: 25.0g;Carbs: 21.9g.

Seafood Cakes With Radicchio Salad

Servings:4 | Cooking Time:30 Minutes

Ingredients:
• 2 tbsp butter
• 2 tbsp extra-virgin olive oil
• 1 lb lump crabmeat
• 4 scallions, sliced
• 1 garlic clove, minced
• ¼ cup cooked shrimp
• 2 tbsp heavy cream
• ¼ head radicchio, thinly sliced
• 1 green apple, shredded
• 2 tbsp lemon juice
• Salt and black pepper to taste

Directions:
1. In a food processor, place the shrimp, heavy cream, salt, and pepper. Blend until smooth. Mix crab meat and scallions in a bowl. Add in shrimp mixture and toss to combine. Make 4 patties out of the mixture. Transfer to the fridge for 10 minutes. Warm butter in a skillet over medium heat and brown patties for 8 minutes on all sides. Remove to a serving plate. Mix radicchio and apple in a bowl. Combine olive oil, lemon juice, garlic, and salt in a small bowl and stir well. Pour over the salad and toss to combine. Serve and enjoy!

Nutrition:
• Info Per Serving: Calories: 238;Fat: 14.3g;Protein: 20g;Carbs: 8g.

Baked Oysters With Vegetables

Servings:2 | Cooking Time: 15 To 17 Minutes

Ingredients:
• 2 cups coarse salt, for holding the oysters
• 1 dozen fresh oysters, scrubbed
• 1 tablespoon almond butter
• ¼ cup finely chopped scallions, both white and green parts
• ½ cup finely chopped artichoke hearts
• ¼ cup finely chopped red bell pepper

- 1 garlic clove, minced
- 1 tablespoon finely chopped fresh parsley
- Zest and juice of ½ lemon
- Pinch salt
- Freshly ground black pepper, to taste

Directions:
1. Pour the salt into a baking dish and spread to evenly fill the bottom of the dish.
2. Prepare a clean work surface to shuck the oysters. Using a shucking knife, insert the blade at the joint of the shell, where it hinges open and shut. Firmly apply pressure to pop the blade in, and work the knife around the shell to open. Discard the empty half of the shell. Using the knife, gently loosen the oyster, and remove any shell particles. Set the oysters in their shells on the salt, being careful not to spill the juices.
3. Preheat the oven to 425°F.
4. Heat the almond butter in a large skillet over medium heat. Add the scallions, artichoke hearts, and bell pepper, and cook for 5 to 7 minutes. Add the garlic and cook for 1 minute more.
5. Remove from the heat and stir in the parsley, lemon zest and juice, and season to taste with salt and pepper.
6. Divide the vegetable mixture evenly among the oysters. Bake in the preheated oven for 10 to 12 minutes, or until the vegetables are lightly browned. Serve warm.

Nutrition:
- Info Per Serving: Calories: 135;Fat: 7.2g;Protein: 6.0g;Carbs: 10.7g.

Salmon And Mushroom Hash With Pesto

Servings:6 | Cooking Time: 20 Minutes

Ingredients:
- Pesto:
- ¼ cup extra-virgin olive oil
- 1 bunch fresh basil
- Juice and zest of 1 lemon
- ⅓ cup water
- ¼ teaspoon salt, plus additional as needed
- Hash:
- 2 tablespoons extra-virgin olive oil
- 6 cups mixed mushrooms (brown, white, shiitake, cremini, portobello, etc.), sliced
- 1 pound wild salmon, cubed

Directions:
1. Make the pesto: Pulse the olive oil, basil, juice and zest, water, and salt in a blender or food processor until smoothly blended. Set aside.
2. Heat the olive oil in a large skillet over medium heat.
3. Stir-fry the mushrooms for 6 to 8 minutes, or until they begin to exude their juices.
4. Add the salmon and cook each side for 5 to 6 minutes until cooked through.
5. Fold in the prepared pesto and stir well. Taste and add additional salt as needed. Serve warm.

Nutrition:
- Info Per Serving: Calories: 264;Fat: 14.7g;Protein: 7.0g;Carbs: 30.9g.

Herby Mackerel Fillets In Red Sauce

Servings:2 | Cooking Time:15 Minutes

Ingredients:
- 1 tbsp butter
- 2 mackerel fillets
- ¼ cup white wine
- ½ cup spring onions, sliced
- 2 garlic cloves, minced
- ½ tsp dried thyme
- 1 tsp dried parsley
- Salt and black pepper to taste
- ½ cup vegetable broth
- ½ cup tomato sauce
- ½ tsp hot sauce
- 1 tbsp fresh mint, chopped

Directions:
1. In a pot over medium heat, melt the butter. Add in fish and cook for 6 minutes in total; set aside. Pour in the wine and scrape off any bits from the bottom. Add in spring onions and garlic; cook for 3 minutes until fragrant. Sprinkle with thyme, parsley, salt, and pepper. Stir in vegetable broth, tomato sauce, and add back the fillets. Cook for 3-4 minutes. Stir in hot sauce and top with mint. Serve and enjoy!

Nutrition:
- Info Per Serving: Calories: 334;Fat: 22g;Protein: 23.8g;Carbs: 7g.

Sicilian-Style Squid With Zucchini

Servings:4 | Cooking Time:25 Minutes

Ingredients:
- 2 tbsp olive oil
- 10 oz squid, cut into pieces
- 2 zucchinis, chopped
- 2 tbsp cilantro, chopped
- 1 jalapeno pepper, chopped
- 3 tbsp balsamic vinegar
- Salt and black pepper to taste
- 1 tbsp dill, chopped

Directions:
1. Warm the olive oil in a skillet over medium heat and sauté squid for 5 minutes. Stir in zucchini, cilantro, jalapeño pepper, vinegar, salt, pepper, and dill and cook for another 10 minutes. Serve right away.

Nutrition:
- Info Per Serving: Calories: 240;Fat: 16g;Protein: 12g;Carbs: 24g.

North African Grilled Fish Fillets

Servings:4 | Cooking Time:15 Minutes

Ingredients:
- 1 tbsp olive oil
- 1 tsp harissa seasoning
- 4 fish fillets
- 2 lemons, sliced
- 2 tbsp lemon juice
- Salt and black pepper to taste

Directions:
1. Preheat your grill to 400 °F. In a bowl, whisk the lemon juice, olive oil, harissa seasoning, salt, and pepper. Coat both sides of the fish with the mixture. Carefully place the lemon slices on the grill, arranging 3-4 slices together in the shape of a fish fillet, and repeat with the remaining slices. Place the fish fillets directly on top of the lemon slices and grill with the lid closed. Turn the fish halfway through the cooking time only if the fillets are more than half an inch thick. The fish is done and ready to serve when it just begins to separate into chunks when pressed gently with a fork. Serve and enjoy!

Nutrition:
- Info Per Serving: Calories: 208;Fat: 12g;Protein: 21g;Carbs: 2g.

Poultry And Meats Recipes

Poultry And Meats Recipes

Chicken Tagine With Vegetables

Servings:6 | Cooking Time:67 Minutes

Ingredients:
- 1 ½ lb boneless skinless chicken thighs, cut into chunks
- 2 zucchini, sliced into half-moons
- 4 tbsp olive oil
- Salt and black pepper to taste
- 1 small red onion, chopped
- 2 cloves garlic, minced
- 1 red bell pepper, chopped
- 2 tomatoes, chopped
- 1 tbsp harissa paste
- 1 cup water
- 1 cup black olives, halved
- ¼ cup fresh cilantro, chopped

Directions:
1. Warm the olive oil in a large skillet over medium heat. Season the chicken with salt and pepper and brown for 6-8 minutes on all sides. Add the onion, garlic, and bell pepper and sauté for 5 minutes until tender. Stir in harissa paste and tomatoes for 1 minute and pour in 1 cup of water. Bring to a boil and lower the heat to low. Cover and simmer for 35-45 minutes until the chicken is tender and cooked through. Stir in zucchini and olives and continue to cook for 10 minutes until the zucchini is tender. Serve topped with cilantro.

Nutrition:
- Info Per Serving: Calories: 358;Fat: 25g;Protein: 25g;Carbs: 8g.

Coriander Pork Roast

Servings:4 | Cooking Time:2 Hours 10 Minutes

Ingredients:
- 2 tbsp olive oil
- 2 lb pork loin roast, boneless
- Salt and black pepper to taste
- 2 garlic cloves, minced
- 1 tsp ground coriander
- 1 tbsp coriander seeds
- 2 tsp red pepper, crushed

Directions:
1. Preheat the oven to 360° F. Toss pork, salt, pepper, garlic, ground coriander, coriander seeds, red pepper, and olive oil in a roasting pan and bake for 2 hours. Serve sliced.

Nutrition:
- Info Per Serving: Calories: 310;Fat: 5g;Protein: 16g;Carbs: 7g.

Pork Chops With Squash & Zucchini

Servings:4 | Cooking Time:40 Minutes

Ingredients:
- 2 tbsp olive oil
- 4 pork loin chops, boneless
- 1 tsp Italian seasoning
- 1 zucchini, sliced
- 1 yellow squash, cubed
- 10 cherry tomatoes, halved
- ½ tsp oregano, dried
- Salt and black pepper to taste
- 3 garlic cloves, minced
- 10 Kalamata olives, halved
- ¼ cup ricotta cheese, crumbled

Directions:
1. Preheat the oven to 370° F. Place pork chops, salt, pepper, Italian seasoning, zucchini, squash, tomatoes, oregano, olive oil, gar-lic, and olives in a roasting pan and bake covered for 30 minutes. Serve topped with ricotta cheese.

Nutrition:
- Info Per Serving: Calories: 240;Fat: 10g;Protein: 29g;Carbs: 10g.

Tzatziki Chicken Loaf

Servings:4 | Cooking Time:70 Min + Chilling Time

Ingredients:
- 1 lb ground chicken
- 1 onion, chopped
- 1 tsp garlic powder
- 1 cup tzatziki sauce
- ½ tsp dried Greek oregano
- ½ tsp dried cilantro
- ½ tsp sweet paprika
- Salt and black pepper to taste

Directions:
1. Preheat oven to 350° F. In a bowl, add chicken, paprika, onion, Greek oregano, cilantro, garlic, salt, and pepper and mix well with your hands. Shape the mixture into a greased loaf pan and bake in the oven for 55-60 minutes. Let sit for 15 minutes and slice. Serve topped with tzatziki sauce.

Nutrition:
- Info Per Serving: Calories: 240;Fat: 9g;Protein: 33.2g;Carbs: 3.6g.

Cream Zucchini & Chicken Dish

Servings:4 | Cooking Time:70 Minutes

Ingredients:
- 3 tbsp canola oil
- 1 lb turkey breast, sliced
- Salt and black pepper to taste
- 3 garlic cloves, minced
- 2 zucchinis, sliced
- 1 cup chicken stock
- ¼ cup heavy cream
- 2 tbsp parsley, chopped

Directions:
1. Warm the olive oil in a pot over medium heat. Cook the turkey for 10 minutes on both sides. Put in garlic and cook for 1 minute. Season with salt and pepper. Stir in zucchinis for 3-4 minutes and pour in the chicken stock. Bring to a boil and cook for 40 minutes. Stir in heavy cream and parsley.

Nutrition:
- Info Per Serving: Calories: 270;Fat: 11g;Protein: 16g;Carbs: 27g.

Chili Beef Stew

Servings:4 | Cooking Time:35 Minutes

Ingredients:
- 2 tbsp olive oil
- 1 lb beef stew, ground
- Salt and black pepper to taste
- 1 onion, chopped
- 2 garlic cloves, minced
- 1 tbsp chili paste
- 2 tbsp balsamic vinegar
- ¼ cup chicken stock
- ¼ cup mint, chopped

Directions:
1. Warm the olive oil in a skillet over medium heat and cook

onion for 3 minutes. Put in beef stew and cook for another 3 minutes. Stir in salt, pepper, garlic, chili paste, vinegar, stock, and mint and cook for an additional 20-25 minutes.
Nutrition:
• Info Per Serving: Calories: 310;Fat: 14g;Protein: 20g;Carbs: 16g.

Mouth-Watering Pork Loin

Servings:4 | Cooking Time:8 Hours 10 Minutes
Ingredients:
• 1 tbsp olive oil
• 2 lb pork loin, sliced
• 1 lb pearl onions
• Salt and white pepper to taste
• 1 tsp Italian seasoning
• 1 cup vegetable stock
• 1 tbsp tomato paste
• 2 bay leaves
Directions:
1. Place pork, olive oil, salt, pepper, pearl onions, Italian seasoning, stock, tomato paste, and bay leaves in your slow cooker. Cover with the lid and cook for 8 hours on Low. Discard the bay leaves and serve.
Nutrition:
• Info Per Serving: Calories: 340;Fat: 15g;Protein: 25g;Carbs: 19g.

Spinach-Cheese Stuffed Pork Loin

Servings:6 | Cooking Time:55 Minutes
Ingredients:
• 1 ½ lb pork tenderloin
• 6 slices pancetta, chopped
• 1 cup mushrooms, sliced
• 5 sundried tomatoes, diced
• Salt and black pepper to taste
Directions:
1. Place a skillet over medium heat and stir-fry the pancetta for 5 minutes until crispy. Add the mushrooms and sauté for another 4-5 minutes until tender, stirring occasionally. Stir in sundried tomatoes and season with salt and pepper; set aside. Preheat the oven to 350°F. Using a sharp knife, cut the pork tenderloin in half lengthwise, leaving about 1-inch border; be careful not to cut through to the other side. Open the tenderloin like a book to form a large rectangle.
2. Flatten it to about ¼-inch thickness with a meat tenderizer. Season the pork generously with salt and pepper. Top all over with pancetta filling. Roll up pork tenderloin and tightly secure with kitchen twine. Place on a greased baking sheet. Bake for 60-75 minutes until the pork is cooked through, depending on the thickness of the pork. Remove from the oven and let rest for 10 minutes at room temperature. Remove the twine and discard. Slice the pork into medallions and serve.
Nutrition:
• Info Per Serving: Calories: 270;Fat: 21g;Protein: 20g;Carbs: 2g.

Greek Beef Kebabs

Servings:2 | Cooking Time: 20 Minutes
Ingredients:
• 6 ounces beef sirloin tip, trimmed of fat and cut into 2-inch pieces
• 3 cups of any mixture of vegetables: mushrooms, summer squash, zucchini, onions, red peppers, cherry tomatoes
• ½ cup olive oil
• ¼ cup freshly squeezed lemon juice
• 2 tablespoons balsamic vinegar
• 2 teaspoons dried oregano

• 1 teaspoon garlic powder
• 1 teaspoon salt
• 1 teaspoon minced fresh rosemary
• Cooking spray
Directions:
1. Put the beef in a plastic freezer bag.
2. Slice the vegetables into similar-size pieces and put them in a second freezer bag.
3. Make the marinade: Mix the olive oil, lemon juice, balsamic vinegar, oregano, garlic powder, salt, and rosemary in a measuring cup. Whisk well to combine. Pour half of the marinade over the beef, and the other half over the vegetables.
4. Put the beef and vegetables in the refrigerator to marinate for 4 hours.
5. When ready, preheat the grill to medium-high heat and spray the grill grates with cooking spray.
6. Thread the meat onto skewers and the vegetables onto separate skewers.
7. Grill the meat for 3 minutes per side. They should only take 10 to 12 minutes to cook, depending on the thickness of the meat.
8. Grill the vegetables for about 3 minutes per side, or until they have grill marks and are softened. Serve hot.
Nutrition:
• Info Per Serving: Calories: 284;Fat: 18.2g;Protein: 21.0g;Carbs: 9.0g.

Curried Green Bean & Chicken Breasts

Servings:4 | Cooking Time:8 Hours 10 Minutes
Ingredients:
• 12 oz green beans, chopped
• 1 lb chicken breasts, cubed
• 1 cup chicken stock
• 1 onion, chopped
• 1 tbsp white wine vinegar
• 1 cup Kalamata olives, chopped
• 1 tbsp curry powder
• 2 tsp basil, dried
• Salt and black pepper to taste
Directions:
1. Place chicken, green beans, chicken stock, onion, vinegar, olives, curry powder, basil, salt, and pepper in your slow cooker. Cover with the lid and cook for 8 hours on Low.
Nutrition:
• Info Per Serving: Calories: 290;Fat: 13g;Protein: 19g;Carbs: 20g.

Herby Beef Soup

Servings:4 | Cooking Time:60 Minutes
Ingredients:
• 2 tbsp olive oil
• ½ lb beef stew meat, cubed
• 1 celery stalk, chopped
• 1 tsp fennel seeds
• 1 tsp hot paprika
• 1 carrot, chopped
• 1 onion, chopped
• Salt and black pepper to taste
• 2 garlic cloves, chopped
• 4 cups beef stock
• ½ tsp dried cilantro
• 1 tsp dried oregano
• 14 oz canned tomatoes, diced
• 2 tbsp parsley, chopped
Directions:
1. Warm the olive oil in a pot over medium heat and cook beef meat, onion, and garlic for 10 minutes. Stir in celery, carrots, fennel seeds, paprika, salt, pepper, cilantro, and oregano for 3 min-

utes. Pour in beef stock and tomatoes and bring to a boil. Cook for 40 minutes. Top with parsley.
Nutrition:
• Info Per Serving: Calories: 350;Fat: 16g;Protein: 38g;Carbs: 16g.

Bell Pepper & Olive Turkey Breasts

Servings:4 | Cooking Time:70 Minutes
Ingredients:
• 4 mixed bell peppers, chopped
• 1 lb turkey breast strips
• 2 leeks, chopped
• 4 garlic cloves, minced
• ½ cup black olives, sliced
• 2 cups chicken stock
• 1 tbsp oregano, chopped
• ½ cup cilantro, chopped
Directions:
1. Preheat the oven to 380° F. Put leeks, bell peppers, garlic, olives, stock, turkey, oregano, and cilantro in a baking pan and roast for 1 hour. Serve right away.
Nutrition:
• Info Per Serving: Calories: 240;Fat: 10g;Protein: 35g;Carbs: 19g.

Turmeric Green Bean & Chicken Bake

Servings:4 | Cooking Time:35 Minutes
Ingredients:
• 1 lb green beans, trimmed and halved
• 1 lb chicken thighs, boneless and skinless
• 2 tsp turmeric powder
• ½ cup sour cream
• Salt and black pepper to taste
• 1 tbsp lime juice
• 1 tbsp dill, chopped
• 1 tbsp thyme, chopped
Directions:
1. Preheat the oven to 380° F. Place chicken, turmeric, green beans, sour cream, salt, pepper, lime juice, thyme, and dill in a roasting pan and mix well. Bake for 25 minutes. Serve.
Nutrition:
• Info Per Serving: Calories: 280;Fat: 13g;Protein: 15g;Carbs: 21g.

Sweet Pork Stew

Servings:4 | Cooking Time:50 Minutes
Ingredients:
• 3 tbsp olive oil
• 1 ½ lb pork stew meat, cubed
• Salt and black pepper to taste
• 1 cup red onions, chopped
• 1 cup dried apricots, chopped
• 2 garlic cloves, minced
• 1 cup canned tomatoes, diced
• 2 tbsp parsley, chopped
Directions:
1. Warm olive oil in a skillet over medium heat. Sear pork meat for 5 minutes. Put in onions and cook for another 5 minutes. Stir in salt, pepper, apricots, garlic, tomatoes, and parsley and bring to a simmer and cook for an additional 30 minutes.
Nutrition:
• Info Per Serving: Calories: 320;Fat: 17g;Protein: 35g;Carbs: 22g.

Stewed Chicken Sausage With Farro

Servings:2 | Cooking Time:55 Minutes
Ingredients:
• 8 oz hot Italian chicken sausage, removed from the casing
• 1 tbsp olive oil
• ½ onion, diced
• 1 garlic clove, minced
• 8 sundried tomatoes, diced
• ½ cup farro
• 1 cup chicken stock
• 2 cups arugula
• 5 fresh basil, sliced thin
Directions:
1. Warm the olive oil in a pan over medium heat. Sauté the onion and garlic for 5 minutes. Add the sun-dried tomatoes and chicken sausage, stirring to break up the sausage. Cook for 7 minutes or until the sausage is no longer pink. Stir in the farro for about 2 minutes. Add the chicken stock and bring the mixture to a boil. Cover the pan and reduce the heat to low. Simmer for 30 minutes or until the farro is tender. Stir in arugula and let it wilt slightly, 2 minutes. Sprinkle with basil and serve.
Nutrition:
• Info Per Serving: Calories: 491;Fat: 19g;Protein: 31g;Carbs: 53g.

Beef Filet Mignon In Mushroom Sauce

Servings:2 | Cooking Time:25 Minutes
Ingredients:
• 8 oz cremini mushrooms, quartered
• 2 tbsp olive oil
• 2 filet mignon steaks
• 1 shallot, minced
• 2 tsp flour
• 2 tsp tomato paste
• ½ cup red wine
• 1 cup chicken stock
• ½ tsp dried thyme
• 1 fresh rosemary sprig
• 1 tsp herbes de Provence
• Salt and black pepper to taste
• ¼ tsp garlic powder
• ¼ tsp shallot powder
• ¼ tsp mustard powder
Directions:
1. Warm 1 tablespoon of olive oil in a saucepan over medium heat. Add the mushrooms and shallot and stir-fry for 5-8 minutes. Stir in the flour and tomato paste and cook for another 30 seconds. Pour in the wine and scrape up any browned bits from the sauté pan. Add the chicken stock, thyme, and rosemary. Bring it to a boil and cook until the sauce thickens, 2-4 minutes. In a small bowl, mix the herbes de Provence, salt, garlic powder, shallot powder, mustard powder, salt, and pepper. Rub the beef with the herb mixture on both sides. Warm the remaining olive oil in a sauté over medium heat. Sear the beef for 2-3 minutes on each side. Serve topped with mushroom sauce.
Nutrition:
• Info Per Serving: Calories: 385;Fat: 20g;Protein: 25g;Carbs: 15g.

Creamy Chicken Balls With Almonds

Servings:4 | Cooking Time:30 Minutes

Ingredients:
- 2 tbsp olive oil
- 1 lb ground chicken
- 2 tsp toasted chopped almonds
- 1 egg, whisked
- 2 tsp turmeric powder
- 2 garlic cloves, minced
- Salt and black pepper to taste
- 1 ¼ cups heavy cream
- ¼ cup parsley, chopped
- 1 tbsp chives, chopped

Directions:
1. Place chicken, almonds, egg, turmeric powder, garlic, salt, pepper, parsley, and chives in a bowl and toss to combine. Form meatballs out of the mixture. Warm olive oil in a skillet over medium heat. Brown meatballs for 8 minutes on all sides. Stir in cream and cook for another 10 minutes.

Nutrition:
- Info Per Serving: Calories: 290;Fat: 10g;Protein: 36g;Carbs: 26g.

Greek-Style Chicken & Egg Bake

Servings:4 | Cooking Time:45 Minutes

Ingredients:
- ½ lb Halloumi cheese, grated
- 1 tbsp olive oil
- 1 lb chicken breasts, cubed
- 4 eggs, beaten
- 1 tsp dry mustard
- 2 cloves garlic, crushed
- 2 red bell peppers, sliced
- 1 red onion, sliced
- 2 tomatoes, chopped
- 1 tsp sweet paprika
- ½ tsp dried basil
- Salt to taste

Directions:
1. Preheat oven to 360° F. Warm the olive oil in a skillet over medium heat. Add the bell peppers, garlic, onion, and salt and cook for 3 minutes. Stir in tomatoes for an additional 5 minutes. Put in chicken breasts, paprika, dry mustard, and basil. Cook for another 6-8 minutes. Transfer the mixture to a greased baking pan and pour over the beaten eggs; season with salt. Bake for 15-18 minutes. Remove and spread the cheese over the top. Let cool for a few minutes. Serve sliced.

Nutrition:
- Info Per Serving: Calories: 480;Fat: 31g;Protein: 39g;Carbs: 12g.

Pork Chops With Green Vegetables

Servings:4 | Cooking Time:70 Minutes

Ingredients:
- 2 tbsp olive oil, divided
- ½ lb green beans, trimmed
- ½ lb asparagus spears
- ½ cup frozen peas, thawed
- 2 tomatoes, chopped
- 1 lb pork chops
- 1 tbsp tomato paste
- 1 onion, chopped
- Salt and black pepper to taste

Directions:
1. Warm olive oil in a saucepan over medium heat. Sprinkle the chops with salt and pepper. Place in the pan and brown for 8 min-

utes in total; set aside. In the same pan, sauté onion for 2 minutes until soft. In a bowl, whisk the tomato paste and 1 cup of water and pour in the saucepan. Bring to a simmer and scrape any bits from the bottom. Add the chops back and bring to a boil. Then lower the heat and simmer for 40 minutes. Add in green beans, asparagus, peas, tomatoes, salt, and pepper and cook for 10 minutes until the greens are soft.

Nutrition:
- Info Per Serving: Calories: 341;Fat: 16g;Protein: 36g;Carbs: 15g.

Marjoram Pork Loin With Ricotta Cheese

Servings:4 | Cooking Time:70 Minutes

Ingredients:
- 2 tbsp olive oil
- 1 ½ lb pork loin, cubed
- 2 tbsp marjoram, chopped
- 1 garlic clove, minced
- 1 tbsp capers, drained
- 1 cup chicken stock
- Salt and black pepper to taste
- ½ cup ricotta cheese, crumbled

Directions:
1. Warm olive oil in a skillet over medium heat and sear pork for 5 minutes. Stir in marjoram, garlic, capers, stock, salt, and pepper and bring to a boil. Cook for 30 minutes. Mix in cheese.

Nutrition:
- Info Per Serving: Calories: 310;Fat: 15g;Protein: 34g;Carbs: 17g.

Mustardy Turkey Ham Stuffed Peppers

Servings:4 | Cooking Time:10 Minutes

Ingredients:
- 1 cup Greek yogurt
- 1 lb turkey ham, chopped
- 2 tbsp mustard
- Salt and black pepper to taste
- 1 celery stalk, chopped
- 2 tbsp balsamic vinegar
- 1 bunch scallions, sliced
- ¼ cup parsley, chopped
- 1 cucumber, sliced
- 1 red bell peppers, halved and deseeded
- 1 tomato, sliced

Directions:
1. Preheat the oven to 360° F. Combine turkey ham, celery, balsamic vinegar, salt, pepper, mustard, yogurt, scallions, parsley, cucumber, and tomatoes in a bowl. Fill bell peppers with the mixture and arrange them on a greased baking dish. Bake in the oven for about 20 minutes. Serve warm.

Nutrition:
- Info Per Serving: Calories: 280;Fat: 13g;Protein: 4g;Carbs: 16g.

Beef, Tomato, And Lentils Stew

Servings:4 | Cooking Time: 10 Minutes

Ingredients:
- 1 tablespoon extra-virgin olive oil
- 1 pound extra-lean ground beef
- 1 onion, chopped
- 1 can chopped tomatoes with garlic and basil, drained
- 1 can lentils, drained
- ½ teaspoon sea salt
- ⅛ teaspoon freshly ground black pepper

Directions:
1. Heat the olive oil in a pot over medium-high heat until shimmering.

2. Add the beef and onion to the pot and sauté for 5 minutes or until the beef is lightly browned.

3. Add the remaining ingredients. Bring to a boil. Reduce the heat to medium and cook for 4 more minutes or until the lentils are tender. Keep stirring during the cooking.

4. Pour them in a large serving bowl and serve immediately.

Nutrition:
• Info Per Serving: Calories: 460;Fat: 14.8g;Protein: 44.2g;Carbs: 36.9g.

Chicken Cacciatore

Servings:2 | Cooking Time: 1 Hour And 30 Minutes

Ingredients:
• 1½ pounds bone-in chicken thighs, skin removed and patted dry
• Salt, to taste
• 2 tablespoons olive oil
• ½ large onion, thinly sliced
• 4 ounces baby bella mushrooms, sliced
• 1 red sweet pepper, cut into 1-inch pieces
• 1 can crushed fire-roasted tomatoes
• 1 fresh rosemary sprig
• ½ cup dry red wine
• 1 teaspoon Italian herb seasoning
• ½ teaspoon garlic powder
• 3 tablespoons flour

Directions:
1. Season the chicken thighs with a generous pinch of salt.

2. Heat the olive oil in a Dutch oven over medium-high heat. Add the chicken and brown for 5 minutes per side.

3. Add the onion, mushrooms, and sweet pepper to the Dutch oven and sauté for another 5 minutes.

4. Add the tomatoes, rosemary, wine, Italian seasoning, garlic powder, and salt, stirring well.

5. Bring the mixture to a boil, then reduce the heat to low. Allow to simmer slowly for at least 1 hour, stirring occasionally, or until the chicken is tender and easily pulls away from the bone.

6. Measure out 1 cup of the sauce from the pot and put it into a bowl. Add the flour and whisk well to make a slurry.

7. Increase the heat to medium-high and slowly whisk the slurry into the pot. Stir until it comes to a boil and cook until the sauce is thickened.

8. Remove the chicken from the bones and shred it, and add it back to the sauce before serving, if desired.

Nutrition:
• Info Per Serving: Calories: 520;Fat: 23.1g;Protein: 31.8g;Carbs: 37.0g.

Zesty Turkey Breast

Servings:4 | Cooking Time:1 Hr 40 Min + Chilling Time

Ingredients:
• 2 tbsp olive oil
• 1 lb turkey breast
• 2 garlic cloves, minced
• ½ cup chicken broth
• 1 lemon, zested
• ¼ tsp dried thyme
• ¼ tsp dried tarragon
• ½ tsp red pepper flakes
• 2 tbsp chopped fresh parsley
• 1 tsp ground mustard
• Salt and black pepper to taste

Directions:
1. Preheat oven to 325° F. Mix the olive oil, garlic, lemon zest, thyme, tarragon, red pepper flakes, mustard, salt, and pepper in a bowl. Rub the breast with the mixture until well coated and transfer onto a roasting pan skin-side up. Pour in the chicken broth. Roast in the oven for 60-90 minutes. Allow to sit for 10 minutes

covered with foil, then remove from the roasting tin and carve. Serve topped with parsley.

Nutrition:
• Info Per Serving: Calories: 286;Fat: 16g;Protein: 34g;Carbs: 0.9g.

Greek Roasted Lamb Leg With Potatoes

Servings:6 | Cooking Time:3 Hours 10 Minutes

Ingredients:
• 3 lb red potatoes, cut into 1-inch chunks
• 1 leg of lamb
• 2 tbsp olive oil
• 1 lemon, juiced
• 1 tsp dried Greek oregano
• ½ tsp dried rosemary
• 2 garlic cloves, minced
• Salt and black pepper to taste
• 3 tbsp butter, melted

Directions:
1. Preheat oven to 300° F. Season the lamb leg with oregano, rosemary, garlic, salt, and pepper and place it in a roasting pan, fat-side up. Brush with olive oil and sprinkle with some lemon juice. Bake for about 2 hours, brushing it occasionally.

2. Increase the oven temperature to 350° F. Spread the potatoes around the lamb. Season them with salt and pepper and drizzle with butter. Add ½ cup of water. Return the pan to the oven and roast for about 50-60 minutes until the lamb is cooked and the potatoes are tender. Remove, slice the lamb, and serve with the potatoes. Enjoy!

Nutrition:
• Info Per Serving: Calories: 770;Fat: 26g;Protein: 82g;Carbs: 42g.

Lamb Kebabs With Lemon-Yogurt Sauce

Servings:4 | Cooking Time:25 Minutes

Ingredients:
• 2 tbsp olive oil
• 1 lb ground lamb
• 2 tbsp chopped fresh mint
• ¼ cup flour
• ¼ cup chopped red onions
• ¼ cup toasted pine nuts
• 2 tsp ground cumin
• Salt to taste
• 1 tsp ground cinnamon
• ½ tsp ground nutmeg
• ½ tsp black pepper
• 1 cup Greek yogurt
• 1 lemon, zested and juiced

Directions:
1. In a small bowl, whisk the yogurt, olive oil, salt, and lemon zest, and lemon juice. Keep in the refrigerator until ready to serve. Warm the olive oil in a pot over low heat. In a large bowl, combine the lamb, mint, flour, red onions, pine nuts, cumin, salt, cinnamon, ginger, nutmeg, and pepper and mix well with your hands. Shape the mixture into 12 patties. Thread the patties onto skewers and place them on a lined cookie sheet. Set under your preheated broiler for about 12 minutes, flipping once halfway through cooking. Serve the skewers with yogurt sauce.

Nutrition:
• Info Per Serving: Calories: 500;Fat: 42g;Protein: 23g;Carbs: 9g.

Smooth Chicken Breasts With Nuts

Servings:4 | Cooking Time:40 Minutes

Ingredients:
- 2 tbsp olive oil
- 1 ½ lb chicken breasts, cubed
- 4 spring onions, chopped
- 2 carrots, peeled and sliced
- ¼ cup mayonnaise
- ½ cup Greek yogurt
- 1 cup toasted cashews, chopped
- Salt and black pepper to taste

Directions:
1. Warm the olive oil in a skillet over medium heat and brown chicken for 8 minutes on all sides. Stir in spring onions, carrots, mayonnaise, yogurt, salt, and pepper and bring to a simmer. Cook for 20 minutes. Top with cashews to serve.

Nutrition:
- Info Per Serving: Calories: 310;Fat: 15g;Protein: 16g;Carbs: 20g.

Baked Beef With Kale Slaw & Bell Peppers

Servings:4 | Cooking Time:35 Minutes

Ingredients:
- 2 tsp olive oil
- 1 lb skirt steak
- 4 cups kale slaw
- 1 tbsp garlic powder
- Salt and black pepper to taste
- 1 small red onion, sliced
- 10 sundried tomatoes, halved
- ½ red bell pepper, sliced

Directions:
1. Preheat the broiler. Brush steak with olive oil, salt, garlic powder, and pepper and place under the broiler for 10 minutes, turning once. Remove to a cutting board and let rest for 10 minutes, then cut the steak diagonally.
2. In the meantime, place sun-dried tomatoes, kale slaw, onion, and bell pepper in a bowl and mix to combine. Transfer to a serving plate and top with steak slices to serve.

Nutrition:
- Info Per Serving: Calories: 359;Fat: 16g;Protein: 38g;Carbs: 22g.

Baked Chicken & Veggie

Servings:4 | Cooking Time:50 Minutes

Ingredients:
- 4 fresh prunes, cored and quartered
- 2 tbsp olive oil
- 4 chicken legs
- 1 lb baby potatoes, halved
- 1 carrot, julienned
- 2 tbsp chopped fresh parsley
- Salt and black pepper to taste

Directions:
1. Preheat oven to 420° F. Combine potatoes, carrot, prunes, olive oil, salt, and pepper in a bowl. Transfer to a baking dish. Top with chicken. Season with salt and pepper. Roast for about 40-45 minutes. Serve topped with parsley.

Nutrition:
- Info Per Serving: Calories: 473;Fat: 23g;Protein: 21g;Carbs: 49g.

Greek-Style Chicken With Potatoes

Servings:4 | Cooking Time:30 Minutes

Ingredients:
- 4 potatoes, peeled and quartered
- 4 boneless skinless chicken drumsticks
- 4 cups water
- 2 lemons, zested and juiced
- 1 tbsp olive oil
- 2 tsp fresh oregano
- Salt and black pepper to taste
- 2 Serrano peppers, minced
- 3 tbsp finely chopped parsley
- 1 cup packed watercress
- 1 cucumber, thinly chopped
- 10 cherry tomatoes, quartered
- 16 Kalamata olives, pitted
- ¼ cup hummus
- ¼ cup feta cheese, crumbled
- Lemon wedges, for serving

Directions:
1. Add water and potatoes to your Instant Pot. Set trivet over them. In a baking bowl, mix lemon juice, olive oil, black pepper, oregano, zest, salt, and Serrano peppers. Add chicken drumsticks in the marinade and stir to coat.
2. Set the bowl with chicken on the trivet in the cooker. Seal the lid, select Manual and cook on High for 15 minutes. Do a quick release. Take out the bowl with chicken and the trivet from the pot. Drain potatoes and add parsley and salt. Split the potatoes among serving plates and top with watercress, cucumber slices, hummus, cherry tomatoes, chicken, olives, and feta cheese. Garnish with lemon wedges. Serve.

Nutrition:
- Info Per Serving: Calories: 726;Fat: 15g;Protein: 72g;Carbs: 75g.

Beef & Vegetable Stew

Servings:6 | Cooking Time:and Total Time: 35 Minutes

Ingredients:
- 2 sweet potatoes, cut into chunks
- 2 lb beef meat for stew
- ¾ cup red wine
- 1 tbsp butter
- 6 oz tomato paste
- 6 oz baby carrots, chopped
- 1 onion, finely chopped
- Salt to taste
- 4 cups beef broth
- ½ cup green peas
- 1 tsp dried thyme
- 3 garlic cloves, crushed

Directions:
1. Heat the butter on Sauté in your Instant pot. Add beef and brown for 5-6 minutes. Add onions and garlic, and keep stirring for 3 more minutes. Add the remaining ingredients and seal the lid. Cook on Meat/Stew for 20 minutes on High pressure. Do a quick release and serve immediately.

Nutrition:
- Info Per Serving: Calories: 470;Fat: 15g;Protein: 51g;Carbs: 27g.

Chicken & Spinach Dish

Servings:4 | Cooking Time:60 Minutes

Ingredients:
- 2 tbsp olive oil
- 2 cups baby spinach
- 1 lb chicken sausage, sliced
- 1 red bell pepper, chopped
- 1 onion, sliced
- 2 tbsp garlic, minced
- Salt and black pepper to taste
- ½ cup chicken stock
- 1 tbsp balsamic vinegar

Directions:
1. Preheat oven to 380° F. Warm olive oil in a skillet over medium heat. Cook sausages for 6 minutes on all sides. Remove to a bowl. Add the bell pepper, onion, garlic, salt, pepper to the skillet and sauté for 5 minutes. Pour in stock and vinegar and return the sausages. Bring to a boil and cook for 10 minutes. Add in the spinach and cook until wilts, about 4 minutes. Serve and enjoy!

Nutrition:
- Info Per Serving: Calories: 300;Fat: 15g;Protein: 27g;Carbs: 18g.

Easy Grilled Pork Chops

Servings:4 | Cooking Time: 10 Minutes

Ingredients:
- ¼ cup extra-virgin olive oil
- 2 tablespoons fresh thyme leaves
- 1 teaspoon smoked paprika
- 1 teaspoon salt
- 4 pork loin chops, ½-inch-thick

Directions:
1. In a small bowl, mix together the olive oil, thyme, paprika, and salt.
2. Put the pork chops in a plastic zip-top bag or a bowl and coat them with the spice mix. Let them marinate for 15 minutes.
3. Preheat the grill to high heat. Cook the pork chops for 4 minutes on each side until cooked through.
4. Serve warm.

Nutrition:
- Info Per Serving: Calories: 282;Fat: 23.0g;Protein: 21.0g;Carbs: 1.0g.

Marsala Chicken With Mushrooms

Servings:4 | Cooking Time:30 Minutes

Ingredients:
- 4 chicken breasts, pounded thin
- ¼ cup olive oil
- Salt and black pepper to taste
- ¼ cup whole-wheat flour
- ½ lb mushrooms, sliced
- 2 carrots, chopped
- 1 cup Marsala wine
- 1 cup chicken broth
- ¼ cup parsley, chopped

Directions:
1. Warm the olive oil in a saucepan on medium heat. Season the chicken with salt and pepper, then dredge them in the flour. Fry until golden brown on both sides, about 4-6 minutes; reserve. Sauté the mushrooms and carrots in the same pan. Add the wine and chicken broth and bring to a simmer. Cook for 10 minutes or until the sauce is reduced and thickened slightly. Return the chicken to the pan, and cook it in the sauce for 10 minutes. Top with parsley and serve.

Nutrition:
- Info Per Serving: Calories: 869;Fat: 36g;Protein: 89g;Carbs: 49g.

Greek Wraps

Servings:2 | Cooking Time:10 Minutes

Ingredients:
- 2 cooked chicken breasts, shredded
- 2 tbsp roasted peppers, chopped
- 1 cup baby kale
- 2 whole-wheat tortillas
- 2 oz provolone cheese, grated
- 1 tomato, chopped
- 10 Kalamata olives, sliced
- 1 red onion, chopped

Directions:
1. In a bowl, mix all the ingredients except for the tortillas. Distribute the mixture across the tortillas and wrap them.

Nutrition:
- Info Per Serving: Calories: 200;Fat: 8g;Protein: 7g;Carbs: 16g.

Vegetable Pork Loin

Servings:4 | Cooking Time:30 Minutes

Ingredients:
- 2 tbsp canola oil
- 2 carrots, chopped
- 2 garlic cloves, minced
- 1 lb pork loin, cubed
- 4 oz snow peas
- ¾ cup beef stock
- 1 onion, chopped
- Salt and white pepper to taste

Directions:
1. Warm the oil in a skillet over medium heat and sear pork for 5 minutes. Stir in snow peas, carrots, garlic, stock, onion, salt, and pepper and bring to a boil; cook for 15 minutes.

Nutrition:
- Info Per Serving: Calories: 340;Fat: 18g;Protein: 28g;Carbs: 21g.

Mushroom & Turkey Pot

Servings:4 | Cooking Time:50 Minutes

Ingredients:
- 2 tbsp canola oil
- 1 turkey breast, cubed
- 1 cup mushrooms, sliced
- 1 onion, chopped
- 2 tbsp tarragon, chopped
- 2 tbsp parsley, chopped
- 1 garlic clove, minced
- 1 cup chicken stock

Directions:
1. Warm the canola oil in a skillet over medium heat. Cook turkey, onion, garlic, and mushrooms for 6 minutes, stirring occasionally. Stir in tarragon and parsley and pour in the stock and bring to a boil. Cook for 35 minutes. Serve.

Nutrition:
- Info Per Serving: Calories: 390;Fat: 14g;Protein: 35g;Carbs: 18g.

Crispy Pesto Chicken

Servings:2 | Cooking Time: 50 Minutes

Ingredients:
• 12 ounces small red potatoes, scrubbed and diced into 1-inch pieces
• 1 tablespoon olive oil
• ½ teaspoon garlic powder
• ¼ teaspoon salt
• 1 boneless, skinless chicken breast
• 3 tablespoons prepared pesto

Directions:
1. Preheat the oven to 425ºF. Line a baking sheet with parchment paper.
2. Combine the potatoes, olive oil, garlic powder, and salt in a medium bowl. Toss well to coat.
3. Arrange the potatoes on the parchment paper and roast for 10 minutes. Flip the potatoes and roast for an additional 10 minutes.
4. Meanwhile, put the chicken in the same bowl and toss with the pesto, coating the chicken evenly.
5. Check the potatoes to make sure they are golden brown on the top and bottom. Toss them again and add the chicken breast to the pan.
6. Turn the heat down to 350ºF and roast the chicken and potatoes for 30 minutes. Check to make sure the chicken reaches an internal temperature of 165ºF and the potatoes are fork-tender.
7. Let cool for 5 minutes before serving.

Nutrition:
• Info Per Serving: Calories: 378;Fat: 16.0g;Protein: 29.8g;Carbs: 30.1g.

Grilled Chicken Breasts With Italian Sauce

Servings:4 | Cooking Time:25 Min + Marinating Time

Ingredients:
• ½ cup olive oil
• 2 tbsp rosemary, chopped
• 2 tbsp parsley, chopped
• 1 tsp minced garlic
• 1 lemon, zested and juiced
• Salt and black pepper to taste
• 4 chicken breasts
• 2 tsp basil, chopped

Directions:
1. Combine the olive oil, rosemary, garlic, lemon juice, lemon zest, parsley, salt, and pepper in a plastic bag. Add the chicken and shake to coat. Refrigerate for 2 hours.
2. Heat your grill to medium heat. Remove the chicken breasts from the marinade and grill them for 6-8 minutes per side. Pour the marinade into a saucepan, add 2 tbsp of water and simmer for 2-3 minutes until the sauce thickens. Sprinkle with basil and serve the grilled chicken. Enjoy!

Nutrition:
• Info Per Serving: Calories: 449;Fat: 32g;Protein: 38g;Carbs: 2.1g.

Pork Chops In Wine Sauce

Servings:4 | Cooking Time:30 Minutes

Ingredients:
• 2 tbsp olive oil
• 4 pork chops
• 1 cup red onion, sliced
• 10 black peppercorns, crushed
• ¼ cup vegetable stock
• ¼ cup dry white wine
• 2 garlic cloves, minced
• Salt to taste

Directions:
1. Warm the olive oil in a skillet over medium heat and sear pork chops for 8 minutes on both sides. Put in onion and garlic and cook for another 2 minutes. Mix in stock, wine, salt, and peppercorns and cook for 10 minutes, stirring often.

Nutrition:
• Info Per Serving: Calories: 240;Fat: 10g;Protein: 25g;Carbs: 14g.

Chicken With Halloumi Cheese

Servings:4 | Cooking Time:40 Minutes

Ingredients:
• 2 tbsp butter
• 1 cup Halloumi cheese, cubed
• Salt and black pepper to taste
• 1 hard-boiled egg yolk
• ½ cup olive oil
• 6 black olives, halved
• 1 tbsp fresh cilantro, chopped
• 1 tbsp balsamic vinegar
• 1 tbsp garlic, finely minced
• 1 tbsp fresh lemon juice
• 1 ½ lb chicken wings

Directions:
1. Melt the butter in a saucepan over medium heat. Sear the chicken wings for 5 minutes per side. Season with salt and pepper to taste. Place the chicken wings on a parchment-lined baking pan. Mash the egg yolk with a fork and mix in the garlic, lemon juice, balsamic vinegar, olive oil, and salt until creamy, uniform, and smooth.
2. Preheat oven to 380° F. Spread the egg mixture over the chicken. Bake for 15-20 minutes. Top with the cheese and bake an additional 5 minutes until hot and bubbly. Scatter cilantro and olives on top of the chicken wings. Serve.

Nutrition:
• Info Per Serving: Calories: 560;Fat: 48g;Protein: 41g;Carbs: 2g.

Pork Loaf With Colby Cheese

Servings:6 | Cooking Time:90 Minutes

Ingredients:
• 1 red onion, chopped
• 2 garlic cloves, minced
• 2 lb ground pork
• 2 tbsp milk
• ¼ cup Colby cheese, grated
• 1 egg, whisked
• 10 black olives, chopped
• 2 tbsp oregano, chopped
• Salt and black pepper to taste

Directions:
1. Preheat oven to 360° F. Combine the onion, garlic, pork, milk, Colby cheese, egg, olives, oregano, salt, and pepper in a bowl. Press the mixture into a lightly greased loaf pan. Bake for 50-60 minutes. Let cool slightly. Serve sliced.

Nutrition:
• Info Per Serving: Calories: 360;Fat: 24g;Protein: 25g;Carbs: 18g.

Chicken Souvlaki

Servings:4 | Cooking Time:20 Min + Cooling Time

Ingredients:
- 1 red bell pepper, cut into chunks
- 2 chicken breasts, cubed
- 2 tbsp olive oil
- 2 cloves garlic, minced
- 8 oz cipollini onions
- ½ cup lemon juice
- Salt and black pepper to taste
- 1 tsp rosemary, chopped
- 1 cup tzatziki sauce

Directions:
1. In a bowl, mix oil, garlic, salt, pepper, and lemon juice and add the chicken, cipollini, rosemary, and bell pepper. Refrigerate for 2 hours. Preheat your grill to high heat. Thread chicken, bell pepper, and cipollini onto skewers and grill them for 6 minutes per side. Serve with tzatziki sauce.

Nutrition:
- Info Per Serving: Calories: 363;Fat: 14.1g;Protein: 32g;Carbs: 8g.

Apricot Chicken Rice Bowls

Servings:4 | Cooking Time:30 Minutes

Ingredients:
- 2 cups cooked chicken breasts, chopped
- ½ cup dried apricots, chopped
- 2 cups peeled and chopped cucumber
- 2 tbsp chicken broth
- 1 cup instant brown rice
- ¼ cup tahini
- ¼ cup Greek yogurt
- 2 tbsp scallions, chopped
- 1 tbsp lemon juice
- 1 tsp ground cumin
- ¾ tsp ground cinnamon
- ¼ tsp kosher or sea salt
- 4 tsp sesame seeds
- 1 tbsp fresh mint leaves

Directions:
1. Place the broth in a pot over medium heat and bring to a boil. Reduce the heat and add the brown rice cook. Simmer for 10 minutes or until rice is cooked through. In a bowl, mix the tahini, yogurt, scallions, lemon juice, 1 tbsp of water, cumin, cinnamon, and salt. Transfer half the tahini mixture to another medium bowl. Mix the chicken into the first bowl. When the rice is done, place it into the second bowl of tahini. Divide the chicken between 4 bowls. Spoon the rice mixture next to the chicken. Next to the chicken, place the dried apricots, and in the remaining empty section, add the cucumbers. Sprinkle with sesame seeds and fresh mint.

Nutrition:
- Info Per Serving: Calories: 335;Fat: 11g;Protein: 31g;Carbs: 30g.

Chicken With Chianti Sauce

Servings:4 | Cooking Time:80 Min + Chilling Time

Ingredients:
- 4 tbsp olive oil
- 2 tbsp butter
- 3 garlic cloves, minced
- 1 tbsp lemon zest
- 2 tbsp fresh thyme, chopped
- 2 tbsp fresh parsley, chopped
- Salt and black pepper to taste
- 4 bone-in chicken legs
- 2 cups red grapes (in clusters)
- 1 red onion, sliced
- 1 cup Chianti red wine
- 1 cup chicken stock

Directions:
1. Toss the chicken with 2 tbsp of olive oil, garlic, thyme, parsley, lemon zest, salt, and pepper in a bowl. Refrigerate for 1 hour. Preheat oven to 400° F. Heat the remaining olive oil in a saucepan over medium heat. Sear the chicken for 3–4 minutes per side. Top chicken with the grapes. Transfer to the oven and bake for 20–30 minutes or until internal temperature registers 180° F on an instant-read thermometer.
2. Melt the butter in another saucepan and sauté the onion for 3–4 minutes. Add the wine and stock, stir, and simmer the sauce for about 30 minutes until it is thickened. Plate the chicken and grapes and pour the sauce over to serve.

Nutrition:
- Info Per Serving: Calories: 562;Fat: 31g;Protein: 52g;Carbs: 16g.

Chicken Sausages With Pepper Sauce

Servings:4 | Cooking Time:30 Minutes

Ingredients:
- 2 tbsp olive oil
- 4 chicken sausage links
- 2 garlic cloves, minced
- 1 onion, thinly sliced
- 1 red bell pepper, sliced
- 1 green bell pepper, sliced
- ½ cup dry white wine
- Salt and black pepper to taste
- ½ dried chili pepper, minced

Directions:
1. Warm the olive oil in a pan over medium heat and brown the sausages for 6 minutes, turning periodically. Set aside. In the same pan, sauté onion and bell peppers and garlic for 5 minutes until tender. Deglaze with the wine and stir in salt, pepper, and chili pepper. Simmer for 4 minutes until the sauce reduces by half. Serve sausages topped with bell peppers.

Nutrition:
- Info Per Serving: Calories: 193;Fat: 12g;Protein: 6.2g;Carbs: 10g.

Parsley Pork Stew

Servings:4 | Cooking Time:8 Hours 10 Minutes

Ingredients:
- 2 tbsp olive oil
- 1 lb pork stew meat, cubed
- ½ cup chicken stock
- Salt and black pepper to taste
- 2 cups tomatoes, chopped
- 2 carrots, chopped
- 1 red bell pepper, chopped
- 1 green bell pepper, chopped
- 1 tbsp parsley, chopped

Directions:
1. Place oil, chicken stock, bell peppers, salt, pepper, pork meat, tomatoes, and carrots in your slow cooker. Cover with the lid and cook for 8 hours on Low. Scatter with parsley.

Nutrition:
- Info Per Serving: Calories: 310;Fat: 16g;Protein: 12g;Carbs: 16g.

Peach Pork Chops

Servings:4 | Cooking Time:30 Minutes

Ingredients:
- 2 tbsp olive oil
- ½ tsp cayenne powder
- 4 pork chops, boneless
- ¼ cup peach preserves
- 1 tbsp thyme, chopped

Directions:
1. In a bowl, mix peach preserves, olive oil, and cayenne powder. Preheat your grill to medium. Rub pork chops with some peach glaze and grill for 10 minutes. Turn the chops, rub more glaze and cook for 10 minutes. Top with thyme.

Nutrition:
- Info Per Serving: Calories: 240;Fat: 12g;Protein: 24g;Carbs: 7g.

Spinach Chicken With Chickpeas

Servings:4 | Cooking Time:25 Minutes

Ingredients:
- 2 tbsp olive oil
- 1 lb chicken breasts, cubed
- 10 oz spinach, chopped
- 1 cup canned chickpeas
- 1 onion, chopped
- 2 garlic cloves, minced
- ½ cup chicken stock
- 2 tbsp Parmesan cheese, grated
- 1 tbsp parsley, chopped
- Salt and black pepper to taste

Directions:
1. Warm the olive oil in a skillet over medium heat and brown chicken for 5 minutes. Season with salt and pepper. Stir in onion and garlic for 3 minutes. Pour in stock and chickpeas and bring to a boil. Cook for 20 minutes. Mix in spinach and cook until wilted, about 5 minutes. Top with Parmesan cheese and parsley. Serve and enjoy!

Nutrition:
- Info Per Serving: Calories: 290;Fat: 10g;Protein: 35g;Carbs: 22g.

Pork Loin With Cilantro-Mustard Glaze

Servings:4 | Cooking Time:35 Minutes

Ingredients:
- 2 tbsp olive oil
- 1 onion, chopped
- 2 lb pork loin, cut into strips
- ½ cup vegetable stock
- Salt and black pepper to taste
- 2 tsp mustard
- 1 tbsp cilantro, chopped

Directions:
1. Warm the olive oil in a skillet over medium heat and cook the onion for 5 minutes. Put in pork loin and cook for another 10 minutes, stirring often. Stir in vegetable stock, salt, pepper, mustard, and cilantro and cook for an additional 10 minutes.

Nutrition:
- Info Per Serving: Calories: 300;Fat: 13g;Protein: 24g;Carbs: 15g.

Cilantro Turkey Penne With Asparagus

Servings:4 | Cooking Time:40 Minutes

Ingredients:
- 3 tbsp olive oil
- 16 oz penne pasta
- 1 lb turkey breast strips
- 1 lb asparagus, chopped
- 1 tsp basil, chopped
- Salt and black pepper to taste
- ½ cup tomato sauce
- 2 tbsp cilantro, chopped

Directions:
1. Bring to a boil salted water in a pot over medium heat and cook penne until "al dente", 8-10 minutes. Drain and set aside; reserve 1 cup of the cooking water.
2. Warm the olive oil in a skillet over medium heat and sear turkey for 4 minutes, stirring periodically. Add in asparagus and sauté for 3-4 more minutes. Pour in the tomato sauce and reserved pasta liquid and bring to a boil; simmer for 20 minutes. Stir in cooked penne, season with salt and pepper, and top with the basil and cilantro to serve.

Nutrition:
- Info Per Serving: Calories: 350;Fat: 22g;Protein: 19g;Carbs: 23g.

Apricot-Glazed Pork Skewers

Servings:6 | Cooking Time:50 Minutes

Ingredients:
- 2 lb pork tenderloin, cubed
- 1 cup apricot jam
- ½ cup apricot nectar
- 1 cup dried whole apricots
- 2 onions, cut into wedges
- ½ tsp dried rosemary

Directions:
1. Coat the pork cubes with apricot jam, cover, and set aside for 10-15 minutes. Bring to a boil the apricot nectar, rosemary, and dried apricots in a saucepan over medium heat. Lower the heat and simmer for 2-3 minutes. Remove the apricots with a perforated spoon and pour the hot liquid over the pork. Stir and drain the pork, reserving the marinade.
2. Preheat your grill to medium-high. Alternate pork cubes, onion wedges, and apricots onto 6 metal skewers. Brush them with some marinade and grill for 10-12 minutes, turning and brushing with some more marinade until the pork is slightly pink and onions are crisp-tender. Simmer the remaining marinade for 3-5 minutes. Serve the skewers with marinade on the side.

Nutrition:
- Info Per Serving: Calories: 393;Fat: 4g;Protein: 34g;Carbs: 59g.

Grilled Chicken And Zucchini Kebabs

Servings:4 | Cooking Time: 20 Minutes

Ingredients:
- ¼ cup extra-virgin olive oil
- 2 tablespoons balsamic vinegar
- 1 teaspoon dried oregano, crushed between your fingers
- 1 pound boneless, skinless chicken breasts, cut into 1½-inch pieces
- 2 medium zucchinis, cut into 1-inch pieces
- ½ cup Kalamata olives, pitted and halved
- 2 tablespoons olive brine
- ¼ cup torn fresh basil leaves
- Nonstick cooking spray
- Special Equipment:
- 14 to 15 wooden skewers, soaked for at least 30 minutes

Directions:

1. Spray the grill grates with nonstick cooking spray. Preheat the grill to medium-high heat.
2. In a small bowl, whisk together the olive oil, vinegar, and oregano. Divide the marinade between two large plastic zip-top bags.
3. Add the chicken to one bag and the zucchini to another. Seal and massage the marinade into both the chicken and zucchini.
4. Thread the chicken onto 6 wooden skewers. Thread the zucchini onto 8 or 9 wooden skewers.
5. Cook the kebabs in batches on the grill for 5 minutes, flip, and grill for 5 minutes more, or until any chicken juices run clear.
6. Remove the chicken and zucchini from the skewers to a large serving bowl. Toss with the olives, olive brine, and basil and serve.

Nutrition:
• Info Per Serving: Calories: 283;Fat: 15.0g;Protein: 11.0g;Carbs: 26.0g.

Chicken Caprese
Servings:4 | Cooking Time:50 Minutes

Ingredients:
• 1 tsp garlic powder
• ½ cup basil pesto
• 4 chicken breast halves
• 3 tomatoes, sliced
• 1 cup mozzarella, shredded
• Salt and black pepper to taste

Directions:
1. Preheat the oven to 390° F. Line a baking dish with parchment paper and grease with cooking spray. Combine chicken, garlic powder, salt, pepper, and pesto in a bowl and arrange them on the sheet. Top with tomatoes and mozzarella and bake for 40 minutes. Serve hot.

Nutrition:
• Info Per Serving: Calories: 350;Fat: 21g;Protein: 33g;Carbs: 5g.

Roasted Chicken Thighs With Basmati Rice
Servings:2 | Cooking Time: 50 To 55 Minutes

Ingredients:
• Chicken:
• ½ teaspoon cumin
• ½ teaspoon cinnamon
• ½ teaspoon paprika
• ¼ teaspoon ginger powder
• ¼ teaspoon garlic powder
• ¼ teaspoon coriander
• ¼ teaspoon salt
• ⅛ teaspoon cayenne pepper
• 10 ounces boneless, skinless chicken thighs
• Rice:
• 1 tablespoon olive oil
• ½ small onion, minced
• ½ cup basmati rice
• 2 pinches saffron
• 1 cup low-sodium chicken stock
• ¼ teaspoon salt

Directions:
1. Make the Chicken
2. Preheat the oven to 350°F.
3. Combine the cumin, cinnamon, paprika, ginger powder, garlic powder, coriander, salt, and cayenne pepper in a small bowl.
4. Using your hands to rub the spice mixture all over the chicken thighs.
5. Transfer the chicken thighs to a baking dish. Roast in the preheated oven for 35 to 40 minutes, or until the internal temperature reaches 165°F on a meat thermometer.
6. Make the Rice

7. Meanwhile, heat the olive oil in a skillet over medium-high heat.
8. Sauté the onion for 5 minutes until fragrant, stirring occasionally.
9. Stir in the basmati rice, saffron, chicken stock, and salt. Reduce the heat to low, cover, and bring to a simmer for 15 minutes, until light and fluffy.
10. Remove the chicken from the oven to a plate and serve with the rice.

Nutrition:
• Info Per Serving: Calories: 400;Fat: 9.6g;Protein: 37.2g;Carbs: 40.7g.

Chicken Bruschetta Burgers
Servings:2 | Cooking Time: 16 Minutes

Ingredients:
• 1 tablespoon olive oil
• 2 garlic cloves, minced
• 3 tablespoons finely minced onion
• 1 teaspoon dried basil
• 3 tablespoons minced sun-dried tomatoes packed in olive oil
• 8 ounces ground chicken breast
• ¼ teaspoon salt
• 3 pieces small Mozzarella balls, minced

Directions:
1. Heat the olive oil in a nonstick skillet over medium-high heat. Add the garlic and onion and sauté for 5 minutes until tender. Stir in the basil.
2. Remove from the skillet to a medium bowl.
3. Add the tomatoes, ground chicken, and salt and stir until incorporated. Mix in the Mozzarella balls.
4. Divide the chicken mixture in half and form into two burgers, each about ¾-inch thick.
5. Heat the same skillet over medium-high heat and add the burgers. Cook each side for 5 to 6 minutes, or until they reach an internal temperature of 165°F.
6. Serve warm.

Nutrition:
• Info Per Serving: Calories: 300;Fat: 17.0g;Protein: 32.2g;Carbs: 6.0g.

Provençal Flank Steak Au Pistou
Servings:4 | Cooking Time:25 Minutes

Ingredients:
• 8 tbsp olive oil
• 1 lb flank steak
• Salt and black pepper to taste
• ½ cup parsley, chopped
• ¼ cup fresh basil, chopped
• 2 garlic cloves, minced
• ½ tsp celery seeds
• 1 orange, zested and juiced
• 1 tsp red pepper flakes
• 1 tbsp red wine vinegar

Directions:
1. Place the parsley, basil, garlic, orange zest and juice, celery seeds, salt, pepper, and red pepper flakes, and pulse until finely chopped in your food processor. With the processor running, stream in the red wine vinegar and 6 tbsp of olive oil until well combined. Set aside until ready to serve.
2. Preheat your grill. Rub the steak with the remaining olive oil, salt, and pepper. Place the steak on the grill and cook for 6-8 minutes on each side. Remove and leave to sit for 10 minutes. Slice the steak and drizzle with pistou. Serve.

Nutrition:
• Info Per Serving: Calories: 441;Fat: 36g;Protein: 25g;Carbs: 3g.

Rosemary Tomato Chicken

Servings:4 | Cooking Time:50 Minutes

Ingredients:
- 2 tbsp olive oil
- 1 lb chicken breasts, sliced
- 1 onion, chopped
- 1 carrot, chopped
- 2 garlic cloves, minced
- ½ cup chicken stock
- 1 tsp oregano, dried
- 1 tsp tarragon, dried
- 1 tsp rosemary, dried
- 1 cup canned tomatoes, diced
- Salt and black pepper to taste

Directions:
1. Warm the olive oil in a pot over medium heat and cook the chicken for 8 minutes on both sides. Put in carrot, garlic, and onion and cook for an additional 3 minutes. Season with salt and pepper. Pour in stock, oregano, tarragon, rosemary, and tomatoes and bring to a boil; simmer for 25 minutes. Serve.

Nutrition:
- Info Per Serving: Calories: 260;Fat: 12g;Protein: 10g;Carbs: 16g.

Pork Butt With Leeks

Servings:4 | Cooking Time:1 Hour 40 Minutes

Ingredients:
- 2 lb boneless pork butt roast, cubed
- 3 tbsp olive oil
- Salt and black pepper to taste
- 2 lb leeks, sliced
- 2 garlic cloves, minced
- 1 can diced tomatoes
- 1 cup dry white wine
- ½ cup chicken broth
- 1 bay leaf
- 2 tsp chopped fresh parsley

Directions:
1. Season the pork with salt and pepper. Warm the oil in a saucepan over medium heat. Brown the pork on all sides, about 8 minutes; transfer to a bowl. Add the leeks, salt, and pepper to fat left in saucepan and sauté for 5-7 minutes, stirring occasionally, until softened and lightly browned. Stir in garlic and cook until fragrant, about 30 seconds. Pour in tomatoes and their juice, scraping up any browned bits, and cook until tomato liquid is nearly evaporated, 10-12 minutes.
2. Preheat oven to 325° F. Add the wine, broth, and bay leaf to the saucepan and return the pork with any accumulated juices; bring to a simmer. Cover, transfer to the oven and cook for about 60 minutes until the pork is tender and falls apart when prodded with a fork. Remove and discard the bay leaf. Sprinkle with parsley. Serve and enjoy!

Nutrition:
- Info Per Serving: Calories: 369;Fat: 14g;Protein: 37g;Carbs: 25g.

Chicken Sausage & Zucchini Soup

Servings:4 | Cooking Time:30 Minutes

Ingredients:
- 2 tbsp olive oil
- 2 chicken sausage, chopped
- 4 cups chicken stock
- 3 garlic cloves, minced
- 1 yellow onion, chopped
- 4 zucchinis, cubed
- 1 lemon, zested
- ½ cup basil, chopped
- Salt and black pepper to taste

Directions:
1. Warm the olive oil in a pot over medium heat and brown the sausages for 5 minutes; reserve. Add zucchini, onion, and garlic to the pot and sauté for 5 minutes. Add in the chicken stock, lemon zest, salt, and pepper and bring to a boil. Simmer for 10 minutes. Return the sausages and cook for another 5 minutes. Top with basil and serve right away.

Nutrition:
- Info Per Serving: Calories: 280;Fat: 12g;Protein: 5g;Carbs: 17g.

Authentic Turkey Kofta

Servings:4 | Cooking Time:35 Minutes

Ingredients:
- 1 lb ground turkey
- ¼ cup breadcrumbs
- 1 egg
- 2 tbsp hot sauce
- ½ tsp celery seeds
- 2 garlic cloves, minced
- ¼ red onion, chopped
- 2 tbsp chopped fresh mint
- Salt and black pepper to taste

Directions:
1. Preheat oven to 350° F. In a bowl, place turkey, breadcrumbs, egg, garlic, red onion, mint, hot sauce, celery seeds, salt, and pepper. Make small balls out of the mixture and arrange them on a lined with parchment paper baking sheet. Bake for 25 minutes until brown. Serve and enjoy!

Nutrition:
- Info Per Serving: Calories: 270;Fat: 14g;Protein: 33.6g;Carbs: 6g.

Beef Kebabs With Onion And Pepper

Servings:6 | Cooking Time: 10 Minutes

Ingredients:
- 2 pounds beef fillet
- 1½ teaspoons salt
- 1 teaspoon freshly ground black pepper
- ½ teaspoon ground nutmeg
- ½ teaspoon ground allspice
- ⅓ cup extra-virgin olive oil
- 1 large onion, cut into 8 quarters
- 1 large red bell pepper, cut into 1-inch cubes

Directions:
1. Preheat the grill to high heat.
2. Cut the beef into 1-inch cubes and put them in a large bowl.
3. In a small bowl, mix together the salt, black pepper, allspice, and nutmeg.
4. Pour the olive oil over the beef and toss to coat. Evenly sprinkle the seasoning over the beef and toss to coat all pieces.
5. Skewer the beef, alternating every 1 or 2 pieces with a piece of onion or bell pepper.
6. To cook, place the skewers on the preheated grill, and flip every 2 to 3 minutes until all sides have cooked to desired doneness, 6 minutes for medium-rare, 8 minutes for well done. Serve hot.

Nutrition:
- Info Per Serving: Calories: 485;Fat: 36.0g;Protein: 35.0g;Carbs: 4.0g.

Traditional Meatball Soup

Servings:6 | Cooking Time:35 Minutes

Ingredients:
- 2 tbsp olive oil
- 1 can diced tomatoes
- ½ cup rice, rinsed
- 12 oz ground beef
- 2 shallots, chopped
- 1 tbsp dried thyme
- 1 carrot, chopped
- 1 tsp garlic powder
- 5 garlic cloves, minced
- 6 cups chicken broth
- ¼ cup chopped basil leaves
- Salt and black pepper to taste

Directions:
1. Combine ground beef, shallots, garlic powder, thyme, salt, and pepper in a bowl. Make balls out of the mixture and reserve. Warm the olive oil in a pot over medium heat and sauté the garlic and carrot for 2 minutes. Mix in meatballs, rice, tomatoes, broth, salt, and pepper and bring to a boil. Lower the heat and simmer for 18 minutes. Top with basil.

Nutrition:
- Info Per Serving: Calories: 265;Fat: 9.8g;Protein: 24g;Carbs: 19g.

Rich Beef Meal

Servings:4 | Cooking Time:40 Minutes

Ingredients:
- 1 tbsp olive oil
- 1 lb beef meat, cubed
- 1 red onion, chopped
- 1 garlic clove, minced
- 1 celery stalk, chopped
- Salt and black pepper to taste
- 14 oz canned tomatoes, diced
- 1 cup vegetable stock
- ½ tsp ground nutmeg
- 2 tsp dill, chopped

Directions:
1. Warm the olive oil in a skillet over medium heat and cook onion and garlic for 5 minutes. Put in beef and cook for 5 more minutes. Stir in celery, salt, pepper, tomatoes, stock, nutmeg, and dill and bring to a boil. Cook for 20 minutes.

Nutrition:
- Info Per Serving: Calories: 300;Fat: 14g;Protein: 19g;Carbs: 16g.

Original Meatballs

Servings:4 | Cooking Time:25 Minutes

Ingredients:
- 2 tbsp olive oil
- 1 lb ground beef meat
- 1 onion, chopped
- 3 tbsp cilantro, chopped
- 1 garlic clove, minced
- Salt and black pepper to taste

Directions:
1. Combine beef, onion, cilantro, garlic, salt, and pepper in a bowl and form meatballs out of the mixture. Sprinkle with oil. Preheat the grill over medium heat and grill them for 14 minutes on all sides. Serve with salad.

Nutrition:
- Info Per Serving: Calories: 240;Fat: 15g;Protein: 13g;Carbs: 17g.

Chicken & Vegetable Skewers

Servings:6 | Cooking Time:20 Minutes

Ingredients:
- 2 tbsp olive oil
- 1 ½ lb chicken breasts, cubed
- 1 tbsp fresh chives, chopped
- 1 zucchini, sliced thick
- 1 tbsp Italian seasoning
- 1 cup bell peppers, sliced
- 1 red onion, cut into wedges
- 1 ½ cups cherry tomatoes

Directions:
1. Preheat grill to high. Toss the chicken cubes with olive oil and Italian seasoning. Thread them onto skewers, alternating with the vegetables. Grill the skewers for 10 minutes, turning them occasionally to ensure even cooking. Top with chives.

Nutrition:
- Info Per Serving: Calories: 295;Fat: 14g;Protein: 36g;Carbs: 6g.

Bell Pepper & Onion Pork Chops

Servings:4 | Cooking Time:30 Minutes

Ingredients:
- 2 tbsp olive oil
- 4 pork chops
- Salt and black pepper to taste
- 1 tsp fennel seeds
- 1 red bell pepper, sliced
- 1 green bell pepper, sliced
- 1 yellow onion, thinly sliced
- 2 tsp Italian seasoning
- 2 garlic cloves, minced
- 1 tbsp balsamic vinegar

Directions:
1. Warm the olive oil in a large skillet over medium heat. Season the pork chops with salt and pepper and add them to the skillet. Cook for 6-8 minutes on both sides or until golden brown; reserve. Sauté the garlic, sliced bell peppers, onions, fennel seeds, and herbs in the skillet for 6-8 minutes until tender, stirring occasionally. Return the pork, cover, and lower the heat to low. Cook for another 3 minutes or until the pork is cooked through. Transfer the pork and vegetables to a serving platter. Add the vinegar to the skillet and stir to combine for 1-2 minutes. Drizzle the sauce over the pork.

Nutrition:
- Info Per Serving: Calories: 508;Fat: 40g;Protein: 31g;Carbs: 8g.

Asparagus & Chicken Skillet

Servings:4 | Cooking Time:30 Minutes

Ingredients:
- 2 tbsp olive oil
- 1 lb chicken breasts, sliced
- Salt and black pepper to taste
- 1 lb asparagus, chopped
- 6 sundried tomatoes, diced
- 3 tbsp capers, drained
- 2 tbsp lemon juice

Directions:
1. Warm the olive oil in a skillet over medium heat. Cook asparagus, tomatoes, salt, pepper, capers, and lemon juice for 10 minutes. Remove to a bowl. Brown chicken in the same skillet for 8 minutes on both sides. Put veggies back to skillet and cook for another 2-3 minutes. Serve and enjoy!

Nutrition:
- Info Per Serving: Calories: 560;Fat: 29g;Protein: 45g;Carbs: 34g.

Green Veggie & Turkey

Servings:4 | Cooking Time:40 Minutes

Ingredients:
- 3 tbsp olive oil
- 1 lb asparagus, halved
- 1 lb turkey breast, sliced
- 1 cup chicken stock
- Salt and black pepper to taste
- 1 cup canned artichoke hearts
- 2 tomatoes, chopped
- 10 Kalamata olives, sliced
- 1 shallot, chopped
- 3 garlic cloves, minced
- 3 tbsp dill, chopped

Directions:
1. Warm the olive oil in a pot over medium heat and cook turkey and garlic for 8 minutes or until the meat is golden brown. Stir in the asparagus, chopped tomatoes, chicken stock, salt, black pepper, artichoke hearts, Kalamata olives, and shallot and bring to a boil. Lower the heat and simmer for 20 minutes. Garnish with dill and serve.

Nutrition:
- Info Per Serving: Calories: 300;Fat: 17g;Protein: 35g;Carbs: 24g.

Pork Chops In Tomato Olive Sauce

Servings:4 | Cooking Time:20 Minutes

Ingredients:
- 2 tbsp olive oil
- 4 pork loin chops, boneless
- 6 tomatoes, crushed
- 3 tbsp basil, chopped
- 10 black olives, halved
- 1 yellow onion, chopped
- 1 garlic clove, minced

Directions:
1. Warm the olive oil in a skillet over medium heat and brown pork chops for 6 minutes on all sides. Share into plates. In the same skillet, stir tomatoes, basil, olives, onion, and garlic and simmer for 4 minutes. Drizzle tomato sauce over.

Nutrition:
- Info Per Serving: Calories: 340;Fat: 18g;Protein: 35g;Carbs: 13g.

Cocktail Meatballs In Almond Sauce

Servings:4 | Cooking Time:30 Minutes

Ingredients:
- 3 tbsp olive oil
- 8 oz ground pork
- 8 oz ground beef
- ½ cup finely minced onions
- 1 large egg, beaten
- 1 potato, shredded
- Salt and black pepper to taste
- 1 tsp garlic powder
- ½ tsp oregano
- 2 tbsp chopped parsley
- ¼ cup ground almonds
- 1 cup chicken broth
- ¼ cup butter

Directions:
1. Place the ground meat, onions, egg, potato, salt, garlic powder, pepper, and oregano in a large bowl. Shape the mixture into small meatballs, about 1 inch in diameter, and place on a plate. Let sit for 10 minutes at room temperature.
2. Warm the olive oil in a skillet over medium heat. Add the meatballs and brown them for 6-8 minutes on all sides; reserve. In the hot skillet, melt the butter and add the almonds and broth. Cook for 3-5 minutes. Add the meatballs to the skillet, cover, and cook for 8-10 minutes. Top with parsley.

Nutrition:
- Info Per Serving: Calories: 449;Fat: 42g;Protein: 16g;Carbs: 3g.

Spanish Chicken Skillet

Servings:4 | Cooking Time:25 Minutes

Ingredients:
- 2 tbsp olive oil
- ½ cup chicken stock
- 4 chicken breasts
- 2 garlic cloves, minced
- 1 celery stalk, chopped
- 1 tbsp oregano, dried
- Salt and black pepper to taste
- 1 white onion, chopped
- 1 ½ cups tomatoes, cubed
- 10 green olives, sliced

Directions:
1. Warm the olive oil in a skillet over medium heat. Season the chicken with salt and pepper and cook for 4 minutes on both sides. Stir in garlic, oregano, stock, onion, celery, tomatoes, and olives and bring to a boil. Simmer for 13-15 minutes.

Nutrition:
- Info Per Serving: Calories: 140;Fat: 7g;Protein: 11g;Carbs: 13g.

Lamb With Couscous & Chickpeas

Servings:6 | Cooking Time:50 Minutes

Ingredients:
- 1 lb lamb shoulder, halved
- 3 tbsp olive oil
- 1 cup couscous
- Salt and black pepper to taste
- 1 onion, finely chopped
- 10 strips orange zest
- 1 tsp ground coriander
- ¼ tsp ground cinnamon
- ½ tsp cayenne pepper
- ½ cup dry white wine
- 2 ½ cups chicken broth
- 1 can chickpeas
- ½ cup dates, chopped
- ½ cup sliced almonds, toasted

Directions:
1. Cover the couscous in a bowl with 1 ½ cups of boiling water and put a lid. Let stand for 5 minutes to absorb the water.
2. Preheat oven to 330° F. Heat 2 tablespoons oil in a pot over medium heat. Season the lamb with salt and pepper and brown it for 4 minutes per side; set aside.
3. Stir-fry onion into the fat left in the pot, 3 minutes. Stir in orange zest, coriander, cinnamon, cayenne, and pepper until fragrant, 30 seconds. Stir in wine, scraping off any browned bits. Stir in broth and chickpeas and bring to a boil.
4. Make a nestle of lamb into the pot along with any accumulated juices. Cover, transfer the pot in the oven, and cook until fork slips easily in and out of the lamb, 1 hour.
5. Transfer the lamb to cutting board, let cool slightly, then shred using 2 forks, discarding excess fat and bones. Strain cooking liquid through a fine mesh strainer set over the bowl. Return solids and 1 ½ cups of cooking liquid to the pot and bring to a simmer over medium heat; discard the remaining liquid. Stir in couscous and dates. Add shredded lamb and almonds. Season to taste and serve.

Nutrition:
- Info Per Serving: Calories: 555;Fat: 31g;Protein: 37g;Carbs: 42g.

One-Pan Sicilian Chicken

Servings:4 | Cooking Time:25 Minutes

Ingredients:
- 1 lb chicken breasts, halved
- Salt and black pepper to taste
- 2 tbsp olive oil
- 1 red onion, thinly sliced
- ½ cup mixed bell pepper strips
- 2 garlic cloves, minced
- 1 tbsp capers, rinsed
- 3 tbsp fresh basil, chopped
- 2 tbsp balsamic vinegar
- ½ tsp red pepper flakes

Directions:
1. Warm the olive oil in a skillet over medium heat. Season the chicken with salt and pepper. Sear chicken for 4-5 minutes on each side until golden brown; remove to a plate. Sauté the onion, garlic, and peppers in the same skillet for 3-4 minutes until soft, stirring often. Stir in vinegar and red pepper flakes. Return the chicken and add the capers. Cover and reduce the heat. Simmer for about 6 minutes until the chicken is cooked through. Serve hot topped with basil.

Nutrition:
- Info Per Serving: Calories: 272;Fat: 17g;Protein: 24g;Carbs: 3g.

Yogurt Chicken Breasts

Servings:4 | Cooking Time: 10 Minutes

Ingredients:
- Yogurt Sauce:
- ½ cup plain Greek yogurt
- 2 tablespoons water
- Pinch saffron
- 3 garlic cloves, minced
- ½ onion, chopped
- 2 tablespoons chopped fresh cilantro
- Juice of ½ lemon
- ½ teaspoon salt
- 1 pound boneless, skinless chicken breasts, cut into 2-inch strips
- 1 tablespoon extra-virgin olive oil

Directions:
1. Make the yogurt sauce: Place the yogurt, water, saffron, garlic, onion, cilantro, lemon juice, and salt in a blender, and pulse until completely mixed.
2. Transfer the yogurt sauce to a large bowl, along with the chicken strips. Toss to coat well.
3. Cover with plastic wrap and marinate in the refrigerator for at least 1 hour, or up to overnight.
4. When ready to cook, heat the olive oil in a large skillet over medium heat.
5. Add the chicken strips to the skillet, discarding any excess marinade. Cook each side for 5 minutes, or until cooked through.
6. Let the chicken cool for 5 minutes before serving.

Nutrition:
- Info Per Serving: Calories: 154;Fat: 4.8g;Protein: 26.3g;Carbs: 2.9g.

Mushroom & Pork Stew

Servings:4 | Cooking Time:8 Hours 10 Minutes

Ingredients:
- 2 tbsp olive oil
- 2 lb pork stew meat, cubed
- 1 lb mushrooms, chopped
- Salt and black pepper to taste
- 2 cups chicken stock
- 1 carrot, chopped
- 1 yellow onion, chopped
- 2 garlic cloves, minced
- 2 cups tomatoes, chopped
- ½ cup parsley, chopped

Directions:
1. Place pork meat, salt, pepper, stock, olive oil, onion, carrot, garlic, mushrooms, and tomatoes in your slow cooker. Cover with the lid and cook for 8 hours on Low. Top with parsley.

Nutrition:
- Info Per Serving: Calories: 340;Fat: 18g;Protein: 17g;Carbs: 13g.

Carrot, Potato & Chicken Bake

Servings:4 | Cooking Time:60 Minutes

Ingredients:
- 2 tbsp olive oil
- 1 lb chicken breasts, cubed
- 1 carrot, chopped
- 2 garlic cloves, minced
- Salt and black pepper to taste
- 2 tsp thyme, dried
- 1 baby potatoes, halved
- 1 onion, sliced
- ¾ cup chicken stock
- 2 tbsp basil, chopped

Directions:
1. Preheat the oven to 380° F. Grease a baking dish with oil. Put carrot, potatoes, chicken, garlic, salt, pepper, thyme, onion, stock, and basil in the dish and bake for 50 minutes. Serve.

Nutrition:
- Info Per Serving: Calories: 290;Fat: 10g;Protein: 15g;Carbs: 23g.

Italian Potato & Chicken

Servings:4 | Cooking Time:50 Minutes

Ingredients:
- 3 tbsp canola oil
- 1 lb chicken breasts, halved
- Salt and black pepper to taste
- 2 garlic cloves, minced
- 2 shallots, chopped
- 1 lb red potatoes, sliced
- 3 tomatoes, chopped
- ¼ cup chicken stock
- 1 tbsp Italian seasoning

Directions:
1. Warm the canola oil in a skillet over medium heat and cook chicken, garlic, salt, and pepper for 6 minutes on both sides. Stir in shallots, potatoes, tomatoes, stock, and Italian seasoning and bring to a boil. Cook for 30 minutes. Serve.

Nutrition:
- Info Per Serving: Calories: 320;Fat: 13g;Protein: 16g;Carbs: 25g.

Potato Lamb And Olive Stew

Servings:10 | Cooking Time: 3 Hours 42 Minutes

Ingredients:
- 4 tablespoons almond flour
- ¾ cup low-sodium chicken stock
- 1¼ pounds small potatoes, halved
- 3 cloves garlic, minced
- 4 large shallots, cut into ½-inch wedges
- 3 sprigs fresh rosemary
- 1 tablespoon lemon zest
- Coarse sea salt and black pepper, to taste
- 3½ pounds lamb shanks, fat trimmed and cut crosswise into

1½-inch pieces
- 2 tablespoons extra-virgin olive oil
- ½ cup dry white wine
- 1 cup pitted green olives, halved
- 2 tablespoons lemon juice

Directions:

1. Combine 1 tablespoon of almond flour with chicken stock in a bowl. Stir to mix well.
2. Put the flour mixture, potatoes, garlic, shallots, rosemary, and lemon zest in the slow cooker. Sprinkle with salt and black pepper. Stir to mix well. Set aside.
3. Combine the remaining almond flour with salt and black pepper in a large bowl, then dunk the lamb shanks in the flour and toss to coat.
4. Heat the olive oil in a nonstick skillet over medium-high heat until shimmering.
5. Add the well-coated lamb and cook for 10 minutes or until golden brown. Flip the lamb pieces halfway through the cooking time. Transfer the cooked lamb to the slow cooker.
6. Pour the wine in the same skillet, then cook for 2 minutes or until it reduces in half. Pour the wine in the slow cooker.
7. Put the slow cooker lid on and cook on high for 3 hours and 30 minutes or until the lamb is very tender.
8. In the last 20 minutes of the cooking, open the lid and fold in the olive halves to cook.
9. Pour the stew on a large plate, let them sit for 5 minutes, then skim any fat remains over the face of the liquid.
10. Drizzle with lemon juice and sprinkle with salt and pepper. Serve warm.

Nutrition:
- Info Per Serving: Calories: 309;Fat: 10.3g;Protein: 36.9g;Carbs: 16.1g.

Baked Root Veggie & Chicken

Servings:6 | Cooking Time:50 Minutes

Ingredients:
- 2 sweet potatoes, peeled and cubed
- ½ cup green olives, pitted and smashed
- ¼ cup olive oil
- 2 lb chicken breasts, sliced
- 2 tbsp harissa seasoning
- 1 lemon, zested and juiced
- Salt and black pepper to taste
- 2 carrots, chopped
- 1 onion, chopped
- ½ cup feta cheese, crumbled
- ½ cup parsley, chopped

Directions:

1. Preheat the oven to 390° F. Place chicken, harissa seasoning, lemon juice, lemon zest, olive oil, salt, pepper, carrots, sweet potatoes, and onion in a roasting pan and mix well. Bake for 40 minutes. Combine feta cheese and green olives in a bowl. Share chicken mixture into plates and top with olive mixture. Top with parsley and parsley and serve immediately.

Nutrition:
- Info Per Serving: Calories: 310;Fat: 10g;Protein: 15g;Carbs: 23g.

Gyro Burgers With Tahini Sauce

Servings:4 | Cooking Time: 10 Minutes

Ingredients:
- 2 tablespoons extra-virgin olive oil
- 1 tablespoon dried oregano
- 1¼ teaspoons garlic powder, divided
- 1 teaspoon ground cumin
- ½ teaspoon freshly ground black pepper
- ¼ teaspoon kosher or sea salt

- 1 pound beef flank steak, top round steak, or lamb leg steak, center cut, about 1 inch thick
- 1 medium green bell pepper, halved and seeded
- 2 tablespoons tahini or peanut butter
- 1 tablespoon hot water (optional)
- ½ cup plain Greek yogurt
- 1 tablespoon freshly squeezed lemon juice
- 1 cup thinly sliced red onion
- 4 whole-wheat pita breads, warmed
- Nonstick cooking spray

Directions:

1. Set an oven rack about 4 inches below the broiler element. Preheat the oven broiler to high. Line a large, rimmed baking sheet with aluminum foil. Place a wire cooling rack on the foil, and spray the rack with nonstick cooking spray. Set aside.
2. In a small bowl, whisk together the olive oil, oregano, 1 teaspoon of garlic powder, cumin, pepper, and salt. Rub the oil mixture on all sides of the steak, reserving 1 teaspoon of the mixture. Place the steak on the prepared rack. Rub the remaining oil mixture on the bell pepper, and place on the rack, cut-side down. Press the pepper with the heel of your hand to flatten.
3. Broil for 5 minutes. Flip the steak and the pepper pieces, and broil for 2 to 5 minutes more, until the pepper is charred and the internal temperature of the meat measures 145°F on a meat thermometer. Put the pepper and steak on a cutting board to rest for 5 minutes.
4. Meanwhile, in a small bowl, whisk the tahini until smooth. Add the remaining ¼ teaspoon of garlic powder and the yogurt and lemon juice, and whisk thoroughly.
5. Slice the steak crosswise into ¼-inch-thick strips. Slice the bell pepper into strips. Divide the steak, bell pepper, and onion among the warm pita breads. Drizzle with tahini sauce and serve.

Nutrition:
- Info Per Serving: Calories: 348;Fat: 15.0g;Protein: 33.0g;Carbs: 20.0g.

Drunken Lamb Bake

Servings:4 | Cooking Time:90 Minutes

Ingredients:
- 3 tbsp butter
- 2 lb leg of lamb, sliced
- 3 garlic cloves, chopped
- 2 onions, chopped
- 3 cups vegetable stock
- 2 cups dry red wine
- 2 tbsp tomato pastes
- 1 tsp thyme, chopped
- Salt and black pepper to taste

Directions:

1. Preheat the oven to 360° F. Melt butter in a skillet over medium heat. Sear lamb for 10 minutes on both sides. Remove to a roasting pan. In the same skillet, add and cook onions and garlic for 5 minutes. Stir in stock, red wine, tomato paste, thyme, salt, and pepper and bring to a boil. Cook for 10 minutes and pour over lamb. Bake for 1 hour.

Nutrition:
- Info Per Serving: Calories: 290;Fat: 22g;Protein: 19g;Carbs: 17g.

Spinach Pesto Chicken Breasts

Servings:4 | Cooking Time:25 Minutes

Ingredients:
- ¼ cup + 1 tbsp olive oil
- 4 chicken breasts
- 1 cup spinach
- ¼ cup grated Pecorino cheese
- Salt and black pepper to taste
- ¼ cup pine nuts
- 1 garlic clove, minced

Directions:
1. Rub chicken with salt and black pepper. Grease a grill pan with 1 tbsp of olive oil and place over medium heat. Grill the chicken for 8-10 minutes, flipping once. Mix spinach, garlic, Pecorino cheese, and pine nuts in a food processor. Slowly, pour in the remaining oil; pulse until smooth. Spoon 1 tbsp of pesto on each breast and cook for an additional 5 minutes.

Nutrition:
- Info Per Serving: Calories: 493;Fat: 27g;Protein: 53g;Carbs: 4g.

Citrusy Leg Lamb

Servings:4 | Cooking Time:7 Hours 10 Minutes

Ingredients:
- 2 cups stewed tomatoes, drained
- 3 ½ lb leg of lamb, cubed
- 1 lb small potatoes, cubed
- 1 grapefruit, zested and juiced
- 4 garlic cloves, minced
- Salt and black pepper to taste
- ½ cup basil, chopped

Directions:
1. Place potatoes, tomatoes, grapefruit juice, grapefruit zest, garlic, leg of lamb, salt, and pepper in your slow cooker. Cover with lid and cook for 8 hours on Low. Top with basil.

Nutrition:
- Info Per Serving: Calories: 300;Fat: 10g;Protein: 19g;Carbs: 16g.

Picante Green Pea & Chicken

Servings:4 | Cooking Time:35 Minutes

Ingredients:
- 2 tbsp olive oil
- 1 lb chicken breasts, halved
- 1 tsp chili powder
- Salt and black pepper to taste
- 1 tsp garlic powder
- 1 tbsp smoked paprika
- ½ cup chicken stock
- 2 tsp sherry vinegar
- 3 tsp hot sauce
- 2 tsp cumin, ground
- 1 cup green peas
- 1 carrot, chopped

Directions:
1. Warm the olive oil in a skillet over medium heat and cook chicken for 6 minutes on both sides. Sprinkle with chili powder, salt, pepper, garlic powder, and paprika. Pour in the chicken stock, vinegar, hot sauce, cumin, carrot, and green peas and bring to a boil; cook for an additional 15 minutes.

Nutrition:
- Info Per Serving: Calories: 240;Fat: 19g;Protein: 14g;Carbs: 16g.

Sides , Salads, And Soups Recipes

Sides , Salads, And Soups Recipes

Moroccan Lamb Soup

Servings:4 | Cooking Time:40 Minutes

Ingredients:
- 2 tbsp olive oil
- 2 carrots, chopped
- 1 red onion, chopped
- 2 celery stalks, chopped
- 2 garlic cloves, minced
- 1 tbsp thyme, chopped
- 4 cups vegetable stock
- 1 cup mushrooms, sliced
- 8 oz leftover lamb, shredded
- 14 oz canned chickpeas
- 2 tbsp cilantro, chopped

Directions:
1. Warm the olive oil in a pot over medium heat and cook onion, garlic, celery, mushrooms, carrots, and thyme for 5 minutes until tender. Stir in vegetable stock and lamb and bring to a boil. Reduce the heat to low and simmer for 20 minutes. Mix in chickpeas and cook for an additional 5 minutes. Ladle your soup into individual bowls. Top with cilantro.

Nutrition:
- Info Per Serving: Calories: 300;Fat: 12g;Protein: 15g;Carbs: 23g.

Classic Aioli

Servings:6 | Cooking Time:10 Minutes

Ingredients:
- ½ cup sunseed oil
- 1 garlic clove, minced
- 2 tsp lemon juice
- 1 tsp lemon zest
- 1 large egg yolk
- Salt to taste

Directions:
1. Blitz all the ingredients in a large bowl with an immersion blender until everything is well combined and thick. Store in an airtight container in the refrigerator for up to 2-3 days.

Nutrition:
- Info Per Serving: Calories: 181;Fat: 9.7g;Protein: 3.3g;Carbs: 4g.

Harissa Chicken Wings

Servings:4 | Cooking Time:45 Min + Marinating Time

Ingredients:
- ½ tsp harissa seasoning
- 4 garlic cloves, minced
- 1 shallot, grated
- 1 tbsp lemon zest
- 1 tbsp lemon juice
- ¼ tsp ground cinnamon
- ¼ tsp smoked paprika
- ½ tsp ground allspice
- Salt and black pepper to taste
- 2 tbsp fresh thyme, chopped
- ¼ cup extra-virgin olive oil
- 2 lb chicken wings

Directions:
1. Combine all ingredients, except for the chicken wings, in a bowl. Add the chicken and toss to coat. Refrigerate for 2 hours. Preheat oven to 425° F. Remove wings from the refrigerator and discard the excess marinade from them. Arrange the wings on a parchment-lined baking sheet. Bake for 30-35 minutes, flipping once until crispy and brown.

Nutrition:
- Info Per Serving: Calories: 417;Fat: 22g;Protein: 50g;Carbs: 3g.

Quick Za´Atar Spice

Servings:4 | Cooking Time:5 Minutes

Ingredients:
- 1 tsp ground cumin
- 1 tsp ground coriander
- ½ cup dried thyme
- 2 tbsp sesame seeds, toasted
- 1 ½ tbsp ground sumac
- ¼ tsp Aleppo chili flakes

Directions:
1. Mix all the ingredients in a bowl. Store in a glass jar at room temperature for up to 7-9 months.

Nutrition:
- Info Per Serving: Calories: 175;Fat: 13.9g;Protein: 5g;Carbs: 12g.

Orange Pear Salad With Gorgonzola

Servings:4 | Cooking Time:10 Minutes

Ingredients:
- 4 oz gorgonzola cheese, crumbled
- 2 tbsp olive oil
- 1 tsp orange zest
- ¼ cup orange juice
- 3 tbsp balsamic vinegar
- Salt and black pepper to taste
- 1 romaine lettuce head, torn
- 2 pears, cored and cut into medium wedges

Directions:
1. Mix orange zest, orange juice, vinegar, oil, salt, pepper, lettuce, pears, and gorgonzola cheese in a bowl. Serve.

Nutrition:
- Info Per Serving: Calories: 210;Fat: 6g;Protein: 4g;Carbs: 11g.

Parmesan Chicken Salad

Servings:4 | Cooking Time:15 Minutes

Ingredients:
- 2 cups chopped cooked chicken breasts
- 1 cup canned artichoke hearts, chopped
- 2 tbsp extra-virgin olive oil
- 2 tomatoes, chopped
- 2 heads romaine lettuce, torn
- 2 cucumbers, chopped
- ½ red onion, finely chopped
- 3 oz Parmesan cheese, shaved
- 4 oz pesto
- 1 lemon, zested
- 2 garlic cloves, minced
- 2 tbsp chopped fresh basil
- 2 tbsp chopped scallions
- Salt and black pepper to taste

Directions:
1. Mix the lettuce, artichoke, chicken, tomatoes, cucumbers, and red onion in a bowl. In another bowl, mix pesto, olive oil, lemon zest, garlic, basil, salt, and pepper and stir to combine. Drizzle the pesto dressing over the salad and top with scallions and Parmesan cheese shavings to serve.

Nutrition:

Herby Yogurt Sauce

Servings:4 | Cooking Time:5 Minutes

Ingredients:
- ¼ tsp fresh lemon juice
- 1 cup plain yogurt
- 2 tbsp fresh cilantro, minced
- 2 tbsp fresh mint, minced
- 1 garlic clove, minced
- Salt and black pepper to taste

Directions:
1. Place the lemon juice, yogurt, cilantro, mint, and garlic together in a bowl and mix well. Season with salt and pepper. Let sit for about 30 minutes to blend the flavors. Store in an airtight container in the refrigerator for up to 2-3 days.

Nutrition:
- Info Per Serving: Calories: 46;Fat: 0.8g;Protein: 3.6g;Carbs: 4.8g.

Red Pollock & Tomato Stew

Servings:4 | Cooking Time:50 Minutes

Ingredients:
- 1 lb pollock fillet
- 4 garlic cloves, crushed
- 1 lb tomatoes, peeled and diced
- 2 bay leaves, whole
- 2 cups fish stock
- Salt and black pepper to taste
- 1 onion, finely chopped
- ½ cup olive oil

Directions:
1. Preheat your Instant Pot on Sauté mode and heat 2 tbsp olive oil. Add onion and sauté until translucent, stirring constantly, for about 3-4 minutes. Add tomatoes and cook until soft. Press Cancel. Add the remaining ingredients and seal the lid. Cook on High Pressure for 15 minutes. When ready, do a quick release. Serve warm.

Nutrition:
- Info Per Serving: Calories: 370;Fat: 27g;Protein: 26.3g;Carbs: 7g.

Moroccan Spiced Couscous

Servings:2 | Cooking Time: 8 Minutes

Ingredients:
- 1 tablespoon olive oil
- ¾ cup couscous
- ¼ teaspoon cinnamon
- ¼ teaspoon garlic powder
- ¼ teaspoon salt, plus more as needed
- 1 cup water
- 2 tablespoons minced dried apricots
- 2 tablespoons raisins
- 2 teaspoons minced fresh parsley

Directions:
1. Heat the olive oil in a saucepan over medium-high heat until it shimmers.
2. Add the couscous, cinnamon, garlic powder, and salt. Stir for 1 minute to toast the couscous and spices.
3. Add the water, apricots, and raisins and bring the mixture to a boil.
4. Cover and turn off the heat. Allow the couscous to sit for 4 to 5 minutes and then fluff it with a fork. Sprinkle with the fresh parsley. Season with more salt as needed and serve.

Nutrition:

Chickpea & Cavolo Nero Soup

Servings:4 | Cooking Time:35 Minutes

Ingredients:
- 2 tbsp olive oil
- 1 lb cavolo nero, torn
- 1 cup canned chickpeas
- Salt and black pepper to taste
- 1 celery stalk, chopped
- 1 onion, chopped
- 1 carrot, chopped
- 14 oz canned tomatoes, diced
- 2 tbsp rosemary, chopped
- 4 cups vegetable stock

Directions:
1. Warm the olive oil in a pot over medium heat and cook onion, celery, and carrot for 5 minutes. Stir in cavolo nero, salt, pepper, tomatoes, rosemary, chickpeas, and vegetable stock and simmer for 20 minutes. Serve warm.

Nutrition:
- Info Per Serving: Calories: 200;Fat: 9g;Protein: 5g;Carbs: 13g.

Traditional Panzanella Salad

Servings:2 | Cooking Time:25 Minutes

Ingredients:
- 1 tbsp olive oil
- 4 French baguette slices, cubed
- 6 cherry tomatoes, halved
- 1 cucumber, cubed
- 1 sweet pepper, chopped
- 4 sweet onion thin slices
- ½ cup fresh basil leaves
- ¼ cup honey balsamic dressing

Directions:
1. Warm the oil in a pan over medium heat. Add the bread and salt and cook for 8-10 minutes, tossing frequently, or until nicely browned; let cool. Mix the cherry tomatoes, cucumber, pepper, onion, basil, and dressing and toss to coat in a large bowl. Top with bread cubes. Leave the salad to sit for about 20 minutes for the flavors to blend. Serve.

Nutrition:
- Info Per Serving: Calories: 525;Fat: 26g;Protein: 16g;Carbs: 61g.

Butternut Squash And Cauliflower Curry Soup

Servings:4 | Cooking Time: 4 Hours

Ingredients:
- 1 pound butternut squash, peeled and cut into 1-inch cubes
- 1 small head cauliflower, cut into 1-inch pieces
- 1 onion, sliced
- 2 cups unsweetened coconut milk
- 1 tablespoon curry powder
- ½ cup no-added-sugar apple juice
- 4 cups low-sodium vegetable soup
- 2 tablespoons coconut oil
- 1 teaspoon sea salt
- ¼ teaspoon freshly ground white pepper
- ¼ cup chopped fresh cilantro, divided

Directions:
1. Combine all the ingredients, except for the cilantro, in the slow cooker. Stir to mix well.
2. Cook on high heat for 4 hours or until the vegetables are ten-

der.
3. Pour the soup in a food processor, then pulse until creamy and smooth.
4. Pour the puréed soup in a large serving bowl and garnish with cilantro before serving.

Nutrition:
• Info Per Serving: Calories: 415;Fat: 30.8g;Protein: 10.1g;Carbs: 29.9g.

Turkish Chickpeas

Servings:4 | Cooking Time:40 Minutes

Ingredients:
• 3 tbsp olive oil
• 2 cans chickpeas
• 2 tsp smoked paprika
• ½ tsp ground coriander
• ½ tsp cumin
• ½ tsp dried oregano
• Salt and white pepper to taste

Directions:
1. Preheat the oven to 400° F. Spread the chickpeas onto a greased baking sheet. In a bowl, combine the olive oil, paprika, ground coriander, cumin, oregano, salt, and white pepper. Pour the mixture over the chickpeas and toss to combine. Bake for 30 minutes or until the chickpeas turn golden brown, shaking once or twice the baking sheet.

Nutrition:
• Info Per Serving: Calories: 308;Fat: 13g;Protein: 11g;Carbs: 40g.

Cheese & Pecan Salad With Orange Dressing

Servings:2 | Cooking Time:10 Minutes

Ingredients:
• Dressing
• 1 tbsp olive oil
• 2 tbsp orange juice
• 1 tbsp cider vinegar
• 1 tbsp honey
• Salt and black pepper to taste
• Salad
• 2 cups packed baby kale
• ½ small fennel bulb, sliced
• 3 tbsp toasted pecans, chopped
• 2 oz ricotta cheese, crumbled

Directions:
1. Mix the orange juice, olive oil, vinegar, and honey in a small bowl. Season with salt and pepper and set aside. Divide the baby kale, orange segments, fennel, pecans, and ricotta cheese evenly between two plates. Drizzle half of the dressing over each salad.

Nutrition:
• Info Per Serving: Calories: 502;Fat: 39g;Protein: 13g;Carbs: 31g.

Tri-Color Salad

Servings:4 | Cooking Time:5 Minutes

Ingredients:
• 2 tbsp olive oil
• 1 cucumber, sliced
• 1 lb tomatoes, sliced
• 1 red onion, chopped
• Salt and black pepper to taste
• 4 oz feta cheese, crumbled
• 2 tbsp parsley, chopped

Directions:
1. Combine tomatoes, onion, cucumber, salt, pepper, feta cheese, parsley, and olive oil in a bowl. Serve.

Nutrition:
• Info Per Serving: Calories: 200;Fat: 5g;Protein: 4g;Carbs: 9g.

Zesty Asparagus Salad

Servings:4 | Cooking Time:10 Minutes

Ingredients:
• 4 tbsp olive oil
• 1 lb asparagus
• 1 garlic clove, minced
• Salt and black pepper to taste
• 1 tbsp balsamic vinegar
• 1 tbsp lemon zest

Directions:
1. Roast the asparagus in a greased skillet over medium heat for 5-6 minutes, turning once. Season to taste. Toss with garlic, olive oil, lemon zest, and vinegar. Serve.

Nutrition:
• Info Per Serving: Calories: 148;Fat: 13.6g;Protein: 3g;Carbs: 5.7g.

Mushroom And Soba Noodle Soup

Servings:4 | Cooking Time: 10 Minutes

Ingredients:
• 2 tablespoons coconut oil
• 8 ounces shiitake mushrooms, stemmed and sliced thin
• 1 tablespoon minced fresh ginger
• 4 scallions, sliced thin
• 1 garlic clove, minced
• 1 teaspoon sea salt
• 4 cups low-sodium vegetable broth
• 3 cups water
• 4 ounces soba noodles
• 1 bunch spinach, blanched, rinsed and cut into strips
• 1 tablespoon freshly squeezed lemon juice

Directions:
1. Heat the coconut oil in a stockpot over medium heat until melted.
2. Add the mushrooms, ginger, scallions, garlic, and salt. Sauté for 5 minutes or until fragrant and the mushrooms are tender.
3. Pour in the vegetable broth and water. Bring to a boil, then add the soba noodles and cook for 5 minutes or until al dente.
4. Turn off the heat and add the spinach and lemon juice. Stir to mix well.
5. Pour the soup in a large bowl and serve immediately.

Nutrition:
• Info Per Serving: Calories: 254;Fat: 9.2g;Protein: 13.1g;Carbs: 33.9g.

Creamy Green Soup

Servings:4 | Cooking Time:20 Minutes

Ingredients:
• 1 tbsp olive oil
• 1 white onion, chopped
• ½ cup Greek yogurt
• 1 celery stalk, chopped
• 4 cups vegetable stock
• 2 cups green peas
• 2 tbsp mint leaves, chopped
• 1 cup spinach
• Salt and black pepper to taste

Directions:
1. Warm the olive oil in a pot over medium heat and cook onion and celery for 4 minutes. Add in stock, green peas, spinach, salt, and pepper and bring to a boil. Simmer for 4 minutes.

2. Take off the heat and let cool the soup for a few minutes. Blend the soup with an immersion blender until smooth. Apportion the soup among bowls and garnish with a swirl of Greek yogurt. Sprinkle with chopped mint and serve.

Nutrition:
- Info Per Serving: Calories: 300;Fat: 12g;Protein: 5g;Carbs: 28g.

Spinach & Bean Salad With Black Olives

Servings:4 | Cooking Time:10 Minutes

Ingredients:
- ½ cup canned cannellini beans, drained
- 2 tbsp olive oil
- 2 cups baby spinach
- 1 cup black olives, halved
- 2 tbsp sunflower seeds
- 1 tbsp Dijon mustard
- 2 tbsp balsamic vinegar

Directions:
1. Combine beans, olive oil, spinach, olives, sunflower seeds, mustard, and vinegar in a bowl. Serve immediately.

Nutrition:
- Info Per Serving: Calories: 290;Fat: 7g;Protein: 13g;Carbs: 11g.

Bell Pepper & Shrimp Salad With Avocado

Servings:4 | Cooking Time:10 Min + Cooling Time

Ingredients:
- 1 lb shrimp, peeled and deveined
- 2 tbsp olive oil
- 1 tbsp lemon juice
- 1 yellow bell pepper, sliced
- 1 Romano lettuce, torn
- 1 avocado, chopped
- Salt to taste
- 12 cherry tomatoes, halved

Directions:
1. Preheat grill pan over high heat. Drizzle the shrimp with some olive oil and arrange them on the preheated grill pan. Sear for 5 minutes on both sides until pink and cooked through. Let cool completely.
2. In a serving plate, arrange the lettuce, and top with bell pepper, shrimp, avocado, and cherry tomatoes. In a bowl, add the lemon juice, salt, and olive oil and whisk to combine. Drizzle the dressing over the salad and serve immediately.

Nutrition:
- Info Per Serving: Calories: 380;Fat: 24g;Protein: 25g;Carbs: 23g.

Herby Tzatziki Sauce

Servings:2 | Cooking Time:10 Minutes

Ingredients:
- 1 medium cucumber, peeled and grated
- Salt to taste
- ½ cup Greek yogurt
- ½ lemon, juiced
- 1 tbsp fresh mint, chopped
- 1 tbsp fresh dill, chopped
- 1 garlic clove, minced

Directions:
1. Place the grated cucumber in a dishtowel and squeeze out the excess moisture. Transfer to a large bowl and add the lemon juice, salt, yogurt, lemon juice, mint, garlic, and dill and whisk the ingredients to combine. Store in an airtight container in the refrigerator for up to 2-3 days.

Nutrition:
- Info Per Serving: Calories: 179;Fat: 2.2g;Protein: 2.9g;Carbs: 7g.

Spring Salad With Mustard Dressing

Servings:4 | Cooking Time:5 Minutes

Ingredients:
- 4 cups spring mix salad greens
- ¼ cup cherry tomatoes
- 1 tbsp fresh parsley, chopped
- 3 tbsp extra-virgin olive oil
- 1 tbsp wine vinegar
- 2 tbsp minced shallots
- ½ tsp yogurt
- ½ tsp Dijon mustard
- Salt and black pepper to taste

Directions:
1. Place parsley, vinegar, shallots, yogurt, mustard, salt, and pepper in a bowl and mix until smooth. Whisking constantly, slowly drizzle in oil until emulsified. In a bowl, combine the salad greens and tomatoes. Pour the dressing over and serve.

Nutrition:
- Info Per Serving: Calories: 64;Fat: 4.1g;Protein: 0.6g;Carbs: 2.2g.

Easy Roasted Cauliflower

Servings:2 | Cooking Time: 20 Minutes

Ingredients:
- ½ large head cauliflower, stemmed and broken into florets
- 1 tablespoon olive oil
- 2 tablespoons freshly squeezed lemon juice
- 2 tablespoons tahini
- 1 teaspoon harissa paste
- Pinch salt

Directions:
1. Preheat the oven to 400°F. Line a sheet pan with parchment paper.
2. Toss the cauliflower florets with the olive oil in a large bowl and transfer to the sheet pan.
3. Roast in the preheated oven for 15 minutes, flipping the cauliflower once or twice, or until it starts to become golden.
4. Meanwhile, in a separate bowl, combine the lemon juice, tahini, harissa, and salt and stir to mix well.
5. Remove the pan from the oven and toss the cauliflower with the lemon tahini sauce. Return to the oven and roast for another 5 minutes. Serve hot.

Nutrition:
- Info Per Serving: Calories: 205;Fat: 15.0g;Protein: 4.0g;Carbs: 15.0g.

Olive Tapenade Flatbread With Cheese

Servings:4 | Cooking Time:35 Min + Chilling Time

Ingredients:
- For the flatbread
- 2 tbsp olive oil
- 2 ½ tsp dry yeast
- 1 ½ cups all-purpose flour
- ¾ tsp salt
- ½ cup lukewarm water
- ¼ tsp sugar
- For the tapenade
- 2 roasted red pepper slices, chopped
- ¼ cup extra-virgin olive oil
- 1 cup green olives, chopped
- 10 black olives, chopped
- 1 tbsp capers
- 1 garlic clove, minced
- 1 tbsp chopped basil leaves
- 1 tbsp chopped fresh oregano
- ¼ cup goat cheese, crumbled

Directions:

1. Combine lukewarm water, sugar, and yeast in a bowl. Set aside covered for 5 minutes. Mix the flour and salt in a bowl. Pour in the yeast mixture and mix. Knead until you obtain a ball. Place the dough onto a floured surface and knead for 5 minutes until soft. Leave the dough into an oiled bowl, covered to rise until it has doubled in size, about 40 minutes.

2. Preheat oven to 400° F. Cut the dough into 4 balls and roll each one out to a ½ inch thickness. Bake for 5 minutes. In a blender, mix black olives, roasted pepper, green olives, capers, garlic, oregano, basil, and olive oil for 20 seconds until coarsely chopped. Spread the olive tapenade on the flatbreads and top with goat cheese to serve.

Nutrition:
- Info Per Serving: Calories: 366;Fat: 19g;Protein: 7.3g;Carbs: 42g.

Sun-Dried Tomato & Spinach Pasta Salad

Servings:4 | Cooking Time:45 Min + Cooling Time

Ingredients:
- 1 ½ cups farfalle
- 1 cup chopped baby spinach, rinsed and dried
- 8 sun-dried tomatoes, sliced
- 1 carrot, grated
- 2 scallions, thinly sliced
- 1 garlic clove, minced
- 1 dill pickle, diced
- ⅔ cup extra-virgin olive oil
- 1 tbsp red wine vinegar
- 1 tbsp lemon juice
- ½ cup Greek yogurt
- 1 tsp chopped fresh oregano
- Salt and black pepper to taste
- 1 cup feta cheese, crumbled

Directions:

1. Bring a large pot of salted water to a boil, add the farfalle, and cook for 7-9 minutes until al dente. Drain the pasta and set aside to cool. In a large bowl, combine spinach, sun-dried tomatoes, carrot, scallions, garlic, and pickle. Add pasta and toss to combine. In a medium bowl, whisk olive oil, vinegar, lemon juice, yogurt, oregano, pepper, and salt. Add dressing to pasta and toss to coat. Sprinkle with feta cheese and serve.

Nutrition:
- Info Per Serving: Calories: 239;Fat: 14g;Protein: 8g;Carbs: 20g.

Creamy Roasted Red Pepper Soup With Feta

Servings:6 | Cooking Time:30 Minutes

Ingredients:
- 8 roasted red peppers, chopped
- 2 roasted chili peppers, chopped
- 3 tbsp olive oil
- 2 shallots, chopped
- 4 garlic cloves, minced
- 2 tsp chopped fresh oregano
- 6 cups chicken broth
- Salt and black pepper to taste
- ¼ cup heavy cream
- 1 lemon, juiced
- ½ cup feta cheese, crumbled

Directions:

1. Puree all of the roasted peppers in your food processor until smooth. Warm the olive oil in a pot over medium heat and add the shallots and garlic. Cook until soft and translucent, about 5 minutes. Add the pepper mixture and oregano, followed by the broth. Bring to a boil on high heat and sprinkle with salt and pep-

per. Lower the heat to low and simmer for 15 minutes. Stir in the heavy cream and lemon juice. Ladle into individual bowls and garnish with feta. Serve immediately.

Nutrition:
- Info Per Serving: Calories: 223;Fat: 6g;Protein: 11g;Carbs: 31g.

Neapolitan Pasta & Fagioli

Servings:4 | Cooking Time:60 Minutes

Ingredients:
- ½ cup canned red kidney beans, drained
- 1 tbsp olive oil
- 1 carrot, diced
- 1 celery stalk, diced
- 1 onion, diced
- 1 large garlic clove, minced
- 2 tsp tomato paste
- 4 cups vegetable broth
- 1 cup kale, chopped
- ½ cup elbow macaroni
- 2 tbsp fresh basil, chopped
- Salt and black pepper to taste

Directions:

1. Warm the olive oil in a stockpot over medium heat. Add the carrot, celery, onion, and garlic and sauté for 5 minutes or until the vegetables start to turn golden. Stir in the tomato paste and cook for about 30 seconds. Add the vegetable broth, beans, and elbow macaroni and bring to a boil. Simmer for 8-10 minutes. Add the kale and cook for 4-5 minutes. Adjust the seasoning with salt and pepper. Serve topped with basil. Enjoy!

Nutrition:
- Info Per Serving: Calories: 215;Fat: 4.2g;Protein: 11g;Carbs: 36g.

Roasted Root Vegetable Soup

Servings:6 | Cooking Time: 35 Minutes

Ingredients:
- 2 parsnips, peeled and sliced
- 2 carrots, peeled and sliced
- 2 sweet potatoes, peeled and sliced
- 1 teaspoon chopped fresh rosemary
- 1 teaspoon chopped fresh thyme
- 1 teaspoon sea salt
- ½ teaspoon freshly ground black pepper
- 2 tablespoons extra-virgin olive oil
- 4 cups low-sodium vegetable soup
- ½ cup grated Parmesan cheese, for garnish (optional)

Directions:

1. Preheat the oven to 400°F. Line a baking sheet with aluminum foil.

2. Combine the parsnips, carrots, and sweet potatoes in a large bowl, then sprinkle with rosemary, thyme, salt, and pepper, and drizzle with olive oil. Toss to coat the vegetables well.

3. Arrange the vegetables on the baking sheet, then roast in the preheated oven for 30 minutes or until lightly browned and soft. Flip the vegetables halfway through the roasting.

4. Pour the roasted vegetables with vegetable broth in a food processor, then pulse until creamy and smooth.

5. Pour the puréed vegetables in a saucepan, then warm over low heat until heated through.

6. Spoon the soup in a large serving bowl, then scatter with Parmesan cheese. Serve immediately.

Nutrition:
- Info Per Serving: Calories: 192;Fat: 5.7g;Protein: 4.8g;Carbs: 31.5g.

Chicken & Mushroom Soup

Servings:4 | Cooking Time:30 Minutes

Ingredients:
- 2 tbsp olive oil
- 1 can diced tomatoes
- ½ lb chicken breasts, cubed
- 4 cups chicken broth
- 2 carrots, chopped
- 1 onion, chopped
- 1 red bell pepper, chopped
- 1 fennel bulb, chopped
- 2 garlic cloves, minced
- ½ tsp paprika
- 1 cup mushrooms, sliced
- 1 tbsp Italian seasoning
- Salt and black pepper to taste

Directions:
1. Warm the olive oil in a pot over medium heat. Place in chicken and brown for 5 minutes. Set aside.
2. Add in onion, carrots, bell pepper, and fennel, sauté for 5 minutes until softened. Throw in garlic and paprika and cook for 30 seconds. Mix in tomatoes, mushrooms, Italian seasoning, broth, chicken, salt, and pepper. Bring to a boil, then decrease the heat and simmer for 20 minutes. Serve.

Nutrition:
- Info Per Serving: Calories: 293;Fat: 14g;Protein: 24g;Carbs: 19g.

Baby Potato And Olive Salad

Servings:6 | Cooking Time: 20 Minutes

Ingredients:
- 2 pounds baby potatoes, cut into 1-inch cubes
- 1 tablespoon low-sodium olive brine
- 3 tablespoons freshly squeezed lemon juice
- ¼ teaspoon kosher salt
- 3 tablespoons extra-virgin olive oil
- ½ cup sliced olives
- 2 tablespoons torn fresh mint
- 1 cup sliced celery
- 2 tablespoons chopped fresh oregano

Directions:
1. Put the tomatoes in a saucepan, then pour in enough water to submerge the tomatoes about 1 inch.
2. Bring to a boil over high heat, then reduce the heat to medium-low. Simmer for 14 minutes or until the potatoes are soft.
3. Meanwhile, combine the olive brine, lemon juice, salt, and olive oil in a small bow. Stir to mix well.
4. Transfer the cooked tomatoes in a colander, then rinse with running cold water. Pat dry with paper towels.
5. Transfer the tomatoes in a large salad bowl, then drizzle with olive brine mixture. Spread with remaining ingredients and toss to combine well.
6. Serve immediately.

Nutrition:
- Info Per Serving: Calories: 220;Fat: 6.1g;Protein: 4.3g;Carbs: 39.2g.

Hearty Veggie Slaw

Servings:4 | Cooking Time: 0 Minutes

Ingredients:
- Salad:
- 2 large broccoli stems, peeled and shredded
- ½ celery root bulb, peeled and shredded
- ¼ cup chopped fresh Italian parsley
- 1 large beet, peeled and shredded
- 2 carrots, peeled and shredded
- 1 small red onion, sliced thin
- 2 zucchinis, shredded
- Dressing:
- 1 teaspoon Dijon mustard
- ½ cup apple cider vinegar
- 1 tablespoon raw honey
- 1 teaspoon sea salt
- ¼ teaspoon freshly ground black pepper
- 2 tablespoons extra-virgin olive oil
- Topping:
- ½ cup crumbled feta cheese

Directions:
1. Combine the ingredients for the salad in a large salad bowl, then toss to combine well.
2. Combine the ingredients for the dressing in a small bowl, then stir to mix well.
3. Dressing the salad, then serve with feta cheese on top.

Nutrition:
- Info Per Serving: Calories: 387;Fat: 30.2g;Protein: 8.1g;Carbs: 25.9g.

Turkish Leek & Potato Soup

Servings:5 | Cooking Time:30 Minutes

Ingredients:
- 2 tbsp butter
- 1 leek, chopped
- 2 cloves garlic, minced
- 4 cups vegetable broth
- 3 potatoes, peeled and cubed
- ½ cup sour cream
- 2 bay leaves
- Salt and black pepper to taste
- 2 tbsp fresh chives, chopped

Directions:
1. Melt butter on Sauté mode in your Instant Pot. Add in garlic and leeks and cook for 3 to 4 minutes, until soft. Stir in bay leaves, potatoes, and broth. Seal the lid and cook on High Pressure for 15 minutes. Release pressure quickly. Remove the bay leaves and discard. Transfer the soup to a food processor and puree it to obtain a smooth consistency. Season with salt and pepper. Top with chives and sour cream. Serve warm in soup bowls.

Nutrition:
- Info Per Serving: Calories: 287;Fat: 7g;Protein: 6g;Carbs: 51g.

Balsamic Potato Salad With Capers

Servings:2 | Cooking Time:30 Minutes

Ingredients:
- 2 tbsp olive oil
- 3 potatoes, peeled and cubed
- 2 tbsp capers
- 1 red onion, chopped
- 1 tbsp balsamic vinegar
- Salt and black pepper to taste

Directions:
1. Place potatoes in a pot over medium heat with enough water and bring to a boil; cook for 20 minutes. Drain and remove to a bowl. Stir in red onion, olive oil, capers, vinegar, salt, and pepper. Serve chilled.

Nutrition:
- Info Per Serving: Calories: 210;Fat: 6g;Protein: 5g;Carbs: 12g.

Greek-Style Pasta Salad

Servings:4 | Cooking Time:10 Minutes

Ingredients:
- 2 tbsp olive oil
- 16 oz fusilli pasta
- 1 yellow bell pepper, cubed
- 1 green bell pepper, cubed
- Salt to taste
- 3 tomatoes, cubed
- 1 red onion, sliced
- 2 cups feta cheese, crumbled
- ¼ cup lemon juice
- 1 tbsp lemon zest, grated
- 1 cucumber, cubed
- 1 cup Kalamata olives, sliced

Directions:
1. Cook the fusilli pasta in boiling salted water until "al dente", 8-10 minutes. Drain and set aside to cool. In a bowl, whisk together olive oil, lemon zest, lemon juice, and salt. Add in bell peppers, tomatoes, onion, feta cheese, cucumber, olives, and pasta and toss to combine. Serve.

Nutrition:
- Info Per Serving: Calories: 420;Fat: 18g;Protein: 15g;Carbs: 50g.

Greens, Fennel, And Pear Soup With Cashews

Servings:4 | Cooking Time: 15 Minutes

Ingredients:
- 2 tablespoons olive oil
- 1 fennel bulb, cut into ¼-inch-thick slices
- 2 leeks, white part only, sliced
- 2 pears, peeled, cored, and cut into ½-inch cubes
- 1 teaspoon sea salt
- ¼ teaspoon freshly ground black pepper
- ½ cup cashews
- 2 cups packed blanched spinach
- 3 cups low-sodium vegetable soup

Directions:
1. Heat the olive oil in a stockpot over high heat until shimmering.
2. Add the fennel and leeks, then sauté for 5 minutes or until tender.
3. Add the pears and sprinkle with salt and pepper, then sauté for another 3 minutes or until the pears are soft.
4. Add the cashews, spinach, and vegetable soup. Bring to a boil. Reduce the heat to low. Cover and simmer for 5 minutes.
5. Pour the soup in a food processor, then pulse until creamy and smooth.

6. Pour the soup back to the pot and heat over low heat until heated through.
7. Transfer the soup to a large serving bowl and serve immediately.

Nutrition:
- Info Per Serving: Calories: 266;Fat: 15.1g;Protein: 5.2g;Carbs: 32.9g.

Authentic Marinara Sauce

Servings:6 | Cooking Time:46 Minutes

Ingredients:
- 2 cans crushed tomatoes with their juices
- 1 tsp dried oregano
- 2 tbsp + ¼ cup olive oil
- 2 tbsp butter
- 1 small onion, diced
- 1 red bell pepper, chopped
- 4 garlic cloves, minced
- Salt and black pepper to taste
- ½ cup thinly sliced basil
- 2 tbsp chopped rosemary
- 1 tsp red pepper flakes

Directions:
1. Warm 2 tablespoons olive oil and butter in a large skillet over medium heat. Add the onion, garlic, and red pepper and sauté for about 5 minutes until tender. Season with salt and pepper. Reduce the heat to low and add the tomatoes and their juices, remaining olive oil, oregano, half of the basil, rosemary, and red pepper flakes. Bring to a simmer and cover. Cook for 50-60 minutes. Blitz the sauce with an immersion blender and sprinkle with the remaining basil.

Nutrition:
- Info Per Serving: Calories: 265;Fat: 19g;Protein: 4.1g;Carbs: 18g.

Party Summer Salad

Servings:4 | Cooking Time:10 Minutes

Ingredients:
- ½ cup extra virgin olive oil
- 2 cucumbers, sliced
- 2 mixed bell peppers, sliced
- 2 tomatoes, sliced
- 2 green onions, thinly sliced
- 2 gem lettuces, sliced
- 1 cup arugula
- 2 tbsp parsley, chopped
- Salt to taste
- 1 cup feta cheese, crumbled
- 3 tbsp lemon juice

Directions:
1. In a bowl, mix the cucumbers, bell peppers, green onions, gem lettuce, and arugula. In a small bowl, whisk the olive oil, lemon juice, and salt. Pour over the salad and toss to coat. Scatter the feta over and top with tomato and parsley.

Nutrition:
- Info Per Serving: Calories: 398;Fat: 34g;Protein: 19g;Carbs: 20g.

Mushroom & Parmesan Risotto

Servings:4 | Cooking Time:25 Minutes

Ingredients:
- 1 ½ cups mixed mushrooms, sliced
- 3 tbsp olive oil
- 1 shallot, chopped
- 1 cup Arborio rice
- 4 cups vegetable stock
- 2 tbsp dry white wine
- 1 cup grated Parmesan cheese
- 2 tbsp butter
- 2 tbsp fresh parsley, chopped

Directions:
1. Pour the vegetable stock into a small saucepan over low heat and bring to a simmer; then turn the heat off.
2. Warm the olive oil in a large saucepan over medium heat. Sauté the mushrooms and shallot for 6 minutes until tender. Stir in rice for 3 minutes until opaque. Pour in the wine and stir. Gradually add the hot stock to the rice mixture, about 1 ladleful at a time, stirring until the liquid is absorbed. Remove the saucepan from the heat, stir in butter and 3 tbsp of Parmesan cheese. Cover and leave to rest for 5 minutes. Scatter the remaining cheese and parsley over the risotto and serve in bowls.

Nutrition:
- Info Per Serving: Calories: 354;Fat: 29g;Protein: 11g;Carbs: 22g.

Fruit Salad With Sesame Seeds & Nuts

Servings:4 | Cooking Time:15 Minutes

Ingredients:
- ¼ cup extra-virgin olive oil
- 2 apples, peeled and sliced
- 1 tbsp lemon juice
- 1 orange, peeled and diced
- ½ cup sliced strawberries
- ½ cup shredded coleslaw mix
- ½ cup walnut halves
- ¼ cup slivered almonds
- ¼ cup balsamic vinegar
- 2 tbsp sesame seeds
- Salt and black pepper to taste

Directions:
1. Place the apples and lemon juice in a bowl and toss to prevent browning. Add the orange, strawberries, coleslaw mix, walnuts, and almonds and toss well to mix. In a bowl, whisk together the balsamic vinegar and olive oil and season with salt and pepper. Pour the dressing over the salad and toss to coat. Top with sesame seeds and serve.

Nutrition:
- Info Per Serving: Calories: 299;Fat: 17g;Protein: 8g;Carbs: 44g.

Carrot & Tomato Salad With Cilantro

Servings:4 | Cooking Time:10 Minutes

Ingredients:
- 2 tbsp olive oil
- 4 tomatoes, chopped
- 1 carrot, grated
- ¼ cup lime juice
- 1 garlic clove, minced
- Salt and black pepper to taste
- 1 lettuce head, chopped
- 2 green onions, chopped
- ½ cup cilantro, chopped

Directions:
1. Toss lime juice, garlic, salt, pepper, olive oil, carrot, lettuce, onions, tomatoes, cilantro in a bowl. Serve cold.

Nutrition:
- Info Per Serving: Calories: 120;Fat: 4g;Protein: 3g;Carbs: 4g.

Tasty Cucumber & Couscous Salad

Servings:4 | Cooking Time:30 Minutes

Ingredients:
- ¼ cup olive oil
- 2 tbsp balsamic vinegar
- 1 cup couscous
- 1 cucumber, sliced
- Salt and black pepper to taste
- 2 tbsp lemon juice

Directions:
1. Place couscous in a bowl with 3 cups of hot water and let sit for 10 minutes. Fluff with a fork and remove to a bowl. Stir in cucumber, salt, pepper, lemon juice, vinegar, and olive oil. Serve immediately.

Nutrition:
- Info Per Serving: Calories: 180;Fat: 6g;Protein: 5g;Carbs: 12g.

Cherry & Pine Nut Couscous

Servings:6 | Cooking Time:10 Minutes

Ingredients:
- 2 tbsp olive oil
- 3 cups hot water
- 1 cup couscous
- ½ cup pine nuts, roasted
- ½ cup dry cherries, chopped
- ½ cup parsley, chopped
- Salt and black pepper to taste
- 1 tbsp lime juice

Directions:
1. Place couscous and hot water in a bowl and let sit for 10 minutes. Fluff with a fork and remove to a bowl. Stir in pine nuts, cherries, parsley, salt, pepper, lime juice, and olive oil.

Nutrition:
- Info Per Serving: Calories: 220;Fat: 8g;Protein: 6g;Carbs: 9g.

Effortless Bell Pepper Salad

Servings:4 | Cooking Time:10 Minutes

Ingredients:
- 2 green bell peppers, cut into thick strips
- 2 red bell peppers, cut into thick strips
- 2 tbsp olive oil
- ½ cup feta cheese, crumbled
- Salt and black pepper to taste

Directions:
1. Combine bell peppers, olive oil, feta cheese, salt, and pepper in a bowl. Serve immediately.

Nutrition:
- Info Per Serving: Calories: 210;Fat: 6g;Protein: 4g;Carbs: 5g.

Simple Mushroom Barley Soup

Servings:6 | Cooking Time: 20 To 23 Minutes

Ingredients:
- 2 tablespoons extra-virgin olive oil
- 1 cup chopped carrots
- 1 cup chopped onion
- 5½ cups chopped mushrooms
- 6 cups no-salt-added vegetable broth
- 1 cup uncooked pearled barley
- ¼ cup red wine
- 2 tablespoons tomato paste
- 4 sprigs fresh thyme or ½ teaspoon dried thyme
- 1 dried bay leaf

- 6 tablespoons grated Parmesan cheese

Directions:
1. In a large stockpot over medium heat, heat the oil. Add the onion and carrots and cook for 5 minutes, stirring frequently. Turn up the heat to medium-high and add the mushrooms. Cook for 3 minutes, stirring frequently.
2. Add the broth, barley, wine, tomato paste, thyme, and bay leaf. Stir, cover, and bring the soup to a boil. Once it's boiling, stir a few times, reduce the heat to medium-low, cover, and cook for another 12 to 15 minutes, until the barley is cooked through.
3. Remove the bay leaf and serve the soup in bowls with 1 tablespoon of cheese sprinkled on top of each.

Nutrition:
- Info Per Serving: Calories: 195;Fat: 4.0g;Protein: 7.0g;Carbs: 34.0g.

Mushroom & Spinach Orzo Soup
Servings:4 | Cooking Time:20 Minutes

Ingredients:
- 2 tbsp butter
- 3 cups spinach
- ½ cup orzo
- 4 cups chicken broth
- 1 cup feta cheese, crumbled
- Salt and black pepper to taste
- ½ tsp dried oregano
- 1 onion, chopped
- 2 garlic cloves, minced
- 1 cup mushrooms, sliced

Directions:
1. Melt butter in a pot over medium heat and sauté onion, garlic, and mushrooms for 5 minutes until tender. Add in chicken broth, orzo, salt, pepper, and oregano. Bring to a boil and reduce the heat to a low. Continue simmering for 10 minutes, partially covered. Stir in spinach and continue to cook until the spinach wilts, about 3-4 minutes. Ladle into individual bowls and serve garnished with feta cheese.

Nutrition:
- Info Per Serving: Calories: 370;Fat: 11g;Protein: 23g;Carbs: 44g.

Fuit & Endive Salad With Gorgonzola
Servings:4 | Cooking Time:10 Minutes

Ingredients:
- 2 tbsp gorgonzola cheese, crumbled
- ¼ cup extra-virgin olive oil
- 4 apples, peeled and sliced
- 2 kiwis, peeled and chopped
- 1 tbsp lemon juice
- ½ cup curly endive, chopped
- ½ cup sliced strawberries
- ½ cup walnuts, chopped
- ¼ cup balsamic vinegar
- 2 tbsp sesame seeds
- Salt and black pepper to taste

Directions:
1. Combine apples with lemon juice in a bowl. Stir in strawberries, kiwis, endive, gorgonzola cheese, and walnuts.In another bowl, mix balsamic vinegar, olive oil, salt, and pepper. Pour over the salad and toss to combine. Share into bowls and top with sesame seeds. Serve.

Nutrition:
- Info Per Serving: Calories: 354;Fat: 16g;Protein: 3g;Carbs: 51g.

Baby Spinach & Apple Salad With Walnuts
Servings:4 | Cooking Time:5 Minutes

Ingredients:
- 2 oz sharp white cheddar cheese, cubed
- 3 tbsp olive oil
- 8 cups baby spinach
- 1 Granny Smith apple, diced
- 1 medium red apple, diced
- ½ cup toasted pecans
- 1 tbsp apple cider vinegar

Directions:
1. Toss the spinach, apples, pecans, and cubed cheese together. Lightly drizzle olive oil and vinegar over the top and serve.

Nutrition:
- Info Per Serving: Calories: 138;Fat: 12.8g;Protein: 1g;Carbs: 7g.

Paprika Ham & Green Lentil Soup
Servings:4 | Cooking Time:30 Minutes

Ingredients:
- 2 tbsp olive oil
- ½ lb ham, cubed
- 1 onion, chopped
- 2 tsp parsley, dried
- 1 potato, chopped
- 3 garlic cloves, chopped
- Salt and black pepper to taste
- 1 carrot, chopped
- ½ tsp paprika
- ½ cup green lentils, rinsed
- 4 cups vegetable stock
- 3 tbsp tomato paste
- 2 tomatoes, chopped

Directions:
1. Warm the olive oil in a pot over medium heat and cook ham, onion, carrot, and garlic for 4 minutes. Stir in tomato paste, paprika, and tomatoes for 2-3 minutes. Pour in lentils, vegetable stock, and potato and bring to a boil. Cook for 18-20 minutes. Adjust the seasoning with salt and pepper and sprinkle with parsley. Serve warm.

Nutrition:
- Info Per Serving: Calories: 270;Fat: 12g;Protein: 15g;Carbs: 25g.

Summer Gazpacho
Servings:6 | Cooking Time:15 Minutes

Ingredients:
- ⅓ cup extra-virgin olive oil
- ½ cup of water
- 2 bread slices, torn
- 2 lb ripe tomatoes, seeded
- 1 cucumber, chopped
- 1 clove garlic, finely chopped
- ½ red onion, diced
- 2 tbsp red wine vinegar
- 1 tbsp fresh thyme, chopped
- Salt to taste

Directions:
1. Put the bread in 1 cup of water mixed with 1 tbsp of vinegar and salt to soak for 5 minutes. Then, blend the soaked bread, tomatoes, cucumber, garlic, red onion, olive oil, vinegar, thyme, and salt in your food processor until completely smooth. Pour the soup into a glass container and store in the fridge until chilled. Serve drizzled with olive oil.

Nutrition:
- Info Per Serving: Calories: 163;Fat: 13g;Protein: 2g;Carbs: 12.4g.

Greek Chicken, Tomato, And Olive Salad

Servings:2 | Cooking Time: 0 Minutes

Ingredients:
• Salad:
• 2 grilled boneless, skinless chicken breasts, sliced
• 10 cherry tomatoes, halved
• 8 pitted Kalamata olives, halved
• ½ cup thinly sliced red onion
• Dressing:
• ¼ cup balsamic vinegar
• 1 teaspoon freshly squeezed lemon juice
• ¼ teaspoon sea salt
• ¼ teaspoon freshly ground black pepper
• 2 teaspoons extra-virgin olive oil
• For Serving:
• 2 cups roughly chopped romaine lettuce
• ½ cup crumbled feta cheese

Directions:
1. Combine the ingredients for the salad in a large bowl. Toss to combine well.
2. Combine the ingredients for the dressing in a small bowl. Stir to mix well.
3. Pour the dressing the bowl of salad, then toss to coat well. Wrap the bowl in plastic and refrigerate for at least 2 hours.
4. Remove the bowl from the refrigerator. Spread the lettuce on a large plate, then top with marinated salad. Scatter the salad with feta cheese and serve immediately.

Nutrition:
• Info Per Serving: Calories: 328;Fat: 16.9g;Protein: 27.6g;Carbs: 15.9g.

Garbanzo & Arugula Salad With Blue Cheese

Servings:4 | Cooking Time:10 Minutes

Ingredients:
• 15 oz canned garbanzo beans, drained
• ½ cup Gorgonzola cheese, crumbled
• 3 tbsp olive oil
• 1 cucumber, cubed
• 3 oz black olives, sliced
• 1 Roma tomato, slivered
• ¼ cup red onion, chopped
• 5 cups arugula
• Salt to taste
• 1 tbsp lemon juice
• 2 tbsp parsley, chopped

Directions:
1. Place the arugula in a salad bowl. Add in garbanzo beans, cucumber, olives, tomato, and onion and mix to combine. In another small bowl, whisk the lemon juice, olive oil, and salt. Drizzle the dressing over the salad and sprinkle with gorgonzola cheese and parsley to serve.

Nutrition:
• Info Per Serving: Calories: 280;Fat: 17g;Protein: 10g;Carbs: 25g.

Home-Style Harissa Paste

Servings:4 | Cooking Time:10 Minutes

Ingredients:
• 1 tbsp ground dried Aleppo pepper
• 1 tbsp lemon juice
• 2 tbsp tomato paste
• 6 tbsp extra-virgin olive oil
• 6 garlic cloves, minced
• 2 tbsp paprika
• 1 tbsp ground coriander
• 1 tsp ground cumin
• ¾ tsp caraway seeds
• ½ tsp salt

Directions:
1. Microwave the oil, garlic, paprika, coriander, Aleppo pepper, cumin, caraway seeds, and salt for about 1 minute until bubbling and very fragrant, stirring halfway through microwaving. Let cool at room temperature. Store in an airtight container in the refrigerator for up to 2-3 days.

Nutrition:
• Info Per Serving: Calories: 162;Fat: 8.4g;Protein: 4.7g;Carbs: 9g.

Yogurt Cucumber Salad

Servings:4 | Cooking Time:10 Min + Chilling Time

Ingredients:
• 1 tbsp olive oil
• 2 tbsp walnuts, ground
• 1 cup Greek yogurt
• 2 garlic cloves, minced
• Salt and white pepper to taste
• 1 tbsp wine vinegar
• 1 tbsp dill, chopped
• 3 medium cucumbers, sliced
• 1 tbsp chives, chopped

Directions:
1. Combine cucumbers, walnuts, garlic, salt, pepper, vinegar, yogurt, dill, olive oil, and chives in a bowl. Let sit in the fridge for 1 hour. Serve.

Nutrition:
• Info Per Serving: Calories: 220;Fat: 13g;Protein: 4g;Carbs: 9g.

Pecorino Basil-Tomato Soup

Servings:4 | Cooking Time:45 Minutes

Ingredients:
• ½ cup Pecorino cheese, grated
• 2 tbsp olive oil
• 2 lb tomatoes, halved
• 2 garlic cloves, minced
• 1 onion, chopped
• Salt and black pepper to taste
• 4 cups chicken stock
• ½ tsp red pepper flakes
• ½ cup basil, chopped

Directions:
1. Preheat the oven to 380° F. Place the tomatoes in a baking tray, drizzle with olive oil, and season with salt and pepper. Roast in the oven for 20 minutes. When ready, peel them
2. Warm the remaining olive oil in a pot over medium heat and sauté onion for 3 minutes. Put in roasted tomatoes, garlic, chicken stock, and red pepper flakes and bring to a boil. Simmer for 15 minutes. Using an immersion blender, purée the soup and stir in Pecorino cheese. Top with basil.

Nutrition:
• Info Per Serving: Calories: 240;Fat: 11g;Protein: 8g;Carbs: 16g.

Uncle's Pork Salad

Servings:4 | Cooking Time:20 Minutes

Ingredients:
- 2 tbsp olive oil
- 1 lb pork loin, cut into strips
- 3 scallions, chopped
- 1 cucumber, sliced
- 1 red chili, sliced
- 1 tbsp parsley, chopped
- ¼ cup pine nuts
- Salt and black pepper to taste
- 1 lime, juiced
- 1 garlic clove, minced

Directions:
1. Warm the olive oil in a skillet over medium heat and brown pork for 10 minutes on all sides. Remove to a bowl. Stir in scallions, cucumber, red chili, parsley, pine nuts, salt, pepper, lime juice, and garlic. Serve immediately.

Nutrition:
- Info Per Serving: Calories: 280;Fat: 14g;Protein: 19g;Carbs: 16g.

Beef Stew With Green Peas

Servings:4 | Cooking Time:40 Minutes

Ingredients:
- 1 lb beef, tender cuts, boneless, cut into bits
- 2 tbsp olive oil
- 2 cups green peas
- 1 onion, diced
- 2 garlic cloves, minced
- 1 tomato, diced
- 3 cups beef broth
- ½ cup tomato paste
- 1 tsp cayenne pepper
- 1 tbsp flour
- Salt to taste
- ½ tsp dried thyme
- ½ tsp red pepper flakes

Directions:
1. Preheat your Instant Pot on Sauté mode and add warm the olive oil. Sear the meat for 6-8 minutes, stirring often. Add the onion, garlic, and salt and sauté for 3 more minutes. Stir in flour, thyme, and cayenne pepper for 1-2 minutes. Add in the tomato and tomato paste, stir, and pour in the stock.
2. Seal the lid, press Manual/Pressure Cook and cook for 20 minutes on High Pressure. When done, release the steam naturally for 10 minutes. Stir in the green peas, press Sauté, and cook for 4-5 minutes. Sprinkle with red pepper flakes.

Nutrition:
- Info Per Serving: Calories: 557;Fat: 16g;Protein: 78g;Carbs: 22g.

Chili Lentil Soup

Servings:4 | Cooking Time:30 Minutes

Ingredients:
- 2 tbsp olive oil
- 1 cup lentils, rinsed
- 1 onion, chopped
- 2 carrots, chopped
- 1 potato, cubed
- 1 tomato, chopped
- 4 garlic cloves, minced
- 4 cups vegetable broth
- ½ tsp chili powder
- Salt and black pepper to taste
- 2 tbsp fresh parsley, chopped

Directions:
1. Warm the olive oil in a pot over medium heat. Add in onion, garlic, and carrots and sauté for 5-6 minutes until tender. Mix in lentils, broth, salt, pepper, chili powder, potato, and tomato. Bring to a boil, lower the heat and simmer for 15-18 minutes, stirring often. Top with parsley and serve.

Nutrition:
- Info Per Serving: Calories: 331;Fat: 9g;Protein: 19g;Carbs: 44.3g.

Sumptuous Greek Vegetable Salad

Servings:6 | Cooking Time: 0 Minutes

Ingredients:
- Salad:
- 1 can chickpeas, drained and rinsed
- 1 can artichoke hearts, drained and halved
- 1 head Bibb lettuce, chopped
- 1 cucumber, peeled deseeded, and chopped
- 1½ cups grape tomatoes, halved
- ¼ cup chopped basil leaves
- ½ cup sliced black olives
- ½ cup cubed feta cheese
- Dressing:
- 1 tablespoon freshly squeezed lemon juice (from about ½ small lemon)
- ¼ teaspoon freshly ground black pepper
- 1 tablespoon chopped fresh oregano
- 2 tablespoons extra-virgin olive oil
- 1 tablespoon red wine vinegar
- 1 teaspoon honey

Directions:
1. Combine the ingredients for the salad in a large salad bowl, then toss to combine well.
2. Combine the ingredients for the dressing in a small bowl, then stir to mix well.
3. Dressing the salad and serve immediately.

Nutrition:
- Info Per Serving: Calories: 165;Fat: 8.1g;Protein: 7.2g;Carbs: 17.9g.

Divine Fennel & Zucchini Salad

Servings:4 | Cooking Time:10 Minutes

Ingredients:
- 2 tbsp olive oil
- 1 cup fennel bulb, sliced
- 1 red onion, sliced
- 2 zucchinis, cut into ribbons
- Salt and black pepper to taste
- 2 tsp white wine vinegar
- 1 tsp lemon juice

Directions:
1. In a large bowl, combine fennel, zucchini, red onion, salt, pepper, olive oil, vinegar, and lemon juice and toss to coat.

Nutrition:
- Info Per Serving: Calories: 200;Fat: 4g;Protein: 3g;Carbs: 4g.

Creamy Tomato Hummus Soup

Servings:4 | Cooking Time:10 Minutes

Ingredients:
- 1 can diced tomatoes
- 1 cup traditional hummus
- 4 cups chicken stock
- ¼ cup basil leaves, sliced
- 1 cup garlic croutons

Directions:

1. Place the tomatoes, hummus, and chicken stock in your blender and blend until smooth. Pour the mixture into a saucepan over medium heat and bring it to a boil. Pour the soup into bowls. Sprinkle with basil and serve with croutons.

Nutrition:
• Info Per Serving: Calories: 148;Fat: 6.2g;Protein: 5g;Carbs: 18.8g.

Red Cabbage Coleslaw With Almonds
Servings:4 | Cooking Time:10 Minutes

Ingredients:
• 2 tbsp olive oil
• 1 head red cabbage, shredded
• 2 tbsp cilantro, chopped
• ½ cup almonds, chopped
• 1 tomato, cubed
• Salt and black pepper to taste
• 1 tbsp white wine vinegar

Directions:
1. Mix red cabbage, cilantro, almonds, olive oil, tomato, salt, pepper, and vinegar in a bowl. Serve cold.

Nutrition:
• Info Per Serving: Calories: 220;Fat: 7g;Protein: 9g;Carbs: 7g.

Mackerel & Radish Salad
Servings:4 | Cooking Time:5 Minutes

Ingredients:
• 3 tbsp olive oil
• 4 oz smoked mackerel, flaked
• 10 radishes, sliced
• 5 oz baby arugula
• 1 cup corn
• 2 tbsp lemon juice
• Sea salt to taste
• 2 tbsp fresh parsley, chopped

Directions:
1. Place the arugula on a serving plate. Top with corn, mackerel, and radishes.Mix olive oil, lemon juice, and salt in a bowl and pour the dressing over the salad. Top with parsley.

Nutrition:
• Info Per Serving: Calories: 300;Fat: 19g;Protein: 19g;Carbs: 23g.

Bell Pepper & Lentil Salad With Tomatoes
Servings:4 | Cooking Time:10 Minutes

Ingredients:
• 2 tomatoes, chopped
• 1 green bell pepper, chopped
• 14 oz canned lentils, drained
• 2 spring onions, chopped
• 1 red bell pepper, chopped
• 2 tbsp cilantro, chopped
• 2 tsp balsamic vinegar

Directions:
1. Mix lentils, spring onions, tomatoes, bell peppers, cilantro, and vinegar in a bowl. Serve immediately.

Nutrition:
• Info Per Serving: Calories: 210;Fat: 3g;Protein: 7g;Carbs: 12g.

Spinach & Bean Salad With Goat Cheese
Servings:4 | Cooking Time:35 Minutes

Ingredients:
• 4 tbsp olive oil
• 1 garlic clove, minced
• ½ tsp cumin
• ½ tsp chili flakes
• 2 tbsp red wine vinegar
• 1 tbsp fresh lemon juice
• 1 tbsp fresh dill
• Salt to taste
• 1 can black beans
• 2 cups fresh baby spinach
• ¼ lb goat cheese, crumbled
• ½ cup spring onions, sliced
• 1 jalapeño pepper, chopped
• 2 bell peppers, chopped

Directions:
1. In a small bowl, combine the garlic, cumin, chili flakes, olive oil, vinegar, lemon juice, dill, and salt. Put in the fridge.
2. Mix the black beans, baby spinach, spring onions, jalapeño pepper, and bell pepper in another bowl. Remove the dressing from the fridge and pour over the salad; toss to coat. Top with the goat cheese and serve.

Nutrition:
• Info Per Serving: Calories: 633;Fat: 25g;Protein: 32g;Carbs: 72g.

Andalusian Lentil Soup
Servings:4 | Cooking Time:25 Minutes

Ingredients:
• 2 tbsp olive oil
• 3 cups vegetable broth
• 1 cup tomato sauce
• 1 onion, chopped
• 1 cup dry red lentils
• ½ cup prepared salsa verde
• 2 garlic cloves, minced
• 1 tbsp smoked paprika
• 2 tsp ground cumin
• ¼ tsp cayenne pepper
• Salt and black pepper to taste
• 2 tbsp crushed tortilla chips

Directions:
1. Warm the olive oil on Sauté in your Instant Pot. Stir in garlic and onion and cook for 5 minutes until golden brown. Add in tomato sauce, broth, salsa verde, cumin, cayenne pepper, lentils, paprika, salt, and pepper. Seal the lid and cook for 20 minutes on High Pressure. Release pressure naturally for 10 minutes. Top with crushed tortilla chips and serve.

Nutrition:
• Info Per Serving: Calories: 324;Fat: 10g;Protein: 14g;Carbs: 47g.

White Bean & Potato Soup
Servings:4 | Cooking Time:50 Minutes

Ingredients:
• 2 tbsp olive oil
• 2 shallots, chopped
• 1 potato, chopped
• 5 celery sticks, chopped
• 1 carrot, chopped
• ½ tsp dried oregano
• 1 bay leaf
• 30 oz canned white beans
• 2 tbsp tomato paste

- 4 cups chicken stock

Directions:

1. Warm the olive oil in a pot over medium heat and cook shallots, celery, carrot, bay leaf, and oregano for 5 minutes. Stir in beans, tomato paste, potato, and chicken stock and bring to a boil. Cook for 20 minutes. Remove the bay leaf. Serve.

Nutrition:

- Info Per Serving: Calories: 280;Fat: 17g;Protein: 8g;Carbs: 16g.

Classic Zuppa Toscana

Servings:4 | Cooking Time:25 Minutes

Ingredients:

- 2 tbsp olive oil
- 1 yellow onion, chopped
- 4 garlic cloves, minced
- 1 celery stalk, chopped
- 1 carrot, chopped
- 15 oz canned tomatoes, diced
- 1 zucchini, chopped
- 6 cups vegetable stock
- 2 tbsp tomato paste
- 15 oz canned white beans
- 5 oz Tuscan kale
- 1 tbsp basil, chopped
- Salt and black pepper to taste

Directions:

1. Warm the olive oil in a pot over medium heat. Cook garlic and onion for 3 minutes. Stir in celery, carrot, tomatoes, zucchini, stock, tomato paste, white beans, kale, salt, and pepper and bring to a simmer. Cook for 10 minutes. Top with basil.

Nutrition:

- Info Per Serving: Calories: 480;Fat: 9g;Protein: 28g;Carbs: 77g.

Egg & Potato Salad

Servings:6 | Cooking Time:25 Minutes

Ingredients:

- ¼ cup olive oil
- 2 lb potatoes, peeled and sliced
- 4 spring onions, chopped
- ½ cup fennel, sliced
- 2 eggs
- 2 tbsp fresh lemon juice
- 1 tbsp capers
- ½ tbsp Dijon mustard
- Salt and black pepper to taste

Directions:

1. Add the eggs to a pot and cover with salted water. Bring to a boil and turn the heat off. Let sit covered in hot water for 10 minutes, then cool before peeling and cutting into slices. In another pot, place the potatoes and cover them with enough water. Bring to a boil, then lower the heat and simmer for 8-10 minutes until tender.

2. In a serving bowl, whisk the olive oil with lemon juice, mustard, salt, and pepper. Add in the potatoes, eggs, capers, spring onions, and fennel slices and toss to combine. Serve.

Nutrition:

- Info Per Serving: Calories: 183;Fat: 10.6g;Protein: 4g;Carbs: 20g.

Cucumber Gazpacho

Servings:4 | Cooking Time: 0 Minutes

Ingredients:

- 2 cucumbers, peeled, deseeded, and cut into chunks
- ½ cup mint, finely chopped
- 2 cups plain Greek yogurt
- 2 garlic cloves, minced
- 2 cups low-sodium vegetable soup
- 1 tablespoon no-salt-added tomato paste
- 3 teaspoons fresh dill
- Sea salt and freshly ground pepper, to taste

Directions:

1. Put the cucumber, mint, yogurt, and garlic in a food processor, then pulse until creamy and smooth.

2. Transfer the puréed mixture in a large serving bowl, then add the vegetable soup, tomato paste, dill, salt, and ground black pepper. Stir to mix well.

3. Keep the soup in the refrigerator for at least 2 hours, then serve chilled.

Nutrition:

- Info Per Serving: Calories: 133;Fat: 1.5g;Protein: 14.2g;Carbs: 16.5g.

Vegetable Fagioli Soup

Servings:2 | Cooking Time: 60 Minutes

Ingredients:

- 1 tablespoon olive oil
- 2 medium carrots, diced
- 2 medium celery stalks, diced
- ½ medium onion, diced
- 1 large garlic clove, minced
- 3 tablespoons tomato paste
- 4 cups low-sodium vegetable broth
- 1 cup packed kale, stemmed and chopped
- 1 can red kidney beans, drained and rinsed
- 1 can cannellini beans, drained and rinsed
- ½ cup chopped fresh basil
- Salt and freshly ground black pepper, to taste

Directions:

1. Heat the olive oil in a stockpot over medium-high heat. Add the carrots, celery, onion, and garlic and sauté for 10 minutes, or until the vegetables start to turn golden.

2. Stir in the tomato paste and cook for about 30 seconds.

3. Add the vegetable broth and bring the soup to a boil. Cover, and reduce the heat to low. Cook the soup for 45 minutes, or until the carrots are tender.

4. Using an immersion blender, purée the soup so that it's partly smooth, but with some chunks of vegetables.

5. Add the kale, beans, and basil. Season with salt and pepper to taste, then serve.

Nutrition:

- Info Per Serving: Calories: 217;Fat: 4.2g;Protein: 10.0g;Carbs: 36.2g.

Pepper & Cheese Stuffed Tomatoes

Servings:2 | Cooking Time:35 Minutes

Ingredients:

- ½ lb mixed bell peppers, chopped
- 1 tbsp olive oil
- 4 tomatoes
- 2 garlic cloves, minced
- ½ cup diced onion
- 1 tbsp chopped oregano
- 1 tbsp chopped basil
- 1 cup shredded mozzarella
- 1 tbsp grated Parmesan cheese

- Salt and black pepper to taste

Directions:

1. Preheat oven to 370° F. Cut the tops of the tomatoes and scoop out the pulp. Chop the pulp and set aside. Arrange the tomatoes on a lined with parchment paper baking sheet.

2. Warm the olive oil in a pan over medium heat. Add in garlic, onion, basil, bell peppers, and oregano, and cook for 5 minutes. Sprinkle with salt and pepper. Remove from the heat and mix in tomato pulp and mozzarella cheese. Divide the mixture between the tomatoes and top with Parmesan cheese. Bake for 20 minutes or until the cheese melts. Serve.

Nutrition:

- Info Per Serving: Calories: 285;Fat: 10g;Protein: 24g;Carbs: 28g.

Italian Tuna & Bean Salad

Servings:4 | Cooking Time:10 Minutes

Ingredients:

- 2 cans can tuna packed in olive oil, drained and flaked
- 4 cups spring mix greens
- 1 can cannellini beans
- ⅔ cup feta cheese, crumbled
- 6 sun-dried tomatoes, sliced
- 10 Kalamata olives, sliced
- 2 thinly sliced green onions
- ¼ medium red onion, sliced
- 3 tbsp extra-virgin olive oil
- ½ tsp dried cilantro
- 3 leaves fresh basil, chopped
- 1 lemon, zested and juiced
- Salt and black pepper to taste

Directions:

1. Place the greens, cannellini beans, tuna, feta, tomatoes, olives, green onions, red onion, olive oil, cilantro, basil, and lemon juice and zest in a large bowl. Season with salt and pepper and mix to coat. Serve and enjoy!

Nutrition:

- Info Per Serving: Calories: 354;Fat: 19g;Protein: 22g;Carbs: 25g.

Zoodles With Tomato-Mushroom Sauce

Servings:4 | Cooking Time:25 Minutes

Ingredients:

- 1 lb oyster mushrooms, chopped
- 2 tbsp olive oil
- 1 cup chicken broth
- 1 tsp Mediterranean sauce
- 1 yellow onion, minced
- 1 cup pureed tomatoes
- 2 garlic cloves, minced
- 2 zucchinis, spiralized

Directions:

1. Warm the olive oil in a saucepan over medium heat and sauté the zoodles for 1-2 minutes; reserve. Sauté the onion and garlic in the same saucepan for 2-3 minutes. Add in the mushrooms and continue to cook for 2 to 3 minutes until they release liquid. Add in the remaining ingredients and cover the pan; let it simmer for 10 minutes longer until everything is cooked through. Top the zoodles with the prepared mushroom sauce and serve.

Nutrition:

- Info Per Serving: Calories: 95;Fat: 6.4g;Protein: 6g;Carbs: 5g.

Fennel Salad With Olives & Hazelnuts

Servings:4 | Cooking Time:5 Minutes

Ingredients:

- 2 tbsp olive oil
- 8 dates, pitted and sliced
- 2 fennel bulbs, sliced
- 2 tbsp chives, chopped
- ½ cup hazelnuts, chopped
- 2 tbsp lime juice
- Salt and black pepper to taste
- 40 green olives, chopped

Directions:

1. Place fennel, dates, chives, hazelnuts, lime juice, olives, olive oil, salt, and pepper in a bowl and toss to combine.

Nutrition:

- Info Per Serving: Calories: 210;Fat: 8g;Protein: 5g;Carbs: 15g.

Zesty Spanish Potato Salad

Servings:6 | Cooking Time: 5 To 7 Minutes

Ingredients:

- 4 russet potatoes, peeled and chopped
- 3 large hard-boiled eggs, chopped
- 1 cup frozen mixed vegetables, thawed
- ½ cup plain, unsweetened, full-fat Greek yogurt
- 5 tablespoons pitted Spanish olives
- ½ teaspoon freshly ground black pepper
- ½ teaspoon dried mustard seed
- ½ tablespoon freshly squeezed lemon juice
- ½ teaspoon dried dill
- Salt, to taste

Directions:

1. Place the potatoes in a large pot of water and boil for 5 to 7 minutes, until just fork-tender, checking periodically for doneness. You don't have to overcook them.

2. Meanwhile, in a large bowl, mix the eggs, vegetables, yogurt, olives, pepper, mustard, lemon juice, and dill. Season with salt to taste. Once the potatoes are cooled somewhat, add them to the large bowl, then toss well and serve.

Nutrition:

- Info Per Serving: Calories: 192;Fat: 5.0g;Protein: 9.0g;Carbs: 30.0g.

Grilled Bell Pepper And Anchovy Antipasto

Servings:4 | Cooking Time: 8 Minutes

Ingredients:

- 2 tablespoons extra-virgin olive oil, divided
- 4 medium red bell peppers, quartered, stem and seeds removed
- 6 ounces anchovies in oil, chopped
- 2 tablespoons capers, rinsed and drained
- 1 cup Kalamata olives, pitted
- 1 small shallot, chopped
- Sea salt and freshly ground pepper, to taste

Directions:

1. Heat the grill to medium-high heat. Grease the grill grates with 1 tablespoon of olive oil.

2. Arrange the red bell peppers on the preheated grill grates, then grill for 8 minutes or until charred.

3. Turn off the grill and allow the pepper to cool for 10 minutes.

4. Transfer the charred pepper in a colander. Rinse and peel the peppers under running cold water, then pat dry with paper towels.

5. Cut the peppers into chunks and combine with remaining ingredients in a large bowl. Toss to mix well.

6. Serve immediately.

Nutrition:

- Info Per Serving: Calories: 227;Fat: 14.9g;Protein: 13.9g;Carbs: 9.9g.

Pesto Ravioli Salad

Servings:6 | Cooking Time:15 Minutes

Ingredients:
- 1 cup smoked mozzarella cheese, cubed
- ¼ tsp lemon zest
- 1 cup basil pesto
- ½ cup mayonnaise
- 2 red bell peppers, chopped
- 18 oz cheese ravioli

Directions:
1. Bring to a boil salted water in a pot over high heat. Add the ravioli and cook, uncovered, for 4-5 minutes, stirring occasionally; drain and place them in a salad bowl to cool slightly. Blend the lemon zest, pesto, and mayonnaise in a large bowl and stir in mozzarella cheese and bell peppers. Pour the mixture over the ravioli and toss to coat. Serve.

Nutrition:
- Info Per Serving: Calories: 447;Fat: 32g;Protein: 18g;Carbs: 24g.

Easy Moroccan Spice Mix

Servings:4 | Cooking Time:15 Minutes

Ingredients:
- 2 tsp ground cayenne pepper
- 16 cardamom pods
- 4 tsp coriander seeds
- 4 tsp cumin seeds
- 2 tsp anise seeds
- ½ tsp allspice berries
- ¼ tsp black peppercorns
- 4 tsp ground ginger
- 2 tsp ground nutmeg
- 2 tsp ground cinnamon

Directions:
1. Place the cardamom, coriander, cumin, anise, allspice, and peppercorns in a dry skillet over medium heat and toast for 1-2 minutes, occasionally shaking the skillet to prevent scorching. Let cool at room temperature. Put the toasted spices, ginger, nutmeg, cayenne pepper, and cinnamon in your spice grinder and process to a fine powder. Store the spices in a glass jar at room temperature for up to 7-9 months.

Nutrition:
- Info Per Serving: Calories: 144;Fat: 7.1g;Protein: 7.8g;Carbs: 4.2g.

Walnut-Cucumber Yogurt Sauce

Servings:4 | Cooking Time:10 Minutes

Ingredients:
- 1 cucumber, peeled and shredded
- 1 tbsp walnuts, chopped
- 2 tbsp extra-virgin olive oil
- 1 cup Greek yogurt
- 2 tbsp minced fresh dill
- 1 garlic clove, minced
- Salt and black pepper to taste

Directions:
1. Place the walnuts, olive oil, yogurt, cucumber, and garlic in a bowl and mix well. Season with salt and pepper. Let sit for about 30 minutes to blend the flavors. Store in an airtight container in the refrigerator for up to 2-3 days. Top with dill.

Nutrition:
- Info Per Serving: Calories: 288;Fat: 17g;Protein: 5.3g;Carbs: 12g.

Caprese Salad With Tuna

Servings:4 | Cooking Time:15 Minutes

Ingredients:
- 2 tbsp extra-virgin olive oil
- 2 oz tuna in water, flaked
- 3 large tomatoes, sliced
- ¼ cup basil leaves, torn
- 4 oz fresh mozzarella, sliced
- ¼ cup balsamic vinegar
- Sea salt to taste
- 10 black olives

Directions:
1. Arrange tomatoes and mozzarella slices on a serving plate. Season with salt, scatter basil all over, and drizzle with vinegar and olive oil. Top with tuna and olives and serve.

Nutrition:
- Info Per Serving: Calories: 186;Fat: 13g;Protein: 13g;Carbs: 6.5g.

Balsamic Brussels Sprouts And Delicata Squash

Servings:2 | Cooking Time: 30 Minutes

Ingredients:
- ½ pound Brussels sprouts, ends trimmed and outer leaves removed
- 1 medium delicata squash, halved lengthwise, seeded, and cut into 1-inch pieces
- 1 cup fresh cranberries
- 2 teaspoons olive oil
- Salt and freshly ground black pepper, to taste
- ½ cup balsamic vinegar
- 2 tablespoons roasted pumpkin seeds
- 2 tablespoons fresh pomegranate arils (seeds)

Directions:
1. Preheat oven to 400ºF. Line a sheet pan with parchment paper.
2. Combine the Brussels sprouts, squash, and cranberries in a large bowl. Drizzle with olive oil, and season lightly with salt and pepper. Toss well to coat and arrange in a single layer on the sheet pan.
3. Roast in the preheated oven for 30 minutes, turning vegetables halfway through, or until Brussels sprouts turn brown and crisp in spots.
4. Meanwhile, make the balsamic glaze by simmering the vinegar for 10 to 12 minutes, or until mixture has reduced to about ¼ cup and turns a syrupy consistency.
5. Remove the vegetables from the oven, drizzle with balsamic syrup, and sprinkle with pumpkin seeds and pomegranate arils before serving.

Nutrition:
- Info Per Serving: Calories: 203;Fat: 6.8g;Protein: 6.2g;Carbs: 22.0g.

Whipped Feta Spread

Servings:6 | Cooking Time:10 Minutes

Ingredients:
- 4 tbsp Greek yogurt
- ½ lb feta cheese, crumbled
- 3 cloves garlic, pressed
- 2 tbsp extra-virgin olive oil
- 2 tbsp finely chopped dill
- 1 tsp dried oregano
- Black pepper to taste

Directions:
1. Combine feta, yogurt, garlic, olive oil, and oregano in your food processor. Pulse until well combined. Keep in the fridge until required. To serve, spoon into a dish and sprinkle with dill and black pepper.

Nutrition:
- Info Per Serving: Calories: 155;Fat: 13g;Protein: 6g;Carbs: 4g.

Roasted Red Pepper & Olive Spread

Servings:6 | Cooking Time:10 Minutes

Ingredients:
- ¼ tsp dried thyme
- 1 tbsp capers
- ½ cup pitted green olives
- 1 roasted red pepper, chopped
- 1 tsp balsamic vinegar
- 2/3 cup soft bread crumbs
- 2 cloves garlic, minced
- ½ tsp red pepper flakes
- 1/3 cup extra-virgin olive oil

Directions:
1. Place all the ingredients, except for the olive oil, in a food processor and blend until chunky. With the machine running, slowly pour in the olive oil until it is well combined. Refrigerate or serve at room temperature.

Nutrition:
- Info Per Serving: Calories: 467;Fat: 38g;Protein: 5g;Carbs: 27g.

Carrot & Celery Bean Soup

Servings:6 | Cooking Time:35 Minutes

Ingredients:
- 3 tbsp olive oil
- 1 onion, finely chopped
- 3 garlic cloves, minced
- 2 cups carrots, diced
- 2 cups celery, diced
- 1 medium potato, cubed
- 2 oz cubed pancetta
- 2 cans white beans, rinsed
- 6 cups vegetable broth
- Salt and black pepper to taste

Directions:
1. Heat the olive oil in a stockpot over medium heat. Add the pancetta, onion, and garlic and cook for 3-4 minutes, stirring often. Add the carrots and celery and cook for another 3-5 minutes until tender. Add the beans, potato, broth, salt, and pepper. Stir and simmer for about 20 minutes, stirring occasionally. Serve warm.

Nutrition:
- Info Per Serving: Calories: 244;Fat: 7.2g;Protein: 9g;Carbs: 36.4g.

Andalusian Gazpacho

Servings:4 | Cooking Time:15 Min + Chilling Time

Ingredients:
- 1 cucumber, peeled and chopped
- ¼ cup extra-virgin olive oil
- ¼ cup bread cubes, soaked
- 3 cups tomato juice
- 6 tomatoes, chopped
- 3 garlic cloves, minced
- 2 red bell peppers, chopped
- 1 red onion, chopped
- 1 green onion, sliced
- ½ red chili pepper, sliced
- ¼ cup red wine vinegar
- ¼ cup basil leaves, torn
- Salt and black pepper to taste

Directions:
1. In a food processor, blend cucumber, soaked bread, tomatoes, garlic, red onion, bell peppers, tomato juice, olive oil, vinegar, basil, salt, and pepper until smooth. Refrigerate for 1-2 hours. Serve topped with 7 chili pepper and green onion.

Nutrition:
- Info Per Serving: Calories: 226;Fat: 13.4g;Protein: 5g;Carbs: 27g.

Fruits, Desserts And Snacks Recipes

Fruits, Desserts And Snacks Recipes

Crunchy Eggplant Fries

Servings:4 | Cooking Time:35 Minutes

Ingredients:
- 2 tbsp olive oil
- 2 eggplants, sliced
- ½ tbsp smoked paprika
- Salt and black pepper to taste
- ½ tsp onion powder
- 2 tsp dried sage
- 1 cup fine breadcrumbs
- 1 large egg white, beaten

Directions:
1. Preheat the oven to 350 °F. Line a baking sheet with parchment paper. In a bowl, mix olive oil, paprika, salt, pepper, onion powder, and sage. Dip the eggplant slices in the egg white, then coat in the breadcrumb mixture. Arrange them on the sheet and roast in the oven for 25 minutes, flipping once.

Nutrition:
- Info Per Serving: Calories: 140;Fat: 8g;Protein: 3g;Carbs: 12g.

Honey & Spice Roasted Almonds

Servings:4 | Cooking Time:15 Minutes

Ingredients:
- 2 tbsp olive oil
- 3 cups almonds
- 1 tbsp curry powder
- ¼ cup honey
- 1 tsp salt

Directions:
1. Preheat oven to 260 °F. Coat almonds with olive oil, curry powder, and salt in a bowl; mix well. Arrange on a lined with aluminum foil sheet and bake for 15 minutes. Remove from the oven and let cool for 10 minutes. Drizzle with honey and let cool at room temperature. Enjoy!

Nutrition:
- Info Per Serving: Calories: 134;Fat: 8g;Protein: 1g;Carbs: 18g.

Walnut And Date Balls

Servings:6 | Cooking Time: 8 To 10 Minutes

Ingredients:
- 1 cup walnuts
- 1 cup unsweetened shredded coconut
- 14 medjool dates, pitted
- 8 tablespoons almond butter

Directions:
1. Preheat the oven to 350°F.
2. Put the walnuts on a baking sheet and toast in the oven for 5 minutes.
3. Put the shredded coconut on a clean baking sheet. Toast for about 3 to 5 minutes, or until it turns golden brown. Once done, remove it from the oven and put it in a shallow bowl.
4. In a food processor, process the toasted walnuts until they have a medium chop. Transfer the chopped walnuts into a medium bowl.
5. Add the dates and butter to the food processor and blend until the dates become a thick paste. Pour the chopped walnuts into the food processor with the dates and pulse just until the mixture is combined, about 5 to 7 pulses.
6. Remove the mixture from the food processor and scrape it into a large bowl.
7. To make the balls, spoon 1 to 2 tablespoons of the date mixture into the palm of your hand and roll around between your hands until you form a ball. Put the ball on a clean, lined baking sheet. Repeat until all the mixture is formed into balls.
8. Roll each ball in the toasted coconut until the outside of the ball is coated. Put the ball back on the baking sheet and repeat.
9. Put all the balls into the refrigerator for 20 minutes before serving. Store any leftovers in the refrigerator in an airtight container.

Nutrition:
- Info Per Serving: Calories: 489;Fat: 35.0g;Protein: 5.0g;Carbs: 48.0g.

Tomato-Cheese Toasts

Servings:4 | Cooking Time:5 Minutes

Ingredients:
- 1 tomato, cubed
- 12 ounces cream cheese, soft
- ¼ cup mayonnaise
- 2 garlic clove, minced
- 1 red onion, chopped
- 2 tbsp lime juice
- 4 slices whole-wheat toast

Directions:
1. In a bowl, blend cream cheese, mayonnaise, garlic, onion, and lime juice until smooth. Spread the mixture onto the bread slices and top with the tomato cubes to serve.

Nutrition:
- Info Per Serving: Calories: 210;Fat: 7g;Protein: 5g;Carbs: 8g.

Two-Cheese Stuffed Bell Peppers

Servings:6 | Cooking Time:20 Min + Chilling Time

Ingredients:
- 1 ½ lb bell peppers, cored and seeded
- 1 tbsp extra-virgin olive oil
- 4 oz ricotta cheese
- 4 oz mascarpone cheese
- 1 tbsp scallions, chopped
- 1 tbsp lemon zest

Directions:
1. Preheat oven to 400 °F. Coat the peppers with olive oil, put them on a baking sheet, and roast for 8 minutes. Remove and let cool. In a bowl, add the ricotta cheese, mascarpone cheese, scallions, and lemon zest. Stir to combine, then spoon mixture into a piping bag. Stuff each pepper to the top with the cheese mixture. Chill the peppers and serve.

Nutrition:
- Info Per Serving: Calories: 141;Fat: 11g;Protein: 4g;Carbs: 6g.

Cantaloupe & Watermelon Balls

Servings:4 | Cooking Time:5 Min + Chilling Time

Ingredients:
- 2 cups watermelon balls
- 2 cups cantaloupe balls
- ½ cup orange juice
- ¼ cup lemon juice
- 1 tbsp orange zest

Directions:
1. Place the watermelon and cantaloupe in a bowl. In another bowl, mix the lemon juice, orange juice and zest. Pour over the fruit. Transfer to the fridge covered for 5 hours. Serve.

Nutrition:
- Info Per Serving: Calories: 71;Fat: 0g;Protein: 1.5g;Carbs: 18g.

Pepperoni Fat Head Pizza

Servings:4 | Cooking Time:35 Minutes

Ingredients:
- 2 tbsp olive oil
- 2 cups flour
- 1 cup lukewarm water
- 1 pinch of sugar
- 1 tsp active dry yeast
- ¾ tsp salt
- 1 tsp dried oregano
- 2 cups mozzarella cheese
- 1 cup sliced pepperoni

Directions:
1. Sift the flour and salt in a bowl and stir in yeast. Mix lukewarm water, olive oil, and sugar in another bowl. Add the wet mixture to the dry mixture and whisk until you obtain a soft dough. Place the dough on a lightly floured work surface and knead it thoroughly for 4-5 minutes until elastic. Transfer the dough to a greased bowl. Cover with cling film and leave to rise for 50-60 minutes in a warm place until doubled in size. Roll out the dough to a thickness of around 12 inches.
2. Preheat oven to 400 °F. Line a round pizza pan with parchment paper. Spread the dough on the pizza pan and top with the mozzarella cheese, oregano, and pepperoni slices. Bake in the oven for 15 minutes or until the cheese melts. Remove the pizza from the oven and let cool slightly. Slice and serve.

Nutrition:
- Info Per Serving: Calories: 229;Fat: 7g;Protein: 36g;Carbs: 0.4g.

Two-Cheese & Spinach Pizza Bagels

Servings:6 | Cooking Time:20 Minutes

Ingredients:
- 2 tbsp olive oil
- 6 bagels, halved and toasted
- 2 green onions, chopped
- 1 cup pizza sauce
- ¼ tsp dried oregano
- 1 cup spinach, torn
- 1 ¼ cups mozzarella, grated
- ¼ cup Parmesan cheese, grated

Directions:
1. Preheat your broiler. Arrange the bagels on a baking sheet. Warm the olive oil in a saucepan over medium heat and sauté the green onions for 3-4 minutes until tender. Pour in the pizza sauce and oregano and bring to a simmer.
2. Spread the bagel halves with the sauce mixture and top with spinach. Sprinkle with mozzarella and Parmesan cheeses. Place under the preheated broiler for 5-6 minutes or until the cheeses melt.

Nutrition:
- Info Per Serving: Calories: 366;Fat: 8g;Protein: 20g;Carbs: 55g.

Fruit And Nut Chocolate Bark

Servings:2 | Cooking Time: 2 Minutes

Ingredients:
- 2 tablespoons chopped nuts
- 3 ounces dark chocolate chips
- ¼ cup chopped dried fruit (blueberries, apricots, figs, prunes, or any combination of those)

Directions:
1. Line a sheet pan with parchment paper and set aside.
2. Add the nuts to a skillet over medium-high heat and toast for 60 seconds, or just fragrant. Set aside to cool.
3. Put the chocolate chips in a microwave-safe glass bowl and microwave on High for 1 minute.

4. Stir the chocolate and allow any unmelted chips to warm and melt. If desired, heat for an additional 20 to 30 seconds.
5. Transfer the chocolate to the prepared sheet pan. Scatter the dried fruit and toasted nuts over the chocolate evenly and gently pat in so they stick.
6. Place the sheet pan in the refrigerator for at least 1 hour to let the chocolate harden.
7. When ready, break into pieces and serve.

Nutrition:
- Info Per Serving: Calories: 285;Fat: 16.1g;Protein: 4.0g;Carbs: 38.7g.

Mini Nuts And Fruits Crumble

Servings:6 | Cooking Time: 15 Minutes

Ingredients:
- Topping:
- ¼ cup coarsely chopped hazelnuts
- 1 cup coarsely chopped walnuts
- 1 teaspoon ground cinnamon
- Sea salt, to taste
- 1 tablespoon melted coconut oil
- Filling:
- 6 fresh figs, quartered
- 2 nectarines, pitted and sliced
- 1 cup fresh blueberries
- 2 teaspoons lemon zest
- ½ cup raw honey
- 1 teaspoon vanilla extract

Directions:
1. Make the Topping:
2. Combine the ingredients for the topping in a bowl. Stir to mix well. Set aside until ready to use.
3. Make the Filling:
4. Preheat the oven to 375°F.
5. Combine the ingredients for the fillings in a bowl. Stir to mix well.
6. Divide the filling in six ramekins, then divide and top with nut topping.
7. Bake in the preheated oven for 15 minutes or until the topping is lightly browned and the filling is frothy.
8. Serve immediately.

Nutrition:
- Info Per Serving: Calories: 336;Fat: 18.8g;Protein: 6.3g;Carbs: 41.9g.

Baked Beet Fries With Feta Cheese

Servings:4 | Cooking Time:40 Minutes

Ingredients:
- 1 cup olive oil
- 1 cup feta cheese, crumbled
- 2 beets, sliced
- Salt and black pepper to taste
- 1/3 cup balsamic vinegar

Directions:
1. Preheat the oven to 340 °F. Line a baking sheet with parchment paper. Arrange beet slices, salt, pepper, vinegar, and olive oil on the sheet and toss to combine. Bake for 30 minutes. Serve topped with feta cheese.

Nutrition:
- Info Per Serving: Calories: 210;Fat: 6g;Protein: 4g;Carbs: 9g.

Healthy Tuna Stuffed Zucchini Rolls

Servings:4 | Cooking Time:5 Minutes

Ingredients:
- 5 oz canned tuna, drained and mashed
- 2 tbsp olive oil
- ½ cup mayonnaise
- 2 tbsp capers
- 2 zucchinis, sliced lengthwise
- Salt and black pepper to taste
- 1 tsp lime juice

Directions:
1. Heat a grill pan over medium heat. Drizzle the zucchini slices with olive oil and season with salt and pepper. Grill for 5-6 minutes on both sides. In a bowl, mix the tuna, capers, lime juice, mayonnaise, salt, and pepper until well combined. Spread the tuna mixture onto zucchini slices and roll them up. Transfer the rolls to a plate and serve.

Nutrition:
- Info Per Serving: Calories: 210;Fat: 7g;Protein: 4g;Carbs: 8g.

Roasted Eggplant Hummus

Servings:4 | Cooking Time:25 Minutes

Ingredients:
- 1 lb eggplants, peeled and sliced
- 1 lemon, juiced
- 1 garlic clove, minced
- ¼ cup tahini
- ¼ tsp ground cumin
- Salt and black pepper to taste
- 2 tbsp fresh parsley, chopped
- ½ cup mayonnaise

Directions:
1. Preheat oven to 350 °F. Arrange the eggplant slices on a baking sheet and bake for 15 minutes until tender. Let cool slightly before chopping. In a food processor, mix eggplants, salt, lemon juice, tahini, cumin, garlic, and pepper for 30 seconds. Remove to a bowl. Stir in mayonnaise. Serve topped with parsley.

Nutrition:
- Info Per Serving: Calories: 235;Fat: 18g;Protein: 4.1g;Carbs: 17g.

Salty Spicy Popcorn

Servings:6 | Cooking Time:10 Minutes

Ingredients:
- 3 tbsp olive oil
- ¼ tsp garlic powder
- Salt and black pepper to taste
- ½ tsp dried thyme
- ½ tsp chili powder
- ½ tsp dried oregano
- 12 cups plain popped popcorn

Directions:
1. Warm the olive oil in a large pan over medium heat. Add the garlic powder, black pepper, salt, chili powder, thyme, and stir oregano until fragrant, 1 minute. Place the popcorn in a large bowl and drizzle with the infused oil over. Toss to coat.

Nutrition:
- Info Per Serving: Calories: 183;Fat: 12g;Protein: 3g;Carbs: 19g.

Cozy Superfood Hot Chocolate

Servings:2 | Cooking Time: 8 Minutes

Ingredients:
- 2 cups unsweetened almond milk
- 1 tablespoon avocado oil
- 1 tablespoon collagen protein powder
- 2 teaspoons coconut sugar
- 2 tablespoons cocoa powder
- 1 teaspoon ground cinnamon
- 1 teaspoon ground ginger
- 1 teaspoon vanilla extract
- ½ teaspoon ground turmeric
- Dash salt
- Dash cayenne pepper (optional)

Directions:
1. In a small saucepan over medium heat, warm the almond milk and avocado oil for about 7 minutes, stirring frequently.
2. Fold in the protein powder, which will only properly dissolve in a heated liquid.
3. Stir in the coconut sugar and cocoa powder until melted and dissolved. Carefully transfer the warm liquid into a blender, along with the cinnamon, ginger, vanilla, turmeric, salt, and cayenne pepper (if desired). Blend for 15 seconds until frothy.
4. Serve immediately.

Nutrition:
- Info Per Serving: Calories: 217;Fat: 11.0g;Protein: 11.2g;Carbs: 14.8g.

Mascarpone Baked Pears

Servings:2 | Cooking Time: 20 Minutes

Ingredients:
- 2 ripe pears, peeled
- 1 tablespoon plus 2 teaspoons honey, divided
- 1 teaspoon vanilla, divided
- ¼ teaspoon ground coriander
- ¼ teaspoon ginger
- ¼ cup minced walnuts
- ¼ cup mascarpone cheese
- Pinch salt
- Cooking spray

Directions:
1. Preheat the oven to 350°F. Spray a small baking dish with cooking spray.
2. Slice the pears in half lengthwise. Using a spoon, scoop out the core from each piece. Put the pears, cut side up, in the baking dish.
3. Whisk together 1 tablespoon of honey, ½ teaspoon of vanilla, ginger, and coriander in a small bowl. Pour this mixture evenly over the pear halves.
4. Scatter the walnuts over the pear halves.
5. Bake in the preheated oven for 20 minutes, or until the pears are golden and you're able to pierce them easily with a knife.
6. Meanwhile, combine the mascarpone cheese with the remaining 2 teaspoons of honey, ½ teaspoon of vanilla, and a pinch of salt. Stir to combine well.
7. Divide the mascarpone among the warm pear halves and serve.

Nutrition:
- Info Per Serving: Calories: 308;Fat: 16.0g;Protein: 4.1g;Carbs: 42.7g.

Goat Cheese Dip With Scallions & Lemon

Servings:4 | Cooking Time:10 Minutes

Ingredients:
- 2 tbsp extra virgin olive oil
- 2 oz goat cheese, crumbled
- ¾ cup sour cream
- 2 tbsp scallions, chopped
- 1 tbsp lemon juice
- Salt and black pepper to taste

Directions:
1. Combine goat cheese, sour cream, scallions, lemon juice, salt, pepper, and olive oil in a bowl and transfer to the fridge for 10 minutes before serving.

Nutrition:
- Info Per Serving: Calories: 230;Fat: 12g;Protein: 6g;Carbs: 9g.

Pecan And Carrot Cake

Servings:12 | Cooking Time: 45 Minutes

Ingredients:
- ½ cup coconut oil, at room temperature, plus more for greasing the baking dish
- 2 teaspoons pure vanilla extract
- ¼ cup pure maple syrup
- 6 eggs
- ½ cup coconut flour
- 1 teaspoon baking powder
- 1 teaspoon baking soda
- ½ teaspoon ground nutmeg
- 1 teaspoon ground cinnamon
- ⅛ teaspoon sea salt
- ½ cup chopped pecans
- 3 cups finely grated carrots

Directions:
1. Preheat the oven to 350°F. Grease a 13-by-9-inch baking dish with coconut oil.
2. Combine the vanilla extract, maple syrup, and ½ cup of coconut oil in a large bowl. Stir to mix well.
3. Break the eggs in the bowl and whisk to combine well. Set aside.
4. Combine the coconut flour, baking powder, baking soda, nutmeg, cinnamon, and salt in a separate bowl. Stir to mix well.
5. Make a well in the center of the flour mixture, then pour the egg mixture into the well. Stir to combine well.
6. Add the pecans and carrots to the bowl and toss to mix well. Pour the mixture in the single layer on the baking dish.
7. Bake in the preheated oven for 45 minutes or until puffed and the cake spring back when lightly press with your fingers.
8. Remove the cake from the oven. Allow to cool for at least 15 minutes, then serve.

Nutrition:
- Info Per Serving: Calories: 255;Fat: 21.2g;Protein: 5.1g;Carbs: 12.8g.

Berry Sorbet

Servings:4 | Cooking Time:10 Min + Freezing Time

Ingredients:
- 1 tsp lemon juice
- ¼ cup honey
- 1 cup fresh strawberries
- 1 cup fresh raspberries
- 1 cup fresh blueberries

Directions:
1. Bring 1 cup of water to a boil in a pot over high heat. Stir in honey until dissolved. Remove from the heat and mix in berries and lemon juice; let cool.
2. Once cooled, add the mixture to a food processor and pulse until smooth. Transfer to a shallow glass and freeze for 1 hour. Stir with a fork and freeze for 30 more minutes. Repeat a couple of times. Serve in dessert dishes.

Nutrition:
- Info Per Serving: Calories: 115;Fat: 1g;Protein: 1g;Carbs: 29g.

Greek Yogurt & Za'Atar Dip On Grilled Pitta

Servings:6 | Cooking Time:10 Minutes

Ingredients:
- 1/3 cup olive oil
- 2 cups Greek yogurt
- 2 tbsp toasted ground pistachios
- Salt and white pepper to taste
- 2 tbsp mint, chopped
- 3 kalamata olives, chopped
- ¼ cup za'atar seasoning
- 3 pitta breads, cut into triangles

Directions:
1. Mix the yogurt, pistachios, salt, pepper, mint, olives, za´atar spice, and olive oil in a bowl. Grill the pitta bread until golden, about 5-6 minutes. Serve with the yogurt spread.

Nutrition:
- Info Per Serving: Calories: 300;Fat: 19g;Protein: 11g;Carbs: 22g.

Chili Grilled Eggplant Rounds

Servings:4 | Cooking Time:25 Minutes

Ingredients:
- 1 cup roasted peppers, chopped
- 4 tbsp olive oil
- 2 eggplants, cut into rounds
- 12 Kalamata olives, chopped
- 1 tsp red chili flakes, crushed
- Salt and black pepper to taste
- 2 tbsp basil, chopped
- 2 tbsp Parmesan cheese, grated

Directions:
1. Combine roasted peppers, half of the olive oil, olives, red chili flakes, salt, and pepper in a bowl. Rub each eggplant slice with remaining olive oil and salt grill them on the preheated grill for 14 minutes on both sides. Remove to a platter. Distribute the pepper mixture across the eggplant rounds and top with basil and Parmesan cheese to serve.

Nutrition:
- Info Per Serving: Calories: 220;Fat: 11g;Protein: 6g;Carbs: 16g.

Turkish Baklava

Servings:6 | Cooking Time:40 Min + Chilling Time

Ingredients:
- 20 sheets phyllo pastry dough, at room temperature
- 1 cup butter, melted
- 1 ½ cups chopped walnuts
- 1 tsp ground cinnamon
- ¼ tsp ground cardamom
- ½ cup sugar
- ½ cup honey
- 2 tbsp lemon juice
- 1 tbsp lemon zest

Directions:
1. In a small pot, bring 1 cup of water, sugar, honey, lemon zest, and lemon juice just to a boil. Remove and let cool.
2. Preheat oven to 350 °F. In a small bowl, mix the walnuts, cinnamon, and cardamom and set aside. Put the butter in a small bowl. Put 1 layer of phyllo dough on a baking sheet and slowly

brush with butter. Carefully layer 2 more phyllo sheets, brushing each with butter in the baking pan and then layer 1 tbsp of the nut mix; layer 2 sheets and add another 1 tbsp of the nut mix; repeat with 2 sheets and nuts until you run out of nuts and dough, topping with the remaining phyllo dough sheets. Slice 4 lines into the baklava lengthwise and make another 4 or 5 slices diagonally across the pan. Bake for 30-40 minutes or until golden brown. Remove the baklava from the oven and immediately cover it with the syrup. Let cool and serve.
Nutrition:
• Info Per Serving: Calories: 443;Fat: 27g;Protein: 6g;Carbs: 47g.

Basic Pudding With Kiwi
Servings:4 | Cooking Time:20 Min + Chilling Time
Ingredients:
• 2 kiwi, peeled and sliced
• 1 egg
• 2 ¼ cups milk
• ½ cup honey
• 1 tsp vanilla extract
• 3 tbsp cornstarch
Directions:
1. In a bowl, beat the egg with honey. Stir in 2 cups of milk and vanilla. Pour into a pot over medium heat and bring to a boil. Combine cornstarch and remaining milk in a bowl. Pour slowly into the pot and boil for 1 minute until thickened, stirring often. Divide between 4 cups and transfer to the fridge. Top with kiwi and serve.
Nutrition:
• Info Per Serving: Calories: 262;Fat: 4.1g;Protein: 6.5g;Carbs: 52g.

Mint-Watermelon Gelato
Servings:4 | Cooking Time:10 Min + Freezing Time
Ingredients:
• ¼ cup honey
• 4 cups watermelon cubes
• ¼ cup lemon juice
• 12 mint leaves to serve
Directions:
1. In a food processor, blend the watermelon, honey, and lemon juice to form a purée with chunks. Transfer to a freezer-proof container and place in the freezer for 1 hour.
2. Remove the container from and scrape with a fork. Return the to the freezer and repeat the process every half hour until the sorbet is completely frozen, for around 4 hours. Share into bowls, garnish with mint leaves, and serve.
Nutrition:
• Info Per Serving: Calories: 149;Fat: 0.4g;Protein: 1.8g;Carbs: 38g.

No-Gluten Caprese Pizza
Servings:4 | Cooking Time:40 Minutes
Ingredients:
• 2 tbsp olive oil
• 2 ¼ cups chickpea flour
• Salt and black pepper to taste
• 1 tsp onion powder
• 1 tomato, sliced
• ¼ tsp dried oregano
• 2 oz mozzarella cheese, sliced
• ¼ cup tomato sauce
• 2 tbsp fresh basil, chopped
Directions:
1. Preheat oven to 360 °F. Combine the chickpea flour, salt, pepper, 1 ¼ cups of water, olive oil, and onion powder in a bowl. Mix

well to form a soft dough, then knead a bit until elastic. Let sit covered in a greased bowl to rise, for 25 minutes in a warm place. Remove the dough to a floured surface and roll out it with a rolling pin into a thin circle.
2. Transfer to a floured baking tray and bake in the oven for 10 minutes. Evenly spread the tomato sauce over the pizza base. Sprinkle with oregano and arrange the mozzarella cheese and tomato slices on top. Bake for 10 minutes. Top with basil and serve sliced.
Nutrition:
• Info Per Serving: Calories: 420;Fat: 26g;Protein: 14g;Carbs: 35g.

The Best Anchovy Tapenade
Servings:4 | Cooking Time:10 Minutes
Ingredients:
• 1 cup roasted red peppers, chopped
• 3 tbsp olive oil
• 2 anchovy fillets, chopped
• 2 tbsp parsley, chopped
• 14 oz canned artichokes
• ¼ cup capers, drained
• 1 tbsp lemon juice
• 2 garlic cloves, minced
Directions:
1. In a food processor, blend roasted peppers, anchovies, parsley, artichokes, oil, capers, lemon juice, and garlic until a paste is formed. Serve at room temperature
Nutrition:
• Info Per Serving: Calories: 210;Fat: 6g;Protein: 5g;Carbs: 13g.

Savory Cauliflower Steaks
Servings:4 | Cooking Time:35 Minutes
Ingredients:
• 1 head cauliflower, cut into steaks
• 2 tbsp olive oil
• Salt and paprika to taste
Directions:
1. Preheat oven to 360 °F.Line a baking sheet with aluminum foil. Rub each cauliflower steak with olive oil, salt, and paprika. Arrange on the baking sheet and bake for 10-15 minutes, flip, and bake for another 15 minutes until crispy.
Nutrition:
• Info Per Serving: Calories: 78;Fat: 7g;Protein: 1g;Carbs: 4g.

Pesto & Egg Avocado Boats
Servings:2 | Cooking Time:15 Minutes
Ingredients:
• 1 halved avocado, pitted
• 2 large eggs
• Salt and black pepper to taste
• 2 tbsp jarred pesto
• 2 sundried tomatoes, chopped
Directions:
1. Preheat oven to 420 °F. Scoop out the middle of each avocado half. Arrange them on a baking sheet, cut-side up. Crack an egg into each avocado half and season to taste. Bake until the eggs are set and cooked to your desired level of doneness, 10-12 minutes. Remove from the oven and top with pesto and sundried tomatoes. Serve and enjoy!
Nutrition:
• Info Per Serving: Calories: 302;Fat: 26g;Protein: 8g;Carbs: 10g.

Lebanese Spicy Baba Ganoush

Servings:4 | Cooking Time:50 Minutes

Ingredients:
• 2 tbsp olive oil
• 2 eggplants, poked with a fork
• 2 tbsp tahini paste
• 1 tsp cayenne pepper
• 2 tbsp lemon juice
• 2 garlic cloves, minced
• Salt and black pepper to taste
• 1 tbsp parsley, chopped

Directions:
1. Preheat oven to 380 °F. Arrange eggplants on a roasting pan and bake for 40 minutes. Set aside to cool. Peel the cooled eggplants and place them in a blender along with the tahini paste, lemon juice, garlic, cayenne pepper, salt, and pepper. Puree the ingredients while gradually adding olive oil until a smooth and homogeneous consistency. Top with parsley.

Nutrition:
• Info Per Serving: Calories: 130;Fat: 5g;Protein: 5g;Carbs: 2g.

White Bean Dip The Greek Way

Servings:6 | Cooking Time:5 Minutes

Ingredients:
• ¼ cup extra-virgin olive oil
• 1 lemon, zested and juiced
• 1 can white beans
• 2 garlic cloves, minced
• ¼ tsp ground cumin
• 2 tbsp Greek oregano, chopped
• 1 tsp stone-ground mustard
• Salt to taste

Directions:
1. In a food processor, blend all the ingredients, except for the oregano, until smooth. Top with Greek oregano and serve.

Nutrition:
• Info Per Serving: Calories: 222;Fat: 7g;Protein: 12g;Carbs: 30.4g.

Fancy Baileys Ice Coffee

Servings:4 | Cooking Time:5 Min + Chilling Time

Ingredients:
• 1 cup espresso
• 2 cups milk
• 4 tbsp Baileys
• ½ tsp ground cinnamon
• ½ tsp vanilla extract
• Ice cubes

Directions:
1. Fill four glasses with ice cubes. Mix milk, cinnamon, and vanilla in a food processor until nice and frothy. Pour into the glasses. Combine the Baileys with the espresso and mix well. Pour ¼ of the espresso mixture over the milk and serve.

Nutrition:
• Info Per Serving: Calories: 100;Fat: 5g;Protein: 4g;Carbs: 8g.

Iberian Spread For Sandwiches

Servings:4 | Cooking Time:10 Minutes

Ingredients:
• 16 pimiento stuffed manzanilla olives
• 4 oz roasted pimientos
• 2/3 cup aioli

Directions:
1. Place the olives and roasted pimientos in your food processor. Pulse until a creamier consistency is formed. Transfer to a bowl and mix well with aioli. Serve and enjoy!

Nutrition:
• Info Per Serving: Calories: 325;Fat: 34g;Protein: 0.1g;Carbs: 2g.

Grilled Pesto Halloumi Cheese

Servings:2 | Cooking Time:9 Minutes

Ingredients:
• 1 tbsp olive oil
• 3 oz Halloumi cheese
• 2 tsp pesto sauce
• 1 tomato, sliced

Directions:
1. Cut the cheese into 2 rectangular pieces. Heat a griddle pan over medium heat. Drizzle the halloumi slices with and add to the pan. After about 2 minutes, check to see if the cheese is golden on the bottom. Flip the slices, top each with pesto, and cook for another 2 minutes, or until the second side is golden. Serve with tomato slices.

Nutrition:
• Info Per Serving: Calories: 177;Fat: 14g;Protein: 10g;Carbs: 4g.

Chili & Lemon Shrimp

Servings:6 | Cooking Time:10 Minutes

Ingredients:
• 24 large shrimp, peeled and deveined
• ½ cup olive oil
• 5 garlic cloves, minced
• 1 tsp red pepper flakes
• 1 lemon, juiced and zested
• 1 tsp dried dill
• 1 tsp dried thyme
• Salt and black pepper to taste

Directions:
1. Warm the olive oil in a large skillet over medium heat. Add the garlic and red pepper flakes and cook for 1 minute. Add the shrimp and cook an additional 3 minutes, stirring frequently. Remove from the pan, and sprinkle with lemon juice, lemon zest, thyme, dill, salt, and pepper. Serve.

Nutrition:
• Info Per Serving: Calories: 198;Fat: 6g;Protein: 9g;Carbs: 28g.

Spiced Nut Mix

Servings:6 | Cooking Time:20 Minutes

Ingredients:
- 1 tbsp olive oil
- 2 cups raw mixed nuts
- 1 tsp ground cumin
- ½ tsp garlic powder
- ½ tsp kosher salt
- ⅛ tsp chili powder
- ⅛ tsp ground coriander

Directions:
1. Place the nuts in a skillet over medium heat and toast for 3 minutes, shaking the pan continuously. Remove to a bowl, season with salt, and reserve. Warm olive oil in the same skillet. Add in cumin, garlic powder, chili powder, and ground coriander and cook for about 20-30 seconds. Mix in nuts and cook for another 4 minutes. Serve chilled.

Nutrition:
- Info Per Serving: Calories: 315;Fat: 29.2g;Protein: 8g;Carbs: 11g.

Spicy Roasted Chickpeas

Servings:2 | Cooking Time:40 Minutes

Ingredients:
- Chickpeas
- 1 tbsp olive oil
- 1 can chickpeas
- Salt to taste
- Seasoning Mix
- ¾ tsp cumin
- ½ tsp ground coriander
- Salt and black pepper to taste
- ¼ tsp chili powder
- ½ tsp cayenne pepper
- ¼ tsp cardamom
- ¼ tsp cinnamon
- ¼ tsp allspice

Directions:
1. Preheat oven to 400 °F. In a small bowl, place all the seasoning mix ingredients and stir well to combine.
2. Place the chickpeas in a bowl and season them with olive oil and salt. Add the chickpeas to a lined baking sheet and roast them for about 25-35 minutes, turning them over once or twice while cooking until they are slightly crisp. Remove to a bowl and sprinkle them with the seasoning mix. Toss lightly to combine. Serve and enjoy!

Nutrition:
- Info Per Serving: Calories: 268;Fat: 11g;Protein: 11g;Carbs: 35g.

Italian Submarine-Style Sandwiches

Servings:4 | Cooking Time:35 Minutes

Ingredients:
- ½ lb sliced deli ham
- ½ lb sliced deli turkey
- 1 Italian loaf bread, unsliced
- ⅓ cup honey mustard
- ½ lb sliced mozzarella cheese

Directions:
1. Preheat oven to 400 °F. Cut the bread horizontally in half. Spread the honey mustard over the bottom half. Layer ham, turkey, and mozzarella cheese over, then top with the remaining bread half. Wrap the sandwich in foil and bake for 20 minutes or until the bread is toasted. Open the foil and bake for 5 minutes or until the top is crisp. Serve sliced.

Nutrition:

- Info Per Serving: Calories: 704;Fat: 17g;Protein: 50g;Carbs: 85g.

Fig & Mascarpone Toasts With Pistachios

Servings:6 | Cooking Time:10 Minutes

Ingredients:
- 4 tbsp butter, melted
- 1 French baguette, sliced
- 1 cup Mascarpone cheese
- 1 jar fig jam
- ½ cup crushed pistachios

Directions:
1. Preheat oven to 350 °F. Arrange the sliced bread on a greased baking sheet and brush each slice with melted butter.
2. Toast the bread for 5-7 minutes until golden brown. Let the bread cool slightly. Spread about a teaspoon of the mascarpone cheese on each piece of bread. Top with fig jam and pistachios.

Nutrition:
- Info Per Serving: Calories: 445;Fat: 24g;Protein: 3g;Carbs: 48g.

Italian Popcorn

Servings:6 | Cooking Time:20 Minutes

Ingredients:
- 2 tbsp butter, melted
- 1 tbsp truffle oil
- 8 cups air-popped popcorn
- 2 tbsp packed brown sugar
- 2 tbsp Italian seasoning
- ¼ tsp sea salt

Directions:
1. Preheat oven to 350 °F. Combine butter, Italian seasoning, sugar, and salt in a bowl. Pour over the popcorn and toss well to coat. Remove to a baking dish and bake for 15 minutes, stirring frequently. Drizzle with truffle oil and serve.

Nutrition:
- Info Per Serving: Calories: 80;Fat: 5g;Protein: 1.1g;Carbs: 8.4g.

Sheet Pan Sweet Potatoes

Servings:4 | Cooking Time:70 Minutes

Ingredients:
- 4 sweet potatoes, pricked with a fork
- 4 tbsp olive oil
- 1 cup arugula
- 1 garlic clove, minced
- 1 red onion, sliced
- 1 lemon, juiced and zested
- 2 tbsp dill, chopped
- 2 tbsp Greek yogurt
- 2 tbsp tahini paste
- Salt and black pepper to taste

Directions:
1. Preheat oven to 340 °F. Line a baking sheet with parchment paper. Arrange potatoes on the sheet and bake for 1 hour. Peel them and slice into wedges. Remove to a bowl and combine with garlic, olive oil, onion, arugula, lemon juice, lemon zest, dill, Greek yogurt, tahini paste, salt, and pepper.

Nutrition:
- Info Per Serving: Calories: 220;Fat: 6g;Protein: 4g;Carbs: 7g.

Artichoke & Curly Kale Flatbread

Servings:4 | Cooking Time:25 Minutes

Ingredients:
- 3 tbsp olive oil
- 1 cup curly kale, chopped
- 1 tbsp garlic powder
- 2 tbsp parsley, chopped
- 2 flatbread wraps
- 4 tbsp Parmesan cheese, grated
- ½ cup mozzarella, grated
- 14 oz canned artichokes
- 12 cherry tomatoes, halved
- Salt and black pepper to taste

Directions:
1. Preheat the oven to 390 °F. Line a baking sheet with parchment paper. Brush the flatbread wrap with some olive oil and sprinkle with garlic, salt, and pepper. Top with half of the Parmesan and mozzarella cheeses. Combine artichokes, tomatoes, salt, pepper, and remaining olive oil in a bowl. Spread the mixture on the top of the wraps and top with the remaining Parmesan cheese. Transfer to the baking sheet and bake for 15 minutes. Top with curly kale and parsley.

Nutrition:
- Info Per Serving: Calories: 230;Fat: 12g;Protein: 8g;Carbs: 16g.

Fruit Skewers With Vanilla Labneh

Servings:4 | Cooking Time:15 Min + Straining Time

Ingredients:
- 2 cups plain yogurt
- 2 tbsp honey
- 1 tsp vanilla extract
- A pinch of salt
- 2 mangoes, cut into chunks

Directions:
1. Place a fine sieve lined with cheesecloth over a bowl and spoon the yogurt into the sieve. Allow the liquid to drain off for 12-24 hours hours. Transfer the strained yogurt to a bowl and mix in the honey, vanilla, and salt. Set it aside.
2. Heat your grill to medium-high. Thread the fruit onto skewers and grill for 2 minutes on each side until the fruit is softened and has grill marks on each side. Serve with labneh.

Nutrition:
- Info Per Serving: Calories: 292;Fat: 6g;Protein: 5g;Carbs: 60g.

Baked Sweet Potatoes With Chickpeas

Servings:4 | Cooking Time:30 Minutes

Ingredients:
- 4 sweet potatoes, halved lengthways
- 2 tbsp olive oil
- 1 tbsp butter
- 1 can chickpeas
- ¼ tsp dried thyme
- Salt and black pepper to taste
- 1 tsp paprika
- ½ tsp garlic powder
- 1 cup spinach
- 1 cup Greek-style yogurt
- 2 tsp hot sauce

Directions:
1. Preheat oven to 360 °F. Drizzle the sweet potatoes with some oil. Place, cut-side down, in a lined baking tray and bake for 8-10 minutes. In a bowl, mix chickpeas with remaining olive oil, paprika, thyme, and garlic powder. Pour them onto the other end of the baking tray and roast for 20 minutes alongside the sweet potatoes, stirring the chickpeas once.
2. Melt the butter in a pan over medium heat and stir-fry the spinach and 1 tbsp of water for 3-4 minutes until the spinach wilts. Stir in the roasted chickpeas. Mix the yogurt with hot sauce in a small bowl. Top the sweet potato halves with chickpeas and spinach and serve with hot yogurt on the side.

Nutrition:
- Info Per Serving: Calories: 97;Fat: 3g;Protein: 5g;Carbs: 14g.

Two Cheese Pizza

Servings:4 | Cooking Time:35 Minutes

Ingredients:
- For the crust:
- 1 tbsp olive oil
- ½ cup almond flour
- ¼ tsp salt
- 2 tbsp ground psyllium husk
- For the topping
- ½ cup pizza sauce
- 4 oz mozzarella, sliced
- 1 cup grated mozzarella
- 3 tbsp grated Parmesan cheese
- 2 tsp Italian seasoning

Directions:
1. Preheat the oven to 400 °F. Line a baking sheet with parchment paper. In a medium bowl, mix the almond flour, salt, psyllium powder, olive oil, and 1 cup of lukewarm water until dough forms. Spread the mixture on the pizza pan and bake in the oven until crusty, 10 minutes. When ready, remove the crust and spread the pizza sauce on top. Add the sliced mozzarella, grated mozzarella, Parmesan cheese, and Italian seasoning. Bake in the oven for 18 minutes or until the cheeses melt. Serve warm.

Nutrition:
- Info Per Serving: Calories: 193;Fat: 10g;Protein: 19g;Carbs: 3g.

Avocado & Dark Chocolate Mousse

Servings:4 | Cooking Time:10 Min + Freezing Time

Ingredients:
- 2 tbsp olive oil
- 8 oz dark chocolate, chopped
- ¼ cup milk
- 2 ripe avocados, deseeded
- ¼ cup honey
- 1 cup strawberries

Directions:
1. Cook the chocolate, olive oil, and milk in a saucepan over medium heat for 3 minutes or until the chocolate melt, stirring constantly. Put the avocado in a food processor, then drizzle with honey and melted chocolate. Pulse to combine until smooth. Pour the mixture into a serving bowl, then sprinkle with strawberries. Chill for 30 minutes and serve.

Nutrition:
- Info Per Serving: Calories: 654;Fat: 47g;Protein: 7.2g;Carbs: 56g.

Strawberry Parfait

Servings:2 | Cooking Time:10 Minutes

Ingredients:
- ¾ cup Greek yogurt
- 1 tbsp cocoa powder
- ¼ cup strawberries, chopped
- 5 drops vanilla stevia

Directions:
1. Combine cocoa powder, strawberries, yogurt, and stevia in a bowl. Serve immediately.

Nutrition:
- Info Per Serving: Calories: 210;Fat: 9g;Protein: 5g;Carbs: 8g.

Crispy Potato Chips

Servings:4 | Cooking Time:40 Minutes

Ingredients:
- 2 tbsp olive oil
- 4 potatoes, cut into wedges
- 2 tbsp grated Parmesan cheese
- Salt and black pepper to taste

Directions:
1. Preheat the oven to 340 °F. In a bowl, combine the potatoes, olive oil, salt, and black pepper. Spread on a lined baking sheet and bake for 40 minutes until the edges are browned. Serve sprinkled with Parmesan cheese.

Nutrition:
- Info Per Serving: Calories: 359;Fat: 8g;Protein: 9g;Carbs: 66g.

Honeyed Pistachio Dumplings

Servings:4 | Cooking Time:25 Minutes

Ingredients:
- 1 cup vegetable oil
- ½ cup warm milk
- 2 cups flour
- 2 eggs, beaten
- 1 tsp sugar
- 1 ½ oz active dry yeast
- 1 cup warm water
- ½ tsp vanilla extract
- 1 tsp cinnamon
- 1 orange, zested
- 4 tbsp honey
- 2 tbsp pistachios, chopped

Directions:
1. In a bowl, sift the flour and combine it with the cinnamon and orange zest. In another bowl, mix the sugar, yeast, and ½ cup of warm water. Leave to stand until the yeast dissolves. Stir in milk, eggs, vanilla, and flour mixture. Beat with an electric mixer until smooth. Cover the bowl with plastic wrap and let sit to rise in a warm place for at least 1 hour.
2. Pour the vegetable oil into a deep pan or wok to come halfway up the sides and heat the oil. Add some more oil if necessary. Using a teaspoon, form balls, one by one, and drop in the hot oil one after another. Fry the balls on all sides, until golden brown. Remove them with a slotted spoon to paper towels to soak the excess fat. Repeat the process until the dough is exhausted. Drizzle with honey and sprinkle with pistachios.

Nutrition:
- Info Per Serving: Calories: 890;Fat: 59g;Protein: 15g;Carbs: 78g.

Mini Meatball Pizza

Servings:4 | Cooking Time:25 Minutes

Ingredients:
- 1 pizza crust
- 1 ½ cups pizza sauce
- ½ tsp dried oregano
- 8 oz bite-sized meatballs
- 1 cup bell peppers, sliced
- 2 cups mozzarella, shredded

Directions:
1. Preheat oven to 400 °F. Spread the pizza crust evenly with pizza sauce and sprinkle with oregano. Arrange the meatballs on the pizza sauce. Sprinkle with bell peppers and mozzarella cheese. Bake for about 20 minutes or until the crust is golden brown and cheese melts. Serve immediately.

Nutrition:
- Info Per Serving: Calories: 555;Fat: 28g;Protein: 30g;Carbs: 45g.

Chocolate-Almond Cups

Servings:6 | Cooking Time:10 Min + Freezing Time

Ingredients:
- ½ cup butter
- ½ cup olive oil
- ¼ cup ground flaxseed
- 2 tbsp cocoa powder
- 1 tsp vanilla extract
- 1 tsp ground cinnamon
- 2 tsp maple syrup

Directions:
1. In a bowl, mix the butter, olive oil, flaxseed, cocoa powder, vanilla, cinnamon, and maple syrup and stir well with a spatula. Pour into 6 mini muffin liners and freeze until solid, at least 2 hours. Serve and enjoy!

Nutrition:
- Info Per Serving: Calories: 240;Fat: 24g;Protein: 3g;Carbs: 5g.

Mini Cucumber & Cream Cheese Sandwiches

Servings:4 | Cooking Time:5 Minutes

Ingredients:
- 4 bread slices
- 1 cucumber, sliced
- 2 tbsp cream cheese, soft
- 1 tbsp chives, chopped
- ¼ cup hummus
- Salt and black pepper to taste

Directions:
1. In a bowl, mix hummus, cream cheese, chives, salt, and pepper until well combined. Spread the mixture onto bread slices. Top with cucumber and cut each sandwich into three pieces. Serve immediately.

Nutrition:
- Info Per Serving: Calories: 190;Fat: 13g;Protein: 9g;Carbs: 5g.

Amaretto Nut Bars

Servings:4 | Cooking Time:10 Minutes

Ingredients:
- 2 tbsp olive oil
- ¼ cup shredded coconut
- 1 cup pistachios
- ½ tsp Amaretto liqueur
- 1 cup almonds
- 2 cups dates, pitted
- ¼ cup cocoa powder

Directions:
1. In a food processor, blend pistachios, dates, almonds, olive oil, Amaretto liqueur, and cocoa powder until well minced. Make tablespoon-size balls out of the mixture. Roll the balls in the shredded coconut to coat. Serve chilled.

Nutrition:
- Info Per Serving: Calories: 560;Fat: 28g;Protein: 11g;Carbs: 79g.

Easy Mixed Berry Crisp

Servings:2 | Cooking Time: 30 Minutes

Ingredients:
- 1½ cups frozen mixed berries, thawed
- 1 tablespoon coconut sugar
- 1 tablespoon almond butter
- ¼ cup oats
- ¼ cup pecans

Directions:
1. Preheat the oven to 350°F.
2. Divide the mixed berries between 2 ramekins
3. Place the coconut sugar, almond butter, oats, and pecans in a food processor, and pulse a few times, until the mixture resembles damp sand.
4. Divide the crumble topping over the mixed berries.
5. Put the ramekins on a sheet pan and bake for 30 minutes, or until the top is golden and the berries are bubbling.
6. Serve warm.

Nutrition:
- Info Per Serving: Calories: 268;Fat: 17.0g;Protein: 4.1g;Carbs: 26.8g.

Easy Blueberry And Oat Crisp

Servings:4 | Cooking Time: 20 Minutes

Ingredients:
- 2 tablespoons coconut oil, melted, plus additional for greasing
- 4 cups fresh blueberries
- Juice of ½ lemon
- 2 teaspoons lemon zest
- ¼ cup maple syrup
- 1 cup gluten-free rolled oats
- ½ cup chopped pecans
- ½ teaspoon ground cinnamon
- Sea salt, to taste

Directions:
1. Preheat the oven to 350°F. Grease a baking sheet with coconut oil.
2. Combine the blueberries, lemon juice and zest, and maple syrup in a bowl. Stir to mix well, then spread the mixture on the baking sheet.
3. Combine the remaining ingredients in a small bowl. Stir to mix well. Pour the mixture over the blueberries mixture.
4. Bake in the preheated oven for 20 minutes or until the oats are golden brown.
5. Serve immediately with spoons.

Nutrition:
- Info Per Serving: Calories: 496;Fat: 32.9g;Protein: 5.1g;Carbs: 50.8g.

Minty Yogurt & Banana Cups

Servings:2 | Cooking Time:5 Minutes

Ingredients:
- 2 bananas, sliced
- 2 cups Greek yogurt
- 1 tsp cinnamon
- 3 tbsp honey
- 2 tbsp mint leaves, chopped

Directions:
1. Divide the yogurt between 2 cups and top with banana slices, cinnamon, honey, and mint. Serve immediately.

Nutrition:
- Info Per Serving: Calories: 355;Fat: 4.2g;Protein: 22g;Carbs: 61g.

Apple And Berries Ambrosia

Servings:4 | Cooking Time: 0 Minutes

Ingredients:
- 2 cups unsweetened coconut milk, chilled
- 2 tablespoons raw honey
- 1 apple, peeled, cored, and chopped
- 2 cups fresh raspberries
- 2 cups fresh blueberries

Directions:
1. Spoon the chilled milk in a large bowl, then mix in the honey. Stir to mix well.
2. Then mix in the remaining ingredients. Stir to coat the fruits well and serve immediately.

Nutrition:
- Info Per Serving: Calories: 386;Fat: 21.1g;Protein: 4.2g;Carbs: 45.9g.

Authentic Greek Potato Skins

Servings:4 | Cooking Time:1 Hour 10 Minutes

Ingredients:
- 2 tbsp extra-virgin olive oil
- 1 cup feta cheese, crumbled
- 1 lb potatoes
- ½ cup Greek yogurt
- 2 spring onions, chopped
- 3 sundried tomatoes, chopped
- 6 Kalamata olives, chopped
- ½ tsp dried dill
- 1 tsp Greek oregano
- 2 tbsp halloumi cheese, grated
- Salt and black pepper to taste

Directions:
1. Preheat oven to 400 °F. Pierce the potatoes in several places with a fork. Wrap in aluminum foil and bake in the oven for 45-50 minutes until tender. Let cool. Split the cooled potatoes lengthwise and scoop out some of the flesh. Put the flesh in a bowl and mash with a fork.
2. Add in the spring onions, sun-dried tomatoes, olives, dill, oregano, feta cheese, and yogurt and stir. Season with salt and pepper. Fill the potato shells with the feta mixture and top with halloumi cheese. Transfer the boats to a baking sheet and place under the broiler for 5 minutes until the top is golden and crisp. Serve right away.

Nutrition:
- Info Per Serving: Calories: 294;Fat: 18g;Protein: 12g;Carbs: 22g.

Eggplant & Pepper Spread On Toasts

Servings:4 | Cooking Time:10 Minutes

Ingredients:
- 1 red bell pepper, roasted and chopped
- 1 lb eggplants, baked, peeled and chopped
- ¾ cup olive oil
- 1 lemon, zested
- 1 red chili pepper, chopped
- 1 ½ tsp capers
- 1 garlic clove, minced
- Salt and black pepper to taste
- 1 baguette, sliced and toasted

Directions:
1. In a food processor, place the eggplants, lemon zest, red chili pepper, bell pepper, garlic, salt, and pepper. Blend while gradually adding the olive oil until smooth. Spread each baguette slice with the spread and top with capers to serve.

Nutrition:
- Info Per Serving: Calories: 364;Fat: 38g;Protein: 1.5g;Carbs: 9.3g.

Artichoke & Sun-Dried Tomato Pizza

Servings:4 | Cooking Time:80 Minutes

Ingredients:
- 2 tbsp olive oil
- 1 cup canned passata
- 2 cups flour
- 1 pinch of sugar
- 1 tsp active dry yeast
- ¾ tsp salt
- 1 ½ cups artichoke hearts
- ¼ cup grated Asiago cheese
- ½ onion, minced
- 3 garlic cloves, minced
- 1 tbsp dried oregano
- 6 sundried tomatoes, chopped
- ½ tsp red pepper flakes
- 5-6 basil leaves, torn

Directions:
1. Sift the flour and salt in a bowl and stir in yeast. Mix 1 cup of lukewarm water, olive oil, and sugar in another bowl. Add the wet mixture to the dry mixture and whisk until you obtain a soft dough. Place the dough on a lightly floured work surface and knead it thoroughly for 4-5 minutes until elastic. Transfer the dough to a greased bowl. Cover with cling film and leave to rise for 50-60 minutes in a warm place until doubled in size. Roll out the dough to a thickness of around 12 inches.
2. Preheat oven to 400 °F. Warm oil in a saucepan over medium heat and sauté onion and garlic for 3-4 minutes. Mix in tomatoes and oregano and bring to a boil. Decrease the heat and simmer for another 5 minutes. Transfer the pizza crust to a baking sheet. Spread the sauce all over and top with artichoke hearts and sun-dried tomatoes. Scatter the cheese and bake for 15 minutes until golden. Top with red pepper flakes and basil leaves and serve sliced.

Nutrition:
- Info Per Serving: Calories: 254;Fat: 9.5g;Protein: 8g;Carbs: 34.3g.

Caramel Peach & Walnut Cake

Servings:6 | Cooking Time:50 Min + Cooling Time

Ingredients:
- ¼ cup coconut oil
- ¼ cup olive oil
- 2 peeled peaches, chopped
- ½ cup raisins, soaked
- 1 cup plain flour
- 3 eggs
- 1 tbsp dark rum
- ¼ tsp ground cinnamon
- 1 tsp vanilla extract
- 1 ½ tsp baking powder
- 4 tbsp Greek yogurt
- 2 tbsp honey
- 1 cup brown sugar
- 4 tbsp walnuts, chopped
- ¼ caramel sauce
- ¼ tsp salt

Directions:
1. Preheat the oven to 350 °F. In a bowl, mix the flour, cinnamon, vanilla, baking powder, and salt. In another bowl, whisk the eggs with Greek yogurt using an electric mixer. Gently add in coconut and olive oil. Combine well. Put in rum, honey and sugar; stir to combine. Mix the wet ingredients with the dry mixture. Stir in peaches, raisins, and walnuts.
2. Pour the mixture into a greased baking pan and bake for 30-40 minutes until a knife inserted into the middle of the cake comes out clean. Remove from the oven and let sit for 10 minutes, then invert onto a wire rack to cool completely. Warm the caramel sauce through in a pan and pour it over the cooled cake to serve.

Nutrition:
- Info Per Serving: Calories: 568;Fat: 26g;Protein: 215g;Carbs: 66g.

Country Pizza

Servings:4 | Cooking Time:45 Minutes

Ingredients:
- For the crust
- 2 tbsp olive oil
- 2 cups flour
- 1 cup lukewarm water
- 1 pinch of sugar
- 1 tsp active dry yeast
- ¾ tsp salt
- For the ranch sauce
- 1 tbsp butter
- 2 garlic cloves, minced
- 1 tbsp cream cheese
- ¼ cup half and half
- 1 tbsp Ranch seasoning mix
- For the topping
- 3 bacon slices, chopped
- 2 chicken breasts
- Salt and black pepper to taste
- 1 cup grated mozzarella
- 6 fresh basil leaves

Directions:
1. Sift the flour and salt in a bowl and stir in yeast. Mix lukewarm water, olive oil, and sugar in another bowl. Add the wet mixture to the dry mixture and whisk until you obtain a soft dough. Place the dough on a lightly floured work surface and knead it thoroughly for 4-5 minutes until elastic. Transfer the dough to a greased bowl. Cover with cling film and leave to rise for 50-60 minutes in a warm place until doubled in size. Roll out the dough to a thickness of around 12 inches.
2. Preheat the oven to 400 °F. Line a pizza pan with parchment

paper. In a bowl, mix the sauce's ingredients butter, garlic, cream cheese, half and half, and ranch mix. Set aside. Heat a grill pan over medium heat and cook the bacon until crispy and brown, 5 minutes. Transfer to a plate and set aside.

3. Season the chicken with salt, pepper and grill in the pan on both sides until golden brown, 10 minutes. Remove to a plate, allow cooling and cut into thin slices. Spread the ranch sauce on the pizza crust, followed by the chicken and bacon, and then, mozzarella cheese and basil. Bake for 5 minutes or until the cheese melts. Slice and serve warm.

Nutrition:
• Info Per Serving: Calories: 528;Fat: 28g;Protein: 61g;Carbs: 5g.

Energy Granola Bites

Servings:5 | Cooking Time:10 Minutes

Ingredients:
• ¾ cup diced dried figs
• ½ cup chopped walnuts
• ¼ cup old-fashioned oats
• 2 tbsp ground flaxseed
• 2 tbsp peanut butter
• 2 tbsp honey

Directions:
1. In a medium bowl, mix together the figs, walnuts, oats, flaxseed, and peanut butter. Drizzle with the honey, and mix everything with a wooden spoon. Freeze the dough for 5 minutes. Divide the dough evenly into four sections in the bowl. Dampen your hands with water—but don't get them too wet, or the dough will stick to them. With hands, roll three bites out of each of the four sections of dough, making 10 energy bites. Store in the fridge for up to a week.

Nutrition:
• Info Per Serving: Calories: 158;Fat: 8g;Protein: 3g;Carbs: 23g.

Banana, Cranberry, And Oat Bars

Servings:16 | Cooking Time: 40 Minutes

Ingredients:
• 2 tablespoon extra-virgin olive oil
• 2 medium ripe bananas, mashed
• ½ cup almond butter
• ½ cup maple syrup
• ⅓ cup dried cranberries
• 1½ cups old-fashioned rolled oats
• ¼ cup oat flour
• ¼ cup ground flaxseed
• ¼ teaspoon ground cloves
• ½ cup shredded coconut
• ½ teaspoon ground cinnamon
• 1 teaspoon vanilla extract

Directions:
1. Preheat the oven to 400°F. Line a 8-inch square pan with parchment paper, then grease with olive oil.
2. Combine the mashed bananas, almond butter, and maple syrup in a bowl. Stir to mix well.
3. Mix in the remaining ingredients and stir to mix well until thick and sticky.
4. Spread the mixture evenly on the square pan with a spatula, then bake in the preheated oven for 40 minutes or until a toothpick inserted in the center comes out clean.
5. Remove them from the oven and slice into 16 bars to serve.

Nutrition:
• Info Per Serving: Calories: 145;Fat: 7.2g;Protein: 3.1g;Carbs: 18.9g.

Mint Raspberries Panna Cotta

Servings:4 | Cooking Time:15 Min + Chilling Time

Ingredients:
• 2 tbsp warm water
• 2 tsp gelatin powder
• 2 cups heavy cream
• 1 cup raspberries
• 2 tbsp sugar
• 1 tsp vanilla extract
• 4 fresh mint leaves

Directions:
1. Pour 2 tbsp of warm water into a small bowl. Stir in the gelatin to dissolve. Allow the mixture to sit for 10 minutes. In a large bowl, combine the heavy cream, raspberries, sugar, and vanilla. Blend with an immersion blender until the mixture is smooth and the raspberries are well puréed. Transfer the mixture to a saucepan and heat over medium heat until just below a simmer. Remove from the heat and let cool for 5 minutes. Add in the gelatin mixture, whisking constantly until smooth. Divide the custard between ramekins and refrigerate until set, 4-6 hours. Serve chilled garnished with mint leaves.

Nutrition:
• Info Per Serving: Calories: 431;Fat: 44g;Protein: 4g;Carbs: 7g.

Poached Pears In Red Wine

Servings:4 | Cooking Time:1 Hour 35 Minutes

Ingredients:
• 4 pears, peeled with stalk intact
• 2 cups red wine
• 8 whole cloves
• 1 cinnamon stick
• ½ tsp vanilla extract
• 2 tsp sugar
• Creme fraiche for garnish

Directions:
1. In a pot over low heat, mix red wine, cinnamon stick, cloves, vanilla, and sugar and bring to a simmer, stirring often until the sugar is dissolved. Add in the pears, make sure that they are submerged and poach them for 15-20 minutes.
2. Remove the pears to a platter and allow the liquid simmering over medium heat for 15 minutes until reduced by half and syrupy. Remove from the heat and let cool for 10 minutes. Drain to discard the spices, let cool, and pour over the pears. Top with creme fraiche and serve.

Nutrition:
• Info Per Serving: Calories: 158;Fat: 1g;Protein: 2g;Carbs: 33g.

Baked Balsamic Beet Rounds

Servings:6 | Cooking Time:45 Minutes

Ingredients:
• 4 tbsp olive oil
• 4 beets, peeled, cut into wedges
• Salt and black pepper to taste
• 3 tsp fresh thyme
• ⅓ cup balsamic vinegar
• 1 tbsp fresh dill, chopped

Directions:
1. Preheat oven to 400 °F. Place the beets into a large bowl. Add 2 tbsp of olive oil, salt, and thyme and toss to combine. Spread the beets onto a baking sheet. Bake for 35-40 minutes, turning once or twice until the beets are tender. Remove and let them cool for 10 minutes. In a small bowl, whisk together the remaining olive oil, vinegar, dill, and black pepper. Transfer the beets into a serving bowl, spoon the vinegar mixture over the beets, and serve.

Nutrition:
• Info Per Serving: Calories: 111;Fat: 7g;Protein: 2g;Carbs: 11g.

White Bean Dip With Pita Wedges

Servings:4 | Cooking Time:25 Minutes

Ingredients:
- ½ cup olive oil
- 1 garlic clove
- 1 can cannellini beans
- 1 lemon, zested and juiced
- Salt to taste
- ½ tsp oregano
- 4 pitas, cut into wedges
- 5 black olives

Directions:
1. Preheat the oven to 350 °F. Arrange the pita wedges on a baking sheet and sprinkle with salt and oregano; drizzle them with some olive oil. Bake for 10-12 minutes until the pita beginning to brown. Place the beans, garlic, lemon juice, lemon zest, and salt and purée, drizzling in as much olive oil as needed until the beans are smooth. Transfer the dip to a bowl and serve the toasted pita bread.

Nutrition:
- Info Per Serving: Calories: 209;Fat: 17g;Protein: 4g;Carbs: 12g.

Apples Stuffed With Pecans

Servings:4 | Cooking Time:55 Minutes

Ingredients:
- 2 tbsp brown sugar
- 4 apples, cored
- ¼ cup chopped pecans
- 1 tsp ground cinnamon
- ¼ tsp ground nutmeg
- ¼ tsp ground ginger

Directions:
1. Preheat oven to 375 °F. Arrange the apples cut-side up on a baking dish. Combine pecans, ginger, cinnamon, brown sugar, and nutmeg in a bowl. Scoop the mixture into the apples and bake for 35-40 minutes until golden brown.

Nutrition:
- Info Per Serving: Calories: 142;Fat: 1.1g;Protein: 0.8g;Carbs: 36g.

Fresh Fruit Cups

Servings:4 | Cooking Time:10 Minutes

Ingredients:
- 1 cup orange juice
- ½ cup watermelon cubes
- 1 ½ cups grapes, halved
- 1 cup chopped cantaloupe
- ½ cup cherries, chopped
- 1 peach, chopped
- ½ tsp ground cinnamon

Directions:
1. Combine watermelon cubes, grapes, cherries, cantaloupe, and peach in a bowl. Add in the orange juice and mix well. Share into dessert cups, dust with cinnamon, and serve.

Nutrition:
- Info Per Serving: Calories: 156;Fat: 0.5g;Protein: 1.8g;Carbs: 24g.

Chocolate, Almond, And Cherry Clusters

Servings:10 | Cooking Time: 3 Minutes

Ingredients:
- 1 cup dark chocolate, chopped
- 1 tablespoon coconut oil
- ½ cup dried cherries
- 1 cup roasted salted almonds

Directions:
1. Line a baking sheet with parchment paper.
2. Melt the chocolate and coconut oil in a saucepan for 3 minutes. Stir constantly.
3. Turn off the heat and mix in the cherries and almonds.
4. Drop the mixture on the baking sheet with a spoon. Place the sheet in the refrigerator and chill for at least 1 hour or until firm.
5. Serve chilled.

Nutrition:
- Info Per Serving: Calories: 197;Fat: 13.2g;Protein: 4.1g;Carbs: 17.8g.

Thyme Lentil Spread

Servings:6 | Cooking Time:10 Minutes

Ingredients:
- 3 tbsp olive oil
- 1 garlic clove, minced
- 1 cup split red lentils, rinsed
- ½ tsp dried thyme
- 1 tbsp balsamic vinegar
- Salt and black pepper to taste

Directions:
1. Bring to a boil salted water in a pot over medium heat. Add in the lentils and cook for 15 minutes until cooked through. Drain and set aside to cool. In a food processor, place the lentils, garlic, thyme, vinegar, salt, and pepper. Gradually add olive oil while blending until smooth. Serve.

Nutrition:
- Info Per Serving: Calories: 295;Fat: 10g;Protein: 10g;Carbs: 16g.

Crispy Kale Chips

Servings:4 | Cooking Time:15 Minutes

Ingredients:
- 2 tbsp olive oil
- 2 heads curly leaf kale
- Sea salt to taste

Directions:
1. Tear the kale into bite-sized pieces. Toss with the olive oil, and lay on a baking sheet in a single layer. Sprinkle with a pinch of sea salt. Bake for 10 to 15 minutes until crispy. Serve or store in an airtight container.

Nutrition:
- Info Per Serving: Calories: 102;Fat: 4g;Protein: 6g;Carbs: 14g.

Garbanzo Patties With Cilantro-Yogurt Sauce

Servings:4 | Cooking Time:20 Minutes

Ingredients:
- ¼ cup olive oil
- 3 garlic cloves, minced
- 1 cup canned garbanzo beans
- 2 tbsp parsley, chopped
- 1 onion, chopped
- 1 tsp ground coriander
- Salt and black pepper to taste
- ¼ tsp cayenne pepper
- ¼ tsp cumin powder
- 1 tsp lemon juice
- 3 tbsp flour
- ¼ cup Greek yogurt
- 2 tbsp chopped cilantro
- ½ tsp garlic powder

Directions:
1. In a blender, blitz garbanzo, parsley, onion, garlic, salt, pepper, ground coriander, cayenne pepper, cumin powder, and lemon juice until smooth. Remove to a bowl and mix in flour. Form 16 balls out of the mixture and flatten them into patties.
2. Warm the olive oil in a skillet over medium heat and fry patties for 10 minutes on both sides. Remove them to a paper towel–lined plate to drain the excess fat. In a bowl, mix the Greek yogurt, cilantro, garlic powder, salt, and pepper. Serve the patties with yogurt sauce.

Nutrition:
- Info Per Serving: Calories: 120;Fat: 7g;Protein: 4g;Carbs: 13g.

Amaretto Squares

Servings:6 | Cooking Time:1 Hour 10 Minutes

Ingredients:
- 1 tsp olive oil
- Zest from 1 lemon
- 3/4 cup slivered almonds
- 2 cups flour
- 3/4 cup sugar
- 1 tsp baking powder
- ¼ tsp salt
- 3 eggs
- 2 tbsp Amaretto liqueur

Directions:
1. Preheat the oven to 280 °F. Combine flour, baking powder, sugar, lemon zest, salt, and almonds in a bowl and mix well. In another bowl, beat the eggs and amaretto liqueur. Pour into the flour mixture and mix to combine.
2. Grease a baking sheet with olive oil and spread in the dough. Bake for 40-45 minutes. Remove from the oven, let cool for a few minutes, and cut diagonally into slices about ½-inch thick. Place the pieces back on the sheet, cut sides up, and bake for 20 more minutes. Let cool before serving.

Nutrition:
- Info Per Serving: Calories: 78;Fat: 1g;Protein: 2g;Carbs: 14g.

Mango And Coconut Frozen Pie

Servings:8 | Cooking Time: 0 Minutes

Ingredients:
- Crust:
- 1 cup cashews
- ½ cup rolled oats
- 1 cup soft pitted dates
- Filling:
- 2 large mangoes, peeled and chopped
- ½ cup unsweetened shredded coconut
- 1 cup unsweetened coconut milk
- ½ cup water

Directions:
1. Combine the ingredients for the crust in a food processor. Pulse to combine well.
2. Pour the mixture in an 8-inch springform pan, then press to coat the bottom. Set aside.
3. Combine the ingredients for the filling in the food processor, then pulse to purée until smooth.
4. Pour the filling over the crust, then use a spatula to spread the filling evenly. Put the pan in the freeze for 30 minutes.
5. Remove the pan from the freezer and allow to sit for 15 minutes under room temperature before serving.

Nutrition:
- Info Per Serving: Calories: 426;Fat: 28.2g;Protein: 8.1g;Carbs: 14.9g.

The Best Trail Mix

Servings:4 | Cooking Time:20 Minutes

Ingredients:
- 1 tbsp olive oil
- 1 tbsp maple syrup
- 1 tsp vanilla
- ½ tsp paprika
- ½ tsp cardamom
- ½ tsp allspice
- 2 cups mixed, unsalted nuts
- ¼ cup sunflower seeds
- ½ cup dried apricots, diced
- ½ cup dried figs, diced
- Salt to taste

Directions:
1. Mix the olive oil, maple syrup, vanilla, cardamom, paprika, and allspice in a pan over medium heat. Stir to combine. Add the nuts and seeds and stir well to coat. Let the nuts and seeds toast for about 10 minutes, stirring often. Remove from the heat, and add the dried apricots and figs. Stir everything well and season with salt. Store in an airtight container.

Nutrition:
- Info Per Serving: Calories: 261;Fat: 18g;Protein: 6g;Carbs: 23g.

Lovely Coconut-Covered Strawberries

Servings:4 | Cooking Time:15 Min + Cooling Time

Ingredients:
- 1 cup chocolate chips
- ¼ cup coconut flakes
- 1 lb strawberries
- ½ tsp vanilla extract
- ½ tsp ground nutmeg
- ¼ tsp salt

Directions:
1. Melt chocolate chips for 30 seconds. Remove and stir in vanilla, nutmeg, and salt. Let cool for 2-3 minutes. Dip strawberries into the chocolate and then into the coconut flakes. Place on a wax paper-lined cookie sheet and let sit for 30 minutes until the chocolate dries. Serve.

Nutrition:
- Info Per Serving: Calories: 275;Fat: 20g;Protein: 6g;Carbs: 21g.

Speedy Granita

Servings:4 | Cooking Time:10 Min + Freezing Time

Ingredients:
- ¼ cup sugar
- 1 cup fresh strawberries
- 1 cup fresh raspberries
- 1 cup chopped fresh kiwi
- 1 tsp lemon juice

Directions:
1. Bring 1 cup water to a boil in a small saucepan over high heat. Add the sugar and stir well until dissolved. Remove the pan from the heat, add the fruit and lemon juice, and cool to room temperature. Once cooled, puree the fruit in a blender until smooth. Pour the puree into a shallow glass baking dish and place in the freezer for 1 hour. Stir with a fork and freeze for 30 minutes, then repeat. Serve and enjoy!

Nutrition:
- Info Per Serving: Calories: 153;Fat: 0.2g;Protein: 1.6g;Carbs: 39g.

Roasted Veggies With Marsala Sauce

Servings:4 | Cooking Time:30 Minutes

Ingredients:
- Vegetables:
- ¼ cup olive oil
- 1 lb green beans, trimmed
- ½ lb carrots, trimmed
- 1 fennel bulb, sliced
- ¼ cup dry white wine
- ¼ tsp oregano
- ½ tsp thyme
- ½ tsp rosemary
- ¼ tsp coriander seeds
- ¼ tsp celery seeds
- ¼ tsp dried dill weed
- 1 head garlic, halved
- 1 red onion, sliced
- Salt and black pepper to taste
- Sauce:
- 2 tbsp olive oil
- 2 tbsp Marsala wine
- 2 tbsp plain yogurt
- 1 tbsp yellow mustard
- 1 tsp honey
- 1 tbsp lemon juice
- 1 yolk from 1 hard-boiled egg
- Salt to taste
- 1 tbsp paprika

Directions:
1. Preheat the oven to 380 °F. In a bowl, combine the olive oil, white wine, oregano, thyme, rosemary, coriander seeds, celery seeds, dill weed, salt, and black pepper and mix well. Add in carrots, green beans, fennel, garlic, and onion and toss to coat. Spread the mixture on a baking dish and roast in the oven for 15-20 minutes until tender.
2. In a food processor, place the honey, yogurt, mustard, lemon juice, Marsala wine, yolk, olive oil, salt, and paprika, and blitz until smooth and uniform. Transfer to a bowl and place in the fridge until ready to use. When the veggies are ready, remove and serve with the prepared sauce on the side.

Nutrition:
- Info Per Serving: Calories: 280;Fat: 20.2g;Protein: 4g;Carbs: 21g.

Prawn & Cucumber Bites

Servings:4 | Cooking Time:5 Minutes

Ingredients:
- 1 lb prawns, cooked and chopped
- 1 cucumber, cubed
- 2 tbsp cream cheese
- Salt and black pepper to taste
- 12 whole-grain crackers

Directions:
1. Combine cucumber, prawns, cream cheese, salt, and pepper in a bowl. Place crackers on a plate and top them with the prawn mixture. Serve right away.

Nutrition:
- Info Per Serving: Calories: 160;Fat: 9g;Protein: 18g;Carbs: 12g.

Portuguese Orange Mug Cake

Servings:2 | Cooking Time:12 Minutes

Ingredients:
- 2 tbsp butter, melted
- 6 tbsp flour
- 2 tbsp sugar
- ½ tsp baking powder
- ¼ tsp salt
- 1 tsp orange zest
- 1 egg
- 2 tbsp orange juice
- 2 tbsp milk
- ½ tsp orange extract
- ½ tsp vanilla extract
- Orange slices for garnish

Directions:
1. In a bowl, beat the egg, butter, orange juice, milk, orange extract, and vanilla extract. In another bowl, combine the flour, sugar, baking powder, salt, and orange zest. Pour the dry ingredients into the wet ingredients and stir to combine. Spoon the mixture into 2 mugs and microwave one at a time for 1-2 minutes. Garnish with orange slices.

Nutrition:
- Info Per Serving: Calories: 302;Fat: 17g;Protein: 6g;Carbs: 33g.

Sicilian Sandwich Muffuletta

Servings:6 | Cooking Time:10 Minutes

Ingredients:
- 1 focaccia bread
- 2 tbsp drained capers
- 2 tbsp black olive tapenade
- ½ lb fontina cheese, sliced
- ¼ lb smoked turkey, sliced
- ¼ lb salami, thinly sliced

Directions:
1. Slice the focaccia bread in half horizontally. Spread each piece with olive tapenade. Layer half of the fontina cheese, a layer of capers, smoked turkey, olive tapenade, salami, capers, and finish with fontina cheese. Top with the remaining focaccia half and press the sandwich together gently. Serve sliced into wedges.

Nutrition:
- Info Per Serving: Calories: 335;Fat: 27g;Protein: 18g;Carbs: 4g.

Salmon-Cucumber Rolls

Servings:4 | Cooking Time:5 Minutes

Ingredients:
- 8 Kalamata olives, chopped
- 4 oz smoked salmon strips
- 1 cucumber, sliced lengthwise
- 2 tsp lime juice
- 4 oz cream cheese, soft
- 1 tsp lemon zest, grated
- Salt and black pepper to taste
- 2 tsp dill, chopped

Directions:
1. Place cucumber slices on a flat surface and top each with a salmon strip. Combine olives, lime juice, cream cheese, lemon zest, salt, pepper, and dill in a bowl. Smear cream mixture over salmon and roll them up. Serve immediately.

Nutrition:
- Info Per Serving: Calories: 250;Fat: 16g;Protein: 18g;Carbs: 17g.

Roasted Garlic & Spicy Lentil Dip

Servings:6 | Cooking Time:40 Minutes

Ingredients:
- 1 roasted red bell pepper, chopped
- 4 tbsp olive oil
- 1 cup split red lentils
- ½ red onion
- 1 garlic bulb, top removed
- ½ tsp cumin seeds
- 1 tsp coriander seeds
- ¼ cup walnuts
- 2 tbsp tomato paste
- ½ tsp Cayenne powder
- Salt and black pepper to taste

Directions:
1. Preheat oven to 370 °F. Drizzle the garlic with some olive oil and wrap it in a piece of aluminum foil. Roast for 35-40 minutes. Remove and allow to cool for a few minutes. Cover the lentils with salted water in a pot over medium heat and bring to a boil. Simmer for 15 minutes. Drain and set aside.
2. Squeeze out the garlic cloves and place them in a food processor. Add in the cooled lentils, cumin seeds, coriander seeds, roasted red bell pepper, onion, walnuts, tomato paste, Cayenne powder, remaining olive oil, salt, and black pepper. Pulse until smooth. Serve with crostiniif desire.

Nutrition:
- Info Per Serving: Calories: 234;Fat: 13g;Protein: 9g;Carbs: 21.7g.

Berry And Rhubarb Cobbler

Servings:8 | Cooking Time: 35 Minutes

Ingredients:
- Cobbler:
- 1 cup fresh raspberries
- 2 cups fresh blueberries
- 1 cup sliced (½-inch) rhubarb pieces
- 1 tablespoon arrowroot powder
- ¼ cup unsweetened apple juice
- 2 tablespoons melted coconut oil
- ¼ cup raw honey
- Topping:
- 1 cup almond flour
- 1 tablespoon arrowroot powder
- ½ cup shredded coconut
- ¼ cup raw honey
- ½ cup coconut oil

Directions:
1. Make the Cobbler
2. Preheat the oven to 350ºF. Grease a baking dish with melted coconut oil.
3. Combine the ingredients for the cobbler in a large bowl. Stir to mix well.
4. Spread the mixture in the single layer on the baking dish. Set aside.
5. Make the Topping
6. Combine the almond flour, arrowroot powder, and coconut in a bowl. Stir to mix well.
7. Fold in the honey and coconut oil. Stir with a fork until the mixture crumbled.
8. Spread the topping over the cobbler, then bake in the preheated oven for 35 minutes or until frothy and golden brown.
9. Serve immediately.

Nutrition:
- Info Per Serving: Calories: 305;Fat: 22.1g;Protein: 3.2g;Carbs: 29.8g.

APPENDIX A : 30 Day Meal Plan

	Breakfast	Lunch	Dinner
Day 1	Oat & Raspberry Pudding	Chicken Tagine With Vegetables	Baked Potato With Veggie Mix
Day 2	5-Ingredient Quinoa Breakfast Bowls	Coriander Pork Roast	Creamy Polenta With Mushrooms
Day 3	Tomato And Egg Breakfast Pizza	Pork Chops With Squash & Zucchini	Zoodles With Beet Pesto
Day 4	Roasted Vegetable Panini	Tzatziki Chicken Loaf	Vegetable And Tofu Scramble
Day 5	Zucchini & Ricotta Egg Muffins	Cream Zucchini & Chicken Dish	Balsamic Cherry Tomatoes
Day 6	Banana Corn Fritters	Chili Beef Stew	Baked Tomatoes And Chickpeas
Day 7	Samosas In Potatoes	Mouth-Watering Pork Loin	Roasted Veggies And Brown Rice Bowl
Day 8	Maple Peach Smoothie	Spinach-Cheese Stuffed Pork Loin	Ratatouille
Day 9	Almond-Cherry Oatmeal Bowls	Greek Beef Kebabs	Roasted Celery Root With Yogurt Sauce
Day 10	Roasted Tomato Paninic	Curried Green Bean & Chicken Breasts	Mini Crustless Spinach Quiches
Day 11	Classic Spanish Tortilla With Tuna	Herby Beef Soup	Sweet Pepper Stew
Day 12	Feta And Spinach Frittata	Bell Pepper & Olive Turkey Breasts	Italian Hot Green Beans
Day 13	Crustless Tiropita (Greek Cheese Pie)	Turmeric Green Bean & Chicken Bake	Vegetable And Red Lentil Stew
Day 14	Goat Cheese & Sweet Potato Tart	Sweet Pork Stew	Veggie Rice Bowls With Pesto Sauce
Day 15	Tomato & Prosciutto Sandwiches	Stewed Chicken Sausage With Farro	Steamed Beetroot With Nutty Yogurt

	Breakfast	Lunch	Dinner
Day 16	Grilled Caesar Salad Sandwiches	Beef Filet Mignon In Mushroom Sauce	Cauliflower Steaks With Arugula
Day 17	Quick & Easy Bread In A Mug	Creamy Chicken Balls With Almonds	Beet And Watercress Salad
Day 18	Creamy Vanilla Oatmeal	Greek-Style Chicken & Egg Bake	Cauliflower Cakes With Goat Cheese
Day 19	Apple & Pumpkin Muffins	Pork Chops With Green Vegetables	Grilled Vegetable Skewers
Day 20	Herby Artichoke Frittata With Ricotta	Marjoram Pork Loin With Ricotta Cheese	Zoodles With Walnut Pesto
Day 21	Cream Peach Smoothie	Mustardy Turkey Ham Stuffed Peppers	5-Ingredient Zucchini Fritters
Day 22	Tomato & Avocado Toast	Beef, Tomato, And Lentils Stew	Chargrilled Vegetable Kebabs
Day 23	Easy Zucchini & Egg Stuffed Tomatoes	Chicken Cacciatore	Lentil And Tomato Collard Wraps
Day 24	Cinnamon Oatmeal With Dried Cranberries	Zesty Turkey Breast	Roasted Vegetables And Chickpeas
Day 25	Feta And Olive Scrambled Eggs	Greek Roasted Lamb Leg With Potatoes	Rainbow Vegetable Kebabs
Day 26	Cheesy Broccoli And Mushroom Egg Casserole	Lamb Kebabs With Lemon-Yogurt Sauce	Stir-Fried Eggplant
Day 27	Spicy Black Bean And Poblano Dippers	Smooth Chicken Breasts With Nuts	Authentic Mushroom Gratin
Day 28	Strawberry Basil Mascarpone Toast	Baked Beef With Kale Slaw & Bell Peppers	Spicy Roasted Tomatoes
Day 29	Eggs Florentine With Pancetta	Baked Chicken & Veggie	Baked Vegetable Stew
Day 30	Zucchini Hummus Wraps	Greek-Style Chicken With Potatoes	Easy Zucchini Patties

Beef Stew With Green Peas 118

Beet
Zoodles With Beet Pesto 33
Beet And Watercress Salad 36
Roasted Caramelized Root Vegetables 44
Baked Beet & Leek With Dilly Yogurt 49
Baked Beet Fries With Feta Cheese 126
Baked Balsamic Beet Rounds 136
Lemon Trout With Roasted Beets 73

Beetroot
Steamed Beetroot With Nutty Yogurt 36

Bell Pepper
Garlic Bell Pepper Omelet 21
Rainbow Vegetable Kebabs 38
Effortless Bell Pepper Salad 115
Grilled Bell Pepper And Anchovy Antipasto 121
Pesto Ravioli Salad 122
Two-Cheese Stuffed Bell Peppers 125

Berry
Breakfast Pancakes With Berry Sauce 29
Granola & Berry Parfait 31

Black Olives
Mozzarella & Olive Cakes 21
Spanish-Style Linguine With Tapenade 57
Chili Flounder Parcels 83
Olive Tapenade Flatbread With Cheese 111

Blueberry
Honey Breakfast Smoothie 26
Berry Sorbet 128
Easy Blueberry And Oat Crisp 134
Berry And Rhubarb Cobbler 140

Broccoli
5-Ingredient Quinoa Breakfast Bowls 16
Roasted Vegetable Panini 16
Cheesy Broccoli And Mushroom Egg Casserole 20
Roasted Veggies And Brown Rice Bowl 34
Quick Steamed Broccoli 41
Minty Broccoli & Walnuts 44
Garlicky Broccoli Rabe 47
Simple Broccoli With Yogurt Sauce 50
Lemon Couscous With Broccoli 56
Pesto Fusilli With Broccoli 58
Hearty Veggie Slaw 113

Brussels Sprout
Veggie Rice Bowls With Pesto Sauce 36
Roasted Vegetables 46
Roasted Vegetable Medley 49
Balsamic Brussels Sprouts And Delicata Squash 122

Butternut Squash
Tahini & Feta Butternut Squash 45
Roasted Butternut Squash And Zucchini With Penne 68
Butternut Squash And Cauliflower Curry Soup 109

C

Cabbage
Baby Kale And Cabbage Salad 41
Sweet Mustard Cabbage Hash 47
Sautéed Cabbage With Parsley 50
Lebanese Flavor Broken Thin Noodles 56

Carrot
Carrot & Pecan Cupcakes 24
Balsamic Grilled Vegetables 41
Pea & Carrot Noodles 48
Simple Honey-Glazed Baby Carrots 49
Carrot & Barley Risotto 64
Couscous With Carrots & Peas 69
Wild Rice, Celery, And Cauliflower Pilaf 70
Neapolitan Pasta & Fagioli 112
Roasted Root Vegetable Soup 112
Chili Lentil Soup 118
Vegetable Fagioli Soup 120
Carrot & Celery Bean Soup 123
Pecan And Carrot Cake 128
Vegetable & Egg Sandwiches 24

Cauliflower
Cauliflower Breakfast Porridge 24
Cauliflower Steaks With Arugula 36
Cauliflower Cakes With Goat Cheese 37
Braised Cauliflower With White Wine 40
Mushroom & Cauliflower Roast 49
Macaroni & Cauliflower Gratin 54
Lentil And Vegetable Curry Stew 59
Rich Cauliflower Alfredo 61
Easy Roasted Cauliflower 111
Savory Cauliflower Steaks 129

Cheese
Crustless Tiropita (Greek Cheese Pie) 18
Strawberry Basil Mascarpone Toast 21
Hummus Toast With Pine Nuts & Ricotta 25
Brown Rice Salad With Cheese 29
Kale & Feta Couscous 67
Whipped Feta Spread 123
Goat Cheese Dip With Scallions & Lemon 128
Grilled Pesto Halloumi Cheese 130
Two Cheese Pizza 132
No-Gluten Caprese Pizza 129
Tomato-Cheese Toasts 125

Cherry Tomato
Feta And Spinach Frittata 18
Cherry Tomato & Mushroom Frittata 27
Cherry Tomato & Zucchini Scrambled Eggs 28
Balsamic Cherry Tomatoes 34
Spicy Roasted Tomatoes 39
Quinoa & Watercress Salad With Nuts 59
Easy Bulgur Tabbouleh 61
Bulgur Pilaf With Kale And Tomatoes 66
Traditional Panzanella Salad 109

Chicken
Parmesan Oatmeal With Greens 25
Veggie & Egg Quinoa With Pancetta 54
Greek Chicken & Fusilli Bake 62
Tzatziki Chicken Loaf 90
Cream Zucchini & Chicken Dish 90
Creamy Chicken Balls With Almonds 93

Roasted Chicken Thighs With Basmati Rice 100
Creamy Tomato Hummus Soup 118

Chicken Breast
Baked Parmesan Chicken Wraps 28
Chicken Linguine A La Toscana 52
Creamy Garlic Parmesan Chicken Pasta 58
Curried Green Bean & Chicken Breasts 91
Greek-Style Chicken & Egg Bake 93
Smooth Chicken Breasts With Nuts 95
Marsala Chicken With Mushrooms 96
Greek Wraps 96
Crispy Pesto Chicken 97
Grilled Chicken Breasts With Italian Sauce 97
Chicken Souvlaki 98
Apricot Chicken Rice Bowls 98
Spinach Chicken With Chickpeas 99
Grilled Chicken And Zucchini Kebabs 99
Chicken Caprese 100
Chicken Bruschetta Burgers 100
Rosemary Tomato Chicken 101
Chicken & Vegetable Skewers 102
Asparagus & Chicken Skillet 102
Spanish Chicken Skillet 103
One-Pan Sicilian Chicken 104
Yogurt Chicken Breasts 104
Carrot, Potato & Chicken Bake 104
Italian Potato & Chicken 104
Baked Root Veggie & Chicken 105
Spinach Pesto Chicken Breasts 106
Picante Green Pea & Chicken 106
Parmesan Chicken Salad 108
Chicken & Mushroom Soup 113
Greek Chicken, Tomato, And Olive Salad 117

Chicken Drumstick
Greek-Style Chicken With Potatoes 95

Chicken Leg
Baked Chicken & Veggie 95
Chicken With Chianti Sauce 98

Chicken Sausage
Stewed Chicken Sausage With Farro 92
Chicken & Spinach Dish 96
Chicken Sausages With Pepper Sauce 98
Chicken Sausage & Zucchini Soup 101

Chicken Thighs
Oregano Chicken Risotto 54
Spicy Chicken Lentils 64
Chicken Tagine With Vegetables 90
Turmeric Green Bean & Chicken Bake 92
Chicken Cacciatore 94

Chicken Wing
Chicken With Halloumi Cheese 97
Harissa Chicken Wings 108

Chickpea
Baked Tomatoes And Chickpeas 34
Roasted Vegetables And Chickpeas 38
Sweet Potato Chickpea Buddha Bowl 43
Hot Turnip Chickpeas 47
Chickpea Lettuce Wraps With Celery 48
Herby Fusilli In Chickpea Sauce 56
Minestrone Chickpeas And Macaroni Casserole 57
Lush Moroccan Chickpea, Vegetable, And Fruit Stew 58
Hot Chickpea & Faro Stew 59

Paprika Spinach & Chickpea Bowl 60
Carrot & Caper Chickpeas 62
Israeli Style Eggplant And Chickpea Salad 67
Veggie & Clam Stew With Chickpeas 83
Chickpea & Cavolo Nero Soup 109
Turkish Chickpeas 110
Sumptuous Greek Vegetable Salad 118
Spicy Roasted Chickpeas 131
Baked Sweet Potatoes With Chickpeas 132

Chocolate
Fruit And Nut Chocolate Bark 126
Avocado & Dark Chocolate Mousse 132
Chocolate, Almond, And Cherry Clusters 137

Coconut
Mango And Coconut Frozen Pie 138

Cod
Baked Cod With Vegetables 72
Herby Cod Skewers 75
Simple Fried Cod Fillets 75
Mom's Cod With Mozzarella & Tomatoes 76
Leek & Olive Cod Casserole 80
Better-For-You Cod & Potatoes 80
Roman-Style Cod 82
Roasted Cod With Cabbage 83
Mediterranean Cod Stew 85
Baked Cod With Lemony Rice 86
Saucy Cod With Calamari Rings 77
Mediterranean Braised Cod With Vegetables 77
Fennel Poached Cod With Tomatoes 86

Couscous
Swiss Chard Couscous With Feta Cheese 52
Harissa Vegetable Couscous 52
Moroccan Spiced Couscous 109
Tasty Cucumber & Couscous Salad 115
Cherry & Pine Nut Couscous 115

Crab
Seafood Cakes With Radicchio Salad 87

Cremini Mushroom
Tasty Lentil Burgers 44
Sautéed Mushrooms With Garlic & Parsley 45
Portuguese Thyme & Mushroom Millet 61
Beef Filet Mignon In Mushroom Sauce 92

Cucumber
Detox Juice 25
Herby Tzatziki Sauce 111
Party Summer Salad 114
Yogurt Cucumber Salad 117
Cucumber Gazpacho 120
Walnut-Cucumber Yogurt Sauce 122
Mini Cucumber & Cream Cheese Sandwiches 133

Tomato & Prosciutto Sandwiches 18
Grilled Caesar Salad Sandwiches 19
Grilled Romaine Lettuce 42

M

Mango
Mango-Yogurt Smoothie 31
Crispy Tilapia With Mango Salsa 87
Fruit Skewers With Vanilla Labneh 132
Milk
Fancy Baileys Ice Coffee 130
Mushroom
Mushroom-Pesto Baked Pizza 30
Creamy Polenta With Mushrooms 33
Chargrilled Vegetable Kebabs 38
Authentic Mushroom Gratin 39
Stuffed Portobello Mushrooms With Spinach 44
Veggie-Stuffed Portabello Mushrooms 46
Asparagus & Mushroom Farro 48
Wild Rice With Cheese & Mushrooms 62
Leftover Pasta & Mushroom Frittata 62
Lentil And Mushroom Pasta 67
Mushroom And Soba Noodle Soup 110
Mushroom & Parmesan Risotto 115
Simple Mushroom Barley Soup 115
Zoodles With Tomato-Mushroom Sauce 121

O

Oat
Oat & Raspberry Pudding 16
Creamy Vanilla Oatmeal 19
Cinnamon Oatmeal With Dried Cranberries 20
Chia & Almond Oatmeal 22
Maple Berry & Walnut Oatmeal 29
Hot Collard Green Oats With Parmesan 64
Energy Granola Bites 136
Olive
Feta And Olive Scrambled Eggs 20
Pork Chops In Tomato Olive Sauce 103
Spinach & Bean Salad With Black Olives 111
Iberian Spread For Sandwiches 130
Onion
Simple Lentil Risotto 63
Orange
Portuguese Orange Mug Cake 139

P

Pea
Scallion Clams With Snow Peas 81
Creamy Green Soup 110
Peach
Maple Peach Smoothie 17
Cream Peach Smoothie 20
Caramel Peach & Walnut Cake 135
Fresh Fruit Cups 137
Pear
Baked Ricotta With Honey Pears 23

Orange Pear Salad With Gorgonzola 108
Greens, Fennel, And Pear Soup With Cashews 114
Mascarpone Baked Pears 127
Poached Pears In Red Wine 136
Pepperoni
Pepperoni Fat Head Pizza 126
Plain Yogurt
Roasted Celery Root With Yogurt Sauce 35
Herby Yogurt Sauce 109
Pork
Green Bean & Pork Fettuccine 65
Coriander Pork Roast 90
Mouth-Watering Pork Loin 91
Sweet Pork Stew 92
Marjoram Pork Loin With Ricotta Cheese 93
Vegetable Pork Loin 96
Pork Loaf With Colby Cheese 97
Parsley Pork Stew 98
Pork Loin With Cilantro-Mustard Glaze 99
Pork Butt With Leeks 101
Mushroom & Pork Stew 104
Uncle´s Pork Salad 118
Pork Chop
Pork Chops With Green Vegetables 93
Pork Chops In Wine Sauce 97
Peach Pork Chops 99
Bell Pepper & Onion Pork Chops 102
Pork Loin Chop
Pork Chops With Squash & Zucchini 90
Easy Grilled Pork Chops 96
Pork Tenderloin
Spinach-Cheese Stuffed Pork Loin 91
Apricot-Glazed Pork Skewers 99
Potato
Samosas In Potatoes 17
Goat Cheese & Sweet Potato Tart 18
Baked Potato With Veggie Mix 33
Cheesy Sweet Potato Burgers 42
Spicy Potato Wedges 45
Swoodles With Almond Butter Sauce 54
Baby Potato And Olive Salad 113
Turkish Leek & Potato Soup 113
Balsamic Potato Salad With Capers 114
Egg & Potato Salad 120
Zesty Spanish Potato Salad 121
Sheet Pan Sweet Potatoes 131
Crispy Potato Chips 133
Authentic Greek Potato Skins 134
Prawn
Prawns With Mushrooms 78
Prawn & Cucumber Bites 139
Prosciutto
Spinach & Prosciutto Crostini 30
Pumpkin Puree
Pumpkin-Yogurt Parfaits 31

W

Z